Cruel and Unusual Punishment

OTHER BOOKS IN AMERICA'S FREEDOMS

Donald Grier Stephenson, Jr., Series Editor

Equal Protection of the Laws, Francis Graham Lee

Freedom of Association, Robert J. Bresler

Freedom of Speech, Ken I. Kersch

Property Rights, Polly J. Price

The Right to Bear Arms, Robert J. Spitzer

The Right to Counsel and Protection against Self-Incrimination, John B. Taylor

The Right to Privacy, Richard A. Glenn

CRUEL AND UNUSUAL PUNISHMENT

Rights and Liberties under the Law

JOSEPH A. MELUSKY
KEITH A. PESTO

ABC CLIO

Santa Barbara, California • Denver, Colorado • Oxford, England

Library of Congress Cataloging-in-Publication Data
Melusky, Joseph Anthony.
Cruel and unusual punishment : rights and liberties under the law / Joseph A. Melusky and Keith A. Pesto.
p. cm. —(America's freedoms)
Includes bibliographical references and index.
ISBN 1-57607-602-4 (hardcover : alk. paper)
1. Capital punishment—United States. I. Pesto, Keith, A. II. Title. III. Series.

KF9227.C2M42 2003
345.73'0773—dc21 2002155574

07 06 05 04 03 10 9 8 7 6 5 4 3 2 1

ABC-CLIO, Inc.
130 Cremona Drive, P.O. Box 1911
Santa Barbara, California 93116-1911
This book is printed on acid-free paper.
Manufactured in the United States of America

To my children, Mike and Jessica,
to my wife, Marie,
to my mom, Eleanor,
and to the memory of my dad, George
—J.A.M.

To my parents, for their many wise answers, and
to my students, for their many wise questions
—K.A.P.

Contents

Series Foreword xi
Preface and Acknowledgments xxi

1 **Introduction,** 1

History, 7
The Constitution and the Death Penalty, 8
Voices of the Capital Punishment Debate, 12
References and Further Reading, 26

2 **Origins and Early Development** 29

America in the Era before Independence, 29
The Founding Era, 39
The Nineteenth Century, 47
References and Further Reading, 65

3 **Twentieth-Century Issues** 67

Continuity and Change, 67
Some Facts, 70
Philosophy, 74
Dreams, 80
From *Weems* to *Furman,* 87
From *Furman* to *Gregg,* 104
After *Gregg,* 111
References and Further Reading, 136

4 **Into the Twenty-First Century** 139

Unresolved and New Issues for the Death Penalty, 139
Penalties Less Than Death, 155
Conditions of Confinement, 162
References and Further Reading, 175

5 **Key People, Cases, and Events** 177

6 **Documents** 197

Code of Hammurabi, c. 1780 B.C., 197
The Bible, Book of Exodus,
The Ten Commandments, c. 1300 B.C., 200
Code of Draco, c. 621 B.C., 201
The Magna Carta, June 15, 1215, 202
The English Bill of Rights, 1689, 203
The American Declaration of Independence, 1776, 204
Ordinance of the Northwest Territory, 1787, 207
Amendments to the U.S. Constitution, 208
"Speech in Favor of Capital Punishment,"
John Stuart Mill, April 21, 1868, 209
Evangelium Vitae (The Gospel of Life),
Encyclical of Pope John Paul II, March 25, 1995, 213
American Bar Association Resolution on
the Death Penalty, February 3, 1997, 214
Message Supporting the Moratorium on
the Death Penalty, the Dalai Lama, 215
Gregg v. Georgia (1976), 217
Woodson v. North Carolina (1976), 226
Coker v. Georgia (1977), 229
Lockett v. Ohio (1978), 235
Enmund v. Florida (1982), 242
Solem v. Helm (1983), 249
Ford v. Wainwright (1986), 256
Tison v. Arizona (1987), 262

McCleskey v. Kemp (1987), 270
Penry v. Lynaugh (1989), 283
Stanford v. Kentucky (1989), 291
Harmelin v. Michigan (1991), 302
Atkins v. Virginia (2002), 314
Ring v. Arizona (2002), 323

Chronology of Capital Punishment 329
Table of Cases 333
Appendix: Data 339
Annotated Bibliography 349
Index 361

Series Foreword

America's Freedoms promises a series of books that address the origin, development, meaning, and future of the nation's fundamental liberties, as well as the individuals, circumstances, and events that have shaped them. These freedoms are chiefly enshrined explicitly or implicitly in the Bill of Rights and other amendments to the Constitution of the United States and have much to do with the quality of life Americans enjoy. Without them, America would be a far different place in which to live. Oddly enough, however, the Constitution was drafted and signed in Philadelphia in 1787 without a bill of rights. That was an afterthought, emerging only after a debate among the foremost political minds of the day.

At the time, Thomas Jefferson was in France on a diplomatic mission. Upon receiving a copy of the proposed Constitution from his friend James Madison, who had helped write the document, Jefferson let him know as fast as the slow sailing-ship mails of the day allowed that the new plan of government suffered one major defect—it lacked a bill of rights. This, Jefferson argued, "is what the people are entitled to against every government on earth." Madison should not have been surprised at Jefferson's reaction. The Declaration of Independence of 1776 had largely been Jefferson's handiwork, including its core statement of principle:

> We hold these truths to be self-evident, that all men are created equal, that they are endowed by their Creator with certain unalienable Rights, that among these are Life, Liberty, and the pursuit of Happiness. That to secure these rights, Governments are instituted among Men, deriving their just powers from the consent of the governed.

Jefferson rejected the conclusion of many of the framers that the Constitution's design—a system of both separation of powers among the legislative, executive, and judicial branches, and a federal division of powers between national and state governments—would safeguard liberty. Even when combined with elections, he believed strongly that such structural checks would fall short.

Jefferson and other critics of the proposed Constitution ultimately had their way. In one of the first items of business in the First Congress in 1789, Madison, as a member of the House of Representatives from Virginia, introduced amendments to protect liberty. Ten were ratified by 1791 and have become known as the Bill of Rights.

America's Bill of Rights reflects the founding generation's understanding of the necessary link between personal freedom and representative government, as well as their experience with threats to liberty. The First Amendment protects expression—in speech, press, assembly, petition, and religion—and guards against a union of church and state. The Second Amendment secures liberty against national tyranny by affirming the self-defense of the states. Members of state-authorized local militia—citizens primarily, soldiers occasionally—retained a right to bear arms. The ban in the Third Amendment on forcibly quartering troops in houses reflects the emphasis the framers placed on the integrity and sanctity of the home.

Other provisions in the Fourth, Fifth, Sixth, Seventh, and Eighth amendments safeguard freedom by setting forth standards that government must follow in administering the law, especially regarding persons accused of crimes. The framers knew firsthand the dangers that government-as-prosecutor could pose to liberty. Even today, authoritarian regimes in other lands routinely use the tools of law enforcement—arrests, searches, detentions, as well as trials—to squelch peaceful political opposition. Limits in the Bill of Rights on crime-fighting powers thus help maintain democracy by demanding a high level of legal scrutiny of the government's practices.

In addition, one clause in the Fifth Amendment forbids the taking of private property for public use without paying the owner just compensation, and thereby limits the power of eminent domain, the authority to seize a person's property. Along with taxation and conscription, eminent domain is one of the most awesome powers any government can possess.

The Ninth Amendment makes sure that the listing of some rights does not imply that others necessarily have been abandoned. If the Ninth offered reassurances to the people, the Tenth Amendment was designed to reassure the states that they or the people retained those powers not delegated to the national government. Today, the Tenth is a reminder of the integral role states play in the federal plan of union that the Constitution ordained.

Despite this legacy of freedom, however, we Americans today sometimes wonder about the origin, development, meaning, and future of our liberties. This concern is entirely understandable, because liberty is central to the idea of what it means *to be American.* In this way, the United States stands apart from virtually every other nation on earth. Other countries typically define their national identities through a common ethnicity, origin, ancestral bond, religion, or history. But none of these accounts for the American identity. In terms of ethnicity, ancestry, and religion, the United States is the most diverse place on earth. From the beginning, America has been a land of immigrants. Neither is there a single historical experience to which all current citizens can directly relate: someone who arrived a decade ago from, say, southeast Asia and was naturalized as a citizen only last year is just as much an American as someone whose forebears served in General George Washington's army at Valley Forge during the American War of Independence (1776–1783). In religious as in political affairs, the United States has been a beacon to those suffering oppression abroad: "the last, best hope of earth," Abraham Lincoln said. So, the American identity is ideological. It consists of faith in the value and importance of liberty for each individual.

Nonetheless, a longstanding consensus among Americans on the *principle* that individual liberty is essential, highly prized, and widely shared hardly assures agreement about liberty *in practice.* This is because the concept of liberty, as it has developed in the United States, has several dimensions.

First, there is an unavoidable tension between liberty and restraint. Liberty means freedom: we say that a person has a "right" to do this or that. But that *right* is meaningless unless there is a corresponding *duty* on the part of others (such as police officers and elected officials) not to interfere. Thus, protection of the liberty of one person necessarily involves restraints imposed on someone else. This is why we speak of a *civil* right or a *civil* liberty: it is a claim on the behavior of another that is enforceable through the legal process. Moreover, some degree of order (restrictions on the behavior of all) is necessary if everyone's liberties are to be protected. Just as too much order crushes freedom, too little invites social chaos that also threatens freedom. Determining the proper balance between freedom and order, however, is more easily sought than found. "To make a government requires no great prudence," declared English statesman and political philosopher Edmund Burke in 1790. "Settle the seat of power; teach obedience; and the work is done. To give freedom is still more easy. It is not necessary to guide; it only requires to let go the rein. But to form a *free government;* that is, to temper together these opposite elements of liberty and restraint in one consistent work, requires much thought; deep reflection; a sagacious, powerful, and combining mind."

Second, the Constitution does not define the freedoms that it protects. Chief Justice John Marshall once acknowledged that the Constitution was a document "of enumeration, and not of definition." There are, for example, lists of the powers of Congress in Article I, or the rights of individuals in the Bill of Rights, but those powers and limitations are not explained. What is the "freedom of speech" that the First Amendment guarantees? What are "unreasonable searches and seizures" that are proscribed by the Fourth Amendment? What is the "due process of law" secured by both the Fifth and Fourteenth Amendments? Reasonable people, all of whom favor individual liberty, can arrive at very different answers to these questions.

A third dimension—breadth—is closely related to the second. How widely shared is a particular freedom? Consider voting, for example. One could write a political history of the United States by cataloging the efforts to extend the vote or franchise to groups such as women and nonwhites that had been previously excluded. Or, consider the First Amendment's freedom of speech. Does it include the expression of *all* points of view or merely *some?* Does the same amendment's protection of the "free exercise of religion" include all faiths, even obscure ones that may seem weird or even irritating? At different times questions like these have yielded different answers.

Similarly, the historical record contains notorious lapses. Despite all the safeguards that are supposed to shore up freedom's foundations, constitutional protections have sometimes been worth the least when they have been desperately needed. In our history the most frequent and often the most serious threats to freedom have come not from people intent on throwing the Bill of Rights away outright, but from well-meaning people who find the

Bill of Rights a temporary bother, standing in the way of some objective they want to reach.

There is also a question that dates to the very beginning of American government under the Constitution. Does the Constitution protect rights not spelled out in, or fairly implied by, the words of the document? The answer to that question largely depends on what a person concludes about the source of rights. One tradition, reflected in the Declaration of Independence, asserts that rights predate government and that government's chief duty is to protect the rights that everyone naturally possesses. Thus, if the Constitution is read as a document designed, among other things, to protect liberty, then protected liberties are not limited to those in the text of the Constitution but may also be derived from experience, for example, or from one's assessment of the requirements of a free society. This tradition places a lot of discretion in the hands of judges, because in the American political system, it is largely the judiciary that decides what the Constitution means. Partly due to this dynamic, a competing tradition looks to the text of the Constitution, as well as to statutes passed consistent with the Constitution, as a *complete* code of law containing *all* the liberties that Americans possess. Judges, therefore, are not free to go outside the text to "discover" rights that the people, through the process of lawmaking and constitutional amendment, have not declared. Doing so is undemocratic because it bypasses "rule by the people." The tension between these two ways of thinking explains the ongoing debate about a right to privacy, itself nowhere mentioned in the words of the Constitution. "I like my privacy as well as the next one," once admitted Justice Hugo Black, "but I am nevertheless compelled to admit that government has a right to invade it unless prohibited by some specific constitutional provision." Otherwise, he said, judges are forced "to determine what is or is not constitutional on the basis of their own appraisal of what laws are unwise or unnecessary."

Black thought that was the job of elected legislators who would answer to the people.

Fifth, it is often forgotten that at the outset, and for many years afterward, the Bill of Rights applied only to the national government, not to the states. Except for a very few restrictions, such as those in Section 10 of Article I in the main body of the Constitution, which expressly limited state power, states were restrained only by their individual constitutions and state laws, not by the U.S. Bill of Rights. So, Pennsylvania or any other state, for example, could shut down a newspaper or barricade the doors of a church without violating the First Amendment. For many in the founding generation, the new central government loomed as a colossus that might threaten liberty. Few at that time thought that individual freedom needed *national* protection against *state* invasions of the rights of the people.

The first step in removing this double standard came with ratification of the Fourteenth Amendment after the Civil War in 1868. Section 1 contained majestic, but undefined, checks on states: "*No State* shall make or enforce any law which shall abridge the privileges or immunities of citizens of the United States; nor shall any *State* deprive any person of life, liberty, or property, without due process of law; nor deny to any person within its jurisdiction the equal protections of the laws" (emphasis added). Such vague language begged for interpretation. In a series of cases mainly between 1920 and 1968, the Supreme Court construed the Fourteenth Amendment to include within its meaning almost every provision of the Bill of Rights. This process of "incorporation" (applying the Bill of Rights to the states by way of the Fourteenth Amendment) was the second step in eliminating the double standard of 1791. State and local governments became bound by the same restrictions that had applied all along to the national government. The consequences of this development scarcely can be exaggerated because most governmental action in the United States is the work of state and local governments. For instance, ordinary citizens are far more likely to encounter a local police officer than an agent of the Federal Bureau of Investigation or the Secret Service.

A sixth dimension reflects an irony. A society premised on individual freedom assumes not only the worth of each person but citizens capable of rational thought, considered judgment, and measured actions. Otherwise democratic government would be futile. Yet, we lodge the most important freedoms in the Constitution precisely because we want to give those freedoms extra protection. "The very purpose of a Bill of Rights was to . . . place [certain subjects] beyond the reach of majorities and officials and to establish them as legal principles to be applied by the courts," explained Justice Robert H. Jackson. "One's right to life, liberty, and property, to free speech, a free press, freedom of worship and assembly, and other fundamental rights may not be submitted to vote; they depend on the outcome of no elections." Jackson referred to a hard lesson learned from experience: basic rights require extra protection because they are fragile. On occasion, people have been willing to violate the freedoms of others. That reality demanded a written constitution.

This irony reflects the changing nature of a bill of rights in history. Americans did not invent the idea of a bill of rights in 1791. Instead it drew from and was inspired by colonial documents such as the Pennsylvania colony's Charter of Liberties (1701) and the English Bill of Rights (1689), Petition of Right (1628), and Magna Carta (1215). However, these early and often unsuccessful attempts to limit government power were devices to protect the many (the people) from the few (the English Crown). With the emergence of democratic political systems in the eighteenth century, however, political power shifted from the few to the many. The right to rule belonged to the person who received the most votes in an election, not necessarily to the firstborn, the wealthiest, or the most physically powerful. So the focus of a bill of rights had to shift too. No longer was it designed to shelter the majority from the minority, but to shelter the minority from the majority. "Wherever the real power in a Government lies, there is the danger of oppression," commented Madison in his exchange of letters with Jefferson in 1788. "In our Government, the real power lies in the majority of the Community, and the invasion of private rights is *chiefly* to be apprehended, not from acts of government contrary to the sense of its constituents, but from acts in which the Government is the mere instrument of the major number of the Constituents."

Americans, however, do deserve credit for having discovered a way to enforce a bill of rights. Without an enforcement mechanism, a bill of rights is no more than a list of aspirations: standards to aim for, but with no redress other than violent protest or revolution. Indeed this had been the experience in England with which the framers were thoroughly familiar. Thanks to judicial review—the authority courts in the United States possess to invalidate actions taken by the other branches of government which, in the judges' view, conflict with the Constitution—the provisions in the Bill of Rights and other constitutionally protected liberties became judicially enforceable.

Judicial review was a tradition that was beginning to emerge in the states on a small scale in the 1780s and 1790s and that would blossom in the U.S. Supreme Court in the nineteenth century and twentieth centuries. "In the arguments in favor of a declaration of rights," Jefferson presciently told Madison in the late winter of 1789 after the Constitution had been ratified, "you omit one which has great weight with me, the legal check which it puts into the hands of the judiciary." This is the reason why each of the volumes in this series focuses extensively on judicial decisions. Liberties have largely been defined by judges in the context of deciding cases in situations where individuals thought the power of government extended too far.

Designed to help democracy protect itself, the Constitution ultimately needs the support of those—the majority—who endure its restraints. Without sufficient support among the people, its freedoms rest on a weak foundation. The earnest hope of *America's Freedoms* is that this series will offer Americans a renewed appreciation and understanding of their heritage of liberty.

Yet there would be no series on America's freedoms without the interest and support of Alicia Merritt at ABC-CLIO. The series was her idea. She approached me originally about the series and was very adept at overcoming my initial hesitations as series editor. She not only helped me shape the particular topics that the series would include, but guided me toward prospective authors. As a result, the topic of each book has been matched with the most appropriate person as author. The goal in each instance has been to pair topics with authors who are recognized teachers and scholars in their field. The results have been gratifying. A series editor could hardly wish for authors who have been more cooperative, helpful, and accommodating.

Donald Grier Stephenson, Jr.

Preface and Acknowledgments

The Eighth Amendment to the U.S. Constitution prohibits "cruel and unusual punishment." State constitutions commonly contain similar provisions. Yet these provisions allow the state to kill us, to imprison us for life, or to keep us in solitary confinement for years in the new Supermax prisons. How do we reconcile this apparent contradiction?

What is cruel and unusual punishment? Few questions generate more debate and passion. But disagreements persist. Context and circumstance frame the controversy. Who was the victim and what was done to him or her? What about prevailing attitudes among judges, elected officials, the media, and the general public? Who stands accused of the crime? Are we questioning the defendant's loved ones or the victim's? Are we questioning the prosecutors or the defense team? This book does not provide definitive answers, but it does attempt to provide an even-handed analysis of the issue.

This book discusses the theoretical and historical evolution of constitutional protections against cruel and unusual punishment. It combines analysis of issues with excerpts from critical documents and landmark court decisions, along with public opinion survey results and statistical data. Some secondary sources are used for historical purposes and for illuminating ongoing debates about the subject. Primary source materials are utilized extensively. Relevant Supreme Court decisions and opinions are summarized and discussed. Carefully selected and edited excerpts from the opinions themselves are included for the convenience of the reader. Readers without formal legal training will find this book accessible, readable, and useful for purposes of following and contributing to our ongoing debate about cruel and unusual punishment.

The book is organized as follows. Chapter 1 provides a brief introduction to the subject and summarizes arguments opposing and supporting capital punishment. Chapter 2 discusses the origins and early development of cruel and unusual punishment from American colonial times through the nineteenth century. Chapter 3 reviews twentieth-century issues and interpretations of constitutional protections against cruel and unusual punishment. Chapter 4 addresses unresolved and new issues for the twenty-first century, including penalties less extreme than death and conditions of confinement. Chapter 5 provides alphabetical entries on key people, organizations, laws, cases, and events discussed in earlier chapters. Chapter 6 provides excerpts from important documents and landmark cases. A chronology and a table of cases follow. An appendix presents data, tables, and charts describing execution patterns, state death penalty statistics, public opinion surveys, and related matters. The book concludes with an annotated bibliography of relevant material and a comprehensive index.

Thanks to all the people at ABC-CLIO who worked to make this project a success. We especially want to acknowledge the support and assistance provided by series editor Donald Grier Stephenson, Jr., Charles A. Dana Professor of Government at Franklin and Marshall College; senior acquisitions editor Alicia S. Merritt, and senior production editor Melanie Stafford. Thank you for your encouragement and patience. We should also mention the Cottage Restaurant in Ebensburg, Pennsylvania, where we met frequently over long breakfasts to discuss this book. Thanks for keeping the coffee pot ready.

Joseph A. Melusky and Keith A. Pesto

1

Introduction

I will not believe an angel from heaven, should he declare that the punishment of death for any crime, was inculcated, or permitted by the spirit of the gospel.

—Benjamin Rush, "An Inquiry into the Consistency of the Punishment of Death with Reason and Revelation" (1792)

Whoever sheds the blood of man, by man shall his blood be shed.

—Genesis 9:6 (RSV)

On April 8, 2002, Ray Krone was released from an Arizona prison. In 1992, he had been convicted of the 1991 stabbing death of a cocktail waitress at a Phoenix bar. Citing the victim's eleven stab wounds and evidence that she had been sexually assaulted, a judge found that Krone had committed murder in a "heinous or depraved manner" and sentenced him to death. On appeal, his attorneys argued that crucial evidence had been hidden—evidence that bite marks on the victim came from someone else and could not have come from Krone—and Arizona's Supreme Court ordered a new trial, at which Krone was again convicted. This time he received a life sentence. Family members hired attorneys who, obtaining newly available DNA tests on the saliva found on the victim's clothing, showed that the odds were 1.3 quadrillion to one that the crime had been committed by a man who had subsequently been convicted of attempted child molestation and was already in prison.

Krone, described as a former proponent of the death penalty, was quoted as saying of his ten years in prison and three years on death row: "To make a mistake is one thing. It's another thing how you correct it afterward" (Weinstein 2002).

On April 26, 2002, at 10:13 A.M., Ohio declared Alton Coleman dead from lethal injection. Coleman, the only man on death row in three states at once, was executed 18 years after the torture murder of Marlene Walters, who had just served lemonade to Coleman and Debra Brown, his girlfriend, after they had talked their way into the Walters's home by expressing interest in purchasing a used camper. Walters was beaten to death with more than twenty blows of a wooden candlestick, and her face and scalp torn a dozen times with a pair of pliers.

Coleman's execution was televised on closed circuit television. There were too many family members of his victims for Ohio's witness room, because Coleman also had been given the death penalty in Indiana and Illinois for other brutal murders he and Brown committed during a campaign of rape, robbery, and murder between May and July of 1984. Leaving out the nonfatal rapings and kidnapings, Coleman was responsible for the strangling death of a 9-year-old girl, the rape and murder of a 7-year-old girl, the strangling of a 35-year-old woman, the rape and strangulation deaths of a 30-year-old mother and her 9-year-old daughter, the kidnaping and murder of a 15-year-old girl, and the kidnaping and murder of a 79-year-old man.

In the week before Coleman's execution, his attorneys had pursued last-minute appeals challenging the effectiveness of his trial attorneys and the alleged improper racial composition of the jury in the 1985 Ohio trial to a three-judge panel of the Court of Appeals for the Sixth Circuit, to the full Court of Appeals, and to the Supreme Court. Coleman's attorneys had also filed an unsuccessful request for clemency with Robert Taft, Jr., the governor of Ohio. Finally, Coleman's attorneys had presented a lawsuit before the Ohio Supreme Court seeking to have the closed-circuit televising of the execution barred. Debra Brown had been on death row in Ohio too, but her sentence had been commuted to life imprisonment by a former governor in 1991. Coleman and Brown were also officially under a sentence of death in Illinois, but in January 2003, Governor George Ryan commuted all Illinois death sentences to life imprisonment after several highly publicized cases of prisoners with death sentences being exonerated by the volunteer efforts of a team of journalism students (Johnson 2002).

The cases of both Krone and Coleman received extensive coverage in the media, as opponents and supporters of capital punishment attempted to persuade undecided members of the public to continue or abolish the death penalty in America. Senator Patrick Leahy of Vermont suggested that Krone's experience demonstrates the need for the passage of federal legislation he has sponsored under the title of The Innocence Protection Act. Meanwhile, the pastor of the Toledo, Ohio, church attended by two of Coleman's victims was quoted as saying, "I wanted to get him before the police. I would have killed him in a real bad way" (Johnson 2002).

The particular case histories of Krone and of Coleman and Brown present the enduring themes in the discussion of the American experience with capital punishment, because they place the spotlight on the most fundamental tensions inherent in establishing and preserving any government that draws its legitimacy from the consent of the governed. What is the primary purpose of any criminal justice system? Is it to maintain order, to accord due process to the accused, to act as moral exemplar to the citizenry?

Of the secondary objectives of punishment, what relative weight must they be given? Is justice dealt out fairly to rich and poor, to black and white, to male and female, in the North and in the South? Should there be a uniform national law on the subject of the death penalty, or is that contrary to the plan of a federal system? What proportion of the power of government should be devoted to seeking convictions, and what proportion to opposing that goal? If it is better that ten guilty go free rather than one innocent suffer, is it better that one hundred guilty go free? How about one thousand? Whose role is it to answer that question—the legislative branch, the executive, or the judicial? Does the death penalty deter crime, and, whether it does or not, should that matter? At what point does a legal system that can execute what hindsight proves to be an innocent person, and allow an unquestionably monstrous criminal to stave off execution indefinitely, lose legitimacy with both proponents and opponents of the death penalty?

It is not our intent to answer these questions, because the terms of the debate as they exist today do not permit anyone other than a demagogue to claim to have the answer. Nor is it to take a position in the debate itself. We hope in this book to present some of the considerations that have led America to its current positions, and to assess fairly both where we are as a country and where we might be going, so that the reader may contribute to the debate as a voice worth hearing, and not just an echo of some pollster's commission to deliver a decibel count.

Part of the problem in determining the scope of the Cruel and Unusual Punishments Clause is determining the purpose of any punishment. Today, when we ask, "What is the cause of crime?" we mean only "What things usually precede crime?" and the question "What is the cause of punishment?" makes no sense at all. But if we want to know whether capital punishment can be justified, we can only do so in light of our understanding of what punishment is for.

There are four distinct ends served by a system of punishments: interdiction, deterrence, rehabilitation, and retribution (Dulles 2001).

The concept of interdiction is so simple that logically it can be viewed as the first end of punishment: a criminal who is incapacitated in some way, whether by imprisonment or execution, cannot harm society further. Interdiction is merely defense against the criminal carried forward in time.

Retribution, although it is perhaps the most ancient of justifications of punishment, is by contrast a subtle and elusive concept requiring moral judgments that are most unfashionable in modern American jurisprudence. The framers of the Constitution and the ratifiers of the Bill of Rights could legitimately look to criminal sanctions as "just desserts," because they generally believed in an order of justice transcending the general will. During the twentieth-century debate in America, the declining strength of the consensus about the ends of the state and the more recent outright denial that violence or coercion in the service of order have any moral legitimacy have demoted retribution to unfashionability.

In the absence of a belief in a moral system to which secular punishment is linked, punishment can still be seen as serving a retributive end, in a debased form, as catharsis. However, the fading echo of moral argument serves to characterize catharsis as simply societal vengeance. Ironically, the quality that formerly served to justify punishment is now seen in corrupted form as the very quality that weakens its legitimacy, and in the case of capital punishment, as a wholly illegitimate usurpation of God's place by Caesar.

Just as interdiction is the defense against crime carried forward in time, deterrence is the end of punishment that seeks to extend the defense across society. Punishment of the criminal is justified as a form of moral and practical education for would-be offenders. Deterrence is certainly the most popular justification for the death penalty, but it has both philosophical and practical problems. Is it just to punish one man, even if he is guilty, just so that another might be "scared straight"? Does it degrade the criminal justice system to punish a man not because of what he has done, but because of what we fear another might do? If sending a message to the public is our goal, does the guilt or innocence of the defendant really matter, or just the perception that the system is effective?

Finally, rehabilitation is at once the most rewarding and most tantalizing end of a system of punishment. It is no accident that efforts to formulate a "rehabilitative" system of punishment arose in the American colonies and the young United States in the same generation as the ratification of the Constitution. Both projects shared a liberal optimism about human nature and the efficacy of reason to transform character. Thus in place of "prison," the rehabilitative ideal offered the "penitentiary." Likewise, it is no accident that as the notion of reforming the criminal through punishment has encountered rising skepticism and outright rejection in recent years, new places for holding convicted criminals are increasingly called "prison camps" instead of "correctional institutions."

The issue of rehabilitation takes on special meaning in the death penalty controversy. Death penalty abolitionists cite cases like Tony Amadeo, whose sentence of death was overturned by a rare unanimous Supreme Court in 1988. On retrial, he was again convicted, but this time was given a life sentence. After years in prison, he was graduated from Mercer University *summa cum laude,* delivering the class valedictory address from prison. Death penalty proponents and friends and relatives of murder victims, on the other hand, often find such "success stories" twice galling, because no rehabilitation can be offered to the victims whose lives were snuffed out. This rejection of rehabilitation as a valid goal of the criminal justice system is, curiously enough, sometimes shared by libertarians who deny that the state has the authority to use coercive confinement to induce any change of behavior by criminal defendants.

History

Daniel Frank was the first person known to have been executed in the American colonies. He was put to death in 1622 in the colony of Virginia for the crime of theft. Since that time, the death penalty has been an almost constant feature of the criminal justice system of the United States. National statistics have been compiled only since about 1930 (*Bureau of Justice Statistics,* U.S. Department of Justice.)

From 1930 through 1967, 3,859 civilians were executed in the United States. During the same years, the U.S. Army executed 160 persons. The U.S. Navy has executed no one since 1849. Over half (54 percent) of the civilians executed were black, 45 percent were white, and the rest were members of other racial groups. Three out of five executions during this period took place in Southern states. On average, 130 executions took place per year. Most executions—3,334 of 3,859 (86 percent)—were for murder, 455 (12 percent) were for rape, and 70 (2 percent) were for other offenses. Ninety percent of prisoners executed for rape were black.

By the late 1960s, all but ten states had laws authorizing capital punishment, but they were rarely used. Federal executions halted after 1963, and legal challenges and political pressure by opponents of the death penalty resulted in a de facto moratorium on executions by the states after 1967.

In 1972, the U.S. Supreme Court *appeared* to strike down the death penalty itself in *Furman v. Georgia.* The decision revealed a severely split Court. Only two of the justices who concurred in the decision—Justices Brennan and Marshall—found capital punishment to be flatly prohibited by the Constitution in all cases. The other three concurring justices—Justices Douglas, Stewart, and White—stressed the appearance of racial bias in, or the arbitrariness of, the *application* of the death penalty. In dissent, Chief Justice Warren Burger pointed out that the Court had not banned capital punishment and invited state legislatures to reform their sentencing procedures.

In response to *Furman,* states began revising their death penalty laws to provide juries with "guided discretion" in sentencing decisions. Such laws called for two-stage trials, with the first stage determining the defendant's guilt or innocence and the second stage determining the sentence upon consideration of aggravating or mitigating circumstances. In 1976, the Supreme Court upheld laws of this kind in three related cases usually known as *Gregg v. Georgia.* Some states attempted to eliminate arbitrariness by providing "mandatory death penalties" for specified crimes: no judicial or jury discretion was permitted beyond determining the defendant's guilt or innocence. In 1978, the Supreme Court invalidated these mandatory death penalty laws.

Capital punishment in the states resumed under revised death penalty laws when convicted murderer Gary Gilmore was executed by a Utah firing squad in 1977. The federal government had never repealed its unused death penalty laws after *Furman,* but after major legislative changes in 1994, federal death rows began a slow expansion. Federal executions resumed, using lethal injection, in 2001.

As of April 2002, there were 3,701 inmates on death row, 25 of them on federal death row. There have been at least ten executions every year in the United States since 1984, with a high of 98 in 1999. Through April 2002, 765 persons had been executed, 2 by the federal government. Of these, 429 (56 percent) were white, and 269 (35 percent) were black; 757 (99 percent) were men, and 8 (1 percent) were women. A total of 38 states and the federal government had the death penalty, and 12 states and the District of Columbia did not (NAACP Legal Defense and Educational Fund 2002, 1, 8).

The Constitution and the Death Penalty

The U.S. Constitution provides the framework for the American political system and places limits on governmental powers by specifying that individuals possess certain rights that may not be infringed. The Constitution, written in 1787, ratified in 1789, contains just 4,223 words. That would be about seventeen double-spaced, typewritten pages. After the Bill of Rights was added in 1791 as the first ten amendments, it has been amended only seventeen times. It is the most durable written governmental document in the world: nearly two-thirds of the world's 160 national constitutions have been written or revised since 1970, and on average each nation has had two constitutions since 1945 (Melusky 2000, 41).

One secret to the Constitution's durability is its language. Many provisions, such as the Eighth Amendment's ban on "cruel and unusual punishments," are written in general, open-ended fashion. What does this phrase mean? The framers did not say. We cover some of the history relevant to the meaning of cruel and unusual punishment in Chapter 2.

Some contend that the Eighth Amendment's language permits it to evolve with changing times. Others assert that the idea of an evolving Constitution is a contradiction in terms, and that what the framers set down can be changed legitimately only by the cumbersome amendment procedure of Article V of the Constitution (Melusky 2000, 40–65).

Regardless of political views, all agree that judges must interpret the Constitution to apply it to contemporary matters. Judges are expected to rely on the actual text of the provision in question, relevant earlier judicial decisions, legislative history, and the intent of the framers, but not to substitute their personal preferences for these authorities (Bork 1989).

This is not a simple matter. Consider trying to construe the Eighth Amendment according to the intent of the framers. It can be difficult to determine what they really intended, because they sometimes disagreed and their records are incomplete. Even deciding who the "framers" are can be a matter of dispute; the delegates to the 1787 constitutional convention in Philadelphia, the delegates to the ratification conventions in the nine states needed before the Constitution became effective in 1789, and the voters in the states who joined the Union after that year could all be considered "framers of the constitution." These problems apply as well to identifying the framers of the Bill of Rights.

Furthermore, even if we could agree on the meaning of "cruel and unusual punishments" when the Eighth Amendment was ratified in 1791, can we ignore more than two hundred years of legal developments since then? Just as the Fourth Amendment's prohibition of "unreasonable searches and seizures" must now address wiretaps, airplane overflights, and facial recognition software, so must interpretation of the Eighth Amendment consider changing views on death and punishment and on the resources available for rehabilitation and incarceration.

Does the Eighth Amendment prohibit only punishments thought cruel in 1791, such as burning at the stake, drawing and quartering, or breaking someone on the wheel? The guillotine and the electric chair were welcomed as humane when they were introduced—the guillotine to replace the inept or drunken executioner who might need several blows to sever a head, and the electric chair to replace an improperly fashioned noose that (if the drop were too short) caused a slow death by strangulation or (if the drop were too long) decapitation.

Because electric chairs have malfunctioned with gruesome results, and because even when they work properly it is uncertain how long the electrocuted individual remains conscious, most states have moved to lethal injections as a more humane method of performing executions. Does the move to lethal injection now make use of the outmoded electric chair "cruel"? If it is not cruel, how about "unusual"? Does that term add an additional limitation on punishment, suggesting that a punishment used only rarely is no longer constitutional? And how should "rarely" be defined? If forty-nine states use lethal injection and one still uses the electric chair, but uses it regularly, is the electric chair an unusual punishment? We present the history of this and similar debates in Chapter 3.

Whether capital punishment is a barbaric punishment that today would absolutely be prohibited by the Eighth Amendment's ban on cruel and unusual punishment, it is certain that the framers of the Constitution and Bill of Rights did not think so, because the Fifth Amendment provides that the federal government shall not deprive persons of "life, liberty, or property without due process of law." If persons *may* be deprived of their lives if they have received due process of law, what is "due process of law"? We will touch on that matter also in chapter 3.

The ban on cruel and unusual punishment extends beyond the death penalty. Some have argued that a sentence disproportionate to the crime should be declared by a court to be unconstitutionally cruel and unusual, whereas others contend that the Constitution commits the length of sentences exclusively to the legislatures. Under today's increasingly popular mandatory sentencing system and "three strikes" laws for repeat offenders, a three-time offender might be sentenced to a maximum of life imprisonment for shoplifting. In 1791 a shoplifter could have been hanged, but today is putting her in jail for twenty-five years cruel and unusual?

What about corporal punishment? Early federal laws required whipping as the punishment for some offenses, but today that seems a relic of the era of slavery. Recall the case of Michael Fay, an American citizen in Singapore, who in 1994 was sentenced to be beaten with a cane. The event provoked public condemnation in the United States but also a call from many to reintroduce public flogging in this country (Hall 1995). Would the practice violate the Eighth Amendment?

The Eighth Amendment also is relevant to prison conditions after a sentence is passed. Solitary confinement, once considered rehabilitative, is now considered a severe disciplinary sanction. Is it cruel? What about mandatory treatment for a repeat sex offender, even after his sentence ends? Is the Eighth Amendment even applicable to rehabilitative programs not intended for punishment? Some have said no, whereas others argue that this would allow return even of the classic chain gang just by billing it as an educational program. We discuss these issues in Chapter 4.

VOICES OF THE CAPITAL PUNISHMENT DEBATE

The Case against Capital Punishment

Proponents of the death penalty argue that it is right and useful. Critics reply that it is morally unacceptable and fails to deter crime. As veteran death penalty defense lawyer Jack Greenberg observes, "Were the subject not so grim and compelling, the exchanges would, by now, be tiresome" (Greenberg 1986). He concedes that proponents of capital punishment want the system to function in such a way that the death penalty is inflicted only on the most reprehensible criminals and is carried out with sufficient frequency to deter other would-be capital offenders. But, Greenberg charges, this idealized system of capital punishment does not exist in the United States, and never has: the death penalty is carried out rarely and erratically, often against the least odious killers, most often against killers of whites, and almost never against killers of blacks.

Some 19,000 homicides are committed in the United States each year, but, Greenberg computes, as of 1986 the average number of executions per year has been about twenty. This, he believes, reflects the public's ambivalence about capital punishment. One reason for the small number of executions is that courts upset the majority of capital convictions, often on grounds unrelated to the heinousness of the crime. The most reprehensible criminals have escaped the death penalty because the defense counsel, the prosecutor, or the judge acted ineffectively or improperly, while less abhorrent criminals have been executed because their trials "went well." The current system of capital punishment, then, violates a central principle of justice, namely, that only the most reprehensible criminals deserve to be executed, and lesser crimes deserve lesser sentences.

Other critics question the deterrent effect of capital punishment. For the death penalty to deter serious crimes such as homicide more effectively than life imprisonment, the criminal would have to have a rough sense of the odds of being caught, convicted, and most important, executed. Most killers cannot engage in the kind of cost-benefit analysis that deterrence requires; many are disturbed or are of low intelligence, and homicides often happen in the heat of passion or anger or under the influence of drugs or alcohol. Even if would-be killers thought about the consequences, critics say they would hear this message: You may in rare cases be executed if you murder a white person in Texas, Florida, or Virginia, cannot afford a private attorney, and waive your right to appeals (Bright 1994).

Because criminals are frequently calculating but not rational, there are times when the death penalty actually has encouraged capital crimes, by defendants who kill and manipulate the death penalty appeals process as just another expression of their sociopathic personalities. Consider David Paul Hammer, serving a prison term of more than 1,000 years, who in April 1996 convinced his cellmate that being injured in an altercation would result in a transfer to a better prison, and after binding him strangled him to death. Hammer pleaded guilty and waived all appeals. Confined at the federal death row facility at Terre Haute, Indiana, Hammer has repeatedly changed his mind, and more than six years later he is still posting content to the death row Web site and does not have a firm execution date (Serrano 2001).

Yet another blow to deterrence comes from the large subset of executions, most famously those of Gary Gilmore and Timothy McVeigh, that are assisted by the prisoner's voluntary discontinuance of appeals. All three executions that have occurred in Pennsylvania in the modern era have been "volunteers for death," and in Nevada seven of eight executions since 1979 were consensual (Liebman et al. 2000, 1865 n.43).

Capital punishment is also opposed by questioning the reasonableness of retribution. Coretta Scott King, widow of slain civil rights leader Martin Luther King, Jr., said in a speech given to the National Coalition to Abolish the Death Penalty on September 26, 1981: "An evil deed is not redeemed by an evil deed of retaliation. Justice is never advanced in the taking of human life. Morality is never upheld by legalized murder" (Bedau 1997, n.54).

The American Civil Liberties Union (ACLU) maintains that the death penalty violates the constitutional provisions concerning not only cruel and unusual punishment but also due process of law and equal protection. In the ACLU's Capital Punishment Project pamphlet, "The Case Against the Death Penalty," philosophy professor Hugo A. Bedau lists reasons why the death penalty is an "intolerable denial of civil liberties" (Bedau 1997):

- Capital punishment is a relic of the early days of penology like slavery, branding, and other forms of corporal punishment, and has no place in civilized society. It is barbarous, even when administered by lethal injection.
- Murder demonstrates disrespect for human life. State-authorized execution is the moral equivalent of murder and does the same.
- Because it is irreversible, capital punishment denies due process of law: a defendant can never benefit from new evidence or legal standards that might warrant the setting aside of a sentence.
- The death penalty is applied both randomly and discriminatorily. It is imposed disproportionally upon those whose victims are white, offenders who are people of color, and on those who are poor and uneducated.
- Changes in death sentencing have been largely cosmetic. The defects in the death penalty laws struck down in the 1970s have not been remedied.

- Experts, including police chiefs, agree that the death penalty is not an effective deterrent. When told that the alternative punishment was life without parole, most proponents of the death penalty change their minds.
- Capital punishment, because it is such an expensive and lengthy process, saps the resources of the criminal justice system.
- The international community regards capital punishment as both cruel and unusual.

On this last point, the trend is clear. All nations in Western Europe have abolished the death penalty, and abolition is a requirement for entry into the European Union. Russia commuted all of its civilian death sentences in 1999. Canada abolished capital punishment in 1976. The South African constitutional court has prohibited the death penalty as inhumane. Between 1989 and 1995, two dozen other countries abolished the death penalty. More than half of all nations have abolished the death penalty. The United Nations General Assembly has passed a formal resolution urging nations to abolish the death penalty. Once used widely, the death penalty today is generally forbidden in most countries outside the United States.

Matthew Stephens, a prison chaplain, also argues against capital punishment on the grounds that it is unevenly applied, defendants sometimes receive inadequate counsel, costs are too high, and it fails to deter crime (Stephens 1999, 160–168). Consider his review of the death penalty data:

- Between 15,000 and 20,000 homicides are committed in the United States each year, but only 200 murderers are sentenced to death. Most persons selected for capital punishment are poor. Many are mentally retarded, with about one-third of death row inmates having an IQ of less than 70. Race is the most important factor in determining who will be sentenced to death: few whites are executed for killing blacks.

- Many capital defendants cannot afford to hire their own attorneys and are represented by poorly paid and inexperienced lawyers working with limited resources. Capital defendants with court-appointed lawyers are more likely to receive death sentences than those who hire their own attorneys. Stephens's "lousy-lawyering" argument was dramatically illustrated by the case of a Texas lawyer who delivered this statement at sentencing: "You are an extremely intelligent jury. You've got that man's life in your hands. You can take it or not. That's all I have to say." His client was executed in 1992 (McCormick 1998, 64).
- Economic costs in capital cases vary from state to state, but they run high. For example, a report from the *Miami Herald* said that keeping a prisoner in jail for life would cost the state in excess of $500,000, based on a forty-year life span in prison. By contrast, the newspaper reported, each execution costs more than $3 million when costs associated with trial and sentencing, mandatory state review, additional appeals, jail costs, and the actual execution are taken into account.
- Some states show an *increase* in violent crime after instituting capital punishment. Calls for the death penalty, then, come more from a desire for revenge than a need for deterrence. In sum, Stephens contends that the death penalty is arbitrary as well as racist in its application.

One of the most often cited objections to the death penalty is that any mistakes cannot be undone. Mistakes undoubtedly occur. Sociology professor Michael Radelet and Bedau have written extensively about cases of men and women who were freed from death row on the strong likelihood—or the certainty—that they were not guilty. In the cases they discuss, the average time from conviction to exoneration was seven years (Radelet et al. 1996). Had the system moved faster, some wrongly convicted people would have been executed. Nevertheless, Radelet and Bedau have documented more than 400 cases since 1900 in which an innocent person was convicted of murder or rape, of which twenty-three were executed (Radelet et al. 1996, 907, and Bedau et al. 1987, 23–24).

The American Bar Association House of Delegates passed a resolution at its 1997 meeting calling for a halt on executions until courts nationwide can ensure that capital cases are administered fairly and impartially, in accordance with due process, and with minimum risk of executing innocent people.

The Case for Capital Punishment

Ernest van den Haag, a sociologist, provides a defense of capital punishment (van den Haag 1986). He admits that because fewer than thirty murderers are executed in the United States in a single year, most convicts sentenced to death are likely to die of old age. Nevertheless, use of the death penalty raises important questions because it is society's harshest punishment, it is irrevocable, and it is the only corporal punishment still applied to adults in this country.

Discussions about the justice and morality of capital punishment are sometimes combined with the criticism that it is applied in a discriminatory fashion. The argument is that the death penalty is immoral because it is most frequently inflicted upon racial, ethnic, and economic minorities. Van den Haag rejects this complaint, maintaining that if capital punishment itself is immoral, then no distribution affects the morality of what is being distributed. Conversely, maldistribution of any punishment among those who deserve it does not affect its justice or morality. Even if poor or black convicts guilty of capital offenses are executed and other equally guilty convicts are not executed, a more equal distribution would not be more *just.* It would merely be more *equal.* Punishments are imposed on individuals, not on racial or ethnic groups. Guilt is personal. The relevant question is: Does *this* individual deserve the punishment? Whether or not others who also deserve the punishment actually receive it is irrelevant. If a person who deserves to be executed escapes the punishment, the guilt of the individual who *is* executed is in no way diminished. In short, if the death penalty were imposed on guilty blacks but not on guilty whites, this irrational and discriminatory distribution would not make the penalty unjust. No individual who did not deserve the penalty would receive it. Van den Haag concedes that distributional inequities offend our sense of equality, but he maintains that equality is less important than justice. Justice is independent of distributional inequalities. Justice requires that as many of the guilty as possible be punished, regardless of whether other guilty persons have avoided the punishment. To let some guilty persons escape punishment does not do justice to them or to society, but it is not unjust to those guilty persons who were executed.

Van den Haag does not doubt that miscarriages of justice occur, even in capital cases. In spite of precautions, innocent persons might be executed. But nearly all human activities, such as trucking or construction, cost the lives of some innocent bystanders. There are always risks. We do not give up these activities because the advantages outweigh unintended losses. It follows that for those who think the death penalty just, occasional miscarriages of justice are offset by the moral benefits of capital justice. For those who think the death penalty unjust even when it does not miscarry, occasional miscarriages are not decisive.

Van den Haag acknowledges that there is no conclusive statistical evidence that the death penalty is a better deterrent than other punishments. However, he does not consider deterrence to be the primary reason for the death penalty. Nonetheless, he believes that the death penalty, because of its finality, is more feared than imprisonment. Even if the death penalty does not deter all murderers, it deters some. Sparing the lives of even a few prospective victims by deterring their murderers is valuable.

It is sometimes argued that inmates on death row, who spend years facing eventual execution, suffer more than their victims, and that this excess suffering is undue under the rule of retaliation. Van den Haag replies that, unlike the murderer, the victim deserved none of the suffering inflicted. Furthermore, punishment is not intended to offset or compensate for the victim's suffering or to be limited by it. This is why, for example, a kidnaper's prison sentence is not limited to precisely the period for which he imprisoned his victim. Punishment is intended to vindicate the social order undermined by the crime.

Van den Haag responds to the argument that the death penalty for murderers endorses killing or is the moral equivalent of murder by pointing out that imprisonment is not thought to legitimize kidnaping. Fines are not thought to legitimize robbery. The difference between murder and execution, between kidnaping and imprisonment, and between robbery and fines, is that the first is unlawful and undeserved and the second is a deserved punishment for an unlawful act.

Is the death penalty unjust? Van den Haag states that the death penalty cannot be unjust to a guilty criminal. By committing a crime, a criminal assumes the risk of receiving a punishment he could have avoided by refraining from committing the crime. The punishment he suffers is one he voluntarily risked suffering.

Is the death penalty excessive? Some believe that no crime, no matter how heinous, can justify capital punishment. Van den Haag says that such a belief can be neither proven nor refuted. It is an article of faith.

As for the assertion that the death penalty is uniquely degrading to human dignity, van den Haag argues that the murderer learns through his punishment that his fellow men and women have found him unworthy of living. Because he has murdered, he is being expelled from the community of the living. His execution does not degrade him. It affirms his humanity by recognizing his rationality and responsibility for his actions.

John Stuart Mill, one of the most influential of the nineteenth-century liberals and hailed today as a patron saint of libertarians, also argued in favor of capital punishment. In a speech given before Parliament on April 21, 1868, he spoke in opposition to a bill banning capital punishment. At the time, the death penalty had been progressively abolished in Great Britain and was reserved for those convicted of aggravated murder. Parliament was deliberating as to whether the penalty should be removed even for this crime. Mill argued that where there is conclusive proof of guilt, depriving the criminal of "the life of which he has proved himself to be unworthy" is the most appropriate punishment (Mill 1868). Mill defended the death penalty on the ground on which it is commonly attacked: humanity to the criminal. The death penalty, he reasoned, is the *least* cruel method of deterring murderers. Subjecting a murderer to imprisonment with hard labor for life places him in "a living tomb" long after memory of his crime has faded. Compared with the "short pang of a rapid death," a long life of arduous and monotonous toil is more cruel. The criminal law merely hastens death. The criminal would have died eventually at any rate, and in all likelihood with a greater amount of bodily suffering.

To those who say that capital punishment does not always deter, Mill responded that its influence should not be measured by its effect on hardened criminals. Those whose way of life keeps them "within sight of the gallows" become hardened and grow to care little about the prospect of capital punishment. As old soldiers are little affected by the chance of dying in battle, professional criminals become indifferent to the gallows. But the effectiveness of capital punishment should be judged by its restraining impact on those who are still innocent and who are inspired to resist temptation. Abolitionists claim that capital punishment fails to deter. After all, we know that some murders occur and that these perpetrators have not been deterred by the death penalty. But we cannot know how many people it *has* deterred. Nor can we know how many human beings have been saved from those who would otherwise have murdered them.

Capital punishment, Mill admitted, should be reserved for the most atrocious crimes. When its use is threatened for lesser offenses, it loses effectiveness. It does not intimidate if criminals do not believe in it. Pickpockets worked the crowd during public executions. According to Mill, however, the thieves did not believe that they would be executed. Mill rejected the abolitionist argument that the death penalty denies the sanctity of human life and that it is absurd to try to teach respect for life by destroying it. As Mill saw it, this argument could be advanced against any form of punishment. The very purpose of the criminal justice system is to inflict suffering on criminals to deter others from inflicting suffering on innocent people. Fining a criminal does not show disrespect for property. Imprisoning a criminal does not show disrespect for personal freedom. Similarly, executing a murderer does not show disrespect for human life. On the contrary, it underscores our regard for human life by enforcing a rule that he who takes a life shall forfeit his own.

Mill admitted that if by an error an innocent person is put to death, the mistake can never be remedied. No compensation is possible. This argument is convincing where the criminal justice system is dangerous to the innocent. However, Mill believed that any defects in the criminal justice system of his time were just the opposite. Rules of evidence favored the prisoner. Courts followed the maxim that it is better for ten guilty persons to escape than for a single innocent person to suffer. The system gave the accused the benefit of the "merest shadow of a doubt." The recognition by judges and juries of the impossibility of correcting errors in capital cases, Mill thought, made judges and juries even more careful in finding a defendant guilty. His arguments are echoed in contemporary debates.

Statistical evidence, like opinion poll evidence, is often put forward on the pro–death penalty side as well. In 1975, economist Isaac Ehrlich published a study in which he concluded that each execution deterred eight murders. Solicitor General Robert Bork used this study in arguing for the constitutionality of the death penalty in *Gregg v. Georgia* in 1976 (Radelet and Akers 1996, 3). Although the study was criticized on methodological grounds, other studies have obtained similar results.

Essayist Robert Lee supports capital punishment on the ground that it deters: it deters the person who has been executed from ever again repeating the crime. But deterrence, he believes, should not be considered the primary reason for administering the death penalty. It is wrong to punish one person merely to serve as an example to others. The most important point is whether or not the punishment is deserved. Besides, any deterrent effect has little to do with the condemned person's guilt or innocence. Deterrence could be achieved, he says, just as effectively if an innocent person were killed. To him, the important question is whether the accused *earned* this penalty. (Lee 1990, 152–159).

As for the argument that capital punishment is financially expensive, Lee charges that the high cost is due to excessive appeals and delaying tactics employed by defense attorneys. In an address to the American Law Institute on May 16, 1990, Chief Justice William Rehnquist recommended that death row inmates be given one chance to challenge their sentence in state courts and one chance to challenge it in federal courts. Lee echoes this belief that appeals should be limited.

Lee rejects the argument that justice should be tempered by mercy. He insists that the state does not have the *moral* right to intervene and extend mercy to a murderer on the part of the murder victim. Consequently, the only responsible alternative is to adopt *justice* as the standard for assigning punishment.

Lee, finally, endorses the argument that capital punishment is supported by society's sense of a need for retribution. He points to public opinion polls showing that three out of four Americans favor capital punishment, and he quotes British jurist Lord Denning, who said in 1953 that punishment is the way in which society "expresses its denunciation of wrongdoing; and in order to maintain respect for law, it is essential that the punishment for grave crimes shall adequately reflect the revulsion felt by a great majority of citizens for them."

Justice Blackmun versus Justice Scalia: Tinkering with the "Machinery of Death"

In Chapters 3 and 4, we explain the importance of the Supreme Court in the administration of the nation's several dozen capital punishment systems. Because in many ways the Supreme Court both speaks for the nation's sense of justice and echoes the nation's divisions over what is justice, it is appropriate to give the last word in this chapter to two Supreme Court justices. They presented their starkly contrasting views on the constitutionality of the death penalty in *Callins v. Collins* (1994), an otherwise run-of-the-mill Texas death penalty case. Justice Harry Blackmun, who had voted to uphold the death penalty in cases earlier in his career on the basis of judicial deference to the democratic process, expressed his personal frustration at the death penalty itself and at the attempt to find constitutional rules that would make capital punishment "work." He set the stage by describing the atmosphere of the execution scene:

> Bruce Edwin Callins will be executed [tomorrow] by the state of Texas. Intravenous tubes attached to his arms will carry the instrument of death, a toxic fluid designed specifically for the purpose of killing human beings. The witnesses . . . will behold Callins . . . strapped to a gurney, seconds away from extinction. Within days, or perhaps hours, the

memory of Callins will begin to fade. The wheels of justice will churn again, and somewhere, another jury or another judge will have the . . . task of determining whether some human being is to live or die.

After detailing all the procedural errors that compromise the reliability of a verdict of guilty and the sentence of death, Blackmun returned to the question of whether we could ever execute with the certainty that the penalty was just:

Our collective conscience will remain uneasy. Twenty years have passed since this court declared that the death penalty must be imposed fairly and with reasonable consistency or not at all, and despite the effort of the states and courts to devise legal formulas and procedural rules to meet this . . . challenge, the death penalty remains fraught with arbitrariness, discrimination . . . and mistake. . . .

Blackmun concluded with this personal plea:

From this day forward, I no longer shall tinker with the machinery of death. For more than 20 years I have endeavored . . . to develop . . . rules that would lend more than the mere appearance of fairness to the death penalty endeavor. . . . Rather than continue to coddle the court's delusion that the desired level of fairness has been achieved . . . I feel . . . obligated simply to concede that the death penalty experiment has failed. It is virtually self-evident to me now that no combination of procedural rules or substantive regulations ever can save the death penalty from its inherent constitutional deficiencies. . . .

Justice Antonin Scalia, known for his conservative views as well as his repeated calls for the judiciary not to overstep the limits placed on it by the Constitution, responded to Justice Blackmun. He began by lecturing Justice Blackmun on history, pointing out that any deficiencies in the death penalty process were largely the fault of the Supreme Court:

> The Fifth Amendment provides that "[n]o persons shall be held to answer for a capital . . . crime, unless on a presentment or indictment of a Grand Jury . . . nor be deprived of life . . . without the due process of law." This clearly permits the death penalty to be imposed, and establishes beyond doubt that the death penalty is not one of the "cruel and unusual punishments" prohibited by the Eighth Amendment. [H]owever, over the years since 1972 this court has attached to the imposition of the death penalty two quite incompatible sets of commands: the sentencer's discretion to impose death must be closely confined, but the sentencer's discretion not to impose death (to extend mercy) must be unlimited. These commands were invented without benefit of any textual or historical support; they are the product of just such "intellectual, moral, and personal" perceptions as Justice Blackmun expresses today, some of which . . . have been made part of what is called "the court's Eighth Amendment jurisprudence."

Justice Scalia implied that Justice Blackmun had written his own discomfort into the Constitution:

> Convictions in opposition to the death penalty are often passionate and deeply held. That would be no excuse for reading them into a Constitution that does not contain them, even if they represented the convictions of a majority of Americans. Much less is there any excuse for using that course to thrust a minority's views upon the people.

Finally, Justice Scalia ended where Justice Blackmun began, by putting a face on the impersonal legal process of capital punishment jurisprudence. Significantly, Justice Scalia chose not the defendant awaiting execution, but his victim, and the other victims of the inmates of death row:

> Justice Blackmun begins his statement by describing with poignancy the death of a convicted murderer by lethal injection. He chooses, as the case in which to make that statement, one of the less brutal of the

murders that regularly come before us, the murder of a man ripped by a bullet suddenly and unexpectedly, with no opportunity to prepare himself and his affairs, and left to bleed to death on the floor of a tavern. The death-by-injection which Justice Blackmun describes looks pretty desirable next to that. It looks even better next to some of the other cases currently before us, which Justice Blackmun did not select as the vehicle for his announcement that the death penalty is always unconstitutional, for example, the case of the 11-year-old girl raped by four men and then killed by stuffing her panties down her throat. How enviable a quiet death by lethal injection compared with that!

As you read on, consider both sides of the issue.

REFERENCES AND FURTHER READING

"ABA Calls for Moratorium on Executions until Death Penalty Fairness Assured." http://www.pbs.org/wgbh/pages/frontline/angel/procon/aba.html.

Bedau, Hugo Adam. 1997. "The Case against the Death Penalty." American Civil Liberties Union Freedom Network at http://www.aclu.org/liberty/case_against_death.html.

Bedau, Hugo A., and Michael L. Radelet. 1987. "Miscarriages of Justice in Potentially Capital Cases." *Stanford Law Review* 40(November):21.

Bork, Robert. 1989. "The Case against Political Judging." *National Review*, December 8.

Bright, Stephen. 1994. "Counsel for the Poor: The Death Penalty Not for the Worst Crime But for the Worst Lawyer." *Yale Law Journal* 103: 1835.

Death Penalty Information Center. *History of the Death Penalty.* Available at http://www.deathpenaltyinfo.org (15 June 2002).

Dulles, Avery. 2001. "Catholicism and Capital Punishment." *First Things* 112(April): 30.

Greenberg, Jack. 1986. "Against the American System of Capital Punishment." *Harvard Law Review* 99(May): 1670; also available at http://www.pbs.org/wgbh/pages/frontline/angel/procon/greenbergarticle.html (February 13, 2002).

Hall, Daniel E. 1995. "When Caning Meets the Eighth Amendment: Whipping Offenders in the United States." *Widener Journal of Public Law* 4: 403.

Johnson, Alan, and Jon Craig. 2002. "Tragic Timing: Alton Coleman's Many Victims Fell Prey to Fate, Circumstances." *Columbus Dispatch*, April 15.

Lee, Robert W. 1990. "Deserving to Die." *The New American*, August 13. Reprinted in *Taking Sides: Clashing Views on Controversial Political Issues*, ed. George McKenna and Stanley Feingold. Guilford, CT: Dushkin/McGraw-Hill, 1999.

Liebman, James S., Jeffrey Fagan, Valerie West, and Jonathan Lloyd. 2000. "Capital Attrition: Error Rates in Capital Cases, 1973–1995." *Texas Law Review* 78(June): 1839.

McCormick, John. 1998. "The Wrongly Condemned: How Many Capital Cases End in False Convictions?" *Newsweek*, November 9.

Melusky, Joseph. 2000. *The American Political System: An Owner's Manual.* New York: McGraw-Hill.

Mill, John Stuart. 1868. "Speech in Favor of Capital Punishment." *Ethics Updates.* Available at http://ethics.acusd.edu/Mill.html.

NAACP Legal Defense and Educational Fund, Inc. 2002. "Death Row U.S.A." Available at http://www.naacpldf.org (June 28, 2002).

Pope John Paul II. *Evangelium Vitae* (The Gospel of Life). March 25, 1995.

Prejean, Sister Helen. 1993. *Dead Man Walking: An Eyewitness Account of the Death Penalty in the United States.* New York: Vintage Books/Random House.

Radelet, Michael L., and Ronald L. Akers. 1996. "Deterrence and the Death Penalty: The Views of the Experts." *Journal of Criminal Law and Criminology* 87(Fall): 1.

Radelet, Michael L., William S. Lofquist, and Hugo A. Bedau. 1996. "Prisoners Released from Death Rows since 1970 Because of Doubts about Their Guilt." *Thomas M. Cooley Law Review* 13(Michaelmas Term): 789.

Serrano, Richard A. 2001. "Forgotten in Life, Jail, and Death." *Los Angeles Times*, January 22.

Stephens, Matthew L. 1990. "Instrument of Justice or Tool of Vengeance?" *Christian Social Action* 3, no. 10 (November). Reprinted in *Taking Sides: Clashing Views on Controversial Political Issues*, ed. George McKenna and Stanley Feingold. Guilford, CT: Dushkin/McGraw-Hill, 1999.

Van den Haag, Ernest. 1986. "The Ultimate Punishment: A Defense." *Harvard Law Review* 99(May): 1662.

Weinstein, Henry. 2002. "Death Penalty Foes Mark A Milestone." *Los Angeles Times,* April 10.

2

Origins and Early Development

The Law is unknown to him that knoweth not the Reason thereof.

—Chief Justice Edward Coke, *The First Part of the Institutes of the Lawes of England* (1628)

America in the Era before Independence

One cannot intelligently consider the merits of the arguments for and against capital punishment in America without considering its history, which literally and figuratively is human history at its worst. Indeed, the book most widely owned by Americans today and most often read as authority by the generation of 1776 and the framers of the Constitution, the Bible, begins its history of humanity with the admonition from God that "in the day that you eat of [the tree of the knowledge of good and evil] you shall die" (Gen. 2:17, RSV).

In the Garden of Eden, death is explained as the inevitable consequence of sin, not as a criminal sanction, but as the framers well knew, by the time of Moses the Jewish people already possessed a well-developed criminal code, complete with at least two levels of courts, which mandated the death penalty for crimes from premeditated murder down to gathering firewood on the Sabbath. Hence to Americans of the era of the drafting of the Constitution and the Bill of Rights, whether relaxed Virginia Anglicans like Thomas Jefferson and James Madison or dour Calvinist New Englanders like Fisher Ames and the Adamses, the death penalty would have been seen not only as historically commonplace but as intrinsically just and even divinely prescribed.

To understand the eighteenth-century attitude toward the death penalty, it would help to reflect on the celebrated but not atypical discussion of God's justice in the sermon "Sinners in the Hands of an Angry God," first delivered in Connecticut in 1741 by Jonathan Edwards, the most important early American theologian, the first president of what is now Princeton University, and the grandfather of Thomas Jefferson's vice president, Aaron Burr. In the milder sections of his warning to the unregenerate of his congregation, Edwards compared eternal justice to earthly justice:

> Sometimes earthly kings have a mind to show how terrible their wrath is, by the extreme punishments they would execute on those that would provoke them. Nebuchadnezzar, that mighty and haughty monarch of the Chaldean empire, was willing to show his wrath enraged with Shadrach, Meschech, and Abednego; and accordingly gave orders that the burning fiery furnace should be heated seven times hotter than it was before; doubtless, it was raised to the utmost degree of fierceness that human art could raise it. But the great God is also willing to show his wrath, and magnify his awful majesty and mighty power in the extreme sufferings of his enemies. . . .
>
> Thus it will be with you. . . .
>
> It is everlasting wrath. It would be dreadful to suffer this fierceness and wrath of Almighty God one moment; but you must suffer it to all eternity. There will be no end to this exquisite horrible misery.

To Edwards's generation, the argument that a quick death by hanging was cruel or unusual would have seemed absurd.

To recapture that worldview, the modern reader must try to put aside the prejudices of our secular culture and the technology of our age and return to a world without closed-circuit television, rapid-fire weapons, and even barbed wire. And one thing more: not only is there no bachelor's degree in criminology and no professional corrections officers' union, but there is no public prosecutor, nor even a regular police force. How can order be maintained, and life and property protected?

One solution is banishment. From the punishment meted out to Cain after the murder of his brother Abel to the choice between death or exile facing Socrates after his conviction for impiety to the settlement of Georgia by James Oglethorpe and company in 1732, an obvious way to control crime is to banish the criminal. Americans should remember that the colonies were originally seen by sober observers not as lands of promise or a city set on a hilltop, as John Winthrop wrote in 1630, but rather as a dumping ground for "persons of low circumstance" (Beverly 1705, 325).

The advantages of a sentence of banishment, or "transportation," especially when the criminal can be sold as an indentured servant to the scarce labor market in the American colonies, are obvious. It is reasonably cheap. This was especially true of the English practice after 1718, when the Crown began subsidizing the merchant shippers at the rate of three pounds a head. It is reasonably permanent, although as trade with the New World increased, Parliament deemed it appropriate to declare English transportees who returned before their time to be felons. The sentence of transportation to the Americas was the classic English response to crime in the eighteenth century. In fact, the modern era in British penal practice can be dated almost exactly to the beginning of the Revolutionary War, when the Americas were closed to Great Britain and the Australian outlet not yet developed (Ignatieff 1978).

Transportation, with or without indentured servitude, still implies that the criminal would remain in some society, even if not in polite society. For those whose crimes proved them unfit to live among any society, the historical choice remained death. Because there are always tasks too dirty, dangerous, or brutal for any person to undertake voluntarily, alternatives almost as good as death for those condemned might be rowing in the harbor galleys of the British fleet or working on a sugar plantation in the West Indies.

Although the possibility of sentencing a criminal to execution or gradual death in slavery certainly permitted cruelty by judges, cruelty was not generally the motivation for such punishments. One can look at historical legal codes from four different eras and cultures, the Code of Hammurabi, c. 1780 B.C., the book of Exodus, c. 1300 B.C., the Code of Draco, c. 621 B.C., and the Twelve Tables of the Roman Republic, c. 451 B.C. The punishment for a typical crime is death. The alternative is banishment or a monetary penalty, in default of payment of which the defendant is often to be sold into slavery. Imprisonment is hardly mentioned.

Similarly, philosophers discussing the ideal state, from Aristotle's *Politics* to Thomas More's *Utopia,* refer to death, fines, banishment, and slavery as methods of dealing with criminals but have a blind spot when it comes to imprisonment.

The lack of alternatives to death was a mirror of social conflicts on a large scale. From the Punic Wars between Rome and Carthage to the Mongol conquests of Persian and Arab states, battles often ended with the total extermination of the losing army, and as late as the seventeenth century, the Dutch jurist Hugo Grotius wrote that by natural law the victor in war had the right to enslave or exterminate the vanquished (Kirk 1991, 325). The war between society and the criminal was modeled on this example of war to the death.

Capital punishment was also a matter of technology and economics. Without an expensive building, one man with a sword or a spear, or even a flintlock musket, could not reliably hold more than one determined man captive. Further, a jailor in a preindustrial farming economy could hardly be expected to see the point in providing lodging, food, and water to an idle criminal. As a result, one should not be surprised to find, in all places and all times until Europe and North America in the eighteenth century, that imprisonment was used almost solely for hostages with monetary or political value, or for the pretrial detention of persons not obviously guilty. Prisons and imprisonment are, in moral and economic terms, luxuries of an advanced society.

If one should not be surprised to find how invariably the death penalty was prescribed, one might be surprised at the relative infrequency with which it was carried out. Michael Ignatieff, studying the original records of proceedings in the Old Bailey, historically London's central criminal court, estimates that by the late 1760s, 70 percent of defendants in English capital cases were not sentenced to be hanged but rather were transported to the American colonies. Of those who were sentenced to death, another significant portion were pardoned, whipped, and jailed for short terms (Ignatieff, 20).

Each of the new United States expressly or tacitly adopted English common law, so examining the English common law of crime and punishment is instructive for determining American attitudes. The preeminently influential text for lawyers in the newly independent United States was William Blackstone's *Commentaries on the Laws of England,* published in four volumes between 1765 and 1769. An American edition was published in 1771 and sold, according to Edmund Burke, almost as many copies in the colonies as the original had sold in England (Kirk, 368).

Blackstone described the large number of crimes that remained capital offenses in English law, from high treason down to what we would consider petty theft, but noted several practices besides the royal pardon on condition of transportation that eased the formal law's severity. One of the meliorating provisions of English law, which had its origin before Magna Carta in the dual system of ecclesiastical and secular courts, was the "benefit of clergy." Because a cleric was to be tried only in the ecclesiastical courts, a man who could prove his clerical state, originally by demonstrating a clerical tonsure and the ability to read a biblical verse in Latin (usually the opening lines of Psalm 51, which became known as the "neck verse"), might escape death for lesser offenses. Over time, the benefit of clergy was extended to more offenses, although not to high treason or heresy. Eventually, Parliament and the courts expanded the benefit to peers (because it could not count on noblemen being literate) and to women and Jews (who could not count on claiming to be tonsured clergy), until finally by the beginning of the eighteenth century it was presumed that an individual would claim "his clergy," and the requirement of reading was abolished. An individual who was convicted of an offense with benefit of clergy was branded on the thumb to prevent a second claim and was whipped or imprisoned for up to a year or, by a 1718 statute of King George I, transported to the American colonies for seven years (Blackstone 1979, vol. 4: 358–367). The possibility always remained, however, that Parliament would withdraw the benefit of clergy from a common law crime, or forget or refuse to extend the benefit of clergy to a new statutory crime. In the Black Act of 1723, for instance, malicious chopping down of trees growing in an orchard, poaching deer or rabbits, and fishing while armed and disguised were made capital offenses without benefit of clergy (Thompson 1975). Hanging was in practice mostly reserved for murderers, burglars, forgers, and counterfeiters, but the combination of harsh penalties and large scope for judicial interpretation of criminal laws made the defendant's risk of facing a capital offense unpredictable at best. At worst it was subject to the arbitrary decision of the trial judge, from whom there was rarely any appeal. The statistical unlikelihood of being executed was of little comfort to the unlucky defendant awaiting trial before such a judge.

Another moderating practice Blackstone described, and approved of in cases of simple theft, was "pious perjury." Theft above the value of twelve pence, a figure traced by Blackstone to its presumed origin in the tenth century under the Saxon king Athelstan, was the capital offense of grand larceny. By the eighteenth century, inflation meant that even a minor theft could lead to a hanging. Conscious of this, Blackstone asserted, "the mercy of juries will often make them strain a point, and bring in larc[e]ny to be under the value of twelvepence, when it is really of much greater value" (Blackstone, vol. 4: 239). A jury's verdict was not subject to revision, and after the seventeenth century, a jury began to have a real freedom to reach a verdict contrary to that sought by the judge. Often the result was that a defendant facing the possibility of death for theft received a fresh start after transportation to America.

Blackstone was not "soft on crime," however, and like contemporary legal thinkers applauded capital punishment in cases of murder and other serious offense, repeating God's injunction to Noah in Genesis 9:6 that "whoso sheddeth man's blood, by man shall his blood be shed" (vol. 4: 9).

If Blackstone was the most influential lawyer in the new United States, the most influential philosopher was John Locke (Corwin 1989, 78). Writing his *Second Treatise on Government* to justify the Glorious Revolution of 1688 and the resulting establishment of Parliament's supremacy over the king, Locke condemned arbitrary use of governmental power that harmed "life, liberty, and estate." However, Locke was concerned with the allocation of the state's power and its proper ends, not its extent. Although Locke opposed the total sovereignty claimed for the monarch in *Leviathan,* Thomas Hobbes's masterwork of the previous generation, Locke and his American following never questioned the assumption that the power of the state extended to life and death. The first generations of Americans after independence therefore inherited without question the view that the death penalty was a harsh penalty, but not a cruel or unusual one.

Another aspect of the criminal law worth considering as American law came to diverge from its British roots is the role of poverty. A substantial proportion of English felons and misdemeanants who were whipped and transported, or sometimes even hanged, were guilty of what we would describe as nonviolent property offenses, or in some cases "victimless crimes." Poaching the rabbits in the landlord's fields and cutting firewood in his forests were crimes that were hard to imagine and harder to prosecute in the colonies, where social classes were less distinct, vacant land plentiful, labor scarce, and the frontier only a short journey away.

As a result, Americans were free to experiment with ideologies that called for less draconian criminal codes. Influenced by the state's Quaker roots and William Penn's 1682 Frame of Government, Pennsylvania's Constitution of 1776 provided, for instance, that punishments should be "less sanguinary and in general more proportionate to the crime," and the preamble to Pennsylvania's murder statute in 1794 proclaimed to the world: "[I]t is the duty of every government to endeavor to reform, rather than exterminate offenders, and the punishment of death ought never to be inflicted where it is not absolutely necessary to the public safety."

The colonists were more free than their British counterparts in another important way. One aspect of the tradition of Anglo-Norman law almost invisible to us was that, in addition to maintaining public order, an important secondary function (and sometimes not even secondary) of the criminal law was the raising of revenue (Haskins 1960, 188). Going all the way back to Magna Carta, one can see that King John's concessions to the barons did not include any limit on the death penalty, but included the prohibition of excessive fines near the top of the list.

Before the establishment of offices of professional prosecutors who acted in the name of the Crown, well into the nineteenth century, justice was still in part a private affair, and in the era of the American Revolution a criminal prosecution could be commenced by a crime victim or his or her family by filing an "appeal," that is, by what we would call a private criminal complaint (Maitland 1908, 128) To return again to the Magna Carta, one of the injustices that the king promised to stop was the indignity of having a man brought to trial on the appeal of a woman.

The sovereign's assertion of the public interest in criminal actions came when the facts of the alleged crime were presented to a grand jury of twenty-three men. If indicted, the accused would stand trial before a petit jury of twelve men of equal social standing. If convicted of treason or felony after indictment, the property and lands of the criminal would be forfeited to the king. Creative interpretations of the law were often used by judges appointed by kings hungry for revenue. However, a royal trial was at first really just one option available to a criminal defendant. Until it was outlawed by the Roman Catholic Church in 1215, a defendant could choose trial by ordeal. For a long while afterward, a defendant could legally choose trial by battle. Even though after the thirteenth century a jury trial was the only option in practice, because it was considered an innovation on prior settled law, a plea to stand trial "upon my country" was considered legally necessary before the king could try a felon and forfeit his property. A man who died but did not enter a plea, even a plea of not guilty, could transmit his lands and goods to his family, whereas a person taking advantage of the king's justice might not only lose his life but also beggar his family. As a result, forcing a defendant to plead became an end in itself, as a matter not of justice but of revenue, and it was lawful to torture a defendant by a combination of starvation, thumbscrews, and *peine forte et dure,* that is, "punishment hard and long" by loading weights on the spreadeagled defendant's chest until he should consent (Fisher 1997, 588–589).

Its practitioners would not have considered these tortures cruel and unusual punishment, but rather pretrial procedure. "Pressing," in fact, was used as late as 1692 in Massachusetts during the

Salem witch trials and was not legally abolished until 1772. Other forms of torture were permitted in the colonies as investigative methods. Although the common law courts traditionally did not employ torture, it was considered lawful for the Court of Star Chamber, which existed from 1487 to 1641, to use torture. Inheriting this practice, the drafters of the Massachusetts Body of Liberties in 1641 saw nothing inconsistent in placing these two provisions in sequence:

> 45. No man shall be forced by Torture to confesse any Crime against himselfe nor any other unlesse it be in some Capitall case where he is first fullie convicted by clear and sufficient evidence to be guilty, After which if . . . it is very apparent there be other conspiratours . . . then he may be tortured, yet not with such tortures as be Barbarous and inhumane.
>
> 46. For bodilie punishments we allow amongst us none that are inhumane Barbarous or cruel.

Even before any legal reform took place, the rise of a mercantile economy and later an industrial one created sources of revenue that rendered the money raising function of the criminal law obsolete in England, and torture in the pursuit of such revenue ended as well. With the exception of the "orgy of confiscations" (McDonald 1985, 21) of Loyalist property in the Revolutionary era, criminal prosecutions for the sake of revenue never established more than a toehold in the new United States. However, some critics of the trend during the last two decades of the twentieth century to revive and greatly expand the scope of criminal forfeitures to combat money laundering and narcotics distribution would say that the United States has gone back into medieval times in reviving the philosophy of criminal justice as a revenue source, whereas other critics would argue that we are just as willing as our forebears to deal out cruel punishments so long as they are not called punishments.

The Founding Era

Like the English Revolution, and unlike the French and Russian revolutions, the American Revolution was not a radical one, but rather a self-consciously conservative act seeking to maintain for the colonists those rights, privileges, and immunities they believed to be theirs by immemorial custom and under attack by innovating ministers of the Crown. Thus the framers of the Constitution in 1787, although paying homage to the writings of Montesquieu and other Continental figures, looked almost exclusively to the English experience for their model of government, and looked for ways to preserve it, not change it (Bradford 1993, 17–33).

Fundamental issues of crime and punishment therefore did not occupy much of the attention of the signers of the Declaration of Independence or the framers of the Constitution, with the notable exception of Benjamin Rush, a Philadelphia physician who, in several pamphlets published after 1787, called for the total abolition of the death penalty on the grounds that it denied the human dignity of the criminal and degraded the morals of the public. Rush also popularized for Americans the "death penalty is no deterrent" argument made in 1764 by the Italian reformer Cesare Beccaria (Post 1944, 41). English translations of Beccaria's *Essay on Crimes and Punishments* were published in Philadelphia and New York in the 1770s, and his thesis that perpetual imprisonment was a more effective deterrent was known to the framers. But, as every student learns in elementary school, taxation without representation and quartering of troops were the chief grievances of the colonists, not the imposition of the death penalty. The only two abuses of English criminal law by King George III and his ministers that were included in the list of grievances in the Declaration of Independence were the deprivation of the right to a jury trial and the right to be tried in the place where the crime was committed and not transported "beyond Seas" to England.

The signers of the Declaration of Independence knew their English law and history well, and knew that if they were captured they could expect to be hanged as traitors at best. At worst, English law permitted them to be burned alive, boiled alive, or hanged until near death, cut down, castrated and disemboweled while alive, and then quartered. If the Continental Congress had denounced the excessiveness of capital punishment it might have been seen as self-serving, but understandable. The silence on the matter in the Articles of Confederation, the first constitution of the United States, is therefore illuminating. Drafted in 1776, adopted by the Congress in November 1777, signed by representatives of the states in 1778 and 1779, and effective at (least in form) from 1781 until the ratification of the Constitution in 1789, the Articles of Confederation contain only one recognizable criminal law provision, a clause requiring any state to extradite any person accused of a crime upon request of the governor of the state where the accusation of crime had been made.

The last legal act of consequence under the Articles of Confederation was the 1787 Ordinance for the Governance of the Northwest Territories. The Northwest Ordinance, an organic document for the governance of a colony expected to be formed into states, did discuss capital punishment in two ways familiar to literate persons of the time and to us. First, the traditional prohibitions of Chapter 39 of the Magna Carta against being fined excessively or being judged other than by one's peers or contrary to the law of the land were stated.

Second, persons charged with crimes were entitled to bail except "for capital offenses, where the proof shall be evident or the presumption great," and "no cruel or unusual punishments shall be inflicted" (Schwartz 1980, vol. 2: 385–387). No attempt was made throughout the drafting of these provisions to define what was a capital offense, nor to define cruel or unusual.

Later in 1787, disputes over trade and debt repayment and concern for the expansion of commerce moved critics of the Articles of Confederation and proponents of a stronger national government to meet in Philadelphia. Although Shays's Rebellion in western Massachusetts in 1786 had alarmed the governors of the new nation and indirectly contributed to the drafting of the Constitution, even that episode did not drive issues of crime and punishment to the forefront of the framers' concerns.

Specific protections against the two grievances listed in the Declaration of Independence were written into the text of the new Constitution, in Article III, Section 2, Clause 3. A guarantee against cruel and unusual punishment was not. In fact, James Madison's notes of the proceedings of the constitutional convention in 1787 reflect little debate on the subject of crimes other than treason.

Why the Confederation Congress should have found it necessary to make provisions for capital offenses in the Northwest Territories and the delegates at the constitutional convention did not find it necessary for the nation at large is not hard to explain. The Northwest Ordinance was conceived of as an organic law for the management of territories until they should form their own governments. The Constitution, though grander in design, was not so ambitious in scope. Like the Articles of Confederation, the Constitution was conceived of primarily as a structural document for allocating power between the states and the national government and for distributing power among the branches of that new government, not as a declaration of rights or a piece of legislation. It was established to form a more perfect Union, not the perfect Union. The framers knew well that they had left some glaring problems, such as the continuation of the slave trade, for another day and papered over others, such as the question of representation in Congress for those states that denied that a slave could be a legal person. Matters we think important, such as the justice of capital punishment, never occurred to them. To them, the current national debate over whether the death penalty is "constitutional" would be puzzling, because to them the death penalty was not, properly speaking, the subject of constitutional law at all.

The states, by contrast, after they declared themselves free of the English sovereign, understandably felt it important to set forth what portions of English common law and Parliamentary practice they believed to be binding in the new states. After the royal governor dissolved Virginia's House of Burgesses in 1774, George Mason drafted for the Virginia Colonial Convention a Declaration of Rights modeled on the English Declaration of Rights of 1688, which included the requirement "That excessive bail ought not to be required nor excessive fines imposed, nor cruel and unusual punishments inflicted." Whether copying English law directly or by way of George Mason, virtually identical prohibitions soon appeared in the 1776 Declarations of Rights by Delaware, Maryland, and North Carolina and in constitutions or bills of rights enacted in New Hampshire in 1783, in New York in 1787, and in South Carolina and Pennsylvania in 1790 (Cogan 1997, 613–617).

Whether the framers did not include similar crime and punishment provisions in the document submitted in 1789 for ratification by the states deliberately or not, the lack of an explicit prohibition in the Constitution against the infliction of cruel and unusual punishments was one of the many perceived flaws that opponents of ratification stressed in their efforts to block ratification or to call for a second constitutional convention. Virginia delegate Patrick Henry, for example, objected vehemently to the lack of a provision banning cruel and unusual punishments (Cogan, 619):

> What has distinguished our ancestors?—That they would not admit of tortures, or cruel and barbarous punishment. But Congress may introduce the practice of the civil law, in preference to that of the common law. They may introduce the practice of France, Spain, and Germany—of torturing, to extort a confession of the crime.

A similar objection was made by Abraham Holmes in the Massachusetts convention: "They are nowhere restrained from inventing the most cruel and unheard-of punishments and annexing them to crimes; and there is no constitutional check on them, but that *racks* and *gibbets* may be amongst the most mild instruments of their discipline" (Cogan, 619).

In the end, Pennsylvania, Virginia, New York, and North Carolina all called for a ban on cruel and unusual punishment along with their ratification of the Constitution. The Constitution's principal draftsman, James Madison, protested that imitating the English Bill of Rights was unnecessary, even counterproductive, because unlike European charters of liberty granted by power, the Constitution was a charter of power granted by liberty. A bill of rights would imply that the government was the master of the people, not its servant.

More famously, Alexander Hamilton, in Federalist Paper No. 84, one of a series of essays written by Madison, Hamilton, and John Jay in support of ratification by New York, wrote that because the Constitution is the charter of the sovereign people granting limited powers to their representatives, the very idea of a bill of rights was inconsistent with the theory of popular sovereignty. Because no power to impose cruel and unusual punishment was ever delegated to the new national government, Hamilton argued, none existed. Worse yet, according to Hamilton, a prohibition of some abuses might tempt would-be aggrandizers of governmental powers to assume that anything not specifically prohibited was permitted, and also to threaten liberty by gradual testing of the limits of what was permitted.

In the end, however, to forestall attempts at undoing the Federalists' work, to answer critics of the new constitution, and to fulfill a campaign promise he made to Virginia voters in the election of 1789, Representative James Madison included George Mason's language from the Virginia Declaration of Rights among the twelve proposed amendments submitted for ratification by the states in 1789. There was little recorded debate on the Eighth Amendment in the first congress, and the only extensive statement on the subject was the opposition expressed by Samuel Livermore of New Hampshire (Cogan, 618):

> The clause seems to express a great deal of humanity, on which account I have no objection to it; but, as it seems to have no meaning in it, I do not think it necessary. What is meant by the terms "excessive bail?" Who are to be the judges? What is understood by "excessive fines?" It lays with the court to determine. No cruel and unusual punishment is to be inflicted; it is sometimes necessary to hang a man, villains often deserve whipping, and perhaps having their ears cut off; but are we, in future, to be prevented from inflicting these punishments because they are cruel? If a more lenient mode of correcting vice and deterring others from the commission of it could be invented, it would be very prudent in the legislature to adopt it; but until we have some security that this will be done, we ought not to be restrained from making necessary laws by any declaration of this kind.

The clause was put to a vote and garnered a considerable majority.

Mr. Livermore notwithstanding, it was almost a foregone conclusion that, once proposed, a ban against cruel and unusual punishments would be adopted. The most influential philosophies are ones that have so seeped into the thoughts of a generation that it cannot recall how and when they were learned. Many of the founding generation looked on their deeds in casting off the rule of George III and establishing a new form of government as a replay of the Parliament's ouster of James II in the Glorious Revolution of 1688. Consciously or not, they made the heroes of that era their heroes, its villains their villains, and its slogans their slogans.

One of the animating causes of the Glorious Revolution of a century earlier was disgust at the excesses of the famous "Bloody Assizes." By the 1680s, the turmoil of the English Civil War and the period of the Commonwealth had ended with the restoration of Charles II. However, the political tensions between Crown and

Parliament and the hostility between the Church of England and its Catholic and Protestant rivals gathered like electrical charges around Charles II's potential successors, his legitimate brother, James the Duke of York, and his illegitimate son, James Scott the Duke of Monmouth. The Duke of York, believed to be overly fond of both Catholicism and absolutist claims for the monarchy, ascended to the throne as James II in February 1685. Raising the banner of popular Protestantism, but without the support of many of the nobles or the wealthy who favored William of Orange, the Duke of Monmouth landed in the west of England in June 1685. He was quickly routed, captured, and beheaded.

James II sent Baron George Jeffreys to the scene of the rebellion with a judicial commission to punish those involved, and Jeffreys did so without stint. Hundreds were hanged, and perhaps a thousand were whipped and transported, not as indentured servants to New England, but as slaves to the sugar plantations of the West Indies. Included among them were the girls who had participated in the treason of Monmouth by sewing his banners. Jeffreys, raised to lord chancellor for his support of James II, dusted off obsolete statutes and precedents to burn alive and behead women guilty of the crime of sheltering fleeing supporters of Monmouth (Brant 1965, 154–155).

No doubt some of the Parliamentary supporters of William of Orange in the winter of 1688 were zealous both in revulsion at the Bloody Assizes and in fear of their repetition if William failed. One of the legal protections Parliament was careful to include in the Declaration of Rights presented to William as a condition of their support, and which was passed as a statute in 1689 as the Bill of Rights, was that "excessive Bail ought not to be required, nor excessive Fines imposed, nor cruel nor unusual Punishments afflicted."

To the Americans of 1787, Jeffreys had already earned his place in infamy in 1683 under Charles II, by his judicial prosecution of Algernon Sidney on a charge of treason. Sidney was put to death on an implausible charge based on the extorted testimony of an alleged coconspirator and on the evidence of an unpublished manuscript, taken from Sidney's ransacked house, that contained what Jeffreys told the jury was the treasonous assertion that kings ruled with the consent of the governed. Sidney's essay, posthumously published as *Thoughts on Government,* was a standard text in the libraries of educated Americans (Bailyn 1992, 34–35).

Jeffreys delivered another judgment infamous in America, in the 1685 trial of one Titus Oates. In several show trials conducted between 1679 and 1682, Oates, falsely asserting that he was a cleric, accused Catholic noblemen of taking part in a fantastic plot to overthrow Charles II and to establish Jesuit rule in England. Oates was richly rewarded for his perjury. But with the shift of political power to James II and the increasing fear on the part of those who had encouraged Oates that he had grown dangerous and would turn on them, the outlandish and contradictory testimony that had sufficed to bring fifteen men to their deaths was used to convict Oates of slander in 1684 and of perjury in 1685. Because perjury was not a capital offense but a misdemeanor and therefore punished at the discretion of the judges, Jeffreys now ordered Oates imprisoned for life, with the further provisions that he be stripped of his clerical status, fined, and flogged twice by the hangman, once from Aldgate to Newgate, and once from Newgate to Tyburn. Furthermore, five times a year, on the anniversaries of his perjurious accusations, Oates was to be placed in the pillory, that is, to be secured hand and foot in a public place, exposed to public ridicule at best and to crippling or fatal stoning at worst (Cogan, 624).

After four years of prison and pillory, with James II having fled and William and Mary on the throne, Oates petitioned Parliament to set aside his sentence. Although the House of Lords denied the petition, nine members dissented that Oates's punishments were contrary to the provisions of the Declaration of Rights. After yet another shift in the political winds, Oates was pardoned and released.

Colonial American laymen, as suspicious of Catholic sovereigns and as ready to believe tales of Jesuit intrigue as their English cousins, undoubtedly saw Oates more sympathetically than did the House of Lords. American lawyers and politicians, even if they believed that Oates's punishments were well earned, undoubtedly would agree with the dissenting lords that Jeffreys had given a "cruel, barbarous, and illegal judgement" in sentencing Oates (Cogan, 625).

At both ends of the American social scale, then, Jeffreys's name would stand for cruel and unjust punishments. And although the Bloody Assizes or the pillory for life were inconceivable in America, the constellation of abuses perpetrated in Sidney's trial was something the orators and pamphleteers of independence could fear as a real possibility, and they kept Baron Jeffreys, Bloody Assizes, and Titus Oates in public memory. As a result, notwithstanding the lack of controversy in 1776, 1787, or 1791 over the severity of American criminal law, most of the new states had guarantees against would-be Jeffreyses as a form of cheap insurance.

The prohibition against "cruel or unusual punishments" in the Northwest Ordinance and "cruel and unusual punishments" in the Eighth Amendment was therefore well rooted in the folk history of the new United States. Familiar phrases often escape definition because no one can imagine that their meaning could be mistaken, yet there was no attempt to define what was cruel and unusual punishment, or to specify what practices were banned by the Eighth Amendment. And, as Samuel Livermore had pointed out, the words were susceptible of different meanings.

The Nineteenth Century

The adoption of the Eighth Amendment did not lead to intense discussion of the nature of cruel and unusual punishment at the national level for almost a century. The causes are several.

First, the states were the primary agents of criminal prosecution and punishment. The importance of the states relative to the federal government may be illustrated by the fact that until 1891, when legislation advanced by Representative Samuel J. Barrow ordered the purchase of three sites to serve as federal prisons (eventually to be built at Fort Leavenworth, Kansas; Atlanta, Georgia; and McNeil Island, Washington), the federal government housed its prisoners in state prisons or, more often, in county and city jails (McKelvey 1977, 194). The states, meanwhile, had active prison building programs throughout the century for their much greater populations of state prisoners, and their wardens, particularly in New York and Pennsylvania, took the lead in developing and promoting their rival theories of reform.

Second, until well after the ratification of the Fourteenth Amendment in 1868, the Bill of Rights was conceived of as a restraint only against the federal government. The Supreme Court had expressly held so in 1833 in *Barron v. Baltimore,* and as a result, despite the prohibition against cruel and unusual punishment in many state constitutions, there was no legal framework for developing or enforcing a national consensus. The Supremacy Clause, Article VI of the Constitution, had provided from the very beginning that federal law took precedence over conflicting state laws or constitutions, but this had little impact on matters of crime and punishment, because criminal laws within the several states were considered matters beyond the competence of the federal government. The Civil War and the Reconstruction Era afterward signaled a de facto alteration in the relation of the states to the federal government but did not perceptibly alter the lack of applicability to the states of federal legal standards. It would not be until the twentieth century that a more expansive definition of the scope of federal law would make itself felt.

Third, until the modern era (beginning, at the earliest, with World War I and, at the latest, with President Franklin D. Roosevelt's second term and the constitutional revolution of 1937) the legislative and executive branches of the federal government possessed, in theory as well as in fact, only limited, delegated powers.

There were relatively few crimes defined by Congress to be within federal jurisdiction, and the executive branch had few resources to investigate or prosecute them. As for the Supreme Court, its relative lack of importance in the nineteenth century can be seen in three incidents that would be startling, even unthinkable, since the middle of the twentieth century. First, John Jay, the first chief justice, resigned to accept the more important office of governor of New York. Other judges, including the second chief justice, John Rutledge of South Carolina, resigned federal appointments for more prestigious state judgeships. Second, in 1832, President Andrew Jackson publicly mocked the effect of one unpopular ruling by the Supreme Court with the words: "[Chief Justice] John Marshall made his decision. Now let him enforce it." Third, at the outset of the Civil War, Abraham Lincoln suspended the writ of habeas corpus, thereby permitting military commanders to arrest civilians and detain them indefinitely beyond the reach of the courts. When Chief Justice Roger Taney ordered the commander of a Maryland military garrison held in contempt for defying a judicial order to bring a suspected Confederate agitator to court, the army denied the U.S. marshal access to the fort to serve the writ. Taney retired to his chambers and drafted an unrefuted demonstration that Lincoln had acted unconstitutionally. Lincoln ignored the opinion; other judges attempting to issue writs of habeas corpus found themselves detained in military custody.

Fourth, the accepted ends of criminal punishment, like the ends of government generally, were those set out by Thomas Jefferson in the Declaration of Independence, that is, that "All men are endowed by their Creator with certain inalienable rights, among which are life, liberty, and the pursuit of happiness, and that governments are instituted to secure these ends. . . ." A typical expression was the unanimous opinion of the Supreme Court in *Hopt v. Utah* (1884), citing only Blackstone, who said, "The great end of punishment is not the expiation or atonement of the offence committed, but the prevention of future offenses of the same kind."

Fifth, although opposition to capital punishment was a subject of debate within the new states, it was not a prominent topic. Before the Civil War, the preservation or abolition of slavery occupied first place in public controversy, and in the postwar era the problems of Reconstruction gave way to the assimilation of immigrants as primary national concerns. An abhorrence of torture and a reluctance to carry out executions for crimes less than murder (at least for the nonslave portion of the populace) had been a universal legacy from England to the new United States. Nevertheless, the first federal crime bill, passed in 1790, defined the federal offenses of treason, murder, piracy and other offenses on the high seas, and made convicted defendants subject to the mandatory penalty of death by hanging. Following the English practice of protecting commercial and financial transactions, forgery was also made subject to a mandatory death penalty. The only substantial controversy over the death penalty in the First Congress was whether the executed criminal's body should be delivered to a doctor for dissection and study. Congress provided that it would (Little 1999, 364).

In general, most opposition to the death penalty was not abolitionist, but only part of a larger nineteenth-century movement taking place in the United States and in Great Britain toward making the criminal law more temperate. Pennsylvania had begun in 1794 by drawing the distinction between premeditated murder, that is, "murder in the first degree," punishable by death, and lesser forms of murder and manslaughter, punishable by imprisonment only. Other states followed Pennsylvania's lead, and in the first half of the nineteenth century, almost every state passed statutes that reduced the number of capital offenses. Capital punishment was typically retained for murder and rape, but Michigan retained the death penalty only for treason after 1847, and there is no history of anyone being prosecuted for treason against a state. In 1852 Rhode Island abolished the death penalty entirely, as did Wisconsin in 1853. Iowa, Maine, and Colorado repealed the death penalty in 1872, 1876, and 1897, and then reinstated it in 1878, 1883, and 1901, respectively.

There were reforms in the imposition of the death penalty. As part of a larger trend toward centralization of state government, many states took the hangman's job away from county sheriffs and wardens of the county jails and provided for execution in a state prison. Well into the nineteenth century, the execution of the condemned was a quasi-religious public ceremony, designed to allow the condemned to express his repentance, and to satisfy the local crowd's desire both for vengeance and to see that the right man was being hanged (Fish 2002, 87, 282–283). But the frequent violations of this sense of ritual by unrepentant prisoners and the general circuslike atmosphere as sometimes tens of thousands gathered to watch executions in the early decades of the nineteenth century led to cooperation by proponents and opponents of the death penalty to abolish public executions. Beginning with legislation in Connecticut in 1830, and spreading from the Northeast to the Midwest and then to the South, executions witnessed by only a handful of representatives of the public became the norm. The Supreme Court held in *Holden v. Minnesota* (1890) that this change in execution practice was constitutional, although public executions in the United States did not end until 1936, when approximately ten thousand people gathered to watch Rainey Bethea hanged in Owensboro, Kentucky.

The short-lived American Society for the Abolition of Capital Punishment was formed in 1845, with President James K. Polk's vice president, George M. Dallas, as its first president, and with expressions of support from prominent politicians, including former President John Quincy Adams (Post, 49–50). However, little attention was given to the death penalty at the federal level until almost the twentieth century. The federal legislative, executive, and judicial branches were preoccupied in turn with the survival of the new nation, its expansion westward and its entry onto the world stage, and with the fundamental social problems caused by a slavery-based economy in the South and then the destruction of that economy, and industrialization and mass migration from Europe. It was not until 1897 that Congress, lagging behind state reform movements, passed a statute that drastically reduced the number of offenses subject to the death penalty, reserving it for treason, murder, and rape. More significantly, at the urging of Civil War general and New York Representative Newton M. Curtis, federal law now provided that for the remaining death penalty offenses, the jury had the power to reach a verdict of guilty "without capital punishment." If the jury so provided, the defendant would be sentenced to life imprisonment instead (Little, 367–368).

Death penalty proponents insisted that death should be the norm and life imprisonment imposed only if there were good reason, but the Supreme Court was quick to rule that the law gave the jury unfettered discretion to order the imposition of a life sentence rather than the death penalty. In *Winston v. United States* (1899), the Court overturned three murder convictions in the District of Columbia in which the trial judges had instructed juries that they should avoid the death sentence only if some good reason had been demonstrated.

Notably, the Supreme Court did not cite the Eighth Amendment in *Winston,* let alone discuss it. In most legal circles, the Eighth Amendment's prohibition of cruel and unusual punishment was regarded as an anachronism, if not as dead a letter as the Third Amendment's prohibition of quartering troops on private property. In 1833, Supreme Court Justice Joseph Story, one of the three outstanding federal jurists of the period before the Civil War, had published *Commentaries on the Constitution,* the most influential legal treatise since Blackstone's *Commentaries.* It was used as a text by Story's students at Harvard Law School and in successive editions as a guide to several generations of lawyers. Dismissing the Eighth Amendment as superfluous, Story wrote (Story 1987, 710–711):

> This is an exact transcript of a clause in the bill of rights, framed at the revolution of 1688. The provision would seem to be wholly unnecessary in a free government, since it is scarcely possible, that any department of such a government should authorize, or justify such atrocious conduct. It was, however, adopted as an admonition to all departments of the national government, to warn them against such violent proceedings, as had taken place in England in the arbitrary reigns of some of the Stuarts.

Succeeding Story in the second half of the nineteenth century as the most important American legal treatise writer was Justice Thomas Cooley of the Michigan Supreme Court, who in 1868 published *A Treatise on the Constitutional Limitations Which Rest Upon the Legislative Power of the States of the American Union.* By 1927, *Constitutional Limitations* had been through eight editions and was in the library of every well-equipped judge. Although successive editions cited in footnotes the progress of cases referring to the Eighth Amendment, the comment remained unchanged (Cooley 1927, vol. 1: 694):

> It is certainly difficult to determine precisely what is meant by 'cruel and unusual punishment.' Probably any punishment declared by statute for an offense which was punishable in the same way at the common law could not be regarded as cruel or unusual, in the constitutional sense. And probably any new statutory offense may be punished to the extent and in the mode permitted by the common law for offenses of similar nature. But those punishments which in any state had become obsolete before its existing constitution was adopted, we think may well be forbidden by it as cruel and unusual.

Finally, a significant reason that the Eighth Amendment's ban on cruel and unusual punishment failed to receive the same attention in the nineteenth century that it would in the twentieth was the common law tradition of Anglo-American jurisprudence.

Then as now, judges announced the developing law case by case, instead of setting forth a comprehensive code. Although this seems at first a technical point of interest only to lawyers, it is perhaps the most important point to grasp in order to understand the changes made in the twentieth century. Some explanation is in order.

First, the modern reader who has learned the familiar tripartite explanation of the American government that "Congress makes the laws, the president enforces the laws, and the courts interpret the laws" must not only unlearn it but also scramble it to understand history. Parliament, on which our Congress was modeled, did not originate as a legislative body that nobles campaigned to get into. It began as a convocation of taxpayers who for centuries regarded a summons to Parliament from the king rather as we regard a summons to jury duty: an expensive and often unpleasant interference with one's business. The king, the executive branch of English government, was likewise not in any modern sense a lawmaker. On the contrary, his coronation oath swore him to "maintain the ancient laws and customs," not to pass good laws. We hear a distant echo of that today when at the inauguration ceremony the president swears to "protect and defend," not to "improve," the Constitution of the United States.

If the legislature was more like taxpayers, the king was more like a judge. We should not forget that the word "court" did not originally bring to mind gavels and black robes, but simply connoted "where the king sat to hear cases."

Lawmaking, as it pertains to crime and punishment, chiefly went on in the courts. Judges not only tried the crimes but also, almost by themselves, decided what the crimes were. Judge Smith, hearing a criminal case, might decide in one case that the accused could not be convicted of burglary because in his opinion, which was not written down but announced orally from the bench at the close of the case, burglary could happen only at night. The next year, an accused fortunate enough to have counsel familiar with

Judge Smith's ruling (because he had been there or had purchased notes of the judge's opinions published by a court reporter) might argue before Judge Jones in another court that his client could not be convicted of burglary because, as established by Judge Smith, there could be no burglary if it was still twilight when he was apprehended. Judge Jones typically would not say that Judge Smith was a fool and his theory about daylight and burglary ridiculous: he would either follow the law as it had been decided in the past, or find some way to distinguish Judge Smith's case from his. Perhaps he would elaborate with some thoughts on whether twilight was day or night. The following decade, after years of dispute over when twilight really faded into night, the Crown might weigh in by appointing judges of the King's Bench with the direction that they determine that for the purposes of the crime of burglary, night, beginning at different times in different seasons, would henceforth be defined as beginning in the city of London at 7:00 P.M. A century later, Parliament might decide that burglary could take place in London day or night. This piecemeal construction of the criminal justice system tended toward limiting change to incremental steps: judicial declarations that burglary was not a felony and that burglars were no longer subject to the death penalty were radical changes that judges could hardly make even if they wanted to.

So, contrary to our modern habit of thought that the courts apply the statutory law given them by the legislative branch, for the greater part of our legal history the legislative body more often simply reacted to a legal code enacted piece by piece by the judges. The judges, for their part, most often considered themselves not as making law, but as humbly discovering and interpreting it from its preexistence in the laws of God and Nature.

Just as the direction of a weight spun at the end of a string changes depending on when it is let go, it was a matter of greatest significance that our country's independent legal system began at the point in history when there was not only a consciousness of this aspect of English legal history but also a perception that this system was an instrument of tyranny that needed to be kept in check.

Parliamentary supremacy over the king had been accomplished in fact with the execution of Charles I and was announced in law with the accession of William and Mary: our framers were determined heirs of that tradition of legislative supremacy. They knew that throughout the seventeenth and eighteenth centuries judges appointed by and subservient to the Crown had undermined or thwarted Parliamentary statutes, and, by creative redefinition of crimes such as treason and criminal libel, often threatened the property, freedom, and lives of opponents of the government.

The framers accordingly sought to remedy those defects by providing that the judicial branch should have specific jurisdictional limits, set by the legislature, that the Senate should advise and consent to any judicial nominations by the president, that judges should not be removable except by impeachment, and that judicial pay should not be left to the caprice of the legislature.

The justices of the Supreme Court shared this common philosophy that the judiciary ought to be, in the words of Alexander Hamilton in Federalist Paper No. 78, the "least dangerous" branch, in the business of exercising judgment, but not force or will. Given this view, early in its existence the Supreme Court took a step, largely forgotten today, that removed the question of the death penalty from serious consideration by the Court for almost a century.

On May 7, 1806, an accusation appeared in the *Connecticut Currant* charging President Jefferson and the Congress with having secretly voted for a present of $2 million dollars to Napoleon Bonaparte "for leave to make a treaty with Spain." The judges of the lower federal courts were divided on the question of whether they had jurisdiction, as did their counterparts in England, to try the publishers of the newspaper for the crime of libel, even though Congress had not passed any statute making libel a crime after the

Alien and Sedition Acts had expired. Without arguments from counsel, without dissent, without footnotes, and without any reference to the Constitution or to any precedent, the Supreme Court held, in *United States v. Hudson and Goodwin* (1812):

> Although this question is brought up now for the first time to be decided by this Court, we consider it as having been long since settled in public opinion. . . .
>
> The only ground on which it has ever been contended that this jurisdiction could be maintained is, that, upon the formation of any political body, an implied power to preserve its own existence and promote the end and object of its creation, necessarily results to it. . . .
>
> But . . . it would not follow that the Courts of that Government are vested with jurisdiction over any particular act done by an individual in supposed violation of the peace and dignity of the sovereign power. The legislative authority of the Union must first make an act a crime, affix a punishment to it, and declare the Court that shall have jurisdiction of the offence.

If the Supreme Court had not withdrawn from the federal judiciary the power to write its own criminal code, the Supreme Court and the lower federal courts might have been forced early on to engage in the kind of internal debate over the permissible scope of criminal sanctions that it came to undertake in the twentieth century.

But as a result of that renunciation of power, the attention of the Supreme Court in the nineteenth century was focused almost exclusively on interpretations of the statutory definitions of federal crimes such as treason and piracy and on the procedural protections surrounding crime and punishment, rather than on the substantive questions of what conduct could be punished and what punishments could be inflicted.

A similar trend occurred in the states. Even though the courts of many of the states retained the power to define and punish offenses as common law, in general throughout the nineteenth century this power was being abolished by legislative enactment of comprehensive criminal codes. As a result, discussion of the cruel and unusual punishment provisions of the state constitutions were not common. Nevertheless, then as now any conscientious criminal defense attorney would make any reasonable argument on behalf of a client, so claims that particular sentences were cruel and unusual were made. These arguments usually failed, for the reasons set forth by the Supreme Court of the New Mexico territory in *Territory v. Ketchum* (1901): "Some courts have thought [the cruel and unusual punishment clause] was never intended as a limitation upon legislative discretion in determining the severity of punishment to be inflicted, but, rather, refers to the mode of infliction." That is, the English Bill of Rights was aimed at the abuse of discretionary punishments by royal judges like Jeffreys, and its American counterparts only prohibited a legislature from ordering defendants to be tortured. So reasoning, the justices of the territory unanimously affirmed the death sentence of a train robber who had wounded but not killed a conductor and mail clerk.

Even in the rare case where a punishment was ruled to be cruel and unusual, the path taken by the court would seem odd to us today. In *State v. Driver* (1878), the Supreme Court of North Carolina overturned not a statute by the legislature, but a judge's imposition of a five-year sentence of imprisonment. While intoxicated, Giles Driver had whipped his wife with several strokes of a switch, and finished with a kick. Admitting that Driver "is a bad man, and not likely to have much of the public sympathy," Justice Reade nevertheless held that confining Driver for so long in the county jail was not lawful. Reade's reasoning illustrates the meaning that "cruel and unusual punishment" had to most judges in the nineteenth century. He noted that none of the justices could remember a five-year sentence for any assault and battery, and that the legislature had until recently permitted imprisonment for felonies not to exceed two years. More severe sentences were now permitted under North Carolina law, but "they are in the Penitentiary, where a man may live and be made useful; but a County jail is a close prison, where life is soon in jeopardy, and where the prisoner is not only useless but a heavy public expense." In other words, idleness in jail was cruel, and a long sentence was so uncommon as to be literally and constitutionally "unusual."

Given the judicial consensus that the Eighth Amendment and similar state provisions had a limited historical meaning, and that the separation of governmental powers commanded judicial deference to the legislature, it is not surprising that the first recognizably modern treatment of the Eighth Amendment did not come until 1878, in the case of *Wilkerson v. Utah*. Wilkerson was a convicted murderer who appealed the judgment of the territorial court that he be executed by a firing squad. He argued that he should not be shot, apparently conceding that he could be hanged; an earlier statute providing that he could be beheaded had been repealed. Justice Clifford delivered the unanimous opinion of the Court affirming the sentence:

> Cruel and unusual punishments are forbidden by the Constitution, but the authorities referred to are quite sufficient to show that the punishment of shooting as a mode of executing the death penalty for the crime of murder in the first degree is not included in that category, within the meaning of the Eighth Amendment. Soldiers convicted of desertion or other capital military offences are in the great majority of cases sentenced to be shot, and the ceremony for such occasions is given in great fulness by the writers upon the subject of courts-martial. . . .
>
> Where the conviction is in the civil tribunals, the rule of the common law was that the sentence or judgment must be pronounced or rendered by the court in which the prisoner was tried or finally condemned, and the rule was universal that it must be such as is annexed to the crime by law. Of these, says Blackstone, some are capital, which

> extend to the life of the offender, and consist generally in being hanged by the neck till dead. . . .
>
> Such is the general statement of that commentator, but he admits that in very atrocious crimes other circumstances of terror, pain, or disgrace were sometimes superadded. Cases mentioned by the author are, where the prisoner was drawn or dragged to the place of execution, in treason; or where he was embowelled alive, beheaded, and quartered, in high treason. Mention is also made of public dissection in murder, and burning alive in treason committed by a female. History confirms the truth of these atrocities, but the commentator states that the humanity of the nation by tacit consent allowed the mitigation of such parts of those judgments as savored of torture or cruelty, and he states that they were seldom strictly carried into effect. . . .
>
> Difficulty would attend the effort to define with exactness the extent of the constitutional provision which provides that cruel and unusual punishments shall not be inflicted; but it is safe to affirm that punishments of torture, such as those mentioned by the commentator referred to, and all others in the same line of unnecessary cruelty, are forbidden by that emendment to the Constitution. . . .
>
> Had the statute prescribed the mode of executing the sentence, it would have been the duty of the court to follow it, unless the punishment to be inflicted was cruel and unusual, within the meaning of the Eighth Amendment to the Constitution, which is not pretended by the counsel of the prisoner. Statutory directions being given that the prisoner when duly convicted shall suffer death, without any statutory regulation specifically pointing out the mode of executing the command of the law, it must be that the duty is devolved upon the court authorized to pass the sentence to determine the mode of execution and to impose the sentence prescribed.

As *Wilkerson* shows, the Eighth Amendment was assumed by the Court to preclude only tortures such as drawing and quartering, public dissection, and burning, which counsel for Wilkerson "could not pretend" resembled death by firing squad.

Technological progress brought a new question of due process to the Supreme Court in 1890: death by electrocution, called by some newspapers "the Kemmler Process," after William Kemmler, the first man condemned to die in an electric chair, at Auburn State Prison in New York. The word electrocute itself entered the language from this case, displacing the alternative proposed by Thomas Edison, who wished to advertise the safety of his direct electrical current as compared with the alternating current system developed by George Westinghouse, that death in the electric chair be termed "Westinghousing." (Gordon 2000, 16). Reviewing a challenge by Kemmler, the justices could not look to history for precedents concerning either the cruelty or the unusualness of the punishment. In denying relief to the condemned, Chief Justice Fuller spoke for a unanimous Supreme Court, avoiding any reexamination of the New York courts' determination, after an evidentiary hearing, that electrocution was humane (*In re Kemmler,* 1890):

> It appears that the first step which led to the enactment of the law was a statement contained in the annual message of the governor of the state of New York, transmitted to the legislature January 6, 1885, as follows: "The present mode of executing criminals by hanging has come down to us from the dark ages, and it may well be questioned whether the science of the present day cannot provide a means for taking the life of such as are condemned to die in a less barbarous manner. I commend this suggestion to the consideration of the legislature." The legislature accordingly appointed a commission to investigate and report "the most humane and practical method known to modern science of carrying into effect the sentence of death in capital cases." This commission reported in favor of execution by electricity. . . .
>
> It is not contended, as it could not be, that the Eighth Amendment was intended to apply to the states, but it is urged that the provision of the Fourteenth Amendment, which forbids a state to make or enforce

> any law which shall abridge the privileges or immunities of citizens of the United States, is a prohibition on the state from the imposition of cruel and unusual punishments, and that such punishments are also prohibited by inclusion in the term "due process of law." . . .
>
> So that, if the punishment prescribed for an offense against the laws of the state were manifestly cruel and unusual as burning at the stake, crucifixion, breaking on the wheel, or the like, it would be the duty of the courts to adjudge such penalties to be within the constitutional prohibition. And we think this equally true of the Eighth Amendment, in its application to congress. . . .
>
> The enactment of this statute was, in itself, within the legitimate sphere of the legislative power of the state, and in the observance of those general rules prescribed by our systems of jurisprudence; and the legislature of the state of New York determined that it did not inflict cruel and unusual punishment, and its courts have sustained that determination. We cannot perceive that the state has thereby abridged the privileges or immunities of the petitioner, or deprived him of due process of law.

Despite the confidence of the Supreme Court, the execution of Kemmler was so gruesome that the next five electrocutions were closed to witnesses (Skelton 1997, 11 n.65). The electric chair was eventually moved to Sing Sing Prison.

In 1892, the majority of the Supreme Court again avoided any reexamination of the Eighth Amendment in *O'Neil v. Vermont,* a case involving not burning, crucifixion, or breaking on the wheel, but a lengthy period of incarceration imposed under the "zero tolerance" laws of the day. The Supreme Court dismissed the challenge to the conviction on procedural grounds, holding that the issue of cruel and unusual punishment had not been properly raised by John O'Neil, a New Yorker who sold alcoholic beverages, some of which were to be delivered to Vermont, a dry state. Justice Field's dissent from the judgment dismissing the appeal tells the story:

The offense charged consisted of selling, furnishing, and giving away intoxicating liquor in Vermont, without authority of law. . . .

The jurors found him guilty of 307 distinct offenses of selling intoxicating liquors without authority and contrary to the laws of Vermont. He was thereupon sentenced to pay a fine of $6,140 to the treasurer of the state, and the costs of prosecution, taxed at $497.96, and stand committed until the sentence was complied with; and, in case the fine and costs were not paid before the 20th day of March, 1883, at 3 o'clock in the afternoon of that day, to be confined at hard labor in the house of correction for the term of 19,914 days,—a period of over 54 years. . . . It was one which, in its severity, considering the offenses of which he was convicted, may justly be termed both "unusual and cruel."

That designation, it is true, is usually applied to punishments which inflict torture, such as the rack, the thumb-screw, the iron boot, the stretching of limbs, and the like, which are attended with acute pain and suffering. Such punishments were at one time inflicted in England, but they were rendered impossible by the declaration of rights, adopted by parliament on the successful termination of the revolution of 1688, and subsequently confirmed in the bill of rights. It was there declared that excessive bail ought not to be required, nor excessive fines imposed, nor cruel and unusual punishments inflicted. From that period this doctrine has been the established law of England, intended as a perpetual security against the oppression of the subject from any of those causes.

The inhibition is directed, not only against punishments of the character mentioned, but against all punishments which by their excessive length or severity are greatly disproportioned to the offenses charged. The whole inhibition is against that which is excessive either in the bail required, or fine imposed, or punishment inflicted. . . .

The state may, indeed, make the drinking of one drop of liquor an offense to be punished by imprisonment, but it would be an unheard-of cruelty if it should count the drops in a single glass, and make

> thereby a thousand offenses, and thus extend the punishment for drinking the single glass of liquor to an imprisonment of almost indefinite duration. The state has the power to inflict personal chastisement, by directing whipping for petty offenses,—repulsive as such mode of punishment is,—and should it, for each offense, inflict 20 stripes, it might not be considered, as applied to a single offense, a severe punishment, but yet, if there had been 307 offenses committed, the number of which the defendant was convicted in this case, and 6,140 stripes were to be inflicted for these accumulated offenses, the judgment of mankind would be that the punishment was not only an unusual, but a cruel one, and a cry of horror would rise from every civilized and Christian community of the country against it. It does not alter its character as cruel and unusual that for each distinct offense there is a small punishment, if, when they are brought together, and one punishment for the whole is inflicted, it becomes one of excessive severity. . . .

This was, of course, a dissent. The majority was untroubled by dismissing the appeal on the technical grounds that the question of cruel and unusual punishment had not first been presented in the lower court.

The Supreme Court's similar attitude toward appeals of state death penalties was expressed pithily by Chief Justice Fuller in *Lambert v. Barrett* (1895), rejecting an argument that a prisoner could not be executed because his federal appeal had not been officially dismissed: "It is natural that counsel for the condemned in a capital case should lay hold of every ground which, in their judgment, might tend to the advantage of their client, but the administration of justice ought not to be interfered with on mere pretexts."

However, the Supreme Court would soon have more opportunities to examine whether the claim that the Eighth Amendment applied to the states and barred the death penalty was a "mere pretext." In the twentieth century, it would not shy away.

References and Further Reading

Bailyn, Bernard. 1992. *The Ideological Origins of the American Revolution,* enlarged edition. Cambridge, MA: Belknap Press of the Harvard University Press.

Beverly, Robert. 1705. *The History and Present State of Virginia.* London, reprinted in *The Annals of America,* vol. 1, ed. Mortimer Adler. Chicago: Encyclopaedia Britannica, 1976.

Blackstone, William. 1979. *Commentaries on the Laws of England.* 4 vols. Chicago: University of Chicago Press. Facsimile of the 1st edition of 1765–1769.

Bradford, M. E. 1993. *Original Intentions: On the Making and Ratification of the United States Constitution.* Athens: University of Georgia Press.

Brant, Irving. 1965. *The Bill of Rights: Its Origin and Meaning.* Indianapolis: Bobbs-Merrill Company.

Cogan, Neil H., ed. 1997. *The Complete Bill of Rights.* New York: Oxford University Press.

Cooley, Thomas M. 1927. *A Treatise on the Constitutional Limitations Which Rest upon the Legislative Power of the States of the American Union,* 8th edition, ed. Walter Carrington. 2 vols. Boston: Little, Brown and Company.

Corwin, Edward S. 1989 [1928]. "The 'Higher Law' Background of American Constitutional Law," in *The Rights Retained by the People,* ed. Randy E. Barnett. Fairfax, VA: George Mason University Press.

Fish, Peter G. 2002. *Federal Justice in the Mid-Atlantic South: United States Courts from Maryland to the Carolinas, 1789–1835.* Washington, DC: Administrative Office of the United States Courts.

Fisher, George. 1997. "The Jury's Rise as Lie Detector." *Yale Law Journal* 107(December): 575.

Gordon, John S. 2000. "Thomas Edison's Deadly Game." *American Heritage* 52(October): 15.

Haskins, Charles Homer. 1960. *Norman Institutions.* New York: Frederick Ungar Publishing Co.

Ignatieff, Michael. 1978. *A Just Measure of Pain: The Penitentiary in the Industrial Revolution, 1750–1850.* New York: Pantheon Books.

Kirk, Russell. 1991. *The Roots of American Order.* Washington DC: Regnery Gateway.

Little, Rory K. 1999. "The Federal Death Penalty: History and Some Thoughts About the Department of Justice's Role." *Fordham Urban Law Journal* 26(March): 347.

Maitland, F. W. 1908. *The Constitutional History of England,* ed. H. A. L. Fisher. Cambridge: Cambridge University Press.

McDonald, Forrest. 1985. *Novus Ordo Seclorum: The Intellectual Origins of the Constitution.* Lawrence: University of Kansas Press.

McKelvey, Blake. 1977. *American Prisons: A History of Good Intentions.* Montclair, NJ: Patterson Smith.

Post, Albert. 1944. "Early Efforts to Abolish Capital Punishment in Pennsylvania." *Pennsylvania Magazine of History and Biography* 68(January): 38.

Schwartz, Bernard, ed. 1980. *The Roots of the Bill of Rights.* 5 vols. New York: Chelsea House.

Skelton, Meghan S. 1997. "Lethal Injection in the Wake of *Fierro v. Gomez.*" *Thomas Jefferson Law Review* 19(Spring): 1.

Story, Joseph. 1987. *Commentaries on the Constitution of the United States.* Durham, NC: Carolina Academic Press.

Thompson, Edward Paul. 1975. *Whigs and Hunters: The Origin of the Black Act.* New York: Pantheon.

3

Twentieth-Century Issues

If we could first know where we are, and whither we are tending, we could better judge what to do, and how to do it.

—Abraham Lincoln, *June 16, 1858*
(The "house divided" speech, given upon acceptance of the Illinois' Republican nomination for Senator)

Continuity and Change

To say that from the beginnings of civilization until the twentieth century the death penalty was not considered to be cruel and unusual punishment puts it too mildly. A more accurate statement is that the question of whether the death penalty was cruel and unusual punishment would not have arisen, but if it had, the answer would certainly have been "no." Rather than be surprised that the state of the death penalty in America remains unsettled, we ought to ask what happened to make this unique point in history possible.

The first fact to leap out at us is that regardless of the statements of religious leaders, writings of abolitionists from Benjamin Rush to Sister Helen Prejean, speeches of political proponents of the death penalty from Ronald Reagan to Bill Clinton, analyses by statisticians, moratoriums by governors, and briefs filed by battalions of lawyers, since 1972 the death penalty has either gone out of the federal and state laws of the United States or has come back in as a result of the shifting majorities of the U.S. Supreme Court. No other center of power in American society comes close to having the influence over the continued use of the death penalty that is wielded by a single justice of the Supreme Court. However, there are two distinct risks inherent in presenting the succession of Supreme Court decisions that address the issue of cruel and unusual punishment in the latter half of the twentieth century history as if the decisions had sprung forth fully formed like Athena from the head of Zeus. For the unwary student, the danger lies in accepting the decisions of the Supreme Court without questioning the Court's fundamental competency, on the mistaken supposition that it is the unique duty of the judiciary to say what cruel and unusual punishment is. As Abraham Lincoln said of this approach in his first inaugural address:

> [T]he candid citizen must confess that if the policy of the Government upon vital questions affecting the whole people is to be irrevocably fixed by decisions of the Supreme Court, the instant they are made in ordinary litigation between parties in personal actions, the people will have ceased to be their own rulers, having to that extent practically resigned their Government into the hands of that eminent tribunal.

Lincoln was of course alluding to the *Dred Scott* decision, which, by professing to end that era's controversy over the spread of slavery by declaring that one position was written into the Constitution and the other not, all but eliminated the chance of a political solution. Although they have not plunged the nation into a second civil war, Supreme Court decisions purporting to resolve intensely disputed issues by appeal to a constitution that does not obviously address the matter continue to generate controversy, from *Roe v. Wade* to *Bush v. Gore.* Blind acceptance of court decisions erodes the capacity for citizenship.

The opposite pitfall threatening observers of the Supreme Court's jurisprudence is cynicism. The more common complaint in modern times, even among the justices themselves, is that it doesn't matter what the Supreme Court decides, because, like the proverbial Scottish weather, it will soon be changing. Some observers, considering the Supreme Court a third legislative branch with nine members and no fear of electoral recall, assert that the Court's decisions are neither wise nor legitimate, but mere products of will that can only be explained by counting noses and only altered by capturing the nominating and confirmation process. This is by no means a new stance: as Mr. Dooley, the fictional bartender of humorist Finley Peter Dunne, observed in 1901, "[T]h' supreme court follows th' iliction returns." But given the virulence of this attitude in recent years, it runs the risk of hardening into an embrace of the position that all change is suspect and that no legitimate development of constitutional doctrine can take place. Worse, it corrodes public trust, the basis of any political system founded on the consent of the governed.

The Supreme Court's twentieth-century decisions on the subject of cruel and unusual punishment can be explained as the result of changes at three intellectual levels. In addition to knowing specific facts or supposed facts ("of defendants condemned to be executed, approximately x percent will be determined to be innocent through DNA testing"), every justice has a philosophy ("better that ten guilty go free than one innocent die" or "kill them all, let God sort them out") that he or she can consciously articulate.

Underlying that philosophy, each judge, like every other person, has what rhetoric professor Richard Weaver (1984) called a "dream of the world"—an attitude toward life that lies beneath the level of examined thought ("the world is a place of amoral struggle" or "people are basically good") and that forms one's philosophy and colors one's interpretation of facts, regardless of political or religious affiliation. Generally the debates over capital punishment and cruel and unusual punishment, particularly as they played out in the Supreme Court in the twentieth century, weave together all three strands—factual, philosophical, and attitudinal—into the narrow legal issues before the justices.

SOME FACTS

First, the acquisition by the United States of overseas possessions (the Philippines, Panama, Puerto Rico, Hawaii, and later the Virgin Islands) and its rise to the status of world power, together with the changing perception of the role of government, led not only to the inevitable expansion of the federal government but also to the centralization of power. The natural increase in the sophistication of the federal government received additional impetus from the successive national and international crises of World War I, the Great Depression, World War II, and the Cold War. This centralization made it possible to enforce a national standard.

Simultaneously, the final decade of the nineteenth century saw not only the beginnings of a federal prison system but also an enlarged and more elaborate federal court system. The Evarts Act, passed in 1891 through the efforts of Senator William Evarts, from New York, created the modern three-tiered structure of district courts that heard trials within the states and territories, courts of appeal that reviewed cases within their "circuits," the multistate regions they comprised, and the Supreme Court. Final review remained in the Supreme Court. By 1925, William Howard Taft, who was president from 1909 to 1913 and chief justice of the Supreme Court from 1921 to 1930, had persuaded Congress to enact the Judiciary Act of 1925. The "Judges Bill" vastly increased the Supreme Court's power to control its own docket by reducing the numbers of cases that could be appealed by right to the Court. Increasingly, the justices could choose to review cases by issuing a writ of certiorari, that is, by an order issued not at the demand of a litigant, but at the discretion of the Court. In receiving control over its own docket, the Court was now able, to a great extent, to control the national legal agenda. This made it possible for a national standard to be declared.

Second, the legal history of cruel and unusual punishment in America in the twentieth century is intertwined with the history of race relations. Economic and political reintegration of the South with the rest of the country as the Reconstruction Era receded, coupled with the migration of blacks to northern industrial cities in the first two decades of the century and the increased national visibility of racial issues after World War I, led to an increasingly national debate over the issue of race in matters of crime and punishment. Beginning early in the twentieth century, the Supreme Court became an increasingly self-conscious participant in this debate, reflecting the concern of members of the Court about legal discrimination against black Americans.

Long before the Court openly addressed the constitutionality of the death penalty itself in *Furman v. Georgia* or began to debate the significance of statistical studies tending to show racial disparities in the imposition of the death penalty, the Supreme Court's concern over prosecutions and penalties being inflicted unfairly on defendants belonging to minority groups can be seen in its decisions. In 1923, in *Moore v. Dempsey,* the Court reversed the murder convictions of five black men sentenced to death for allegedly being involved in gun battle between blacks and whites in Arkansas in 1919 that had resulted in the death of a white deputy sheriff. Although the form of a trial had been observed, the Court found that the verdicts could not stand because, among other errors, they had been obtained with the pressure of a lynch mob standing literally right outside the courthouse to ensure that the right verdict was reached. Sixty-seven other defendants had pleaded guilty to avoid the risk of the death penalty; all were released by 1925 (Kluger 1975, 114). In

1932, in *Powell v. Alabama,* the justices sent back the case of the Scottsboro Boys for retrial on the basis that the defendants had not received effective representation because of the last-minute nature of the appointment of counsel. The defendants were black teenage boys sentenced to death for the alleged rape of two white women on a train after a scuffle between rival black and white groups of hoboes. Some of the defendants had been maneuvered into accusing their codefendants of rape, but there was strong evidence tending to show that neither rape nor even consensual sexual intercourse had occurred (Carter 1969, 33–34). Given the conflicting nature of the evidence, the Supreme Court could easily have upheld the verdicts, or simply declined to hear the case. However, the Supreme Court heard the case and reversed the convictions. Moreover, the Court took up the case a second time after the second round of trials, in *Norris v. Alabama* (1935), and again reversed the death sentences, this time on the basis that blacks had been unfairly excluded from jury service. Because there was an international outcry over the Scottsboro Boys case, one might think the Court's interest was unusual, but three years later the Court drove home the point in *Hale v. Kentucky* (1938), reversing a death sentence for murder imposed on a black man by a jury chosen from an all-white jury list. The opinion was issued per curiam, that is, "by the Court" and not, as is normally the case, by an individual judicial author, indicating that to the Court the issue was so settled that it did not require personal discussion.

Absent the intersection of race and the death penalty, it was rare to see the Supreme Court taking interest in routine state criminal trials. Similarly, the Court's current rule that only a subset of the worst murders will make a defendant eligible for the death penalty has clearly developed as a result of some of the justices' concerns that allowing the death penalty for a wider range of offenses would permit its imposition to be more racially skewed. The history of unjust imposition of the death penalty made it possible for a national standard for imposition or abolition of the death penalty to be seen as morally right.

Third, the Supreme Court's death penalty rulings throughout the twentieth century influenced the criminal law in two ways. One was the Court's use of death penalty cases to change criminal procedure within the legal system generally. The other was the Court's producing significant changes in capital punishment law by procedural rulings that were technical in nature and thus less easily understood by the nonlawyer public to be capital punishment decisions. Both types of rulings, abstracted as they were from the merits of the particular case, rested on a more universal and impartial rationale than a bare ruling in favor of or against the death penalty and therefore were less controversial.

Powell v. Alabama is a good example. Beyond its importance to the Scottsboro Boys, the ruling would be the cornerstone of the Supreme Court's expansion of the constitutional right to the effective assistance of appointed counsel in all criminal prosecutions in which the accused faced imprisonment. The expansion followed a common sequence. First, a legal position of relatively modest scope would be established in a case presenting extreme facts. As the ruling became of sufficient vintage to be considered settled law, its application to a wider universe of facts would be announced in case-by-case decision making. Finally, the Supreme Court would sweep away the need for case-by-case analysis and announce a new universal rule of substantive law. The most famous example of this evolution is the history of the step-by-step undermining of legal segregation that took place in the path from *Plessy v. Ferguson* (1896) to *Brown v. Board of Education* (1954). Similarly, in the jurisprudence of the death penalty, the paradigm was followed in the line of cases dealing with the use of confessions. Long before *Miranda v. Arizona* (1966), which held that every questioning in police custody was presumably coercive and therefore required warnings, the Court began with *Brown v. Mississippi* (1936). There, the Court reviewed the convictions of three black men for murder, where the only evidence of guilt was their confessions. Sheriff's deputies extracted confessions from two of the defendants by tying them to chairs and beating them with belt buckles until they were bloody; the third was hanged at the end of a rope and whipped until he would admit his guilt. Their confessions were then taken down, and they were convicted and sentenced to death. This was certainly not the first (or last) use of the "third degree" to obtain a confession, but the Supreme Court had previously been unwilling to assert any supervisory power over use of evidence in state courts. The use of a death penalty decision to announce an innovating decision allowed the innovation to be seen as legally legitimate.

PHILOSOPHY

Although America had deep thinkers from the outset, by the dawn of the twentieth century its philosophy had matured as a discipline. That maturation produced three changes in American legal philosophy that had independent origins but related effects on how the death penalty would be reviewed in the Supreme Court. They were changes in the way judges viewed (1) what the United States was for; (2) what law was for; and (3) what judges were for.

The United States

From Plato through the Christian philosophers of the scholastic period, it had been generally agreed that the state was a moral community that existed for the purpose of making its citizens virtuous. As Aristotle remarked, a state that aimed merely to provide a living might as well be made up of slaves or animals.

By the beginning of the eighteenth century, after Europe's era of religious wars had rocked England and its colonies, the costs in blood and the hypocrisy of forcing subjects to adopt the virtues of their princes led philosophers to adopt a more modest aim for the state. At the time the United States was founded, political thinkers expected the state to provide order and justice. James Madison could count on the readers of his Federalist Paper No. 51 to agree without further argument that "justice is the end of the state. It is the end of civil society." And justice, every thinker understood, was the securing to individuals their rights in life, liberty, and the pursuit of happiness.

By 1900, a new idea had gained currency: that the government exists to promote not just the general welfare but also the welfare of individuals. Influential educators such as John Dewey (Horwitz 1987, 858) and Roscoe Pound (Pound 1999, 196) held that it is the duty of the state to provide its citizens not only with formal justice, but a fair share of the goods of life as well. This idea eventually trickled down into the popular political platforms of the New Deal and the Great Society.

Now, there is no logical contradiction in an economic liberal's being a proponent of the death penalty, or in a death penalty abolitionist's being a supply-side economist. Nevertheless, just as the promoters of the welfare state tended to evaluate other policies by criteria of public welfare rather than by a standard of individual rights, so did they tend to measure the success or failure of the death penalty according to how well it met the public functions of interdiction, deterrence, and rehabilitation, and not the retributive goal of giving the criminal his "just desserts." The most respected of the judges of the new century were in step with, if not leading, this change: Supreme Court Justices Oliver Wendell Holmes, Jr., and Benjamin Cardozo praised the social engineering function of law and rejected retribution in criminal punishment as the relic of a bygone era. Popular writers of the time such as H. L. Mencken similarly rejected the idea of retribution.

If one discounts Samuel Johnson's reflection that nothing so concentrates a man's thoughts as the knowledge he is to be hanged in the morning, the death penalty obviously has no rehabilitative effect. Because a prison term incapacitates a criminal almost as well as a death sentence, once the retributive ideal fell into disfavor, the remaining prop for the death penalty was the belief that the death penalty deters crime. This proved to be a weak prop.

The deterrence theory can be supported anecdotally: any experienced prosecutor can tell the story of at least one criminal who testified that the reason he spared victims or witnesses was to avoid the death penalty, or of a criminal who killed with the assurance that he could suffer no additional penalty by doing so. But even the testimony of the killers themselves is equivocal: most murders are not the result of much advance thought, and of the truly foresighted criminals, some have purposely committed murders in a death penalty state expressly for the purpose of facing the death penalty. And when the central collection of crime statistics began in the twentieth century, simple statistical comparisons of states with and without the death penalty showed that the evidence for the claim that the death penalty deters crime was inconclusive at best.

Law

Because the government is the guardian and the enforcer of the law, the twentieth-century change in the measurement of government was closely tied to a change in how the law itself was viewed. Today we think, or assume without thinking, that government creates the laws. But from antiquity through the founding of our country, it was just the opposite: laws created the government. The Judeo-Christian tradition was based on a divinely revealed law that was not subject to amendment; the Greek philosophers similarly drew the distinction between unchanging "laws" and relatively trivial "legislation" (Kitto 1991, 94). To Cicero, writing in the first century B.C., "True law is Reason. . . . Its validity is universal; it is immutable and eternal." To Locke, one of the last inheritors of the classical tradition, a magistrate passing laws against theft or adultery acts "superfluously and seems to be not so much to make new law as to declare and enforce the old" (Locke 1967, 223). The notion that there are preexisting laws that result in preexisting rights is spelled out in the Declaration of Independence's twin statements that all men are endowed by their creator with certain inalienable rights and that governments are instituted to preserve these rights.

By the early 1900s, the images of unchanging law and natural rights had been severely eroded both by the practical experience of busy legislatures passing obviously new laws to meet new economic conditions and by legal philosophies that, in Justice Cardozo's summary (Cardozo 1924, 124–127), proposed that law was anything that a legislature would enact, a court construe, or a sheriff enforce. As historian Richard Hofstadter wrote, the "supreme achievement" of this new philosophical movement came in 1913 with the publication of Charles A. Beard's *An Economic Interpretation of the Constitution of the United States,* which asserted that the framers of the Constitution could not have been seeking justice, but rather had been motivated by economic self-interest (Hofstadter 1955, 199). This was not to blame the framers, because according to the new thinking there could be no such thing as justice until the legislature decided what it was. The idea that justice was a universal standard to which lawmakers could conform was derided, in the words of Justice Holmes, as a superstitious belief that law was a "brooding omnipresence in the sky."

Judges

If the state existed for purposes other than to secure justice, and if justice was no more transcendent a matter than what happened to come out of the legislative hopper, a reasonable judge might ask in a thoughtful moment, what am I doing here? Chief Justice Marshall's statement in 1803 that it was the duty of the judiciary "to declare what the law is," was as out of date as powdered wigs to the generation of 1903, who had been taught that there was no law until the judge made a ruling.

In 1870, Professor Charles Langdell had become dean of the Harvard Law School, and had immediately set about reforming the way future judges would be trained. No more would students read law in offices of older attorneys and memorize treatises by Blackstone, Story, and Cooley: students were to go to law schools to dissect the actual texts of judicial decisions, from which they were to deduce general legal principles as if constructing a geometric proof. Law was to be developed like logic.

Just as with the dinosaurs, in law the most highly developed forms came right before extinction. Although the law school was here to stay, Langdell's arid but influential "case method" was eventually submerged by the new schools of sociological jurisprudence and legal realism. To the rising generation, the life of the law was not logic but experience, and the question "What does a judge do?" should not be answered "He decides cases according to law" but rather "He makes law, just as a legislator does." Justice Cardozo significantly entitled the third of his landmark lectures at Yale Law School in 1921 "The Judge as Legislator." The attitude of politicians was characteristically described in a May 3, 1907, speech to the Elmira Chamber of Commerce by New York Governor Charles Evans Hughes, later to be Chief Justice from 1930 to 1941: "We are a nation under the Constitution, but the Constitution is what the judges say it is." Although holdovers from the nineteenth century like Hughes did not entirely approve of this change in style, the newer generation of judges, like Jerome Frank of the Second Circuit Court of Appeals (a public opponent of capital punishment) would argue that their approach was not only more honest but also more humble (Frank 1947, 1271):

> A judge . . . who publicly admits that at times he cannot help legislating, is far more demanding of himself, far more restrained when doing

> so. Such a judge will do his best to enforce the policy of a statute, even when he detests its aim. If he is a so-called conservative, he will not deliberately try to frustrate a distastefully liberal statute, if he is a so-called liberal, he will deal similarly with what he considers perniciously reactionary legislation.

Throughout the nineteenth century, legislatures had been increasingly active in drafting comprehensive civil and criminal codes, in many cases abolishing the power of courts to declare the elements of criminal offenses or the severity of punishment. At the very moment in history when judges had generally surrendered to the legislature the role of making law, they were widely adopting the ideology that they, like legislatures, should be lawmakers.

And like lawmakers, the new breed of judge often employed draftsmen for the tedious work of preparing opinions. Law clerks, recent graduates of top law schools, came into use at the end of the nineteenth century, around the same time that law reviews, student-led scholarly journals analyzing social and legal issues, cases, and legislation, were being started or expanded in the Ivy League and beyond. The influx of these younger lawyers into the decision-making process accelerated the spread of the philosophies they had acquired from their professors. The effect of this shift was intensified by the heavy concentration of clerks coming from elite law schools such as Harvard, Yale, Columbia, and the University of Pennsylvania. Writing approvingly in an introduction to a legal textbook in 1931, Justice Cardozo remarked, "[T]he sobering truth is that leadership in the march of legal thought has been passing in our day from the benches of the courts to the chairs of universities." Liberal Harvard Law School professor and conservative Supreme Court Justice Felix Frankfurter, no less than liberal Justice William Douglas, both appointed by Franklin Delano Roosevelt, relied on their law clerks and cited law review articles far more often than the justices appointed by previous presidents.

According to Richard Posner, a prominent judge of the Court of Appeals for the Seventh Circuit, by the late twentieth century most opinions were no longer even written by the judges, but by their clerks (Posner 1995, 1432). It became a two-way street: law clerks became professors, and their protégés became law clerks. The academy cheered progressive Supreme Court opinions, as when the Court decided *Weems v. United States* in 1910. The Supreme Court, as in *Trop v. Dulles* in 1958, sometimes relied heavily on law review scholarship. Often the circle was completed when a law clerk returned as a judge. To illustrate this pattern only at the nation's highest court, of the justices serving at the start of the twenty-first century, Chief Justice Rehnquist clerked for Justice Robert Jackson, Justice John Paul Stevens clerked for Justice Wiley Rutledge, and Justice Stephen Breyer clerked for Justice Arthur Goldberg.

These changes did not have an immediate effect on the jurisprudence of the death penalty. In fact, the first effect of the new school of judicial thought was increased judicial deference to economic legislation. Nevertheless, the legal tools that had been created would be put to use in the death penalty rulings of a later generation.

DREAMS

Finally, the history of cruel and unusual punishment has been influenced, most significantly though least obviously, by shifts in the nation's unspoken consensus about crime and criminals. Both the Supreme Court's decisions and the controversy they generate can be explained in large part by the fact that as members of society the justices have unexamined opinions too, and that as nine out of 275 million citizens they almost always are running ahead of or lagging behind the center of gravity of the country. Because of the Court's lack of reliability as a measurer of public opinion, conservative Justice Antonin Scalia wrote in 1990 that the Court had no better idea of how to decide some constitutional issues than nine persons chosen at random from the Kansas City phone book. Other justices, such as liberal Justice Arthur Goldberg, denied that public opinion should matter. In 1963, he argued that the "Court traditionally has guided rather than followed public opinion."

Divisions in the courts reflect the divisions in society. From the days when Puritan mercantile New Englander and Cavalier agrarian Southerner looked askance at one another, there have been differing cultures in America, and in a country as large and diverse as the United States is today it is impossible for there to be a general philosophy. Nevertheless, it is possible to identify three successively dominant modes of viewing crime and criminals. In the first period, stretching from the settlement of the nation until the end of the nineteenth century, the general view may be called the retributive model. Man was seen as a moral actor freely engaged in a moral struggle in the world, and when he committed a serious crime he deserved, in a moral sense, to shed blood for the blood he had shed. If he committed a lesser crime he might not be capable of being led out of his sins, but he could be made to "pay for his crime," and perhaps in the process others could see the error of his criminal ways.

By the end of the nineteenth century the decline of the conservative Protestant consensus, caused by the rise in urbanization and the influx of immigrants from southern and eastern Europe, ended the reign of the retributive theory of punishment. The twin pressures of religious skepticism and philosophies loosely derived from the theories of natural selection advanced by Charles Darwin's 1859 work *On the Origin of Species,* forced America into a second era, that of the "medicinal rehabilitative" model. It had been sketched out as a philosophical program in the early 1800s by Jeremy Bentham, and its triumph over the retributive ideal was hailed as a sign of progress by utopian writers such as Edward Bellamy in his popular 1888 novel *Looking Backward.* Where

Aristotle and More had assumed that crime would be punished by death, the new visionaries imagined a world in which criminals were healed and returned to society. Moral explanations of crime and justifications of punishment declined or were expressly rejected in favor of environmental explanations of crime and rehabilitative theories of punishment. Ironically, the rise of this trend in punishment coincided with the rise of a crude Darwinism, popularized by writers such as Cesare Lombroso in his 1889 work *The Criminal Man,* which asserted that there were criminal types, evolutionary throwbacks with immutable physical characteristics. This pseudoscience, with its transparently racist implications, gave birth to a minor eugenics movement in early twentieth-century American criminal punishment that attempted to address crime by sterilizing some classes of criminals.

In the mainstream, however, the classic statement of the new orthodoxy on crime and punishment came in midcentury, in an opinion by Justice Hugo Black for the Supreme Court in *Williams v. New York* (1949):

> A sentencing judge, however, is not confined to the narrow issue of guilt. His task within fixed statutory or constitutional limits is to determine the type and extent of punishment after the issue of guilt has been determined. Highly relevant—if not essential—to his selection of an appropriate sentence is the possession of the fullest information possible concerning the defendant's life and characteristics. And modern concepts individualizing punishment have made it all the more necessary that a sentencing judge not be denied an opportunity to obtain pertinent information by a requirement of rigid adherence to restrictive rules of evidence properly applicable to the trial. . . .
>
> The belief no longer prevails that every offense in a like legal category calls for an identical punishment without regard to the past life and habits of a particular offender. This whole country has traveled far from the period in which the death sentence was an automatic and commonplace result of convictions—even for offenses today deemed

> trivial. Today's philosophy of individualizing sentences makes sharp distinctions for example between first and repeated offenders. Indeterminate sentences, the ultimate termination of which are sometimes decided by nonjudicial agencies have to a large extent taken the place of the old rigidly fixed punishments. The practice of probation which relies heavily on nonjudicial implementation has been accepted as a wise policy. . . .
>
> Retribution is no longer the dominant objective of the criminal law. Reformation and rehabilitation of offenders have become important goals of criminal jurisprudence. . . .
>
> [I]ndeterminate sentences and probation have resulted in an increase in the discretionary powers exercised in fixing punishments. In general, these modern changes have not resulted in making the lot of offenders harder. On the contrary a strong motivating force for the changes has been the belief that by careful study of the lives and personalities of convicted offenders many could be less severely punished and restored sooner to complete freedom and useful citizenship. This belief to a large extent has been justified.

The justices announced this concern with rehabilitation in rejecting Williams's constitutional challenge to the imposition of the death penalty by a judge, after the jury that convicted him of first degree murder had recommended life imprisonment. No doubt it was small comfort to Williams at his execution that the lot of defendants had improved because judges were permitted to sentence them on the basis of presentence reports containing evidence that would not be admissible at trial.

The period when the medical model of crime was dominant, from the beginning of the twentieth century until its last quarter, also saw juvenile criminal law become a separate specialty, based on the presumably distinct needs of younger criminals. The use of probation and "suspended sentences," had begun in the last quarter of the nineteenth century and spread widely in the new century, as did the use of indeterminate sentences and parole boards to determine not the severity of the crime but rather when an offender was fit to rejoin society. A criminal sentence, because it no longer represented a "debt to society" but rather a diagnosis of how badly the offender had strayed, was to be tailored to the individual. The language used in standard texts shows this clearly. Professor Daniel Glaser's landmark study, commissioned by the Bureau of Prisons and endorsed by Attorney General Robert F. Kennedy, discusses an offender's imprisonment, from initial incarceration through release to what significantly was called a community treatment program, in the style of a medical case history. Glaser even refers to the role of the probation officer as involving the competing duties of "diagnosis" and "treatment." He implicitly approves of the view that crime is like disease and that "one can change the criminal's behavior by altering his learning experience, and especially by changing the social influences at work on him" and disapproves of "the tendency to think of the person whose experiences make him a criminal as profoundly and consistently different from the noncriminal" (Glaser 1969, 317).

Of course, outside elite circles, the medical model of crime never gained full acceptance, even at its height of influence. In large part this was because the merits of the model, being subtle, were hard to grasp, and its faults, being obvious, were easy to lampoon. A classic parody that struck a chord with America was the famous "Gee Officer Krupke" song of the juvenile delinquents in the 1957 musical *West Side Story,* depicting young hoodlums mocking the rehabilitative apparatus of juvenile court with excuses for crime like "I'm depraved on account of I'm deprived." Indeed, by the 1950s it had become a staple of popular crime fiction books and movies that there was a universal dichotomy in the law enforcement system between hardheaded police officer, private detective, or vigilante, who understood the nature of evil, and softhearted judge, social worker, or soon-to-be victim, who believed that the villain had reformed. But even given allowances for the need of popular entertainment to simplify the matter, there truly was a change in style. Where a judge in 1850 might sentence a man to hang (or to prison) with the thought "there but for the grace of God go I," the judge of 1950 more typically would sentence a man to prison (or to hang) with the regret that "there but for the lack of a good education and social support structures goes a potentially useful citizen."

By the time President Richard Nixon began his first term in office in 1969, the medical model consensus about crime was beginning to fray. Nixon's inauguration followed the 1968 assassinations of presidential candidate Robert Kennedy and civil rights leader Martin Luther King, Jr. Whereas the assassination attempt on President Truman and the murder of a guard by Puerto Rican separatists in 1950 had caused no deep impression on the nation, and Truman's 1952 commutation of the death penalty imposed on would-be assassin Oscar Collazo went little noticed, by the late 1960s America was well into the television age. Americans had seen the film of the assassination of President Kennedy by Lee Harvey Oswald, and then seen Oswald murdered by Jack Ruby. Deprived of the catharsis that putting Oswald on trial might have provided had he not been killed so soon after his capture, the country watched as Robert Kennedy and King's assassins received life imprisonment (or had their death sentences overturned and reduced to life) and even became eligible for parole.

Also darkening the nation's mood as the 1970s began were televised scenes of antiwar protests and summertime rioting in major American cities, a wave of airplane hijackings, bizarre and seemingly inexplicable murders such as those of Charles Manson's "family" (also made eligible for parole by the overturning of their death sentences), and the depiction of crime as sometimes glamorous *(Butch Cassidy and the Sundance Kid)*, sometimes successful *(The Sting)*, and sometimes both *(The Godfather)*, by a Hollywood free from the censorship of earlier decades.

Finally, joining the perennial objection to rehabilitative models by conservatives, by 1970 libertarians and radical liberals had begun to assail as despotic the indeterminate jail sentences and discretionary parole systems that had been acclaimed as progressive in 1900. America's prisons historically had been mostly white institutions, because most crime was committed by members of the local community and therefore was intraracial, and law enforcement had traditionally underserved black communities. Once there was a sustained attempt to provide consistent police protection to majority black communities, prisons experienced a rise in the proportion of black inmates. Of course, just as not every failure of the justice system in the early twentieth century was due to racism, not every step in the right direction was untainted by injustice. Sometimes with evidence, black inmates argued that indeterminate parole dates were used as tools of racism. All inmates protested that long maximum prison terms, where the real power to order release was held by unaccountable and invisible bureaucracies, led to arbitrary decision making.

Outside the academic and legal community, George Orwell's bleak prediction of universal tyranny in his work *1984* and Anthony Burgess's *A Clockwork Orange,* made into a hit movie in 1971 by Stanley Kubrick, acquainted the public at large with the idea that ideologies that treated crime like disease could themselves be a recipe for cruel and unusual punishment.

By the end of the 1970s, even though it was the high summer of the Supreme Court's upheaval in death penalty jurisprudence, the medical model of crime and punishment was dead. Its obituary was written for the legal community in 1984 with the bipartisan passage of the federal Bail Reform Act and the Sentencing Reform Act. To the public at large, the death of the medical model was confirmed during the 1988 presidential campaign by the famous "Willie Horton" series of attack ads that equated leniency toward criminals with complicity in their crimes, developed during the Democratic primary races by Tennessee Senator Al Gore, Jr., and used with devastating effect in the general election by Vice President George H. W. Bush against Governor Michael Dukakis of

Massachusetts. Dukakis's principled statement during a presidential debate that he would continue to oppose the death penalty even if his wife were raped and murdered alienated voters, because the Willie Horton ads resonated with a public that for the most part had settled comfortably into a third consensus, the "just war" model.

In the current era, the line between police and military action is blurred because the criminal is no longer an individual, whether sinful or sick, at all. Regardless of his individual merits or lack thereof, he is part of an army at war with society that must be neutralized. In an era when explicitly moral judgments are not fashionable and consensus may not be possible, the justification for criminal policy is necessarily the same as for other military policies: it is the bottom line that counts. Increasingly, the bottom line is almost solely expressed in terms of aggregate crime statistics.

From *Weems* to *Furman*

The coming momentous changes of the twentieth century were not apparent to anyone in 1910, when in *Weems v. United States* for the first time the Supreme Court overturned a criminal sentence because it inflicted cruel and unusual punishment. Paul Weems, a disbursing officer of the U.S. government in the Philippines, was convicted of falsifying public documents. Under the Philippine criminal law, which had incorporated with few changes the preexisting Spanish penal code, Weems had to be sentenced to at least twelve years of *cadena temporal,* that is, a term of hard and painful labor, complete with chains hanging from wrists to ankles. Weems was forbidden visitors while in prison, and after release he was obliged for the rest of his life to report his whereabouts to the authorities, submitting at any time to official inspection.

Justice McKenna, writing for the majority, exhaustively canvassed the congressional debates over the Eighth Amendment, the commentaries by Story, Cooley, and others, cases from the states and territories applying their prohibitions of cruel and unusual punishment, and *Wilkerson, Kemmler,* and *O'Neil.* Conceding that almost all of the authorities cited commanded the judiciary to keep its hands off a legislative schedule of punishments, McKenna nevertheless distilled two significant principles from precedent. Adopting the position of the dissent in *O'Neil,* McKenna reasoned that the ban on cruel and unusual punishment was directed not just against torture "but against all punishments which, by their excessive length or severity, are greatly disproportioned to the offenses charged." More important, he examined the Eighth Amendment and found: "The clause of the Constitution in the opinion of learned commentators may be therefore progressive, and is not fastened to the obsolete but may acquire meaning as public opinion becomes enlightened by a humane justice."

Disparaging the cruelty of Spanish law, even though moderation in punishment had only recently become a feature of federal law, the Court held that the severity of Weems's punishment, of itself and in comparison to other federal crimes, the indifference of the statute to whether Weems had profited from his falsification, and the accessory punishments of chains, isolation, and surveillance by the authorities made it cruel and unusual.

Easing the way to the decision in *Weems* was the fact that in the previous fifteen years the Court had in other fields of law been reconsidering and reinterpreting the meaning of other constitutional provisions. As Justice McKenna observed, the Court had steadily been expanding the scope of Congress's power to legislate in economic matters by interpreting Article I's grant of the power to regulate interstate commerce more broadly than in Chief Justice Marshall's day. Most portentous for the future was that Justice McKenna also referred, as an example of an evolving interpretation of the Constitution, to the judicial "construction of the Fourteenth Amendment." In 1873, in the first decision construing the

Fourteenth Amendment, the Supreme Court had doubted that the Fourteenth Amendment had any other purpose than to invalidate laws that "discriminate against Negroes as a class." By 1910, McKenna pointed out that the extent to which "the Amendment has expanded beyond that limitation" was so well known that it "need not be instanced."

The reason McKenna felt it unnecessary to give examples was not because he thought they were unpersuasive, but because to his fellow justices the scope of the Fourteenth Amendment was the hottest topic of the age. Section 1 of the Amendment commands: "nor shall any State deprive any person of life, liberty, or property, without due process of law."

What that meant had not been elaborated by the drafters of the amendment, nor had there been any real discussion of its meaning in the states when it was ratified, in large part because requiring "due process of law" was understood to be, like Magna Carta's parallel phrase that judgments be given according to "the law of the land," a command to judges that customary rules of procedure must be followed in court.

After the ratification of the Fourteenth Amendment, the Supreme Court had first looked to historical custom to judge the scope of due process. In *Hurtado v. California* (1884), the defendant, sentenced to death for murder in a prosecution started by the filing of an "information" by the prosecutor, not by indictment returned by a grand jury, argued that he had been denied due process in violation of the Fourteenth Amendment. The Fifth Amendment required the federal government to afford a criminal defendant due process in federal courts, and also specifically required that the prosecution of capital cases begin by the evidence being heard by a grand jury. Did the Fourteenth Amendment's requirement of due process mean that California must use this procedure against Hurtado in a capital case, or not? Both Justice Stanley Matthews's majority opinion and the dissent by the first Justice John Marshall Harlan are notable for their exclusive use of the history of English criminal procedure to answer this question. The Court upheld the conviction.

By the late nineteenth century, however, justices of what could be considered the conservative wing of the Court, generally more sympathetic to claims of individual rights than to legislation realigning those rights, had declared that due process meant more than simply procedures followed in court. In *Missouri Pacific Railway v. Nebraska* (1896) and *Chicago, Burlington, and Quincy Railroad Co. v. Chicago* (1897), the Court announced that states and municipalities could not take railroad property unless it was for public use and the railroad received just compensation. The Fifth Amendment imposed that constraint on the federal government, but even though the Fifth Amendment did not apply to the states, its requirements of public use and just compensation, said the Court, were principles of "due process of law" binding on states and cities under the Fourteenth Amendment.

This left the judges and legislators who were generally more sympathetic to legislation limiting work hours or establishing minimum wages in a quandary. In a mirror image of the rhetorical exchanges at the end of the twentieth century, at the beginning of the 1900s liberals urged "strict construction" of the Constitution and charged that the conservative justices were legislating their own values through the Fourteenth Amendment.

On the other hand, the liberal justices had to deal with the philosophical notion of an expanding and evolving Constitution. Justice Louis Brandeis, who as a practicing lawyer had been a strong advocate of minimum wage, maximum hour, and other working conditions legislation and one of the first attorneys to use economic and social statistics in addition to legal precedents in his legal briefs, was named to the Supreme Court by President Woodrow Wilson in 1916. Throughout his tenure on the Court, Brandeis pointed out that to accept that only economic rights such as just compensation and freedom of contract were protected by the Due Process Clause would mean that other freedoms named in the Bill of Rights would be left as second-class rights, open to invasion by states and localities. Hence by the 1920s, both liberal and conservative justices had embarked on the expansion of the meaning of due process to include other portions of the Bill of Rights, such as freedom of speech and freedom of the press.

This process, called "incorporation" of rights into the Due Process Clause, was slow and uneven as justices groped for a theoretical basis for their actions. The result in *Weems* had been made easier by the fact that the Court was free to construe the meaning of cruel and unusual punishment to strike down a foreign, and therefore inferior, law applicable in a foreign possession, not a law enacted by Congress or a state. Only five years after *Weems,* the Court rejected a claim that a fourteen-year sentence for perjury was excessive punishment prohibited by the Due Process Clause, holding in *Collins v. Johnston* (1915), that "to establish appropriate penalties for the commission of crime . . . [is a] function peculiarly belonging to the several States." The Eighth Amendment was not incorporated yet.

What other provisions were or were not part of due process? The Supreme Court had already held in *Hurtado* that the Fifth Amendment's guarantee of indictment by grand jury was not part of due process, and affirmed Hurtado's death sentence. In *Powell v. Alabama* in 1932, the court incorporated part of the Sixth Amendment's guarantee of the assistance of counsel, on the basis that the effective assistance of counsel was "at the base of all our civil and political institutions." But in 1937, in *Palko v. Connecticut,* the Court allowed the prosecution to appeal Frank Palko's second-degree murder conviction for the killing of his wife. On retrial, Palko had been convicted of first-degree murder and sentenced to death. Rejecting Palko's argument that the Fifth Amendment's Double Jeopardy Clause was part of the due process of law, Justice Cardozo, hardly a conservative, held that only rights "of the very essence of a scheme of ordered liberty" were incorporated. Palko was executed.

As the New Deal era of the 1930s was brought to an end by U.S. entry into World War II, the Supreme Court finally had embraced the federal government's broad power to legislate in economic affairs, but it tended to be skeptical of or even hostile to civil rights claims. A significant exception was Justice Hugo Black. Black, formerly a Democratic senator from Alabama, appointed in 1937 as President Roosevelt's first pick for the Court because of his strong support for New Deal policies, believed despite the absence of historical evidence that the Fourteenth Amendment had been written to incorporate all of the protections of the Bill of Rights. Nevertheless, although a Bill of Rights absolutist, Justice Black was no "evolutionist" when it came to cruel and unusual punishment. Black reasoned that because the death penalty had existed side by side with the Eighth Amendment since the nation's founding, the Amendment could not possibly be interpreted to outlaw use of the death penalty. The other justices on the Court through the 1930s and 1940s reached the same conclusion through different means.

In 1947, the Court confronted its first Eighth Amendment incorporation claim in *Louisiana ex. rel. Francis v. Resweber.* Willie Francis, age sixteen, had been sentenced to die in the electric chair for a murder committed when he was fifteen. Louisiana was one of the few states that had not fully centralized its execution process: it sent a truck with a portable generator and traveling electric chair to the parish jails when needed to execute a criminal (Prettyman 1961, 95). Due to a malfunction, possibly because the executioner was intoxicated, the first attempt to electrocute Francis had failed. Would a second attempt to kill Francis be cruel and unusual punishment? Four members of the Court said no, it was just as if Francis had suffered from an accidental fire in his cell. Four members said yes: Louisiana could not torture a prisoner to death by repeated shocks, and it made no difference whether the first attempt was an accident. Casting the deciding vote was Justice Frankfurter, an opponent of the death penalty who authored books calling for its abolition. Personally liberal and judicially conservative, Frankfurter found that because the first failure was not intentional, a second attempt would not be unconstitutional. Francis was executed at age seventeen.

There matters stood at the Supreme Court for a decade. Below the nation's highest court, however, changes were taking place. As part of the general trend of the legal realist school toward a rational and systematic presentation of the law, the American Law Institute had been formed in 1923. Its members and supporters, including the justices of the Supreme Court and of the highest courts of the forty-eight states, began codification projects designed to provide uniform treatment of important areas of law throughout the nation. Drafting of uniform sales and commercial codes began. Another project was to develop restatements, comprehensive treatments of the laws of contracts, property, and torts, designed to synthesize cases throughout the nation and explain the policy choices thought to underlie the variety of state legal rules. By the 1930s, the first fruits of this effort began to appear in legal libraries.

By the 1950s, the ALI had selected Professor Herbert Wechsler of Columbia University to draft a Model Penal Code. Supplemented by the sociological work of Thorsten Sellin of the University of Pennsylvania, who had worked on the Royal Commission that successfully recommended the abolition of capital punishment in Great Britain, Wechsler took no official position for or against total abolition of the death penalty, but noted the risk of executing innocent defendants, recommended that the death penalty be reserved only for murder with aggravating circumstances, and prescribed a bifurcated process for capital cases. Under the Model Penal Code, completed in 1962, a capital trial that resulted in a guilty verdict would proceed to determine the sentence after a hearing in which the judge or jury received aggravating and mitigating evidence not necessarily relevant to the guilt-determining phase. Variations on the Model Penal Code's procedure were adopted in several states.

Meanwhile, the states and the federal government had been imposing the death penalty less and less. Between 1930 and 1939, executions had been carried out, on average, 167 times per year. In the period between 1940 and 1949, the annual average had dropped to 128, and in 1950 through 1959, to 72. A report to the House of Representatives in 1829 showed that in the first thirty-six years of the nation's history, the federal hangman had executed forty-two criminals (Little 1999, 366). In the thirty-six years between 1927 and 1963, only twenty-four federal executions had been carried out, and eight of them had been for espionage or wartime sabotage. After the hanging in 1957 of brothers George Krull and Michael Krull for rape committed in a federal park and the hanging of Victor Feguer in 1963 for the kidnaping and murder of a young doctor, the federal government would not seek the death penalty for another thirty years (Little 1999, 357). The Supreme Court denied review in each of the last three federal death penalty cases.

The Federal Bureau of Prisons, meanwhile, had been established in 1930 under President Herbert Hoover, and for its first director, Hoover chose Sanford Bates. Bates came to the post after almost a decade of experience as head of the Massachusetts state prison system, and was strongly committed to a rehabilitative model. Although Blackstone had in 1769 described wardens as "a merciless race of men . . . conversant in scenes of misery, steeled against any tender sensation" (Blackstone IV, 297), and despite the legendary mystique of names like Alcatraz and Leavenworth, federal penal institutions were early promoters of the science of treatment in preference to retributive punishment. Bates, his successor James Bennett, the head of the California prison system Richard A. McGee, and many of the wardens of the mid–twentieth century, including John Ryan of the federal prison in Milan, Michigan, James Johnston of the federal prison at Alcatraz, Clinton Duffy of the California state penitentiary at San Quentin, and Lewis Lawes, warden of New York's Sing Sing Prison and president of the American Prison Association (which in 1954 would become the American Correctional Association), strongly and publicly opposed the death penalty (Bennett 1972, 144; McGee 1972, 161–175).

By the late 1950s, most of the justices appointed by Presidents Roosevelt and Truman—justices who were deferential to government regulation of the economy but, in this era of the Cold War, were skeptical about claims that the constitution protected individual liberties—had left the Court. Remaining were Justice Black and Justice William Douglas, formerly a professor at Columbia University Law School and head of the Securities and Exchange Commission. As his tenure on the Court (1939–1975) lengthened, Douglas would become increasingly vocal against traditional criminal practices in favor of a strongly libertarian model of individual rights. President Dwight D. Eisenhower added to the Court four justices who were important to the history of the death penalty: Chief Justice Earl Warren, former governor of California and candidate for vice president, most famous for his unanimous opinion in *Brown v. Board of Education;* John Marshall Harlan, the grandson of the first justice to bear that name; William Brennan, of the New Jersey Supreme Court; and Potter Stewart, one of the youngest judges ever to be appointed to the Court of Appeals for the Sixth Circuit.

Chief Justice Warren, once joined by Justice Brennan in 1956, led the Supreme Court through a due process revolution. By 1968, virtually all of the criminal law provisions of the Bill of Rights were incorporated into the Due Process Clause and therefore binding on the states. But first, in 1958 the justices would decide an Eighth Amendment case that seemed at first to have little to do with due process or the death penalty, *Trop v. Dulles.*

Albert Trop was a twenty-year-old private in the U.S. Army serving in French Morocco in 1944. He deserted for one day after escaping from the stockade, returned, was court-martialed, and was dishonorably discharged. He returned home. In 1952 he applied for a passport, only to find that it was denied because he was no longer a citizen of the United States. Under a federal law passed in 1865 to stem the flood of desertions from the Union Army in the Civil War, Trop had, by being court-martialed for desertion, been stripped of his citizenship. He unsuccessfully argued in the lower federal courts that this penalty violated the Cruel and Unusual Punishments Clause of the Eighth Amendment.

Chief Justice Warren, speaking for four members of the Court, and no doubt influenced by the fact that there were approximately 7,000 former soldiers like Trop, held that the forfeiture of citizenship was unconstitutional (Justice Brennan, the fifth vote for Trop, wrote separately). Announcing a constitutional principle that echoed *Brown v. Board of Education*'s approach to the Equal Protection Clause and that would be employed throughout the next three decades, Warren wrote of the Eighth Amendment that it "must draw its meaning from the evolving standards of decency that mark the progress of a maturing society."

Just as significant for the history of the death penalty was the chief justice's reply to the four dissenters, led by Justice Frankfurter, who argued that because a deserter in wartime could have been and still could be shot by a firing squad, the loss of citizenship could hardly be cruel and unusual punishment. Warren countered:

> At the outset, let us put to one side the death penalty as an index of the constitutional limit on punishment. Whatever the arguments may be against capital punishment, both on moral grounds and in terms of accomplishing the purposes of punishment—and they are forceful—the death penalty has been employed throughout our history, and, in a day when it is still widely accepted, it cannot be said to violate the constitutional concept of cruelty. But it is equally plain that the existence of the death penalty is not a license to the Government to devise any punishment short of death within the limit of its imagination.

Warren signaled to all the members of the legal community who cared to see that a considerable bloc on the Court acknowledged that there were "forceful" moral and practical arguments against the death penalty. It would not be long before the Court would accept that these were constitutional arguments as well.

Incidentally, without fuss, in *Trop* the Court had put to an end to banishment as a constitutionally allowable punishment. Before *Trop,* and well after *Trop* where counsel and judges chose to ignore the opinion, a sentencing judge could tell a defendant that "if he got on the next bus and never came back" there would be no further penalty. It was a traditional way of getting rid of vagrants and petty offenders, especially in rural counties. The practice had the same merits as in the eighteenth century: it was an inexpensive and often effective way of reforming a delinquent. The defects of "Greyhound therapy" were that too often it was employed to spare the locality trouble and expense, regardless of what happened to the next town, and regardless of the guilt or innocence of the defendant.

Meanwhile, in the 1950s, public opinion was being shaped by celebrity cases beyond the courthouse, from the execution of Julius and Ethel Rosenberg at Sing Sing in 1953 to the execution of Caryl Chessman at San Quentin in 1960. Chessman was arrested and convicted in 1948 of a series of crimes, including sexual assaults and two kidnapings for which he received the death penalty. During twelve years on death row, the "Red Light Bandit," so-called because he had tricked his victims into stopping by flashing a red light from his automobile, achieved fame by writing books proclaiming his innocence and denouncing the death penalty. By the end, clemency petitions with more than ten million signatures, plus statements from religious leaders and celebrities, were submitted on Chessman's behalf. At first the public had focused on the question of Chessman's guilt, but by 1960, after numerous trips to the Supreme Court had exhausted even Justice Douglas's patience, Chessman sparked international debate over the justice of the death penalty especially for crimes less than murder, and national debate over how long a condemned man could delay his execution simply by filing legal pleadings (Joyce 1961, 20).

While the Chessman drama was playing out, Barbara Graham was executed at San Quentin in 1955. The 1958 film *I Want to Live*, which won Susan Hayward an Academy Award, portrayed Graham as a down-and-out small-time criminal framed by her male associates, tricked by unscrupulous police officers into falsely incriminating herself, and abandoned by incompetent attorneys and judges indifferent to the methods used to convict someone of a capital crime. Its not-so-subtle message was made more effective by its showing the defendant's last visit with her young son and her last moments in the gas chamber (Foster 1997).

In 1962, President John F. Kennedy made two appointments to the Supreme Court: Byron White, formerly Assistant Attorney General for Civil Rights and an architect of Kennedy's desegregation efforts, and Arthur Goldberg, a respected labor lawyer who had negotiated the merger of the American Federation of Labor and the Congress of Industrial Organizations (AFL-CIO). Although the death penalty would not be declared unconstitutional for another decade, as a practical matter 1962 marked the end of capital punishment. The next year the two new justices joined Justice Brennan's opinion for the Court in *Fay v. Noia* (1963), a little-known case construing the federal habeas corpus statute. *Fay v. Noia* reversed the life sentence imposed on Noia for a 1942 murder on the grounds that his confession had been coerced, even though Noia had not appealed on that ground in the state court. As long as he had not "deliberately bypassed" the issue in state court, the Court held, a defendant in state custody could claim that his conviction violated the federal Constitution. The importance of the opinion (other than to Noia, who was released) was that by opening such a broad new avenue of relief to defendants in state custody, a death row inmate did not need to be one of the few defendants whose cases were reviewed by the Supreme Court each year. He could be sure his execution would be stayed, and his claim would be heard, because he could file an original proceeding before hundreds of federal district judges, followed by a second round of appeals to the federal appellate courts, followed by a petition to the Supreme Court. This could add years to the average time a sentenced inmate could spend before risking execution, especially because an inmate did not need to file his first federal habeas corpus petition until he actually faced an execution date, and as long as a judge would hear them, there was no limit on the number of times he could file new petitions.

Fay v. Noia applied to prisoners in state custody. In the same term of court, the Supreme Court declined the petition of Victor Feguer to review the decision affirming his federal death sentence for interstate kidnaping under the "Lindbergh law," passed in 1934, after the national sensation caused by the 1932 kidnaping and murder of the son of aviation hero Charles Lindbergh. The opinion affirming the death sentence had been written by Judge Harry Blackmun of the Eighth Circuit Court of Appeals. Despite a plea from the governor of Iowa not to execute Feguer because the death penalty was cruel and unusual punishment, Feguer was hanged by the neck for nine minutes until dead. Feguer's would be the last federal execution until that of Timothy McVeigh in 2001.

Later in 1963, the justices would receive a memorandum from Justice Goldberg, who believed the time had come for a frontal assault on the death penalty. In his memorandum, Justice Goldberg urged that even though none of the defendants in the six death penalty cases before the Court had attacked the constitutionality of the death penalty, the Court should, as it had in *Weems,* disregard its general rule of not addressing arguments not made by the litigants and confront the issue on its own. He laid out the arguments, legal and practical (Goldberg 1986):

1. *Weems* marked a turning point in interpreting the Eighth Amendment because in it the Court focused on the disproportionate severity of the punishment, not

merely whether the method of carrying it out involved torture.

2. After *Weems* and *Trop,* the meaning of the Eighth Amendment could evolve and was not limited to the understanding of 1791.
3. There was a worldwide move toward abolishing the death penalty. Although public opinion in the United States was evenly divided, it was the duty of the Court to guide rather than reflect public opinion.
4. A punishment was unconstitutionally severe if it went beyond what anyone would reasonably find necessary to satisfy the proper ends of punishment.
5. The proper ends of punishment were deterrence and rehabilitation. The Court had declared, in *Williams v. New York,* that vengeance was not an acceptable goal of punishment.
6. Obviously the death penalty could not rehabilitate. Further, there was no conclusive evidence that the death penalty had any deterrent effect over and above life imprisonment.
7. Finally, death was different. The Court had called the constitutionality of many convictions into doubt, but if the death penalty were carried out, a defendant could hardly benefit from a rule subsequently announced in another case. A penalty that made enforcement of constitutional rights meaningless should be ruled out. Goldberg concluded that the death penalty was in all cases unconstitutionally severe, but was especially so where it was imposed for offenses not involving the taking of life.

The court denied review in each of the six cases Goldberg identified in his memorandum. In *Rudolph v. Alabama* (1963), Justice Goldberg, joined by Douglas and Brennan, dissented with a written opinion that substantially repeated the questions posed in Justice Goldberg's memorandum. A bloc on the Court was clearly inviting counsel to ask for the death penalty to be struck down.

Justice Goldberg left the Court in 1965 at President Lyndon B. Johnson's urging to become Ambassador to the United Nations, and the Court regularly continued to deny review to death penalty cases. Nevertheless, after *Fay v. Noia,* the rate of executions slowed to a trickle because defendants were challenging their convictions in federal court. There were 56 executions in 1960, 42 in 1961, 47 in 1962, 21 in 1963, and 15 in 1964. From 1965 to 1967 there were a total of ten. In 1967, the National Association for the Advancement of Colored People (NAACP) Legal Defense and Educational Fund began filing class-action lawsuits, usually in federal court, on behalf of death row inmates, accompanied by requests for stays of execution while constitutional challenges to the death penalty were litigated. The stays were always granted (Greenberg and Himmelstein 1972, 239–240). After 1967, although there was no permanent legal bar to the death penalty, and although states continued to sentence defendants to death at the rate of about 100 per year, there were no executions.

The 1960s were years of ferment in the Court's thinking about the issue of cruel and unusual punishment beyond the death penalty. In *Robinson v. California* (1962), the Court held that it violated the Eighth Amendment to make narcotics addiction a criminal offense. This could have been the beginning of a much more revolutionary change than outlawing capital punishment.

Some crimes are hard to prove and so they are attacked by attacking the related crime. Possession of burglary tools is severely punished not because they are believed to be inherently evil, but because it is easier to prove what was in a burglar's pocket than what was on his mind. Similarly, loitering was a criminal offense not because of some puritanical distaste for idleness but because loitering was perceived to be the first step in disruptive criminal conduct.

The Court in *Robinson* said that this logic could not be extended to so called "status crimes." Because the state of being addicted was something by definition a defendant had no control over, criminal punishment could not deter it and was not useful to rehabilitate it. Therefore, imprisonment was unconstitutionally cruel. The implications of *Robinson*—that the Eighth Amendment allowed the Supreme Court to use drug addiction, or perhaps mental illness, poverty, or religious beliefs to invalidate criminal penalties—were profoundly disturbing. In 1968, Justice White provided the fifth vote, which backed the Court away from extending this reasoning to the crime of public intoxication, in *Powell v. Texas.* Justice White began in his written opinions to move away from the exclusive focus on deterrence and rehabilitation as permissible goals of the criminal law, and increasingly would become the spokesman on the Court for the point of view that society could express its moral disapproval of conduct without engaging in the type of cost-benefit analysis that Justices Goldberg and Douglas believed the Eighth Amendment required. Although the Court held in *Bearden v. Georgia* (1983) that a state could not imprison a poor person for inability to pay (as opposed to refusal to attempt to repay) a fine, it did so without relying on the Eighth Amendment rationale put forward in *Robinson. Robinson* appears to be a dead end in constitutional analysis of the Eighth Amendment.

Thinking about the death penalty changed in the executive branch as well. Although there was no serious effort to repeal federal capital punishment, it was the position of the Johnson administration that the death penalty should be abolished, in part because it was applied in a racially discriminatory fashion: U.S. Attorney General Ramsey Clark (the son of former Supreme Court Justice Tom Clark) testified before the Senate Judiciary Committee in July 1968 that according to federal statistics, 405 of the 455 persons executed for rape since 1930 were black men (Clark 1972, 179).

Although few state death sentences were making it past the lower courts, the Supreme Court continued to tinker with the death penalty without making any fundamental changes, while the nation's death rows continued to expand slowly as defendants were sentenced to death but not executed. In 1968, the Supreme Court held in *United States v. Jackson* that the moribund federal death penalty for kidnaping was unconstitutional. Under the 1897 revision of the federal mandatory death penalty statute, a federal jury had the discretion to recommend a life sentence or fix a sentence of death; inattentive legislative drafting of the kidnaping statute allowed a judge who took a guilty plea to kidnaping to sentence a defendant to a maximum of life imprisonment. This disparity, reasoned the Court, coerced a defendant into forgoing the constitutional right to a trial before a jury. In *Witherspoon v. Illinois* (1968), the Court held that a juror who voiced objections to capital punishment could not be excluded from jury service in a capital case. In *Boykin v. Alabama* (1969), the Supreme Court reversed the death sentence imposed on a young black man who had pleaded guilty to five armed robberies, on the ground that the defendant did not make a knowing and voluntary waiver of his rights. The dissent pointed out that the defendant had challenged the excessiveness of the sentence, but not the voluntariness of the guilty plea. This would imply that in 1969 the Supreme Court did not have a majority opposed to the death penalty, but could pick up a decisive vote by invalidating the procedures used to reach it.

In a case presenting almost every element of the death penalty controversy in the 1960s, the Supreme Court reversed a death sentence for a rape committed by a black man against a white woman in Arkansas, in *Maxwell v. Bishop* (1970). The defendant was represented by veteran anti–death penalty litigators Anthony Amsterdam and Jack Greenberg. The case was before the Court after the lower federal court, in an opinion by Harry Blackmun, had rejected a second federal habeas corpus petition. The defendant contended on the basis of statistical evidence that the death penalty was being disproportionately used against black men, but the Court chose the narrower grounds that jurors opposed to the death penalty had been excluded.

From *Furman* to *Gregg*

By the end of President Johnson's tenure in office, Justice Thurgood Marshall, the longtime chief litigator for the NAACP Legal Defense and Educational Fund, had moved from the Court of Appeals for the Second Circuit to become the first black Supreme Court justice. Like Justices Douglas and Brennan, Marshall was strongly opposed to the death penalty; unlike other members of the Court, he had seen the practical consequences of the death penalty issue as counsel on the defendant's side of the courtroom.

In 1971, the last of the cases expressing deference to the states in death penalty procedures was decided. *McGautha v. California* upheld death sentences from California and Ohio; Justice Harlan and four members of the Court held that the Due Process Clause of the Fourteenth Amendment did not require a separate sentencing hearing after the guilt phase of the trial, or guidance about how to weigh aggravating and mitigating factors, as recommended by the Model Penal Code. Justice Black wrote separately, rejecting on historical grounds the claim that the Eighth Amendment barred the death penalty. Although giving the jury unfettered discretion to return a life sentence instead of mandatory death had been a humane advance when introduced, Justices Douglas, Brennan, and Marshall argued in dissent that in 1971 this discretion was being used to permit the arbitrary and capricious imposition of death instead of life.

By the opening of the Court's next term, Justices Harlan and Black had retired and been replaced by President Nixon's last two appointees, Lewis Powell of the Court of Appeals for the Fourth Circuit, and Assistant Attorney General William Rehnquist. They joined Justices Douglas, Brennan, Stewart, White, and Marshall, as well as two previous Nixon appointees: Chief Justice Warren Burger of the Court of Appeals for the District of Columbia Circuit, who had succeeded Earl Warren, and Harry A. Blackmun of the Eighth Circuit, who had been unanimously confirmed after political controversy had derailed two previous nominees. The newly reconstituted Supreme Court granted review to a trio of cases, decided under the name of *Furman v. Georgia* (1972), to consider again whether the death penalty violated the Eighth Amendment.

Given the Supreme Court's almost total control over the decision whether to review a case from a state court or lower federal court, and its complete power to choose which issue or group of issues it wished to consider, the selection of a case for review often gives a strong hint as to how the Court will rule. The three defendants before the Court were William Furman, sentenced to death in Georgia after he was convicted of murder, but not a particularly aggravated one: Furman shot a man, perhaps accidentally, through a closed door during a burglary. The other two defendants were young black men convicted of raping but, unlike the petitioner in *Maxwell v. Bishop,* not otherwise seriously injuring white women: Lucious Jackson had been sentenced to death by the state of Georgia, Elmer Branch by the state of Texas.

The decision in *Furman* was only six sentences long. In each case the court reversed the death penalty per curiam. The concurring and dissenting opinions, however, took up more space in the United States Reports than any other case in Supreme Court history, and all nine justices wrote separate opinions. Although the Court works year-round, its official term runs from the first Monday in October, when it begins hearing oral arguments; written opinions begin to be issued in these cases around the beginning of January. As a matter of folklore, it is assumed that the Court issues its least divisive opinions early in January, and more contentious decisions do not appear until the end of the term, usually in late June. *Furman* was issued on June 29, 1972.

There were approximately 560 inmates on death row when *Furman* was decided. About 100 others had already been spared the death penalty when the California Supreme Court decided, in *People v. Anderson* (1972), that under California's state constitution, the death penalty was cruel and unusual punishment. It is probable that, just as in *Trop,* in which the Supreme Court was moved to act as it did in part by the large number of persons in the same difficulty as Albert Trop, so in *Furman* the Court was able to issue the decision that it did because of the lead given by *Anderson,* the relatively small numbers of inmates on death row, and the fact that it was practically speaking issuing an advisory opinion, because no one had been executed in any state in the previous five years.

Furman's concurrences and dissents are as important for what they did not say as for what they did say. The five justices who voted to overturn the death penalties wrote individually, depriving their rulings of the prestige or clarity of a majority position. Justices Douglas, Brennan, and Marshall formed a core of total abolitionists, and each tracked with minor variations the arguments laid out by Justice Goldberg in 1963. Justice Brennan and Justice Marshall each wrote eloquently that it was time to consign the death penalty to the fate of the pillory and whipping post. Justice Douglas, with emotion but less legal precision, scored the death penalty because it was disproportionately imposed on poor and minority defendants, a point also stressed by Marshall.

Justices Stewart and White, who had concluded the year before in *McGautha* that the imposition of the death penalty did not violate the Due Process Clause of the Fourteenth Amendment, moved to the opposite conclusion in considering the Eighth Amendment in *Furman.* Stewart's narrow concurrence avoided sweeping condemnation of the death penalty, and implied that these three death sentences were cruel and unusual punishment because they were "wantonly and freakishly" imposed. He and Justice White agreed that because the death penalty had become such a rare sentence in America, its imposition was more likely to offend the prohibition against "unusual" punishments. Unlike the abolitionists, White admitted the constitutionality of retribution as a justification for the death penalty. He stressed that for him the constitutional infirmity was that in each case the jury had been left without any legal guidance to determine whether this defendant was one of the rare defendants who deserved the death penalty.

All four of the Nixon appointees dissented. Significantly, Justice Blackmun wrote in a solo dissent that he personally agreed with the abolitionists that the death penalty was unwise and unjust, but that he felt constrained by his duty as an unelected judge not to usurp the role of the legislature. Justice Powell wrote a scholarly dissent joined by the other three dissenters, admitting the force of Justices Douglas and Marshall's concerns about equal protection of law raised by the disproportionate execution of black men for rape, but suggesting that a narrower constitutional attack on these verdicts was appropriate.

Chief Justice Burger's dissent, joined by the other three dissenters, was a how-to guide directed to state and federal legislators who wished to impose the death penalty. Burger pointed out that the votes of Justices Stewart and White to overturn the death penalty compelled states to revise their sentencing procedures to overcome the problem of lack of formal standards. Burger noted with irony that since the death penalty had been declared cruel and unusual punishment in decisive part because it was so rare and juries had such complete discretion to impose or withhold it, it seemed that one way for a state to comply with the Eighth Amendment was to put more people on death row and give juries less chance to show them mercy.

The federal government reacted to *Furman* as it had to the Court's rulings in the 1960s: with inaction. Congress passed an antihijacking law in 1974 with a death penalty provision that was probably unconstitutional but that sat on the books unused. Not until 1994 would the federal government revise its death penalty procedures.

The states, which had reacted little to the practical closing of death row by the procedural decisions of the 1960s, were stirred to action by *Furman.* Thirty-five states reenacted the death penalty in the four years following *Furman.* California, immediately after *Anderson,* ratified by about a two-to-one vote an amendment to its constitution restoring the death penalty.

Understandably, in response to *Furman* most of the states used for their new capital punishment law the model most likely to be held constitutional, namely, that provided by the Model Penal Code, while some states reacted to the "too much discretion" flaw identified by Justices White and Stewart by enacting mandatory death penalties.

Both of these fixes received review in 1976, when the Supreme Court heard arguments in a quintet of cases: *Gregg v. Georgia, Profitt v. Florida, Jurek v. Texas, Woodson v. North Carolina,* and *Roberts v. Louisiana.* Justice Douglas had retired in 1975 after his record term of service on the Court and was replaced by President Gerald Ford's appointee, John Paul Stevens of the Court of Appeals for the Seventh Circuit.

Troy Gregg was convicted of the murder and robbery of two men who had given him a ride while he hitchhiked from Florida through Georgia; he was sentenced to death by a jury after a separate sentencing hearing. Justice Stewart, writing for himself and Justices Powell and Stevens, found that Georgia's murder statute sufficiently directed the jury that it minimized the risk of arbitrary imposition of the death sentence. Justice White, writing in a separate opinion joined by Chief Justice Burger and Justice Rehnquist, added that Georgia's sentencing plan required the state's appellate court to review the sentence to determine whether the criteria the jury used to impose the sentence were sufficiently supported. In contrast with some pre-*Furman* statutes (like Ohio's in *McGautha*) in which no trial judge or appellate court could review the punishment imposed by the jury, the Georgia Supreme Court was required to compare the sentence imposed on the defendant to the sentences imposed on other defendants convicted of the same crime, and to reverse the death penalty if juries only rarely imposed death for the crime in question.

Thus the two justices who were the key to the decision in *Furman* pronounced themselves satisfied by the enactment of death penalty statutes that provided for guided jury discretion backed up by judicial review. Justice Blackmun provided a seventh vote to uphold Georgia's law, citing his statement in *Furman* of personal opposition but judicial deference. Justice Brennan and Justice Marshall reiterated their view that the death penalty was in all cases unconstitutional. Justice Brennan argued that the death penalty was inconsistent with human dignity. Justice Marshall wrote at greater length, making two points. First, despite the legislative reenactment of the death penalty in many states since *Furman,* the American people knew little about the death penalty. Marshall asserted that if well informed, the public would reject the death penalty. Second, Marshall assailed the acceptability of retribution as an end in punishment generally, and especially the idea that if retribution was desired that it could be provided only by the death penalty rather than life imprisonment.

Proffitt v. Florida also featured a murderer even less sympathetic than most: he had stabbed a sleeping man with a butcher knife while burglarizing his home, and while awaiting trial had volunteered to a psychiatrist that he had an uncontrollable desire to kill again. The same alignments on the Court approved Florida's two-step death penalty procedure, which provided that the jury, if it convicted a defendant of a capital crime, would return an advisory verdict. The trial judge was then required to make the decision of death or life imprisonment, with written findings stating the aggravating and mitigating factors shown by the evidence, and whether the aggravating factors outweighed the mitigating ones. The Florida Supreme Court automatically reviewed all death sentences to determine whether the death penalty was being evenly applied throughout the state, and had overturned eight of the twenty-one death sentences imposed in Florida as of 1976.

In *Jurek v. Texas,* for a third time the trio of Stewart, Powell, and Stevens combined with the trio of Burger, White, and Rehnquist to uphold one more variant on the two-step death penalty statute, with Blackmun again taking a "personally opposed but deferential" position. Once again, the Court chose to review a murderer more unsympathetic than most: Jerry Jurek had kidnaped a ten-year-old girl to rape her, and then had choked her and thrown her body into a river.

Texas limited the death penalty to five kinds of murder: murder of a peace officer or fireman, murder in the course of a felony (such as kidnaping or rape), murder for hire, murder during a prison escape, and murder of a prison employee by an inmate. If the jury convicted a defendant of one of these forms of murder, it proceeded to a penalty phase in which it had to answer three "special issue" questions. If the jury unanimously agreed: (1) that the defendant intended to kill, (2) would probably commit violent crimes in the future that would constitute a continuing threat to society, and (3) had responded unreasonably to provocation (if any) by the victim, then the jury would impose the death sentence. Again, the decision was automatically reviewed by the appellate courts.

The majority pointed out that although a Texas jury did not at the penalty phase consider specific aggravating or mitigating factors as in Florida or Georgia, it had done effectively the same thing in the guilt phase, because Texas defined the crimes eligible for death with aggravating factors built in, and permitted the jury to consider any mitigating factors the defendant cared to argue in answering the question about future dangerousness.

In *Woodson v. North Carolina,* the court struck down North Carolina's mandatory death penalty for first-degree murder. The two defendants sentenced to die had participated in a convenience store robbery, James Woodson contending unsuccessfully that he had been coerced into the crime by the other three robbers, and Luby Waxton admitting his participation but contending that the murder of the store clerk had been committed by a codefendant who had pleaded guilty and testified for the prosecution.

In *Roberts v. Louisiana* the Court held invalid Louisiana's mandatory death penalty for first-degree murder. Stanislaus Roberts had been convicted of killing the owner of a gas station during a robbery; his three codefendants had testified for the prosecution. As in North Carolina, once a Louisiana jury found that a murder had been intentionally committed in the course of a robbery, the death penalty was automatic.

The Court split 5–4 both times. The trio of Stewart, Powell, and Stevens sided with abolitionists Brennan and Marshall, finding that mandatory death penalties had been abolished in every state by 1963 and therefore violated both *Trop*'s evolving standard of decency and *Furman*'s problem of excessive jury discretion. As these three justices viewed the problem, juries in states with a mandatory death penalty could not limit the death penalty to the most offensive of criminals and might therefore revert to acquitting obviously guilty defendants because they did not approve of the punishment. This would make the penalty more freakishly imposed and not subject to judicial review, because the only important decision, made at the guilt phase, would be an up or down verdict of guilty or not guilty.

The dissenting trio of White, Burger, and Rehnquist suggested that because ten states had enacted mandatory death penalty statutes since *Furman*, mandatory penalties clearly did not offend contemporary standards. As for the problem of uncontrolled jury discretion, these three reasoned that the statutes obviously reduced the unlimited jury discretion that had troubled White and Stewart in *Furman*, and found the suggestion that juries would return to acquitting guilty defendants wholesale to be unconvincing.

After *Gregg*

To know the constitutional meaning of cruel and unusual punishment in the first 180 years after the ratification of the Bill of

Rights, an observer of the American justice system would have needed to know only one Supreme Court case, and it would not have mattered whether it was *Weems, Wilkerson, Kemmler,* or *Francis v. Resweber.* After 1976, there would be hundreds of Supreme Court rulings exploring the permissible permutations of aggravating factors, mitigating factors, and evidentiary issues relevant to capital punishment in the states, but the four years from *Furman* to *Gregg* represented the rise, high noon, and sunset of constitutional thought about capital punishment in America. After 1976, the Court settled down into intellectual trench warfare, with the deferentialist wing that took a hands-off position on state sentencing schemes and the abolitionists each competing for the votes of a decisive center bloc. New justices were studied by prosecutors and defense lawyers, much as bookies would inspect scorecards, to see where they would line up. Death penalty proponents reviled Justice Blackmun when in 1994 he abandoned his stance of judicial deference and openly joined the abolitionist camp; each side accused the other of engaging in exercises of power and not judgment. Despite the legal necessity for lawyers and legislators to study closely the annual pronouncements of the Supreme Court, as the century ended productive developments in thinking about capital punishment would lie elsewhere, in moratorium movements, in death penalty innocence projects taking advantage of improved forensic identification technologies, and in legislative repeal of the death penalty.

In states from California to Texas to Tennessee, judges and justices dependent on the voters for election or retention found themselves likely to be out of work if they consistently overturned capital convictions. In a reversal of the practice before 1776, judges no longer defined the crimes and set their punishments: crimes and their penalties now defined the judges. On the other hand, governors from Bill Clinton of Arkansas to Tom Ridge of Pennsylvania found it prudent to campaign on pro–death penalty platforms, then pursue courses that prevented them from having to carry out more than a few exemplary executions.

On the Supreme Court, the death penalty moved to a back burner. Through the 1980s and 1990s, the justices were known to the small portion of the public that cared who they were by their stances on abortion, and moving into the new century the most urgent question asked by presidents and senators about prospects for the high Court was how they viewed congressional reapportionment, campaign finance reform, and disputes over electoral results.

Because of the numerous labyrinthine rulings of the Supreme Court and the shifting alignments of state politics, by the end of the twentieth century, virtually all important death penalty decisions were being made in the federal Courts of Appeals. The least noticed of the three levels of federal courts, the Courts of Appeals became the court of last resort for most death row inmates after Warren Burger retired in 1986 and the most deferential member of the Court, William Rehnquist, became chief justice. Mirroring the pattern Justice Brennan had followed in moving an abolitionist agenda forward, Chief Justice Rehnquist accepted the principled opposition of the abolitionists on the Court, but moved steadily toward procedural reforms that reduced the Court's engagement in review of capital cases.

Meanwhile, the proportion of abolitionists and deferentialists in the lower federal courts resembles that on the Supreme Court. Although with rare exceptions lower court judges have sufficient prudence not to categorically denounce the death penalty, an abolitionist could easily find in the intricate layers of precedent a legally defensible basis for overturning virtually any capital sentence. This led to unusually public clashes between the Court of Appeals for the Ninth Circuit and the Supreme Court over the executions of Robert Alton Harris in 1992 and Thomas Thompson in 1998 (Reinhardt 1999), but an appellate judge who wished to block an execution could do so without much fear of reversal by the Supreme Court. As a result of the historical role of senators in selection and approval of the judges of these lower courts and the generally more conservative views of senators from the South about capital punishment, the imposition of the death penalty, which had always been more common in the South, became even more geographically concentrated in the Fifth and Eleventh Circuits, in the belt from Texas to Florida. Although at the end of the twentieth century the three largest sources of death row inmates were Los Angeles, Houston, and Philadelphia, only the Texas inmates faced a realistic chance of being executed.

When Can You Get the Death Penalty?

At the beginning of the post-*Gregg* era, the Court had to decide whether the constitutional limitation on the death penalty was a right of the condemned defendant that could be subject to a knowing and voluntary waiver much in the same way that a suspect could waive his *Miranda* rights, or whether the Eighth Amendment was a limitation on governmental power. In *Gilmore v. Utah* (1976), the majority of the Court appeared to disregard the language of the Eighth Amendment, which forbids the imposition of "cruel and unusual punishment" regardless of a defendant's desire to commit governmentally assisted suicide. Dismissing an appeal by Gary Gilmore's mother Bessie, the Court cleared the way for Gary Gilmore to be the first person executed in the modern era, in 1997. Fourteen years later, the Court held that because the Eighth Amendment created a personal right, not a limit on state power, an inmate on death row could not object to a fellow inmate's waiver of his rights to appeal. In *Whitmore v. Arkansas* (1990), the court rejected the claim that by volunteering for death, mass murderer Ronald Simmons was bringing other inmates on death row closer to death by depriving them of the argument that Ronald Simmons was still alive and at least they weren't as deserving of death as Ronald Simmons.

In *Gilmore* and *Whitmore,* the majority of the Supreme Court, correct or not, was at least consistent with the traditional approach toward interpreting other provisions of the Bill of Rights. With few exceptions, however, the Court's decisions after its pronouncement in *Woodson v. North Carolina* in 1976 that "death is a punishment different from all other sanctions" began to define two different Eighth Amendments, one for capital offenses, and one for all lesser offenses. In some cases, notably in *Booth v. Maryland* (1987), discussed below, the majority expressly held that its ruling was restricted to capital punishment cases because "death is a punishment different from all other sanctions." Similarly, in *United States v. Jackson* the Court had invalidated a statute that allowed a jury but not a judge to impose the death penalty, but ten years later in *Corbitt v. New Jersey* (1978), the Court held that it did not coerce a defendant into giving up a jury trial if he were subject to a mandatory life sentence if convicted but could receive a lesser term if he pleaded guilty. The principal difference, the Court acknowledged, was that the death penalty was not at issue.

Similar special rules for death were applied in one direction in *Roberts v. Louisiana* (1976), where the Court struck down Louisiana's mandatory death penalty because it allowed the jury to avoid the death penalty by convicting the defendant of any lesser offense, whether in evidence or not, and then in the other direction in *Beck v. Alabama* (1980), striking down an Alabama statute that forbade a judge from giving a jury the option of convicting the defendant of a lesser offense. Both times, the Court reasoned that the options available would impermissibly coerce a jury into returning death sentences.

In *Bullington v. Missouri* (1981), the Court reinterpreted the Double Jeopardy Clause of the Fifth Amendment to bar the state from seeking the death penalty on a retrial after a conviction in which the first jury had not imposed the death penalty. Because the Double Jeopardy Clause literally and traditionally prevents retrial after acquittal for a "crime," this in effect split every capital murder into two offenses. A defendant could no longer be guilty of murder or not: he was either not guilty, guilty of murder, or guilty of murder with the death penalty. Thus, if a judge or jury makes an error in sentencing a defendant to death, the Double Jeopardy Clause does not bar "getting it right" the second time around, according to *Poland v. Arizona* (1986), but if the jury or trial judge imposes a life sentence, the defendant is in effect "acquitted of the death penalty" and on resentencing the death penalty cannot be given, according to *Arizona v. Rumsey* (1984).

The justices have also bent the rules of evidence and arguably the First Amendment in death cases. Although a judge in a noncapital case can consider information not admissible at trial, including even evidence of a count for which a defendant was acquitted, in *Dawson v. Delaware* (1992), the Court held that informing the jury that an inmate given a life sentence belonged to a racist prison gang called the "Aryan Brotherhood" violated the defendant's First Amendment rights, because there was no evidence that the defendant had engaged in the gang's crimes. In dissent, Justice Clarence Thomas argued that it was absurd for the Court to require a court to permit a defendant to introduce evidence that he had joined Alcoholics Anonymous or went to church while in prison, as the Court had held in *Skipper v. South Carolina* (1986), but forbid the prosecution to respond with negative character evidence.

As for jury selection, the Supreme Court has held, in *Turner v. Murray* (1986), that in a capital case involving a victim and murderer of different races the defense is entitled to question the jurors about racial bias. Holding to the position that a capital case was really two trials, one on guilt and one on punishment, the majority held that failure to allow this inquiry required the death penalty, but not the conviction of first degree murder, to be overturned. The dissent noted that the Court's precedent in crimes not subject to the death penalty required such questioning only if issues of racial bias were inextricably bound up in the case, and pointed out that of the twelve jurors who returned a unanimous sentence against a black man who repeatedly shot the white proprietor of a jewelry store, four, including the foreman, were black.

Finally, in *Ake v. Oklahoma* (1985), the Supreme Court held it is constitutionally required that a defendant in a capital case who makes a showing that his sanity is likely to be at issue must be provided not only with an attorney but a psychiatric expert as well. The lower federal courts have read *Ake* as applying to non-capital cases, but most states, with smaller budgets and higher case loads, have held that only capital cases require such assistance. The Supreme Court has not resolved that conflict yet.

Murderers. The three 1976 decisions approving death penalty procedures involved murders. Despite the position of Justice White that mandatory penalties were generally constitutional because they eliminated the unchecked jury discretion that he believed made the death penalty too random a sanction, the Court made it clear that same year that mandatory death penalties would not pass muster. Yet, the two decisions striking down mandatory death sentence provisions involved participants in robbery murders, who, as murderers go, were not too bad. But what about the classic case of a murderer who kills because he has little or nothing to lose, such as a prisoner already serving a life term who kills a fellow inmate, or a prison guard, perhaps in an escape attempt? What about a serial killer, a contract killer, or a criminal who kills to dispose of witnesses? Even in those cases, the Court has held that a jury must retain the discretion not to sentence a defendant to death: mandatory death penalties, no matter how heinous the crime, have been ruled a violation of the Eighth Amendment. In *Sumner v. Shuman* (1987), the Court held 6–3 that a mandatory death penalty for murder by a prisoner serving a life sentence was unconstitutional because it deprived the jury of the ability to consider the unique characteristics of the defendant and any mitigating circumstances.

It is important to understand, however, that merely because a statute says a jury "must" impose the death penalty if it finds certain facts does not make it a mandatory statute: in *Blystone v. Pennsylvania* (1990), for instance, the jury was instructed that the jury must impose the death sentence "if" it unanimously found an aggravating factor and there were no mitigating factors of any kind. As the Court explained, that simply was another way of telling the jury that it had to find that a defendant truly deserved death before imposing the penalty.

The Court has been consistent in emphasizing the importance of presenting mitigating evidence and allowing unfettered consideration of mitigating factors. In *Lockett v. Ohio* (1978), seven justices invalidated an Ohio statute requiring the trial judge to impose the death penalty if the jury had convicted the defendant of murder with one or more of seven statutory aggravating factors and the judge found that none of the statute's three specific mitigating factors (provocation by the victim or coercion or mental impairment of the defendant) was present. The Court held that the Eighth Amendment required individualized consideration of mitigating factors, and therefore that the defendant could not be limited to the three specified by Ohio. The justices in *Lockett* were obviously troubled by a death sentence given to a woman who was an accomplice with a relatively minor role in a robbery, while her codefendant, who committed the murder, escaped with a life sentence by testifying for the prosecution.

In *Mills v. Maryland* (1988), the Court reversed a death penalty where the jury instructions could have led the jury to believe that it needed to find a mitigating factor unanimously. Two years later, building on *Mills*, the Court struck down a North Carolina's statute that did require that a mitigating factor be proved unanimously, in *McKoy v. North Carolina* (1990). And in 1987, the Court held in a rare unanimous opinion, *Hitchcock v. Dugger,* that a sentencing jury or judge had to consider evidence believed to be mitigating, whether or not it fit into the statutory mitigating factors. The jury had been told that it could not consider the defendant's poor upbringing, and the sentencing judge had stated that he would not consider mitigating evidence that was not part of the statutory scheme.

Aggravating factors, by contrast, must be statutorily defined in advance and must narrow the universe of intentional murderers into a subset that especially deserves the death penalty. To impose the death penalty because a murder was "outrageously or wantonly vile, horrible, or inhuman" was just too vague for four Justices (joined by the two abolitionists) in *Godfrey v. Georgia* (1980). Godfrey had gone to his mother-in-law's residence and shot his estranged wife to death with a shotgun, as she, his mother-in-law, and his eleven-year-old daughter sat playing a card game. Godfrey then entered the residence, struck his fleeing daughter with the barrel of the gun, and shot his mother-in-law to death. The Court held that unless the statutory term were limited, as in previous Georgia Supreme Court decisions, to murders involving torture, virtually any murder could be considered as being "outrageous" or wantonly vile. The Court held that a statutory aggravating circumstance that the murder was "especially heinous, atrocious, or cruel" was just as broad and just as unconstitutional in *Maynard v. Cartwright* (1988). The state court could not cure the risk that the unguided jury had too little guidance by its own review of the case, in which a disgruntled ex-employee had shot his former employer to death and shot and stabbed the employer's wife after entering their home.

However, a judge who puts a narrowing construction on an otherwise vague term to guide the jury or show how the judge reached the sentencing decision might be able to save a verdict from reversal: in *Arave v. Creech* (1993), Thomas Creech, a serial killer, beat to death a handicapped fellow inmate in the Idaho State Penitentiary, then pleaded guilty. The Supreme Court held that the aggravating factor that the murderer acted with "utter disregard of human life" was construed to mean that the murderer was a "cold-blooded pitiless slayer." Although the dissent pointed out that one set of undefined terms had been exchanged for another, the majority of the court was satisfied that the sentencing judge's discretion was sufficiently guided to satisfy the Eighth Amendment.

An aggravating factor must truly be aggravating, not something that applies to every murder, but the jury need not be told in mathematical terms how to weigh the factors or, for instance, when told to consider a defendant's age, even whether the fact that he is twenty-five is an aggravating factor (because he has a long criminal career ahead of him) or a mitigating factor (because he has a long reformed life ahead of him).

And, so long as the class of eligible defendants is narrowed, it does not matter whether the narrowing is done at the guilt or penalty stage, and it does not offend the Eighth Amendment if the jury imposes the death penalty at the penalty stage on the basis of an aggravating factor that duplicates an element of the crime that was found at the guilt stage. To illustrate, in *Lowenfield v. Phelps* (1988), Leslie Lowenfield was convicted of two counts of manslaughter and three counts of first-degree murder for killing the woman he lived with, three members of her family, and one of her friends. The jury found as its sole aggravating factor that Lowenfield intended to kill or harm more than one person, which of course it had already found in finding him guilty of murder. That was permissible, said the Court.

The Supreme Court does not treat aggravating and mitigating factors symmetrically: a durable majority of the justices clearly wish to have the former narrowly defined and the latter broadly defined. The problem is that although there is no logical contradiction in such a stance, the Court is trying to reach both of two irreconcilable goals and not a compromise between them. On the one hand, the Court had held that capital punishment cannot be imposed universally or arbitrarily. To promote the goal of uniformity, aggravating factors must limit the penalty to truly the worst murders. To promote the goal of individual determination of culpability, mandatory sentences and restrictions on mitigating evidence are out, so that death is imposed only on the worst murderers. It seems that the unfettered discretion to return a verdict of life that made the death penalty unconstitutional to Justices White and Stewart in *Furman* cannot be eliminated.

The conclusion drawn from this impasse depends on one's attitude toward the death penalty: abolitionists conclude that because juries can't give individualized consideration to every murderer without possessing too much discretion to deal out arbitrary sentences, the death penalty can never be constitutionally imposed. On the deferential side, the conclusion is that the Court should get out of the business of writing a penal code and defer to virtually any choice of aggravating and mitigating factors.

Accomplices to Murder. Having rejected mandatory death penalties and limitations on mitigating evidence, through the 1980s the Supreme Court groped for a set of concepts that would, among participants in murder other than the murderer himself, draw a line between defendants who are eligible for death and those who are not. First, in *Enmund v. Florida* (1982), the Supreme Court held, in a 5–4 opinion authored by Justice White, that Earl Enmund, who drove the car used in a robbery of an elderly couple who were shot to death by one of the robbers who went into the house, could not be executed where the record showed that he "neither took life, attempted to take life, nor intended to take life."

Five years later, Justice White moved to the other side, giving Justice O'Connor a 5–4 majority in *Tison v. Arizona* (1987), holding that accomplices to a murder—two boys who helped their father escape from prison and stood by while he and another escapee massacred a family they had helped to kidnap—are liable for the death penalty if their participation in the crime is "major" and they were "recklessly indifferent" to the prospect that human life be taken, even if they themselves did not intend to kill anyone.

Rapists. In *Coker v. Georgia* (1977), the Supreme Court held that the death penalty could not be imposed for the rape of an adult woman. Unlike many questionable rape verdicts of previous decades, here there was no doubt that Ehrlich Coker raped a woman shortly after escaping from the penitentiary where he was serving a life sentence for previous rapes and the murder of one of his victims. Nevertheless, in addition to the Brennan-Marshall abolitionist vote, Justices White, Stewart, Blackmun, and Stevens noted that only Georgia permitted the death penalty for rape of an adult, and that under the *Weems-Trop* evolving standards approach death was a disproportionate sentence for rape. Justice Powell concurred that in this case, because there was no serious bodily injury beyond the rape itself, death was disproportionate, but he agreed with Chief Justice Burger and Justice Rehnquist that death might be appropriate for some rapes.

In cases after *Coker*, the Court has assumed only a subset of the worst murderers is subject to the death penalty, but the opinions in *Coker*, noting that Florida and Mississippi also made rape a capital offense if the victim was a child, appear to leave open the door to making rape of a child a capital offense. Mississippi sentenced a man to death for raping a child in 1986, but the conviction was overturned on other issues, and there was no occasion to decide whether the defendant could receive the death penalty under the Eighth Amendment. Subsequently, Louisiana has made aggravated sexual assault on a child a capital offense, but as of 2002 there have been no prosecutions resulting in the death penalty.

Traitors. One of the first offenses to be punished without benefit of clergy or any other safety valve was treason, that is, "imagining the death of the king." Treason was narrowly defined in the Constitution to be waging war against the United States or giving aid and comfort to its enemies. Moreover, to avoid the repetition of royal judges creatively defining treason and punishing political enemies in the Parliament, the Constitution specifically reserved to Congress the power to declare the punishment of treason. Since 1790, the punishment for treason against the United States has been death. The last execution for the related crime of espionage, that of Julius and Ethel Rosenberg, took place in June 1953.

After *Coker,* can the death penalty be imposed without proof that the treason caused death? In the early twenty-first century, with the experience of traitors like CIA agent Aldrich Ames and FBI agent Robert Hanssen, and with freelance "Taliban John" Walker Lindh in custody, will the Supreme Court hold to its position that only murder can be punished with death, or will it, as it often has done, create a "wartime exception?"

Who Can Get the Death Penalty?

Is There Such a Thing As Too Young to Die? In *Thompson v. Oklahoma* (1988), a 4–1–4 decision, the Court sparred over whether it could discern a national and international consensus against executing fifteen-year-olds. William Thompson was certified to adult court for participating in the murder of his former brother-in-law after a judge found that there was no reasonable prospect for his rehabilitation. A jury heard evidence of the shooting, stabbing, and disposal of the victim, as well as of Thompson's criminal record, and condemned him to death. Justice Stevens and three other justices, relying on *Trop*'s evolving standard of the Eighth Amendment to find a societal consensus against executing Thompson, noted that fifteen-year-olds were not treated like adults under state drinking, driving, voting, or marriage laws, and that although nineteen states permitted capital punishment without specifying a minimum age, the last execution of such a young criminal had taken place in 1948, while eighteen states expressly permitted the death penalty to be imposed only on those sixteen or older at the time of the offense. Significantly, Justice Stevens noted in support of a consensus that the death penalty had been abolished in the balance of the states and in most Western European countries. Justice O'Connor, who provided the swing vote, left the question open whether fifteen-year-olds could ever be executed but thought that because Oklahoma had not set a minimum age, its insufficient attention to the issue violated the Eighth Amendment. For the four dissenters, Justice Scalia charged that the Court could hardly determine a consensus against executing Thompson when nineteen states and the federal government permitted any juvenile certified as an adult to be executed, and that the rarity of executions (which he argued was due to the rarity of murders by juveniles) should not be a consideration in determining their constitutionality.

A year later, in *Stanford v. Kentucky* (1989), Justice O'Connor moved to the other side, joining Justice Scalia's plurality of four to find no national consensus against executing older teens. The Court upheld death sentences for seventeen-year-old Kevin Stanford, who robbed and raped a gas station attendant, then shot her to death to prevent her from identifying him, and for sixteen-year-old Heath Wilkins, who during a robbery stabbed to death the convenience store clerk as she pleaded for her life. Although the plurality noted that twenty-two of thirty-seven states permitted the death penalty for sixteen-year-olds and that twenty-five permitted it for seventeen-year-olds, Justice Brennan's dissent found a consensus against executions established by the fact that only about 2 percent of executions in the United States involved juveniles.

As long as the consensus theory of the Eighth Amendment holds, it is unlikely that executions of otherwise guilty juveniles will be halted on Eighth Amendment grounds, given that after *Stanford* three states added the death penalty but only for those eighteen and older, and two other states abandoned their previous minimum age of 17.

In *Johnson v. Texas* (1993), the Court held that Texas's requirement that the jury consider the defendant's future dangerousness allowed sufficient consideration of the defendant's youth as a mitigating factor. In dissent, four members of the Court wanted an explicit instruction to consider the defendant's age. In general, as the Court stressed in *Buchanan v. Angelone* (1998), the Eighth Amendment does not require a state to specify what weight the sentencer must give to particular factors, either in aggravation or mitigation: what the Eighth Amendment requires is that the jury hear all the relevant evidence. In that case, Douglas Buchanan had murdered his father, stepmother, and two younger brothers. The state court allowed the jury to hear evidence but had refused to give an instruction that Buchanan's young age and emotional turmoil at the time of the murders over the death of his mother were mitigating factors.

To illustrate the dilemma faced by the judge, how should the defendant's age be judged, in the case of a juvenile who commits a heinous enough murder to be eligible for the death penalty? Although Justices Stevens and Brennan imply in *Stanford v. Kentucky* and *Thompson v. Oklahoma* that youth is a mitigating factor in calling for reserving the death penalty for adults (if it is to be imposed at all), Paul McNulty, former Chief Counsel to the House of Representatives' Subcommittee on Crime and now a United States attorney, stops just short of calling for a defendant's youth to be treated as an aggravating factor. McNulty observed in 1995 that more than one-third of murders were committed by offenders under the age of twenty-one, and the number of thirteen- to fifteen-year-olds arrested for murder jumped from 390 in 1982 to 740 in 1992. He concludes that the United States will experience a resurgence of violent crime in the period from 2005 onward as a new cohort of teenage criminals comes of age and that rehabilitation of juveniles should be scrapped as a goal of the criminal system (McNulty 1995).

Insanity or Incompetence. Since before the publication of Blackstone's *Commentaries*, it was the law that insane defendants cannot be tried for their actions. In 1986, the Court, observing that no state had permitted the execution of a defendant who had become insane since the time of his conviction, held 5–4 in *Ford v. Wainwright* that the Eighth Amendment prohibited such an execution.

Under some circumstances, the state can force a convicted inmate to take medication against his will for his own safety. However, the Court reversed the conviction and death sentence of the defendant in *Riggins v. Nevada* (1992) on the grounds that the state failed to show that it had medicated Riggins at his trial for his own safety. Given that the state's interest in medicating Riggins was to make him healthy enough to put to death, one must wonder how the Supreme Court thought allowing involuntary administration of medication could be (other than on a temporary basis) for Riggins's safety. Nevertheless, the Supreme Court stated that its ruling was not to be taken as answering the question of whether a government could medicate an incompetent defendant just for the purpose of making him competent enough to convict. The Supreme Court will soon have to confront this issue head on in the death penalty context because the lower federal courts are beginning to hold that states can medicate a mentally ill defendant involuntarily in order to convict him.

In *Perry v. Louisiana* (1990) the Court came close to addressing the related issue of whether a state can rehabilitate a mentally ill inmate against his will for the purpose of making him sane enough to execute. On remand, Louisiana's Supreme Court held that the state could not "cure" an inmate just to kill him.

Affirming the death sentence imposed on a defendant who murdered three persons during a series of armed robberies, the Court held in 1992 in *Medina v. California* that a state can presume that a defendant is competent and require him to prove his incompetency. How much proof does a defendant need? In *Cooper v. Oklahoma* (1996), the defendant was convicted of the brutal murder of an 86-year-old man and sentenced to death. Justice Stevens wrote for the Court reversing the conviction because Oklahoma law required the defendant to prove his incompetence by clear and convincing evidence. This was too high a burden, said the unanimous Court: a defendant need only show that it is more likely than not that he is incompetent. Again, it made a difference to the Court in determining the "evolving standard" that at the time only four states used the higher standard of proof.

Mental Retardation. A person who is so profoundly retarded that he lacks the capacity to appreciate the wrongfulness of his conduct is not competent and cannot be executed. The Supreme Court formerly held, in *Penry v. Lynaugh* (1989), that less profound mental retardation was no bar to the death penalty. The Justices followed the *Trop* and *Coker* model of looking to state legislation to determine whether a consensus had developed concerning the execution of the mentally retarded, and found that because only Georgia and Maryland had passed laws barring capital punishment for the mentally retarded, it could not be said that the death penalty for such defendants was constitutionally unusual. The Court nevertheless vacated the death penalty, because it found that the three "special issues" procedure it had approved in the case of *Jurek* in Texas did not permit the jury to consider mental retardation to be a mitigating factor.

Johnny Paul Penry was retried and again sentenced to death for the brutal rape and murder of a twenty-two-year-old woman. In 2001, the Supreme Court again vacated the death penalty on procedural grounds. Texas held a third hearing for Penry in 2002 and again found him competent. However, the landscape has changed behind Penry: after the first *Penry* decision, sixteen more states enacted legislation prohibiting the execution of mentally retarded defendants (Governor Rick Perry of Texas vetoed similar legislation there in 2001 after *Penry II*), and in 2001 the Tennessee Supreme Court declared that its state constitution banned such executions. Faced with the Supreme Court's grant of certiorari in

2001 to review the death sentence imposed on mentally retarded murderer Ernest McCarver, the North Carolina legislature also changed its law to ban executions of the mentally retarded. The Supreme Court was determined to revisit *Penry,* however, and granted certiorari in *Atkins v. Virginia* (2002), in which Virginia upheld the death penalty for Daryl Atkins, a man with an IQ of 59, a long criminal record, and a conviction for robbery and murder. Justice Stevens wrote for six justices in declaring that the number of states that had banned execution of the mentally retarded and the absence of states moving in the opposite direction showed that under *Trop*'s evolving standard doctrine, executing the mentally retarded was cruel and unusual punishment. Justice Scalia's dissent predicted a flood of new-found retardation on death row, while Chief Justice Rehnquist expressed concern over the majority's seeming reliance on public opinion polls and trends in international law, neither of which he argued were relevant to the meaning of the Eighth Amendment.

Who Decides?

Whether a trial by judge or by jury is a better risk is one of the most crucial decisions a death penalty lawyer can make. A judge known to oppose the death penalty is the defendant's better choice in cases of obvious guilt, and prosecutors have successfully lobbied in some states for the prosecution's right to choose a jury trial for that reason. On the other hand, an elected judge might be unwilling to show mercy for fear of electoral defeat, whereas a jury that has never been in a courthouse before might be reluctant to impose the ultimate penalty. These complex considerations get completely erased in the Supreme Court: because every capital case heard is one of a defendant already sentenced to death, the condemned must argue that no matter how he was sentenced, it was unconstitutional. In *Proffitt v. Florida,* the Supreme Court had approved Florida's sentencing statute providing that the jury verdict was advisory and the sentence was to be imposed by the trial judge. The most constitutionally troublesome combination, of course, would be a jury recommendation of life and a trial judge imposition of the death penalty, a step that Florida law had held should be taken only if no reasonable person (the jury presumably not being reasonable in refusing the death penalty) could disagree that the death penalty was proper. The Court confronted that case in *Spaziano v. Florida* (1984). The jury had recommended life for a young black man who had murdered a white hitchhiker in a juvenile plot to incite a race war; affected by his experiences in liberating Nazi death camps during World War II, the trial judge found Spaziano's conduct and motives deserving of death and overrode the jury recommendation. Splitting 5–4 in favor of the death sentence, the deferential wing of the Court held that neither the Eighth Amendment nor the Sixth Amendment required that the life or death decision be imposed by a jury.

Four years later, the Court held that in addition to making the decision on the basis of the facts and recommendation of a jury, the aggravating facts used to justify the imposition of the death penalty could be found by a judge. *Walton v. Arizona* (1990) also permitted a judge to construe otherwise vague statutory aggravating circumstances to avoid violation of the Eighth Amendment. However, in 2002, in *Ring v. Arizona,* an unusual seven-justice coalition of liberals and conservatives cast doubt on the constitutionality of all judge sentencing: building on several recent Sixth Amendment right-to-jury trial cases, the justices struck down Arizona's sentencing procedure. The majority held that the facts used to justify a death sentence must be found by a jury; only the two justices from Arizona (O'Connor and Rehnquist) disagreed. The Court stopped short of invalidating procedures in states where a jury finds all the necessary facts and a judge decides the sentence, but further decisions are anxiously awaited by the death row inmates of the other eight states (Alabama, Colorado, Delaware, Florida, Idaho, Indiana, Montana, and Nebraska) that permit judicial capital sentencing. By the end of 2002, Arizona and Colorado amended their laws to require juries to decide on life or death. Delaware now requires juries to find aggravating circumstances but, like Florida, still allows a judge to make the ultimate decision.

Qualifying the Jury. As mentioned above, even before *Furman*, the Court held in *Witherspoon v. Illinois* that a death sentence could not stand if the jury recommending it had been purged of any person who expressed general objections to the death penalty. Only if a juror admitted that he would never vote for the death penalty could he be excluded. After *Gregg*, the Supreme Court loosened this standard in *Wainwright v. Witt* (1985), permitting the exclusion for cause of any prospective juror whose opposition to the death penalty would "substantially impair" performance of the duties of a juror.

In *Lockhart v. McCree* (1986), the Supreme Court rejected McCree's claim that excluding opponents of the death penalty from jury service deprived him of a fair trial on charges of robbery and murder, based on statistics allegedly showing that juries subject to "death qualification" (or dismissing anyone who could not meet the *Witherspoon-Wainwright* standard) were more conviction prone. The following year, in *Buchanan v. Kentucky* (1987), which arose out of the same robbery-murder that gave rise to *Stanford v. Kentucky*, the Court rejected a variant of this argument, this time by Stanford's codefendant, Buchanan. The prosecution had not sought the death penalty, but Buchanan had been convicted and received a life sentence from a death-qualified jury, despite his claim that this gave the prosecution a "hanging" jury.

The Supreme Court subsequently held, in *Morgan v. Illinois* (1992), that a jury must be "life-qualified" as well. That is, a defendant was entitled in a capital case to question jurors about whether they would readily vote for the death penalty and, if so, to challenge them for cause.

What Evidence Must Be Heard? What Can Be Heard? What Cannot?

The Eighth Amendment has been interpreted as a law of evidence, limiting the information that the jury may consider during both the trial, at which guilt is determined, and at the penalty phase, at which the jury determines whether death is an appropriate penalty. The Supreme Court observed in *Johnson v. Mississippi* (1988) that the weighing process may be impermissibly skewed if the sentencing jury considers an invalid sentencing factor and that a jury that sentences on the basis of a conviction that was later overturned commits error.

In *Caldwell v. Mississippi* (1985), the Court noted that a jury must be aware of its awesome responsibility and held that for the prosecutor or the trial judge to tell them that their decision is not the final one because it will be the subject of lengthy review unconstitutionally diminishes the jury's sense of responsibility for the death of the defendant. An instruction not to be swayed by sentiment or public opinion is permissible, the Court held in *California v. Brown* (1987), and in *Romano v. Oklahoma* (1994) it found that informing the jury that the defendant had already received the death sentence in another case does not improperly diminish its sense of responsibility.

The Court since *Caldwell* has continued to grapple with the problem of ensuring two incompatible goals: that the jury feels its responsibility fully in making the decision for the death penalty, and at the same time is aware of the possible legal alternatives to the death penalty. In *Simmons v. South Carolina* (1994), the Court held that where a state has a sentencing system that provides for life without parole, the jury must be informed of that sentencing option if a defendant's future dangerousness is at issue. At the time only South Carolina, Pennsylvania, and Virginia refused to inform juries that life without parole was the alternative to the death penalty. In *Shafer v. South Carolina* (2001), the Supreme

Court reversed a death sentence imposed under a statute revised after *Simmons,* and came very close to saying that a defendant's future dangerousness is always at issue in a capital case. It is hard to imagine a sentencing proceeding where future dangerousness is not at issue, if only because the defendant claims the existence of mitigating evidence, and so if life without parole is an option, the jury must be so informed.

However, the jury is not required to be invited to deadlock. Under the 1994 Federal Death Penalty Act, if a jury cannot unanimously agree on a sentence of death or life without parole, the judge must impose a sentence of life without parole. The defendant in *Jones v. United States* (1999), who had received a death sentence for the kidnapping and murder of a young soldier from her Texas military base, argued that the jury should have been instructed of this fact. The Court rejected this misplaced analogy to *Simmons.*

What about the Victim?

In *Booth v. Maryland* (1987), the Supreme Court held that it violates the Constitution to read a so-called victim impact statement to a jury. Two heroin users were convicted of the robbery and brutal slaying of an elderly couple in their neighborhood while seeking to find money to buy drugs. The prosecutor read a summary of interviews with the victims' relatives discussing the character of the victims and the impact their death had on the family, and giving the survivors' opinions that the defendants deserved punishment. According to the majority of the Supreme Court, led by Justice Powell, this focus on the impact of the crime on the victims ran the risk of encouraging a jury to impose capital punishment not on the worst murderers, but on the killers of the best victims, and thus unconstitutionally risked the kind of arbitrary and capricious imposition of the death penalty condemned in *Furman.* Justice White, who had been in the majority in *Furman,* led the dissent, charging the majority with illogically creating a rule that only applied to capital punishment cases and that barred the prosecution from countering a defendant's mitigating evidence with evidence about the true impact of a defendant's crime.

Two years later, the justices overturned a South Carolina verdict in *South Carolina v. Gathers* (1989). That the defendant had rummaged through the victim's personal possessions looking for valuables was fair game for comment, but the Court held that the prosecutor's closing argument, which praised the victim's religious nature and quoted a religious tract he had carried unfairly emphasized the qualities of the victim not known to the murderer.

The majorities in *Booth* and *Gathers* were the bare minimum, and after Justice Powell was replaced by Justice Anthony Kennedy in 1988 and Justice Brennan by Justice David Souter in 1990, the deferential wing lost no time in granting review to *Payne v. Tennessee* (1991). Payne had stabbed to death a mother and her two-year-old daughter and severely wounded her three-year-old son. The victim's mother testified at the sentencing how her grandson "cries for his mom. . . . And he cries for his sister Lacie. He . . . asks me, 'Grandma, do you miss my Lacie?' And I tell him yes."

To the majority, the amount of harm caused by a defendant was particularly relevant to the determination of an appropriate punishment, and it was not unconstitutional because it merely balanced the mitigating evidence the jury was required to consider. Giving constitutional approval to the growing victims' rights movement in the United States, the Supreme Court overruled *Booth.*

Some liberal Supreme Court rulings live on despite their reversal by the more recent conservative majority, because state court judges find that their state constitutions require what the Supreme Court now says the U.S. Constitution does not. *Booth* is unlikely to be in that company: today more than thirty state constitutions contain victims' rights provisions. Ironically, it is now often the case that the most effective evidence in opposition to the death penalty is the plea to the jury, by grieving relatives of the victim, to spare the life of the murderer.

How Is a Court to Review the Determination that the Death Penalty Is Appropriate?

In the trio of death penalties approved in 1976, the Court dwelled at some length on the fact that in each state the highest court of the state conducted a review of the sentence of death to compare it with other sentences imposed throughout the state. Almost every state that retains the death penalty requires such a "proportionality review" as a matter of state law. Is it required by the Eighth Amendment? The Court seems to have answered that one in the negative. In *Pulley v. Harris* (1984), with only the dissent of the two abolitionists, the Court held that the Eighth Amendment does not require a comparison of penalties imposed in similar cases.

How Long Should All This Take?

A new issue has become the subject of debate on the Court: whether excessive delay on death row itself constitutes cruel and unusual punishment. At the close of the twentieth century, a pointed exchange on this subject took place between Justice Thomas and Justice Breyer in their opinions in *Knight v. Florida* (1999):

> Justice THOMAS, concurring in denial of certiorari.
>
> . . . I am unaware of any support in the American constitutional tradition or in this Court's precedent for the proposition that a defen-

dant can avail himself of the panoply of appellate and collateral procedures and then complain when his execution is delayed. . . .

It is worth noting, in addition, that, in most cases raising this novel claim, the delay in carrying out the prisoner's execution stems from this Court's Byzantine death penalty jurisprudence. . . . It is incongruous to arm capital defendants with an arsenal of "constitutional" claims with which they may delay their executions, and simultaneously to complain when executions are inevitably delayed.

Justice BREYER, dissenting from the denial of certiorari.

Where a delay, measured in decades, reflects the State's own failure to comply with the Constitution's demands, the claim that time has rendered the execution inhuman is a particularly strong one. . . .

[T]he longer the delay, the weaker the justification for imposing the death penalty in terms of punishment's basic retributive or deterrent purposes. . . .

Finally, the constitutional issue, even if limited to delays approaching—or even exceeding—twenty years, has considerable practical importance. Available statistics indicate that as of December 1997, twenty-four prisoners sentenced to death had been on death row for more than twenty years. At that time 125 prisoners on death row had been sentenced in or before 1980 and therefore may now fall within two-decade category. Given these figures and the nature of the question, despite the absence of a division among the lower federal courts, this Court should consider the issue.

The Court has repeatedly rejected the claim that delay itself could invalidate the death penalty. It remains to be seen whether, with the next shift in the composition of the Court, this claim will someday be added to the other issues the Court has considered in the quarter century after *Gregg*.

REFERENCES AND FURTHER READING

Bennett, James V. 1972 [1970]. "The Death Penalty," in *Capital Punishment,* ed. James McCafferty, 140–156. Chicago: Aldine-Atherton.

Cardozo, Benjamin. 1921. *The Nature of the Judicial Process.* New Haven: Yale University Press.

———. 1924. *The Growth of the Law.* New Haven: Yale University Press.

Carter, Dan T. 1969. *Scottsboro: A Tragedy of the American South.* Baton Rouge: Louisiana State University Press.

Clark, Ramsey A. 1972 [1968]. "To Abolish the Death Penalty," in *Capital Punishment,* ed. James McCafferty, 176–180. Chicago: Aldine-Atherton.

Foster, Teree E. 1997. "I Want to Live! Federal Judicial Values in Death Penalty Cases." *Oklahoma City University Law Review* 22: 63.

Frank, Jerome. 1947. "Words and Music." *Columbia Law Review* 47: 1259.

Glaser, Daniel. 1969. *The Effectiveness of a Prison and Parole System.* Indianapolis: Bobbs-Merrill Company.

Goldberg, Arthur J. 1986. "Memorandum to the Conference Re: Capital Punishment." *South Texas Law Review* 27: 493.

Greenberg, Jack, and Jack Himmelstein. 1972 [1969]. "Varieties of Attack on the Death Penalty," in *Capital Punishment,* ed. James McCafferty, 231–244. Chicago: Aldine-Atherton.

Hofstadter, Richard. 1955. *The Age of Reform.* New York: Alfred A. Knopf.

Holmes, Oliver W., Jr., 1881. *The Common Law.* Boston: Little, Brown.

Horwitz, Robert. 1987. "John Dewey," in *History of Political Philosophy,* ed. Leo Strauss and Joseph Cropsey. Chicago: University of Chicago Press.

Joyce, James A. 1961. *Capital Punishment: A World View.* New York: Thomas Nelson & Sons.

Kitto, H. D. F. 1991. *The Greeks.* London: Penguin Books.

Kluger, Richard. 1975. *Simple Justice: The History of* Brown v. Board of Education *and Black America's Struggle for Equality.* New York: Alfred A. Knopf.

Little, Rory K. 1999. "The Federal Death Penalty: History and Some Thoughts about the Department of Justice's Role." *Fordham Urban Law Journal* 26(March): 347.

Locke, John. 1967 [1660]. *Two Tracts on Government.* Edited by Philip Abrams. Cambridge: Cambridge University Press.

McGee, Richard A. 1972 [1964]. "Capital Punishment as Seen by a Correctional Administrator," in *Capital Punishment,* ed. James McCafferty, 161–175. Chicago: Aldine-Atherton.

McNulty, Paul. 1995. "Natural Born Killers?" *Policy Review* 71(Winter): 84.

Mencken, H. L. 1985 [1926]. "The Penalty of Death," in *Elements of Argument,* ed. Annette T. Rottenberg, 394–396. New York: St. Martin's Press.

Posner, Richard A. 1995. "Judges' Writing Styles (and Do They Matter?)." *University of Chicago Law Review* 62(Fall): 1421.

Pound, Roscoe. 1999. *The Spirit of the Common Law.* New Brunswick, NJ: Transaction Publishers.

Prettyman, Barrett, Jr. 1961. *Death and the Supreme Court.* New York: Harcourt, Brace & World.

Reinhardt, Stephen. 1999. "The Anatomy of an Execution: Fairness v. Process." *NYU Law Review* 74: 313.

Weaver, Richard M. 1984 [1948]. *Ideas Have Consequences.* Chicago: University of Chicago Press.

4

Into the Twenty-First Century

Many that live deserve death. And some die that deserve life. Can you give it to them? Then do not be too eager to deal out death in judgment.

—J. R. R. Tolkien, *The Fellowship of the Ring* (1954)

Unresolved and New Issues for the Death Penalty

The Legal Issues

After the retirement of Justices Brennan, Marshall, and Blackmun, the Supreme Court has had no openly abolitionist members, but although it no longer couches its debate in the same terms as it did in 1972, the justices still predictably divide between those who believe the death penalty is unreliably imposed and unthinkingly reviewed and those who believe that the procedural tangle that accompanies every case where the accused does not volunteer for the death penalty degrades the justice system far more. On the antiexecution wing are Justice Stevens, who now occupies the most abolitionist position, and President Bill Clinton's appointees, Justices Ruth Ginsburg and Stephen Breyer, joined by President George H. W. Bush's second appointee, Justice David Souter. President Ronald Reagan's picks, Chief Justice Rehnquist, Justice Scalia, and Justice Anthony Kennedy, and President Bush's first appointee, Justice Clarence Thomas, occupy the deferentialist wing. This split leaves the balance of power in the hands of another Reagan appointee, Justice Sandra O'Connor, the only member of the Court who has held elective office, as majority leader of the Arizona Senate.

The chief justice has the most important institutional role on the Court. A majority decision requires five votes. As a result of these two facts, the two capital punishment issues the Supreme Court has focused on in the past two decades have been narrow issues of particular interest to the chief justice and to Justice O'Connor: lawyer competency and the procedural rules governing the way that a death row inmate must present his appeals in federal court. In many cases, lawyers' arguments are little more than competing appeals to Justice O'Connor's sense of fairness to the accused and to her deference to state decision making.

Competent Counsel and Habeas Corpus Reform. A startling difference between the legal profession and other occupations such as practicing medicine or driving a tractor trailer, is its lack of a requirement of practical experience before one is presumed competent to solo. The day that a new lawyer receives a license and joins the approximately one million lawyers in practice, that lawyer can sit as a justice on the Supreme Court, conduct the merger of two Fortune 500 corporations, and represent a man on trial in a capital murder case. The Senate and corporate directors can be counted on to screen out the first two hazards, but it is common for trial attorneys to get their experience in trying cases by representing indigent criminal defendants, even in capital cases, before going on to make "real" money. Although the standard of professionalism is high in the federal public defender system and in the state's public defender offices for most larger metropolitan areas, many of the worst cases in the nation's criminal courts are defended by the worst lawyers because only the newest or hungriest attorneys will represent a capital defendant for what often ends up being near the minimum wage (Paduano and Smith 1991). This is not a new complaint: Barrett Prettyman, Jr., who clerked at the Supreme Court in the 1950s, relates that in 1955, counsel for one death row inmate in Georgia wrote to the Supreme Court declining to come to oral argument because he had a client with an alimony hearing scheduled for the same week, and he could not neglect a paying customer for a client he was representing for free. The client was subsequently executed (Prettyman 1961, 277).

At the same time, there is a small cadre—Professor Austin Sarat of Amherst College estimates it at about 200 lawyers—of very highly qualified attorneys who focus on capital cases (Sarat 1998, 12 n.55). Some of them are ideological opponents of the death penalty, some are just interested in a good fight, and others see potential for money from book and movie rights. Unfortunately, these attorneys almost always enter the case after the initial trial. This leads abolitionists to argue that the capital punishment process is irretrievably contaminated by an unacceptably sloppy first trial, and proponents to argue that counsel are, in the words of Judge Edith Jones of the Court of Appeals for the Fifth Circuit, "playing chicken" with the court, by filing appeals only as the defendant is heading to the execution chamber (Dow 1996, 692 n.6).

To understand how this works in practice, it is necessary to understand the various methods of review available to a convicted defendant. Although the Supreme Court has repeatedly held that the Constitution does not even require a state to give a defendant convicted of crime the right to an appeal, almost every state has both a direct appeal system, and some form of collateral review, available after direct appeals are completed.

In the direct appeal process, garden variety grounds (evidence should have been suppressed, pretrial publicity required a change of venue) for overturning a guilty verdict or death sentence can be raised. Most states, like the federal government, allow one direct appeal, and thereafter permit further appeals to be reviewed only if the court believes the issue raised to be of general importance. In the federal government, the appeal "of right" is to the Court of Appeals; in the states this direct appeal usually proceeds to a similar middle-level court, or often in death cases bypasses that level and goes to the state's highest court. After that, review of the trial can be granted at the discretion of the state's highest court (if the case is not already there). Review of the decision of the highest court of a state (or of a judgment of a Court of Appeals in a federal case) can be sought by a petition for certiorari in the U.S. Supreme Court.

Next, a defendant can avail himself of the state's (or, if a federal prisoner, the federal government's) collateral review process. In theory, the object of these proceedings is to review only those claims of errors that compromise the fairness or reliability of the trial. Typically, the defendant will claim here that his trial or appeal attorneys were incompetent and that he was therefore deprived of counsel in violation of the Sixth Amendment, but claims that a witness has recanted or that new evidence has come to light can also be raised.

For state prisoners, there is a third avenue for relief, namely, a federal writ of habeas corpus, which permits a federal court to discharge from custody or order a new trial for a defendant who is in custody in violation of the federal Constitution, federal laws, or federal treaties. Although errors of state law cannot be a basis for relief in habeas corpus, it is normal for petitioners, often proceeding without a lawyer at this point, to include every piece of paper in their possession that has ever been filed.

This three-tiered system makes death penalty review not only cumbersome, but expensive. In an article that sent tremors throughout the legal community and briefly splashed into the popular press, James Liebman of Columbia University Law School estimated that 68 percent of the death penalty sentences imposed between 1973 and 1995 were eventually overturned, after an average of more than nine years of review (Liebman et al. 2000). In the process, he contended, the state spends between $1 million and $23 million more to convict and execute a murderer than it would cost to house the inmate for life (Liebman et al., 2000).

From the figures three conclusions can be drawn. A small minority of observers believes that the system should be left as it is because the delays and expense of the death penalty are worth it. Many death row inmates are in this camp: given that less than 3 percent of the inmates on death row are likely to be executed in any year, and most of those are volunteers, a death row inmate is more likely to die of old age than as a result of a death sentence.

Abolitionists argue that a system so fraught with error and so expensive must be scrapped. If, after twenty-five years of tinkering, accurate verdicts still cannot be guaranteed, this should prove the unworkability of capital punishment.

Death penalty proponents argue that any unworkability of the system is due to the continual redefinition of what the Constitution requires and that the delay and expense are the fault of a marathon review process. Their remedy for the high cost of the death penalty is to reduce the cost. Sometimes this approach takes the form of attempts to ensure that defendants facing capital sentences have competent counsel from the outset, but more often it results in legislative or judicial streamlining or elimination of the existing remedies available.

At the close of the twentieth century, the streamliners controlled the political agenda, while the abolitionist movement won the public relations battle. In 1988, Chief Justice Rehnquist appointed retired Justice Powell to head a commission to study federal habeas corpus reform. The Powell Commission report, completed in 1989, noted three urgent problems: (1) the repetitive nature of many habeas corpus petitions; (2) the low quality of counsel in postconviction proceedings; and (3) the difficulty of making proper decisions under the pressure of imminent execution dates (Rundlet 1999, 691).

Although in the years following *Fay v. Noia* repeated federal habeas corpus petitions challenging aspects of a capital case could be and were filed, by the late 1970s the Court began to reduce or eliminate the ability of state prisoners to raise federal claims for the first time in federal court. Before and after the Powell Commission report, the Court began moving case by case toward a general rule that one federal habeas corpus petition was the limit, and by 1991 it had held that repeating claims or withholding claims for a later habeas corpus petition was an abuse of the writ justifying dismissal of the petition.

More ominous for death row inmates, beginning in 1983 the Court began to separate the consideration of the merits of a case from the issuance of a stay of execution. In 1992, in *Gomez v. United States District Court,* the Supreme Court held that a judge could take the last-minute nature of even a meritorious second or subsequent petition into account in deciding whether to stay an execution. After an all-night seesaw exchange of judicial opinions between California and Washington, D.C., the Supreme Court vacated four separate stays of execution issued by lower courts, and finally ordered that no further stays could be issued. Later on the morning of April 21, 1992, Robert Alton Harris became the first person executed by California in twenty-five years, after thirteen years on death row for the 1978 kidnapping and murder of two teenage boys because he wanted their car to use in a robbery.

In 1993, the Supreme Court limited the grounds for federal review still further. In *Herrera v. Collins,* the Court expressly held that habeas corpus was not for the purpose of correcting errors of fact: a last-minute confession by the death row inmate's brother or a recantation by a prosecution witness, in the absence of an independent claim that federal rights were violated, does not result in a stay of execution or a writ of habeas corpus.

The Supreme Court's new limitations did not entirely satisfy the objections of death penalty proponents to the delays caused by review in the lower federal courts. The unprecedented action taken by the Supreme Court in the *Harris* execution was decried by death penalty opponents as judicial murder, but proponents saw it as proof that a judge opposed to the death penalty would also be unlikely to find that a prisoner's last-minute filing was an abuse of the writ.

Death penalty proponents' proposals for a legislative fix resulted in the passage in 1996 of the Antiterrorism and Effective Death Penalty Procedures Act. The law, called AEDPA, attempted to solve two of the three problems identified by the Powell Commission by imposing a time limit on filing federal habeas corpus petitions, requiring them to be filed within one year of the date that the state court judgment became final, and except in exceptional circumstances (such as DNA or other forensic proof of innocence) limiting prisoners to one habeas corpus petition. It also commanded federal courts to refuse relief to petitioners unless they had properly raised the constitutional violation in the state court, and required in most cases that federal judges defer to the facts found by the state courts, not conduct their own independent hearing. The Supreme Court declared the AEDPA constitutional in 1996 in *Felker v. Turpin.* As Congress was passing AEDPA, several states passed similar, though stricter, time limits on the filing of collateral attacks on convictions.

In 1998, the Supreme Court and the Court of Appeals for the Ninth Circuit clashed again over an execution, this time over the new limits AEDPA placed on attempts to file second habeas corpus petitions. Despite the contention by the lower federal court that it had simply decided to review a first habeas corpus petition, the Supreme Court found in *Calderon v. Thompson* that some of the federal judges had essentially lain in wait until the state court's fourth collateral appeal and the governor's clemency review had both been completed. When Thompson's state appeals failed to halt his execution, the Ninth Circuit reopened a decision that had denied Thompson relief, and vacated the death sentence. This abused the federal courts' discretion, said the Supreme Court. All stays of execution were vacated by the justices, and Thomas Thompson was executed on July 14, 1998, for a rape and murder committed in 1981.

The third concern expressed by the Powell Commission, that competent counsel assist defendants in their one round of appeals, has been mostly ignored. The American Bar Association recommended, in the same year as the Powell Commission report, that every capital trial be defended by two counsel, at least one of whom had five years' experience and tried nine jury trials before, including at least one capital case. Federal statutes require the appointment of counsel at all stages of federal capital cases who have at least five years' experience, at least three years of which must be spent trying cases in the court where the trial or appeal is being heard. However, in 1995, Congress ended a program begun in 1987 to fund attorneys to handle postconviction work in state death penalty cases.

AEDPA contains an incentive to states to establish their own staff of competent death penalty counsel by imposing even stricter time limits on the filing of habeas corpus petitions and a six-month deadline for a federal court to make a decision on a petition if a state provides "competent" counsel to defendants in capital cases. As of 2001, however, only Arizona had attempted to create a system for assuring the appointment of competent counsel beyond the trial of capital cases. Many states continue to provide no assistance of counsel to indigent defendants beyond the first appeal, and some states pay only a token amount.

To understand the importance of competent counsel and the significance of the fact that, of the states that maintain the death penalty, only one has decided to ensure minimum standards of representation, one needs to know what the Supreme Court means by competent counsel.

First, the Sixth Amendment guarantees the assistance of counsel at trial. This means that counsel must be provided to a poor defendant at trial, and also that the attorney provided be competent, or as the Supreme Court described it in *Strickland v. Washington* (1984), "not ineffective." This is true as well about any first appeal of right.

After that first level of appeals, however, a convicted defendant has no constitutional right to appointed counsel in any discretionary appeal in the state court or in any collateral proceeding attacking his sentence. This is true even of a death sentence, the Court held in *Murray v. Giarratano* (1989). Because a defendant has no constitutional right to the assistance of counsel, the Supreme Court reasoned in *Coleman v. Thompson* (1991), if a prisoner does have an attorney at these posttrial stages there is no constitutional right that the attorney be effective.

This may seem a little abstract. To explain how it works in practice, Coleman was executed without the appeal of his petition for habeas corpus being heard because his attorney filed it on the thirty-third day instead of the thirtieth day after the trial court's decision, as required by Virginia law. Missing a filing date is generally conceded to be ineffective assistance of counsel, but because it did not happen at trial or in the first appeal, no constitutional right of Coleman's was violated.

On the other hand, ineffective assistance of counsel is not always as clear-cut as missing a deadline. The Supreme Court in *Strickland v. Washington,* rejecting a challenge to a death sentence imposed after a guilty plea, held that for counsel to be ineffective, there must be more than poor judgment or lack of skill, and the deficiencies of counsel must actually have resulted in some harm to the defendant. That is, in a case with overwhelming evidence, even the worst attorney can't do any constitutional harm.

Under that standard, consider some of the "competent" counsel whose clients have been sentenced to death (Bright 1996):

An attorney who slept through most of trial

An attorney who was drunk at the start of a trial, whom the judge sent to jail with his client to sober up

An attorney (in Georgia, no less) who had never heard of either *Furman v. Georgia* or *Gregg v. Georgia*

An attorney who filed a one-page brief

Additionally, 20 percent of the lawyers who represented defendants executed in North Carolina were later suspended or disbarred for ethical or competency failures (Alexander 2000).

Of great significance for the future of this issue, Justice O'Connor commented in a July 2, 2001, speech to a group of lawyers in Minnesota that "the system may well be allowing some innocent defendants to be executed" and, echoing public remarks by Justice Ginsburg in April 2001, that it was time to look at minimum standards for counsel in capital cases.

It is unlikely that setting minimum standards of experience or number of cases tried will solve the problem, and unless the attorney is disbarred, drunk, or asleep, the judgment of what is effective assistance is a difficult one to make in hindsight. Most recently, in *Bell v. Cone* (2002), the Court decided 8–1 (with only Justice Stevens dissenting) that an attorney who declined to call any witnesses or make a closing argument on behalf of his client at the penalty phase of a capital trial was not ineffective because, under Tennessee law, by doing so he prevented the prosecution, which had delivered a "low-key" statement calling for the death penalty, from having a second and more dramatic opportunity to argue in rebuttal.

Now, Gary Cone is unquestionably guilty, and even admits to the brutal murder of an elderly couple whose home he broke into while on the run after an armed robbery. The problem with a legal shrug of the shoulders when the evidence of guilt is so overwhelming that even a silent attorney is deemed to have been harmless, is that the death penalty always is discretionary. Even if guilt is not in doubt, the appropriateness of a death sentence is never a foregone conclusion. Where an attorney fails in presenting some kind of reason why this defendant should not receive the death penalty, one must always question whether the defendant has received the sentence fairly.

Methods of Execution. The Greeks let Socrates take poison. The Romans beheaded citizens and crucified slaves. For some centuries, English law permitted the burning of heretics, and the hanging, drawing, and quartering of traitors. In America, the traditional method of execution has been hanging, but the firing squad, gas chamber, electric chair, and lethal injection have all been introduced in the quest to make the death penalty more humane. Motives are mixed on both sides of the capital punishment issue. Some proponents of the death penalty openly assert that an easy death is too good for murderers; others see executions as necessary but as no occasion for excessive pain; yet others urge painless methods of death in order to reduce opposition to capital punishment. On the other side of the glass, some murderers, where given a choice of methods under state law, have chosen the grisliest death in the hopes that it would be declared unconstitutional. Usually this tactic fails: in a 1999 case, Arizona executed a man after the Supreme Court held that he had waived the challenge to the constitutionality of the gas chamber by choosing it instead of lethal injection. But in 1994, Mitchell Rupe gained a federal court order stopping his hanging, in part because he had deliberately ballooned up to 410 pounds while in prison and successfully argued that Washington state would violate the Eighth Amendment by hanging him because it would likely result in his decapitation (Kirchmeier 2000, 637). In a mirror image of the NAACP's long campaign of litigation against separate but equal school systems, death penalty opponents succeeded at first with a frontal assault on capital punishment in general, but into the twenty-first century have been forced to litigate case by case to attack particular methods of execution as cruel and unusual.

In *Fierro v. Gomez* (1996), the Court of Appeals for the Ninth Circuit held that the gas chamber, invented in 1924, inflicts a lingering and painful death and therefore is cruel and unusual punishment. This marked the first time any court has ruled that a method of execution violated the Eighth Amendment.

Hanging, once used by 48 states but now limited to Washington, was declared by the Ninth Circuit in *Campbell v. Wood* (1994) not to be cruel and unusual punishment (at least for normally sized defendants), even though opponents contended that, rather than quickly breaking the condemned's neck, the noose produces death by suffocation or decapitation.

The Supreme Court of Georgia, after complaints of frequent gruesome malfunctions in the electric chair, declared death by electrocution unconstitutional under its state constitution in October 2001. On April 13, 2000, the Supreme Court declined to review Alabama's mandatory use of the electric chair. Robert Lee Tarver was electrocuted the next day (Willing 2000). In January 2001, Florida's legislature changed its law to permit lethal injection in lieu of electrocution. In part Florida did so because the Supreme Court had decided to reexamine its 110-year-old holding in *Kemmler* that electrocution was not inhumane. In Nebraska, the only other state to mandate the electric chair, a state court judge held the punishment cruel and unusual under the state constitution in May 2000, leading to adoption of lethal injection there.

In 1878, the Supreme Court in *Wilkerson* came very close to implying that death by firing squad was a more honorable method of death than Wilkerson deserved. Since that time the Supreme Court has not reviewed another firing squad case, and because only Utah, Idaho, and the military continue to employ a firing squad as options, it is unlikely that future challenges will be successfully raised.

Abolitionists often object to lethal injection not because it is inhumane but because it is too antiseptic. Afraid that the public attitude, particularly in the executions of the grisliest of murderers, that "he got an easier death than he deserved" will lead to a more rapid pace of executions, abolitionists have so far been unable to raise a credible legal challenge to this form of execution. Attempts to persuade medical doctors to condemn physician participation in lethal injection as a violation of the Hippocratic Oath have been occasionally successful. The long-term success of such opposition is doubtful, both because the medical profession remains divided on the legitimacy of capital punishment and because the technology of lethal injection does not require the assistance of medical professionals.

The World beyond the Supreme Court

Despite the continuing ability of the Supreme Court to have the last say on the scope of the Eighth Amendment, in the new century the focus has shifted to the executive branch and the state and federal legislatures, and therefore increasingly back into the hands of the public. It is safe to say that voters know the death penalty stance of candidates for their state and federal offices far more than they know the candidates' positions on trade, taxation, and education. What accounts for this attention to an issue that will never have a direct effect on more than a minuscule fraction of the public? In part, willingness to argue about legal rules that will affect only several hundred persons each year is precisely because the issue remains largely academic. Unless one is conducting the debate in a death row cell or at the funeral of a murder victim, one risks no personal offense to the beliefs of one's opponents and is free by being "for the death penalty" or "against the death penalty" to signal at no cost one's position on a whole host of political and social controversies. But the issue deserves our time because it is literally a matter of life and death to those concerned.

And just as coal miners kept canaries as a sensitive indicator of a poisonous atmosphere, attention to the issues of cruel and unusual punishment alerts us to the defects and dangers of our justice system at large. A nation that is indifferent to how the death penalty is applied to murderers is likely to care even less about innocence, justice, and proportionate punishment for burglars, drunk drivers, and petty thieves.

One of the issues of proportionality that currently occupies first place in the death penalty debate outside the Supreme Court is the claim by abolitionists that the death row population is disproportionately black. As discussed in Chapter 3, the Supreme Court sidestepped or rejected statistical evidence in *Maxwell v. Bishop, Lockhart v. McCree,* and *Buchanan v. Kentucky,* and even though the historical record shows that the death penalty for rape was almost exclusively used as a punishment in the South for black men accused of raping white women, the Supreme Court in *Coker* struck down the death penalty for rape under the *Weems-Trop* theory of evolving standards without reference to this evidence. When presented with statistical evidence in support of a claim that use of the death penalty for murder is likewise tainted by racism, the Supreme Court again rejected the idea that statistical correlation proves causation, in *McCleskey v. Kemp* (1987). Warren McCleskey, a black man who had killed a white police officer during a robbery, contended that he received the death penalty in part because of his race and in part because of the race of his victim. He offered in support a complex statistical review by David Baldus of more than 2,000 murder verdicts handed down in Georgia during the 1970s. Baldus's figures showed, among other things, that defendants who killed whites were eleven times more likely to receive the death penalty than defendants who killed blacks. On the other hand, white defendants in murder cases received death sentences 7 percent of the time while only 4 percent of black defendants received death sentences. Baldus concluded that when the circumstances of the crimes and other nonracial factors were taken into account, black defendants generally received the death penalty 1.1 times more often than white defendants, and that killers of whites received the death penalty 4.3 times more often than the killers of blacks.

The majority of the Court was unconvinced that this showed any racial discrimination. Unlike an employer who rejects ten black applicants and hires fifty white applicants, jury verdicts are delivered one at a time by separate juries uniquely chosen for the purpose from panels that represent a fair cross-section of the community. Unless one assumes that every jury regardless of its composition and every reviewing judge is biased, the Baldus study proves correlation but not causation. The Supreme Court's rejection of the Baldus study is consistent with its holding in other areas that only conscious discrimination violates the Constitution.

However, the Court has also repeatedly declared that Congress has the power to go beyond the constitutional minimum to prohibit practices with discriminatory effects, even if prejudice cannot be proved. This is the basis for the Equal Employment Opportunity Commission's prohibition of employment tests or other workplace measures with a discriminatory impact in employment cases governed by Title VII of the Civil Rights Act of 1964. Since *McCleskey v. Kemp,* death penalty opponents have called for similar legislation to eliminate what they contend is the discriminatory impact the death penalty has on blacks.

Such legislation has never approached a floor vote in Congress. First, Congress tends to lag behind the states in movements to limit or abolish the death penalty, and the only way a death penalty "Title VII" would be constitutional would be to end the death penalty. The Supreme Court has uniformly held that each defendant must be treated as an individual by the sentencing jury or judge: requiring explicit consideration of the race of previous defendants in imposing sentence in order to achieve a hypothetically fair distribution of the death penalty would mean selecting defendants to die not because of their crime or their individual circumstances, but because of their race. No one now on the Supreme Court would support that. Second, looking at the race of the murderer (as was traditional before the Baldus study) shows that there is at least an equally persuasive claim that the death penalty is stacked against whites. Not only did Baldus's study itself show a higher rate of death sentences for white defendants, but also it is now a standard claim in every white defendant's pretrial motions in a capital case that he is being prosecuted as a capital murderer just to "balance the numbers." Third, there are unquestionable imbalances other than racial ones: while 2 percent of men convicted of murder receive the death penalty, only one-tenth of 1 percent of women convicted of murder do (Rapaport 1991, 368). This twenty-to-one disparity could easily be cited by every man on death row as a reason to bar his execution. Fourth, because of the small numbers of persons on death row in most states, racial imbalances in different states may change directions over a relatively brief period as a result of only a few executions, and one can use statistics to draw almost any conclusion simply by careful selection of the sample to be studied. If Congress ever attempts to implement legislation to eliminate claimed racial inequalities, it will only be sure of doing so by eliminating the death penalty entirely.

The other issue receiving attention outside the courts over the future of the death penalty is the use of forensic evidence to exonerate defendants convicted on less than conclusive proof. On January 31, 2000, Illinois Governor George Ryan imposed a formal moratorium on executions in Illinois pending study of ways to improve the reliability of verdicts: between 1976 and 2000, Illinois had executed twelve death row inmates and had freed thirteen on the grounds of innocence. Evidence exonerating some of the death row inmates came from work done by students at Northwestern University studying investigative journalism. On May 9, 2002, Maryland Governor Parris Glendening, echoing Ryan, also formally declared a moratorium on executions. Meanwhile, Governor Jeb Bush, of Florida, has rejected a moratorium, stating, "Here in Florida, there is no competent evidence that suggests an innocent person has been wrongly executed."

Both Ryan, a Republican, and Glendening, a Democrat, were lame ducks in states where executions are hardly ever scheduled, whereas Jeb Bush was running for reelection. Although abolitionists have hailed Ryan's actions as the beginning of a national movement, in historical perspective the pattern of concern over innocent defendants being executed mirrors executive clemency decisions, which almost always come from lame-duck governors (Rapaport 2001, 982).

Penalties Less Than Death

When Is Punishment Not Punishment?

The Supreme Court, whether dominated by conservatives or liberals, follows the same three stages in balancing conflicts between governmental power and individual rights. First, the Supreme Court holds that a matter is not governed by constitutional law. This does not mean that the matter is not subject to law, but rather that it is a matter for state governments, or for the federal legislative and executive branches. At the second stage, the Supreme Court subjects an area of law to what it calls constitutional standards, but is rather fuzzy about where these standards are located in the Constitution, often resorting to "principles of due process" as if the Due Process Clause of the Fifth and Fourteenth Amendments were a reservoir of good policies. In the final mode of constitutional analysis, the Court locates a relevant text from the Constitution or the Bill of Rights and inquires into its original meaning as a source of present standards. In many areas where the Eighth Amendment might apply, the Justices have either unthinkingly remained at stage one or are wandering in stage two. Early in the post-*Furman* era the Supreme Court faced the claim that corporal punishment in schools was a violation of the Eighth Amendment. In 1968, while still on the Court of Appeals, Justice Blackmun had held that use of a lash on Arkansas prisoners was cruel and unusual punishment, and in the Vietnam War era, the justices had subjected student dress codes and even the librarian's choice of books to constitutional scrutiny. However, in *Ingraham v. Wright* (1977), the Supreme Court refused to wade into the issue of school discipline by construing corporal punishment by a governmental body—a school district—not to be "punishment." Although it is likely that this was a practical policy, the four justices in the dissent pointed out that it is completely illogical to say that a warden paddling a juvenile (or adult) prisoner is administering "criminal punishment" subject to the Eighth Amendment, whereas a school principal paddling a student for the same infraction is delivering an educational lesson not subject to the Eighth Amendment.

As has already been discussed, in *Trop* the Court held that stripping a court-martialed soldier of his citizenship was banned by the Eighth Amendment. However, the deportation of aliens, even though it may inflict a much more grievous loss on the deportee, has for more than a century, since *Fong Yue Ting v. United States* (1893), been held not to be subject to the Eighth Amendment, because it is not a punishment for crime.

The Court has also steadfastly refused to find incarceration for civil contempt, that is, when a court imprisons someone to force compliance with a court order, to be punishment subject to Eighth Amendment limitations, as it held in *Uphaus v. Wyman* (1959). Cases of spouses in divorce and custody cases remaining imprisoned for years to keep the whereabouts of children or financial assets secret are not uncommon, but so far they remain invisible to the Eighth Amendment.

What about being placed in jail at the request of a law enforcement officer? The federal Bail Reform Act of 1984 presumes that individuals who have been indicted for serious crimes, but also for some routine street crimes, are too dangerous to the community to be released and must be held in custody even though there is no claim that they would flee and even though legally they are presumed innocent. Although this sounds like criminal punishment governed by the Eighth Amendment, the Supreme Court upheld the constitutionality of the Bail Reform Act of 1984 by a 6–3 vote in *United States v. Salerno* (1987). The Supreme Court rejected the claim that the law violates the Eighth Amendment's prohibition of excessive bail, and also rejected the claim that it violates due process to punish a defendant before trial, on the grounds that pretrial detention is "regulatory, not penal."

What about the flip side of the suggestion that the Supreme Court made in *Robinson v. California* that narcotics addiction could not be punished as a criminal offense because a treatment program would be more effective? In most states serial sex offenders are not subject to life imprisonment for their criminal offenses, but after hundreds of newsworthy cases of released sex offenders, especially pedophiles, committing new, similar crimes, several states, including Louisiana and Kansas, enacted statutes that provide for the involuntary civil commitment of a defendant convicted of offenses such as rape and indecent assault. Kansas's Sexually Violent Predator Act provides, for instance, that a defendant who is proved to have a mental abnormality or personality disorder that makes him likely to commit "predatory acts of sexual violence" can despite the expiration of his prison term be confined indefinitely. The Supreme Court, in *Kansas v. Hendricks* (1997), rejected the claim that this is punishment, even though from the defendant's point of view, whether he remains behind bars as a criminal or as a patient mattered little.

California takes another approach to sex offenders. In 1996, it enacted a law that required repeat offenders of sexual offenses committed on children under thirteen to be "chemically castrated" with medroxyprogesterone as a precondition of parole. So far no cases have tested its constitutionality (Beckman 1998).

Proportionality

Is there is any constitutional requirement that "the punishment fit the crime?" If so, does the Court today have any better measuring stick to judge when the severity of a sentence less than death is too great to pass muster under the Eighth Amendment than it did in 1910 in *Weems?*

Before *Robinson v. California* held in 1962 that states were subject to the Eighth Amendment because it was incorporated into the Due Process Clause of the Fourteenth Amendment, the Court was able to reach the validity of state criminal law enactments by applying other constitutional provisions. Consider how the court might rule differently or reach the same result by better reasoning today.

In 1914, in *United States v. Reynolds,* the Supreme Court held that under the Thirteenth Amendment Alabama's criminal surety laws were illegal. These laws provided that when a "surety" paid a defendant's fines and costs for a petty offense and a defendant entered into an agreement to "work off" the debt at a minimal rate, the breach of the labor contract could be treated as a criminal offense. This system had been used since the formal end of slavery by agricultural employers to meet their need for low-cost seasonal labor. In practice, after a farm laborer was convicted for a petty offense, he was, in the words of the Supreme Court, "chained to an everturning wheel of servitude," because the employer could charge the laborer with violating the contract, have him punished for the new offense, pay the laborer's new fine, and again have him work off the debt in a new season (Klarman 1998, 921–924).

In 1942, the Supreme Court struck down state mandatory sterilization laws under the Equal Protection Clause of the Fourteenth Amendment, in *Skinner v. Oklahoma.* Oklahoma, like other states participating in the so-called eugenics movement, provided for the sterilization of a "probable potential parent of socially undesirable offspring." Skinner had been convicted of stealing chickens and twice convicted of armed robbery, all felonies involving moral turpitude under state law, and therefore was legally subject to an involuntary vasectomy. The Supreme Court found that the statute was unconstitutional, not because it was cruel and unusual punishment, but because it failed to punish other similar offenses with sterilization. Fortunately for Skinner, the case came before the Court in the middle of World War II and smacked too much of practices in Nazi Germany.

In the past four decades, the Court has had to analyze state punishments in light of the Eighth Amendment's prohibition of cruel and unusual punishment, but is reluctant to interfere with noncapital sentencing statutes. In 1980, in *Rummel v. Estelle,* five members of the Court joined to uphold what could potentially be a life sentence law for a third offense of obtaining money by false pretenses. William Rummel had been convicted of fraudulent use of a credit card to obtain $80, then of passing a forged check in the amount of $28.36. When he obtained $120.75 by false pretenses, he became subject as a recidivist to Texas's mandatory maximum sentence of life imprisonment, without parole eligibility for twelve years. In 1982, in *Hutto v. Davis* (1982), a divided Court issued a per curiam opinion that a Virginia sentence of forty years for possessing less than nine ounces of marijuana was not excessive under the Eighth Amendment.

One year later, however, in *Solem v. Helm* (1983), the Court vacated a mandatory life sentence without parole, imposed on a South Dakota man for passing a $100 bad check. Although normally the maximum penalty was five years' imprisonment, Helm had six prior felony convictions and was therefore a recidivist. His other crimes, third-degree burglary, obtaining money under false pretenses, grand larceny, and driving while intoxicated, were all nonviolent offenses. Attempting to provide objective standards for sentences less than capital punishment, Justice Powell wrote that the Eighth Amendment prohibited a sentence grossly disproportionate to the crime, and that this could be measured by considering whether Helm's life sentence was deserved because of the seriousness of the offense that triggered the recidivist statute, whether his punishment was similar to penalties imposed on similar offenses in South Dakota, or similar to the penalties imposed in other states for the same offense.

Solem v. Helm did not signal open season on mandatory sentencing statutes, however. In *Harmelin v. Michigan* (1991), the Court upheld Michigan's law imposing mandatory life without parole for possession of 650 grams of cocaine. Although the Court was divided in its reasoning, five justices rejected the claim that individualized sentencing, required in capital cases, was also necessary for life sentences without parole. In other words, mandatory sentences for crimes, except for the death penalty, are constitutional.

Going further than their colleagues, Justice Scalia and Chief Justice Rehnquist rejected the idea that the Eighth Amendment contained any requirement that sentences had to be proportionate to some judicially declared standard, while Justices Kennedy, O'-Connor, and Souter took an approach similar to that of Justice Powell in *Solem v. Helm,* but found that the sentence was constitutional because it was not grossly disproportionate to the serious crime committed.

For a decade after *Harmelin,* the Supreme Court shied away from reviewing the severity of state laws under the Eighth Amendment, leaving the matter to the political process. Some severe laws were amended. For example, Michigan Governor John Engler signed legislation in 1998 permitting Harmelin to be paroled after fifteen years in prison. In 1999, the justices denied review to California's "three strikes" law despite a claim that the Eighth Amendment prohibited a sentence of twenty-five-years to life for stealing a bottle of vitamins from a supermarket.

Because of the split of the justices in *Harmelin,* the lower federal courts have assumed that proportionality is required in criminal sentences. In 2001, the Court of Appeals for the Eighth Circuit struck down an Arkansas life sentence imposed for a first-offense delivery of one one-hundredth of an ounce of crack cocaine for $20, and the Court of Appeals for the Ninth Circuit declared that California's "three strikes" law inflicted cruel and unusual punishment on Leandro Andrade, who received a life sentence (he would be eligible for parole after fifty years) for shoplifting a total of nine videotapes worth $153 from two K-Mart stores. It appears that the Supreme Court will confront the issue again in 2003, because it has granted a writ of certiorari to review the Ninth Circuit ruling.

Fines and Forfeitures

The Excessive Fines Clause of the Eighth Amendment did not come before the Supreme Court until 207 years after it became part of our nation's charter. Modern efforts to combat drug trafficking by controlling the flow of cash across international borders unintentionally brought the issue before the Supreme Court in *United States v. Bajakajian* (1998). Hosep Bajakajian was traveling to Cyprus with his wife and children when customs dogs alerted on his suitcase, which was checked in with the airline at the Los Angeles International Airport. Customs officers opened the bag and found almost a quarter of a million dollars in cash. When Bajakajian was approached by customs officials and told that he had to disclose and report any cash in the amount of $10,000 or more, he falsely claimed that he carried only $8,000 and his wife only $7,000. A search led to the discovery of a total of $357,000 in cash, all of which was subject to forfeiture under federal law simply because it had not been reported.

At trial, the judge found that the money was being used to repay a lawful debt, was not connected to any crime, and that Bajakajian lied about transporting the money in cash because as an ethnic Armenian who grew up in Syria, he distrusted the government. The lower federal courts found that forfeiting such a large sum for technical infraction of currency transfer laws would violate the Eighth Amendment. Justice Thomas, joined by the four liberal members of the Court, agreed that a sentence that was so grossly disproportionate to the crime violated the Eighth Amendment, while Justice Kennedy stressed for the four dissenters that Bajakajian had never told a true story at any point about where the money came from and that the difficulty in proving the illegal source of laundered money was why even seemingly harsh forfeiture laws were not disproportionate.

It is too soon after *Bajakajian* to tell whether the opinion, like *Furman,* marks the beginning of a new era of scrutiny of fines and forfeitures, or a judicial dead end.

Conditions of Confinement

That the conditions of punishment can be cruel and unusual punishment might seem a tautology, but for most of the nation's history the state of affairs behind prison walls, although a matter for debate among legislators and governors and concern by philanthropists in society, was tacitly conceded to be no business of the courts or the Constitution. The classic statement was made by the Supreme Court of Virginia, in *Ruffin v. Commonwealth* (1871):

> The bill of rights is a declaration of general principles to govern a society of freemen, and not of convicted felons and men civilly dead. . . . They are slaves of the State undergoing punishment for heinous crimes . . . [and] must be subject to the regulations of the institution of which they are inmates, and the laws of the State to whom their service is due in expiation of their crimes.

This not so benign neglect was not as severe a problem in the early days of the country, because during the first part of the nineteenth century the relative shortage of labor, coupled with a desire to have prisons be self-sufficient entities, led to widespread use of prison trade programs. By 1900, opposition from skilled craftsmen and later from the labor movement to this cheap source of goods put an end to widespread use of prison labor in any but the more unpleasant chain-gang-like occupations. Matters in the federal prison system never became desperately bad, because from the outset the Bureau of Prisons had adopted an explicitly rehabilitative philosophy. This philosophy did not always filter down to the cell block; nevertheless, conditions in federal prisons were by and large considerably more humane than one might expect.

The state prisons were another story. The penitentiary movement had gained momentum in the nineteenth century as a response to the twin forces of centralization of state governments and a philosophy of rehabilitation through work. Once these movements had run their course, the removal of state prisons from a place in the state economy aggravated the physical isolation of prisoners from society. By the mid–twentieth century, many American state prisons were far worse places to be than when they had been built a century before.

Nevertheless, the courts, state and federal, retained their deferential attitude toward prison conditions. For one thing, the primary expenditure of political capital by the federal courts was taking place in the school desegregation effort. For another, prior to the 1960s the courts were groping for legal tools to confront complaints of abuses in state prisons. Typical of judicial decisions in the years before the 1970s were statements like these, from the Ninth Circuit in *Stroud v. Swope* (1951): "[I]t is well settled that it is not the function of the courts to superintend the treatment and discipline of prisoners in penitentiaries, but only to deliver from imprisonment those who are illegally confined."

In the occasional case that did bubble up to the Supreme Court, little relief could be foreseen: in *Johnson v. Dye* (1949), the Court of Appeals for the Third Circuit granted a habeas corpus petition of a black prisoner who escaped from a Georgia chain gang and was rearrested in Pittsburgh. Finding that the petitioner's treatment in the chain gangs was cruel and unusual punishment, the lower court said:

> We shall not set out in this opinion the revolting barbarities which Johnson and his witnesses state were habitually perpetrated as standard chain gang practice. To perpetrate these atrocities in an opinion is to be unfair to the American scene as a whole and to reflect little credit on this generation for posterity. It is enough to state that leg-irons and most frequent beatings were among the "minor" constant cruelties.

The Supreme Court reversed, in a one-sentence per curiam opinion. The jurisprudence in this area, as with the death penalty cases, had its greatest decade of development in the 1970s, an era of prison riots that drew national attention, particularly those in Attica, New York, and in Soledad, California. Turning for the first time to the prison system, the Court initially emphasized the Due Process Clause of the Fourteenth Amendment as a constraint on prison decision making. Announcing that "[t]here is no iron curtain drawn between the Constitution and the prisons of this country," in *Wolff v. McDonnell* (1974), the Court held that disciplinary procedures in jails and prisons had to meet federal standards. In doing so, the Court opened one of the most divisive chapters in constitutional jurisprudence. *Wolff* required some adherence to due process for prisoners whose "good time" credits were being revoked for misconduct, because that would delay the day that they would return to society. After two decades of bitter litigation, the Supreme Court has returned to a hands-off approach for the majority of disciplinary proceedings, which do not involve delays of parole or release. In *Sandin v. Conner* (1995), the Court held that a prisoner who was already in prison did not, by being placed in the "restrictive housing unit" (that is, in solitary confinement), suffer any "atypical, significant deprivation," that would implicate the Due Process Clause. This had the effect of removing a great deal of prison litigation from federal court, and therefore, because most state prison bureaucracies are at least as politically formidable as state courts, from judicial supervision altogether. So long as prison officials did not inflict cruel and unusual punishment, prisoners could be removed from the general population without a hearing and placed in isolation for disciplinary or administrative reasons indefinitely.

On a day-to-day basis, most prisoners care less about the procedures at disciplinary hearings than they do about whether anyone will write to or visit them, whether the food will be edible, whether another inmate will assault them or steal their possessions, and whether the corrections officers will be professional or hostile. The Supreme Court first attempted to formulate how the Constitution related to these issues in the 1970s. In *Estelle v. Gamble* (1976), the Court, speaking through Justice Marshall, held that the Eighth Amendment's prohibition of excessive punishment and torture applied to inhumane conditions of confinement as well. In more recent years, Justice Thomas has argued that it is a historical mistake to consider conditions of confinement not intended as punishment as governed by the Eighth Amendment, but the Court is unlikely to uproot thirty years of jurisprudence. For the reasons, consider some of the cases cited by the Supreme Court in *Estelle,* which held that although medical malpractice did not violate the Constitution, deliberate indifference to serious medical needs did:

1. a prison doctor's choice of the "easier and less efficacious treatment" of throwing away the prisoner's ear and stitching the stump rather than treating the prisoner after an altercation;
2. a doctor's injection of a prisoner with penicillin despite knowledge that he was allergic, and refusal to treat the allergic reaction;
3. the stoppage of a prescribed painkiller by the prison doctor after surgery on a prisoner's leg, and requiring prisoner to stand despite the contrary instructions of the surgeon, negating the effect of the operation.

As the Court implied in *Estelle,* a significant cause of the problem was not sadism but indifference to the consequences of taking the cheapest course of action. The Court returned to this theme in 1978 in *Hutto v. Finney,* affirming a series of remedial decrees imposed by the lower federal courts on the Arkansas prison system. The routine conditions that the ordinary Arkansas convict had to endure were characterized by the district court as "a dark and evil world completely alien to the free world." That characterization was amply supported by the evidence. The punishments for misconduct not serious enough to result in punitive isolation were cruel, unusual, and unpredictable.

The Court elaborated:

> Cummins Farm, the institution at the center of this litigation, required its 1,000 inmates to work in the fields 10 hours a day, six days a week, using mule-drawn tools and tending crops by hand. The inmates were sometimes required to run to and from the fields, with a guard in an automobile or on horseback driving them on. They worked in all sorts of weather, so long as the temperature was above freezing, sometimes in unsuitably light clothing or without shoes. The inmates slept together in large, 100-man barracks and some convicts, known as "creepers," would slip from their beds to crawl along the floor, stalking their sleeping enemies. In one 18-month period, there were 17 stabbings, all but 1 occurring in the barracks. Homosexual rape was so common and uncontrolled that some potential victims dared not sleep; instead they would leave their beds and spend the night clinging to the bars nearest the guards' station.
>
> Inmates were lashed with a wooden-handled leather strap five feet long and four inches wide. Although it was not official policy to do so, some inmates were apparently whipped for minor offenses until their skin was bloody and bruised.
>
> The "Tucker telephone," a hand-cranked device, was used to administer electrical shocks to various sensitive parts of an inmate's body.

> Most of the guards were simply inmates who had been issued guns. Although it had 1,000 prisoners, Cummins employed only eight guards who were not themselves convicts. Only two nonconvict guards kept watch over the 1,000 men at night. While the "trusties" maintained an appearance of order, they took a high toll from the other prisoners. Inmates could obtain access to medical treatment only if they bribed the trusty in charge of sick call. As the District Court found, it was "within the power of a trusty guard to murder another inmate with practical impunity," because trusties with weapons were authorized to use deadly force against escapees. "Accidental shootings" also occurred; and one trusty fired his shotgun into a crowded barracks because the inmates would not turn off their TV. Another trusty beat an inmate so badly the victim required partial dentures.

This was all by way of background to the issue before the Court, decrees affecting the disciplinary sanction of "punitive isolation." The Court explained:

> Confinement in punitive isolation was for an indeterminate period of time. An average of 4, and sometimes as many as 10 or 11, prisoners were crowded into windowless 8'x10' cells containing no furniture other than a source of water and a toilet that could only be flushed from outside the cell. At night the prisoners were given mattresses to spread on the floor. Although some prisoners suffered from infectious diseases such as hepatitis and venereal disease, mattresses were removed and jumbled together each morning, then returned to the cells at random in the evening. Prisoners in isolation received fewer than 1,000 calories a day; their meals consisted primarily of 4-inch squares of "grue," a substance created by mashing meat, potatoes, oleo, syrup, vegetables, eggs, and seasoning into a paste and baking the mixture in a pan.

Hutto v. Finney was rare in reaching the Supreme Court, because conditions in many state prisons were so obviously bad that once legal attention was drawn to them, attorneys for prisoners and the state attorney general together drafted consent decrees calling for reforms, including the construction of new prisons. Congress responded to the issue in 1976 by making changes to federal civil rights statutes to make it easier for prisoners represented by counsel to obtain attorneys fees, and in 1980 by enacting the Civil Rights of Institutionalized Persons Act, permitting the Department of Justice to enter lawsuits where a pattern of abuse could be shown.

Although there were some ridiculous decisions in the lower federal courts of which jailhouse lawyers were quick to take advantage, the Supreme Court itself never became a force for prison reform, and contrary to its role in supervising death penalty statutes, tended to rein in the rulings of the Courts of Appeals rather than be the source of innovations. In *United States v. Bailey* (1980), the Supreme Court reviewed the claims of three federal prisoners who escaped from the District of Columbia jail by climbing down knotted bed sheets from a window from which the bars had been removed. After they were recaptured and convicted for escaping from federal custody, the Court of Appeals reversed the verdicts, holding that the jury should have been instructed that evidence of allegedly inhumane conditions at the jail could support the inmates' defense that they had escaped out of necessity. The Supreme Court, over the dissent of Justices Blackmun and Brennan, held that inmates could not claim they were "forced" to escape by poor conditions unless they proved that they had surrendered as soon as the necessity ended, that is, by immediately turning themselves in. Anything less, said the Court, would turn every escape trial into a lengthy suit over prison conditions.

In *Rhodes v. Chapman* (1981), the Court dismissed the argument that double celling in Ohio prisons constituted cruel and unusual punishment. The Constitution, said the Court, "does not mandate comfortable prisons."

As the twentieth century ended and a new one began, isolation and not overcrowding has been in the forefront of litigation. One of the late-eighteenth-century experiments in rehabilitative methods in the new United States was the "Pennsylvania system" of solitary confinement. Designed to replace the group idleness of the debtors prison or common jail, the total isolation of an inmate was designed to allow and require him to reflect and repent, after which he might be allowed to work in solitary silence in his cell, and thus ultimately be reformed. The practice was a disaster, both in England and in Pennsylvania. Describing the experiment from the perspective of 1890, the Supreme Court noted in *In re Medley* (1890):

> Solitary confinement . . . [was] little known prior to the experiment in Walnut Street Penitentiary, in Philadelphia, in 1787. The peculiarities of this system were the complete isolation of the prisoner from all human society, and his confinement in a cell of considerable size, so arranged that he had no direct intercourse with or sight of any human being, and no employment or instruction. Other prisons on the same plan, which were less liberal in the size of their cells and the perfection of their appliances, were erected in Massachusetts, New Jersey, Maryland, and some of the other states. But experience demonstrated that there were serious objections to it. A considerable number of the prisoners fell, after even a short confinement, into a semifatuous condition, from which it was next to impossible to arouse them, and others became violently insane; others still, committed suicide; while those who stood the ordeal better were not generally reformed, and in most cases did not recover sufficient mental activity to be of any subsequent service to the community. It became evident that some changes must be made in the system, and the separate system was originated by the Philadelphia Society for Ameliorating the Miseries of Public Prisons, founded in 1787. . . . [I]t is within the memory of many persons interested in prison discipline that some 30 or 40 years ago the whole subject attracted the general public attention, and its main feature of solitary confinement was found to be too severe.

What was too severe in 1890 was popular again in 1990, but this time isolation was conceived as a method of managing the worst of prison inmates, not as a method of reform. So far Eighth Amendment challenges to the so-called "supermax" facilities have met with little success. Consider the findings of the district court in *Jones'El v. Berge* (2001), ordering mentally ill prisoners removed from Wisconsin's most restrictive prison:

> Supermax Correctional Institution is a 500 bed supermaximum security facility in Boscobel, Wisconsin, designed to incarcerate the worst of the worst offenders. Supermax prisoners experience limited social interaction and almost total idleness, are fed in their cells and have very limited out-of-cell activities. Almost every aspect of daily life is controlled and monitored. Remote controlled doors minimize contact even further. There is little natural light and no access to the outdoors. . . . Inmates in Alpha Unit are housed in single-person cells separated from the corridor by a solid steel door, a vestibule and a second solid steel door. Officers do not walk in front of prisoners' cells unless they have a specific reason to do so. It is impossible for a prisoner in Alpha Unit to see what is happening in the area adjacent to his cell unless the shutter of his door is opened. Because of the way in which the cells are constructed, inmates have little face-to-face contact with staff. . . . All of the cells at Supermax have "boxcar doors" that are constructed of solid metal. . . . [T]here is a constant muffled sound broken intermittently by loud yells and slamming gates.
>
> A five-inch strip of opaque glass runs along the top edge of one wall of each cell. By standing on the bed and craning his neck, an inmate can glimpse the sky through a small sealed skylight. Inmates are not allowed to wear watches or have clocks and it is not easy for them to gauge time from the restricted view they have of the sky. Cells remain illuminated 24 hours a day. . . . At night, inmates are required to sleep in such a way as to allow guards to see skin when they perform hourly checks of the inmates. Guards will wake inmates if they have covered their faces in such a way that the guards cannot see any of the inmate's skin. . . .
>
> Inmates in Level One in Alpha Unit are allowed four hours of exercise a week in an exercise cell, which is nothing more than a slightly

> larger version of a regular cell. It has no windows. . . . Inmates are not allowed face-to-face visits, other than with their lawyers. The institution provides only video visitation. Inmates remain in their cell block and visitors at the front of the institution. Inmates and their visitors see each other on small video screens that are located across the room from the inmate. The audio quality is poor. . . . During the video visits, inmates remain handcuffed, shackled and belly chained. Prison log books show that only 10% of inmates receive visits, an unusually low number. The low number of visitors is also a result of Boscobel's distance from Madison and Milwaukee, making it difficult for families without private transportation to make the trip to Boscobel. . . . Level One inmates at Supermax are allowed only one six-minute telephone call a month. They are not allowed to have any electronic equipment in their cells or to participate in any programs. Their canteen privileges are limited. Inmates in Level One are not allowed to have library books in their cells but may have one box or two shopping bags of legal materials, a soft-cover Bible or Koran or the equivalent and up to 25 letters. Sometimes a chaplain will come to the door of a cell. Inmates have no congregate activity until Level Five and then only on a case by case basis. Inmates who start in Level One spend a minimum of 30 days there. If they move to another level and are demoted back, they must remain in Level One a minimum of 45 days before being reviewed for movement to the next level; if returned a third time, they must spend at least 60 days there before they can be evaluated for transfer to a higher level. Inmates who advance to a higher level may be demoted at any time if staff determine they have engaged in negative behavior.

This level of restriction has been upheld for inmates who are not mentally ill.

In *Whitley v. Albers* (1986), the Court began to grope for a way to distinguish how the Eighth Amendment applied to the particular actions of corrections officers and not generally imposed conditions. The justices focused on the intent of the corrections officer rather than on the effect of his actions on the inmate, holding that a guard who had shot an innocent inmate in the leg during a prison riot had been responding to an emergency and not unnecessarily and wantonly. Therefore, despite seriously injuring the inmate, the guard did not inflict cruel and unusual punishment. By contrast, the Court subsequently held in *Hudson v. McMillian* (1992) that a corrections officer who used unnecessary force by beating a shackled and handcuffed prisoner did not have to inflict "serious" injury on him to violate the Eighth Amendment.

The general rule that the Court has settled on is that conditions that show a "deliberate indifference" to "the minimal civilized measure of life's necessities," violate the Eighth Amendment. The Court has tended to leave the details of defining these two terms to the lower federal courts, although the justices have held that involuntarily subjecting nonsmoking prisoners to tobacco smoke for a long period of time and deliberate indifference to the risk that an inmate would be assaulted by another inmate could constitute cruel and unusual punishment.

In 2002, the justices gave their latest views in *Hope v. Pelzer.* The Eleventh Circuit had held that Alabama corrections officers who shackled a disobedient inmate to a post in the prison yard and left him in the sun without a shirt, water, or a bathroom break for seven hours violated the Eighth Amendment, but dismissed the prisoner's lawsuit on the grounds that the corrections officers were protected by a doctrine known as qualified immunity. Because corrections officers and other government officials are not expected to be lawyers or to consult with judges on a daily basis, under the doctrine of qualified immunity they may not be held liable unless they knowingly violate or disregard clearly established law. Six justices held in *Hope v. Pelzer* that the guards could be liable because use of the hitching post for punishment "obviously" violated the Eighth Amendment. Two facts key to the majority's ruling were that the guards allegedly taunted the prisoner while he stood in the sun, and that only Alabama used this form of punishment.

The punishment considered in *Hope v. Pelzer* is far milder than some of the disciplinary practices from the 1970s, such as the treatment of Arkansas inmates discussed in *Hutto v. Finney,* or Mississippi's practice of using cattle prods on inmates or forcing them to drink laxatives. As a result of the elimination of the worst abuses in prisons and a hardening of public opinion toward criminals generally, the tide of public opinion that had supported much-needed change in the 1970s and 1980s had by 2000 not only turned, but split.

First, with the national decline in heavy manufacturing, particularly affecting employment in unionized jobs in the Northeast, prison construction had quietly become a boom industry eagerly sought by communities desperate for employment. The new prisons were far more livable than the poorly located, overcrowded firetraps they replaced, and corrections officers vastly better equipped and trained. Many critics of the justice system charged that throughout the United States too many persons were now being incarcerated not because the public fears crime, but because prisons provide large sources of patronage jobs.

Second, regardless of the changing political climate and conditions in prisons, lawyers and inmates continued to use the tools available to seek improved prison conditions through judicial interpretation of the Eighth Amendment, to harass the prison administration, or in some cases to kill time. Although in 1970 only about 2,000 lawsuits were filed by prisoners in state and county prisons, by 1995 nearly 40,000 were being filed annually. Quantity adversely affected the quality of these suits. Opponents of these lawsuits, led by the National Association of Attorneys General, publicized cases such as the suit filed by a death row inmate in Arizona who sued when guards took his Nintendo Gameboy, the Indiana inmate who sued when his cable television service was interrupted, and the Nevada inmate who sued because the prison replaced crunchy peanut butter with creamy. On a more serious note, law enforcement officials contended that more than 100 murders had been committed by inmates who had been released solely to comply with judicially imposed population caps (Branham 2001).

In response, Congress passed the Prison Litigation Reform Act (PLRA) in 1996, which made significant changes in the way inmate litigation would be conducted and in the relief judges could grant. First, the practice of allowing inmates to file unlimited complaints *in forma pauperis,* that is, without payment of filing fees, was abolished: an inmate who now had three lawsuits dismissed as meritless would have to pay the full $150 filing fee at the outset of the case. This significantly cut back on the filing of frivolous lawsuits by inmates not represented by counsel. To limit the attractiveness of even meritorious prison lawsuits, the PLRA amended the 1976 amendments in the attorneys fees statute to cap, at a modest level, the fee that a lawyer could earn from even a successful lawsuit.

Second, prisoners were now required to pursue their complaints within the prison grievance system before filing a lawsuit in federal court. This permitted resolution of many minor complaints short of the courthouse but acted as a serious impediment to genuine cases of abuse or injury, because prisoners had to use the grievance system whether or not it could provide them with the relief they sought.

Finally, federal judges were all but forbidden to issue injunctive orders releasing prisoners on the grounds of overcrowding, and orders directing judicial supervision of state and local prisons were made subject to automatic sunset provisions, encouraging an end to the practice of sometimes decades-long judicial management of state prison systems. So far, constitutional challenges to the PLRA have been uniformly unsuccessful, and prison lawsuits in federal court have dropped markedly.

As the new century opens, the most serious Eighth Amendment issues are not legal issues dealing with capital punishment. The Eighth Amendment problems facing America in the twenty-first century are political and social ones affecting inmates in America's prisons who are not on death row: Do we incarcerate too many persons? How should we deal with racial violence, gangs, and other challenges to maintaining order in prison? What priority should we give to attempts at rehabilitation? For good or for ill, these problems will be most likely be addressed in court as lawyers battle over the scope of the Eighth Amendment. But if it is true that war is too important to be left to the generals, it is even more the case that crime and punishment are too important to be left to the Supreme Court justices.

References and Further Reading

Alexander, Ames, et al. 2000. "Uncertain Justice." *Charlotte Observer*, September 10.

Beckman, Linda. 1998. "Chemical Castration." *West Virginia Law Review* 100: 853.

Branham, Lynn S. 2001. "The Prison Litigation Reform Act's Enigmatic Exhaustion Requirement." *Cornell Law Review* 86(March): 483.

Bright, Stephen B. 1996. "The Electric Chair and the Chain Gang: Choices and Challenges for America's Future." *Notre Dame Law Review* 71(July): 845.

Dow, David R. 1996. "The State, the Death Penalty, and Carl Johnson." *Boston College Law Review* 37(July): 691.

Klarman, Michael J. 1998. "Race and the Court in the Progressive Era." *Vanderbilt Law Review* 51: 881.

Liebman, James S., Jeffrey Fagan, Valerie West, and Jonathan Lloyd. 2000. "Capital Attrition: Error Rates in Capital Cases, 1973–1995." *Texas Law Review* 78 (June): 1839.

Paduano, Anthony, and Clive A. S. Smith. 1991. "The Unconscionability of Sub-minimum Wages Paid Appointed Counsel in Capital Cases." *Rutgers Law Review* 43(Winter): 281.

Powell, Lewis. 1989. "Ad Hoc Committee on Federal Habeas Corpus in Capital Cases, Judicial Conference of the United States, Committee Report." Reprinted in *Criminal Law Reporter* 45: 3239.

Prettyman, Barrett, Jr. 1961. *Death and the Supreme Court.* New York: Harcourt, Brace & World.

Rapaport, Elizabeth. 1991. "The Death Penalty and Gender Discrimination." *Law and Society Review* 25: 367.

———. 2001. "Staying Alive: Executive Clemency, Equal Protection, and the Politics of Gender in Women's Capital Cases." *Buffalo Criminal Law Review* 4: 967.

Rundlet, Alexander. 1999. "Opting for Death: State Responses to the AEDPA's Opt-in Provisions and the Need for a Right to Post-conviction Counsel." *University of Pennsylvania Journal of Constitutional Law* 1(Spring): 661.

Sarat, Austin. 1998. "Recapturing the Spirit of *Furman*: The American Bar Association and the New Abolitionist Politics." *Law and Contemporary Problems* 61(Autumn): 5.

Schabos, Willaim A. 2001. "The Federal Death Penalty and International Law." *Federal Sentencing Reporter* 14(July/August): 32.

Willing, Richard. 2000. "Appeal of Alabama Execution Denied by High Court Law." *USA Today,* February 28.

5

Key People, Cases, and Events

American Bar Association

Founded in 1878 to promote improvement in the American justice system, with approximately 400,000 lawyer members, this is the largest association of lawyers in the world. Officially calls for a moratorium on executions and assurance of effective counsel for all criminal defendants. Historically, approval by the ABA has been necessary for appointment to the federal bench, but in recent years ABA advocacy of Democratic Party positions has caused Republican Party to attempt to reduce its role in screening candidates. Web site: http://www.abanet.org.

American Civil Liberties Union

Originally founded in 1920 in New York as advocate of free speech rights under First Amendment, the nation's most famous liberal organization seeks to overturn the death penalty because it is an "intolerable denial of civil liberties" and violates constitutional protections found in the Fifth, Eighth, and Fourteenth Amendments. Web site: http://www.aclu.org.

American Correctional Association

Founded in 1870 as the National Prison Association, this group of approximately 20,000 corrections professionals attempts to upgrade the effectiveness and humanity of prisons and correctional institutions. The ACA's official position on the death penalty is neutrality, but the organization is committed to the view that the object of criminal punishment should be the "moral regeneration" of the criminal. Web site: http://www.aca.org.

Amnesty International

Founded in 1961 in London to call attention to the plight of political prisoners worldwide, winner of Nobel Peace Prize in 1977, AI and its U.S. organization, AI-USA, seek an end to the death penalty worldwide. Web site: www.amnesty-usa.org.

Amsterdam, Anthony

Professor of law at New York University and lawyer with NAACP Legal Defense and Educational Fund, opposing the death penalty in numerous Supreme Court cases, such as *Woodson v. North Carolina*, *Roberts v. Louisiana*, and *Furman v. Georgia.*

Antiterrorism and Effective Death Penalty Act of 1996

Legislation by Congress codifying some of the restrictions the Supreme Court had been placing on federal habeas corpus petitions, also imposes a one-year statute of limitations on filing a federal petition and requires federal courts to defer to the findings made in proceedings by state courts unless they are not just wrong but also "unreasonable." The Supreme Court upheld AEDPA's constitutionality in *Felker v. Turpin* (1996).

Appeal of Right

Although not required by the Constitution, every state and the federal government provides at least one review of a criminal verdict by a higher court, in which a defendant is guaranteed the effective assistance of counsel.

Atkins v. Virginia (2002)

Supreme Court decision prohibiting execution of mentally retarded murderers as a disproportionate penalty under the Eighth Amendment.

Attorney General

Head of the Department of Justice, the federal government's chief criminal lawyer. Has ultimate veto power over decision to seek federal death penalty.

Bail Reform Act of 1984

Reformed the system of bail in federal court. Although bail had been traditionally set for the purpose of assuring the defendant's presence at trial, this law expressly ordered judges to consider the safety of the community as well and to presume that defendants charged with certain offenses, particularly drug offenses, were a danger to the community and should be detained pending trial.

Beccaria, Cesare

Eighteenth-century nobleman of Milan, wrote landmark *On Crimes and Punishments* in 1764, arguing that because it is better to prevent crimes than to punish them cruelly, the death penalty was unjust.

Bedau, Hugo Adam

Professor of political philosophy at Tufts University and a long-time opponent of capital punishment. Author-editor of the 1964 classic *The Death Penalty in America.*

Bennett, James

Successor to Sanford Bates as director of the federal prison system and one of the twentieth century's most influential prison administrators.

Bethea, Rainey

The last man executed in public in United States, in Owensboro, Kentucky, in 1936. Approximately twenty thousand watched him hanged for rape.

Bill of Rights, English and American

The English Bill of Rights is a statute passed in 1689 expressing Parliament's limits on the king's power. The same name was given in the United States to the first ten amendments to the Constitution, ratified in 1791. In theory, they are unalterable limits on the power of the government generally.

Bird, Rose

Former chief justice of California Supreme Court, opponent of the death penalty, defeated for retention in 1986 (along with two other justices) based on campaign by death penalty proponents. A fourth justice changed his voting on death penalty cases and was retained.

Blackmun, Justice Harry A.

Early in his career as lower court judge and on the Supreme Court (after 1970) rejected challenges to the death penalty. Steadily became more abolitionist until shortly before retirement in 1994, announced his most unequivocal opposition to capital punishment.

Bork, Robert

Former judge of Court of Appeals for the D.C. Circuit, nominated to Supreme Court in 1987 but not confirmed by Senate; a critic of Supreme Court invalidation of laws based on personal philosophies of the justices. As solicitor general in 1976, argued in support of the death penalty in *Gregg v. Georgia.*

Brennan, Justice William J., Jr.

Believed that the Eighth Amendment flatly prohibits the death penalty because it is a form of cruel and unusual punishment, but also issued key procedural rulings allowing successful challenges to capital punishment. On the Supreme Court from 1956 to 1990, the most influential justice of twentieth century.

Brooks, Charles, Jr.

First prisoner executed by lethal injection, in Texas, on December 7, 1982.

Cannon, Joe Frank

Houston, Texas, lawyer who represented many death row defendants. Death penalty opponents say that Cannon is a symbol of the poor representation indigent defendants receive from appointed counsel. One of Cannon's clients was executed despite claim that Cannon fell asleep during trial; another defendant obtained a new trial based on the claim.

Chessman, Caryl

Convicted in 1948 of kidnaping, he spent twelve years on California's death row as he filed motions seeking to obtain a new trial. Became international celebrity based on books such as *Cell 2455, Death Row* (1954). Executed in 1960.

Coker v. Georgia (1977)

Supreme Court decision striking down the death penalty for rape of an adult as disproportionate under the Eighth Amendment.

Collateral Attack

A suit brought by a defendant after appellate review of his verdict is completed, which alleges constitutional errors. In federal court collateral attack is accomplished by a petition for a writ of habeas corpus.

Common Law

Generally refers to the Anglo-American system, especially prior to the twentieth century, in which the law was primarily developed on a case-by-case basis by judicial decisions. Currently, the term is also used to refer to a collection of judicial decisions interpreting and applying statutory law.

Concurrence

An opinion agreeing with the decision reached by the majority or plurality, but not necessarily for the same reasons. Important because decisive votes on issues are often held by concurring judges.

Death Penalty Information Center

Clearinghouse by death penalty opponents for information about the death penalty in United States. Maintains informative Web site: www.deathpenaltyinfo.org.

Death Penalty Review Unit

Committee within the Department of Justice created by Attorney General Janet Reno to review decisions to seek the death penalty, and eliminate racial or geographical disparity in federal capital punishment cases.

Douglas, Justice William

New Deal appointee to the Supreme Court from 1939 to 1945. A reliable vote to overturn death penalties and criminal convictions generally, on the basis of his libertarian view of the Bill of Rights.

Evarts, William

Impeachment counsel for President Andrew Johnson, election counsel for President Rutherford Hayes. As Senator from New York he sponsored legislation in 1891 that created modern three-tier federal court system: District Courts, Circuit Courts of Appeal, Supreme Court.

Fay, Michael

An American citizen who in 1994 committed vandalism in Singapore and was sentenced to be beaten with a cane. The incident inspired public debate about the legitimacy of such sentences for crimes committed in the United States.

Federal Death Penalty Act of 1994

Using a variant of the Model Penal Code's bifurcated guilt and penalty procedure, this law greatly expanded the number of federal offenses subject to the death penalty, including murders by federal prisoners, terrorist killings, and use of weapons of mass destruction. As of 2002, the two persons charged, convicted, sentenced to death, and executed under this law are Timothy McVeigh, for the 1995 bombing of the federal building in Oklahoma City, and Juan Garza, for murders committed in aid of drug trafficking.

Federal *Habeas Corpus* Statutes

Modern federal habeas statutes permit an attack on a conviction after an appeal is completed for both state prisoners under Title 28 United States Code section 2254 and federal prisoners under 28 U.S.C. sections 2241 and 2255. As added by AEDPA in 1996, special procedures at 28 U.S.C. sections 2261–2266 apply to habeas corpus petitions attacking death sentences in a state where the defendant was guaranteed representation by effective counsel, requiring a federal court to make a decision within six months of the filing of the petition.

Frank, Daniel

The first person known to have been executed in the American colonies. He was put to death in 1622 in Virginia for the crime of theft.

Frankfurter, Justice Felix

Vocal opponent of the death penalty, but while on the Supreme Court from 1939 to 1962 consistently rejected challenges to death penalty as beyond the power of the judicial branch.

Furman v. Georgia (1972)

One of three Supreme Court decisions in 1972 striking down death penalty statutes under the Eighth Amendment.

Gilmore, Gary

The first person executed in the United States after a ten-year moratorium on capital punishment was ended by the Supreme Court's decision in *Gregg v. Georgia,* by a Utah firing squad on January 17, 1977.

Goldberg, Justice Arthur

Although on the Supreme Court from 1962 to 1965, had great influence on death penalty jurisprudence by writing key memorandum in 1963 opposing capital punishment.

Gregg v. Georgia (1976)

One of three Supreme Court decisions in 1976 holding that some death penalty statutes could comply with the Eighth Amendment.

Greenberg, Jack

Thurgood Marshall's successor as lead counsel of the NAACP Legal Defense and Educational Fund, and professor of law at Columbia University, who with Anthony Amsterdam has argued against the death penalty in several key cases in the U.S. Supreme Court.

Hughes, Chief Justice Charles Evans

Pivotal figure in early twentieth century: governor, Supreme Court justice from 1910 to 1916, presidential candidate, secretary of state, chief justice from 1930 to 1941. Wrote key early death penalty decisions of *Norris v. Alabama* and *Brown v. Mississippi.*

Human Rights Watch

Formed in 1978 to monitor compliance with the Helsinki Accords, this now worldwide organization calls for an end to the death penalty, especially for juveniles. Web site: http://www.hrw.oig.

Incorporation

Refers to the theory that specific guarantees of rights, particularly those mentioned in the Bill of Rights, are part of the "due process of law," and so are enforceable against state and local governments under the Fourteenth Amendment.

Ineffective Assistance of Counsel

Counsel whose performance is not merely negligent, but so poor that a defendant has been deprived of the protection of the Sixth Amendment.

Jeffreys, George

First Baron of Wem, chief justice of Court of Common Pleas under Charles II, and later lord chancellor under James II. His notoriously cruel punishments in the Bloody Assizes of 1685 led to the adoption of a prohibition on cruel and unusual punishments in the new United States.

Lawes, Lewis E.

Warden at Sing Sing Prison, home of New York's electric chair, and public opponent of the death penalty in books such as *Mans' Judgment of Death* and *Twenty Thousand Years in Sing Sing.* President of the American Prison Association.

Liebman, James

Professor of law at Columbia University, author of numerous scholarly articles about the death penalty, anti–death penalty litigator in Supreme Court, including case of *Enmund v. Florida.*

Lombroso, Cesare

Nineteenth-century Italian criminologist whose 1876 book, *The Criminal Man,* argued that criminals were evolutionary throwbacks and could be detected by physical characteristics. Later, the father of the "lie detector."

Madison, President James

Principal drafter of the Constitution of 1787. As Representative from Virginia, 1789–1797, introduced resolution calling for a Bill of Rights in 1789. Voted for first federal death penalty statute in 1790, including provision providing for dissection of executed criminals. Fourth president of the United States, 1809–1817.

Marshall, Justice Thurgood

First head of the NAACP Legal Defense and Educational Fund, key figure in the school desegregation movement. On the Court from 1967 to 1991, wrote that the death penalty was prohibited by the Eighth Amendment as cruel and unusual punishment, and because it was imposed unfairly on poor and minority defendants.

McVeigh, Timothy

Convicted of murder in the truck bombing of the federal building in Oklahoma City in 1995, he became on June 11, 2001, the first person executed under federal death sentence since Victor Feguer in 1963.

Mill, John Stuart

An influential nineteenth-century liberal and advocate of utilitarian philosophy, he outlined his support for capital punishment in an April 21, 1868, speech before Parliament.

"Moderate Middle"

The bloc of justices on the Supreme Court between the abolitionist and deferential wings. Because they hold the key fifth vote, they are the most influential justices in interpreting the Eighth Amendment. Since the early 1990s, the center has been Justice O'Connor. In the 1980s, the center was Justices Powell and White. In the 1970s, the center was Justices Stewart, White, Powell, and Stevens.

National Association for the Advancement of Colored People Legal Defense and Educational Fund

Created by Thurgood Marshall in 1940 as a litigating arm of the NAACP, and independent of the NAACP after 1957, this organization boasts it has been before the Supreme Court more times than any organization except the Department of Justice. In addition to school desegregation cases, has taken numerous death penalty cases where inequality on basis of race has been at issue. Publishes useful roster of death row inmates and issues "Death Row U.S.A." Web site: www.naacpldf.org.

National Association of Attorneys General

Since 1907, this has been the umbrella organization of the top law enforcement officials of the states. A longtime supporter of habeas corpus reform, instrumental in 1996 passage of federal statutes restricting federal habeas corpus and inmate civil rights lawsuits. Web site: http://www.naag.org.

National Association of Criminal Defense Attorneys

Founded in 1958, this 10,000-lawyer group seeks to promote access to effective representation to all criminal defendants. Strongly condemns the death penalty as unjust and unfairly applied. Its magazine, *The Champion,* is an excellent source of news and legal developments for those interested in criminal law. Web site: www.nacdl.org.

National Coalition to Abolish the Death Penalty

Small group working nationally since its founding in 1976 for legislation abolishing the death penalty. Its director is Steven Hawkins. Web site: www.ncadp.org.

O'Connor, Justice Sandra Day

A moderate to conservative former state legislator appointed to the Court in 1981. Since the late 1980s usually represents the decisive vote in death-penalty cases, particularly in procedural cases.

Opinion

A document issued by a judge or group of judges explaining the reasoning for a decision.

Pardon (Commutation)

An inheritance from government by a monarch, these are orders from the executive branch (president or governor) that, regardless of guilt or innocence, a convicted person should be released from prison or have a sentence reduced.

Penn, William

Granted proprietorship of colony of Pennsylvania by Charles II in 1681, his Quaker-inspired Frame of Government, which reserved the death penalty only for murder, was the model for milder penal laws in the American colonies.

Per Curiam

A decision issued by the Court without an opinion by any particular justice. Used to indicate both that the Court believes an issue is so settled it does not need a signed opinion, and also that the Court is too badly fragmented to agree on an approach to a constitutional issue.

Plurality

In a nine-member Supreme Court, at least five justices are needed to issue a decision. If fewer than five justices agree on an opinion for their action, the largest bloc of justices agreeing with the outcome is referred to as the plurality. Unlike the opinion of a majority, a plurality's opinion generally does not have value as precedent.

Post-Conviction Defender Organizations (PCDOs)

Established by Congress in 1988 to provide expert representation to death row inmates in order to make federal habeas corpus review more effective, these organizations won several publicized reversals of death sentences. Funding for PCDOs was withdrawn in 1996, returning to practice of appointing counsel on a case-by-case basis.

Powell, Justice Lewis

Appointed to the Court in 1972 as part of President Nixon's "Southern strategy." In 1980s, frequently became a key vote against the death penalty. After his 1987 retirement headed commission recommending reforms in habeas corpus procedure, and voiced his personal opposition to the death penalty.

Prejean, Sister Helen

A spiritual advisor to death row prisoners in Louisiana's Angola State Prison, and author of the 1993 book, *Dead Man Walking: An Eyewitness Account of the Death Penalty in the United States.* A 1995 film adaption of the book won Susan Sarandon an Academy Award (Best Actress) for her portrayal of Sister Prejean. Her movement to collect signatures for a moratorium on executions maintains a Web site at www.moratoriumcampaign.org.

Prettyman, Barrett

Law clerk for Justices Jackson, Frankfurter, and Harlan, and son of a judge of the Court of Appeals for the D.C. Circuit, noted lawyer and author of *Death and the Supreme Court* (1961), a prizewinning examination of the stories behind several key death penalty decisions.

Prison Litigation Reform Act of 1996

Legislation reforming federal law to limit inmate civil rights lawsuits. Reduces the ability of inmates to file suits without payment of costs, requires prisoners to attempt to resolve grievances within prison administrative process before filing suit, and orders federal courts to inspect the inmate's complaint and, if it is without merit, to dismiss it before requiring a response.

Public Defender

Attorney or group of attorneys funded by federal, state, or local government, to provide defense for indigent persons accused of crime. Although the federal government and many states appointed counsel for defendants in capital cases from the founding of the country, most offices date from the 1960s, when the Supreme Court held that all defendants facing imprisonment were entitled to counsel. Some states continue to appoint counsel to poor defendants on a case-by-case basis from the local bar, leading to complaints that defendants especially in capital cases receive ineffective assistance of counsel.

Rehnquist, Chief Justice William H.

Appointed in 1972, chief justice since 1986. Has been a consistent advocate of a hands-off policy to state capital punishment laws, and has led the deferential wing of the Court in limiting inmates' federal challenges to criminal convictions and the death penalty.

Reinhardt, Stephen

Judge of Court of Appeals for the Ninth Circuit and outspoken opponent of the conservative trend in Supreme Court jurisprudence.

Rush, Benjamin

Signer of Declaration of Independence and prominent Philadelphia physician, by 1787 was an advocate of abolition of the death penalty because of its inhumanity, failure as deterrent, and coarsening effect on public.

Scalia, Justice Antonin

On the Supreme Court since 1986, is consistently deferential to state capital punishment procedures and critical of Supreme Court attempts to write a detailed set of constitutional rules governing the death penalty. He is the most prominent of the "original meaning" interpreters of the Constitution and the Bill of Rights.

Sentencing Reform Act of 1984

Drastically reformed federal sentencing from rehabilitative to punitive model, abolished parole for federal offenses and created United States Sentencing Commission. The Commission's Sentencing Guidelines restrict the discretion of federal judges to give sentences deemed to be too lenient by Congress.

Solicitor General

The federal government's chief civil lawyer, responsible for presenting the position of the United States in cases before the Supreme Court in death penalty cases.

Southern Center for Human Rights

Atlanta-based nonprofit organization of approximately ten lawyers, founded in 1976 to litigate death penalty and inhumane condition of confinement cases. Stephen Bright, author of many articles in opposition to capital punishment, has been its director since 1982. Web site: www.schr.org.

Spaziano v. Florida (1984)

Supreme Court decision upholding the imposition of the death penalty by judge after a jury recommended life. In 2002, the Court held, in *Ring v. Arizona,* that only a jury could find the facts on which a sentence of death was based.

Spenkelink, John

First prisoner executed after *Gregg v. Georgia* who did not volunteer for death. Electrocuted in Florida on May 25, 1979.

Stay of Execution

An order preventing an execution while a court hears a challenge to the death penalty. A stay of execution is mandatory when considering a first habeas corpus petition, but after that the Supreme Court may deny a stay even if some members of the Court believe a challenge may have merit.

Taft, President William H.

President from 1909 to 1913, named chief justice (1921–1930) by President Warren Harding, brought Supreme Court into twentieth century by spurring passage of Judiciary Act of 1925, which gave Supreme Court greater control over its own workload.

Three Strikes Laws

Generic name for enormously popular statutes that impose harsh penalties on repeat offenders, particularly in drug cases.

van den Haag, Ernest

Professor of jurisprudence and public policy at Fordham University, wrote extensively in defense of capital punishment.

"Volunteering for Death"

The waiver or discontinuance of appeals and other challenges by a death row inmate. Since 1976, approximately 1 in 6 executions have been of a volunteer, and in some states a majority of executions are of volunteers.

Warren, Chief Justice Earl

Appointed in 1953 and best known for *Brown v. Board of Education,* also led the due process incorporation revolution of the

1960s. In *Trop v. Dulles* wrote that scope of the Eighth Amendment should be judged by an evolving standard.

Washington, David

Committed three random murders in a crime spree in September 1976. Sought to avoid the death penalty by claiming his attorney was ineffective. In *Strickland v. Washington,* Supreme Court announced that attorney was ineffective only if his performance was highly deficient and the deficiency resulted in harm to client. Washington was executed on July 13, 1984, in Florida.

Wechsler, Herbert

Professor of law at Columbia University, director of the American Law Institute, reporter (principal author) of the influential Model Penal Code, and strong adherent to the rehabilitative theory of punishment.

White, Justice Byron

On the Court from 1962 to 1993, a key vote to invalidate the death penalty in *Furman v. Georgia.* One of the rare justices who became more conservative on the Supreme Court, generally deferential to state attempts to impose the death penalty with consistency.

Writ of Certiorari

The procedural device through which most criminal cases are chosen by the Supreme Court for review.

6

Documents

Excerpts from selected U.S. Supreme Court opinions are presented in this chapter so you can read the words of the justices for yourself. Footnotes and internal citations are omitted to make them user-friendly and to highlight the essentials. Excerpts from important documents, papers, statements, and speeches on capital punishment are also included. We encourage you to read the unedited opinions and documents, which are available in print and on-line.

Code of Hammurabi, c. 1780 B.C.

Hammurabi was king of Babylonia from 1792 through 1750 B.C. *His Code of Laws appears on a stone slab discovered in 1901 and preserved in the Louvre Museum, in Paris.*

1. If any one ensnare another, putting a ban upon him, but he can not prove it, then he that ensnared him shall be put to death.

2. If any one bring an accusation against a man, and the accused go to the river and leap into the river, if he sink in the river his accuser shall take possession of his house. But if the river prove that the accused is not guilty, and he escape unhurt, then he who had brought the accusation shall be put to death, while he who leaped into the river shall take possession of the house that had belonged to his accuser.

3. If any one bring an accusation of any crime before the elders, and does not prove what he has charged, he shall, if it be a capital offense charged, be put to death. . . .

6. If any one steal the property of a temple or of the court, he shall be put to death, and also the one who receives the stolen thing from him shall be put to death.

7. If any one buy from the son or the slave of another man, without witnesses or a contract, silver or gold, a male or female slave, an ox or a sheep, an ass or anything, or if he take it in charge, he is considered a thief and shall be put to death.

8. If any one steal cattle or sheep, or an ass, or a pig or a goat, if it belong to a god or to the court, the thief shall pay thirtyfold therefor; if they belonged to a freed man of the king he shall pay tenfold; if the thief has nothing with which to pay he shall be put to death.

9. If any one lose an article, and find it in the possession of another: if the person in whose possession the thing is found say: "A merchant sold it to me, I paid for it before witnesses," and if the owner of the thing say, "I will bring witnesses who know my property," then shall the purchaser bring the merchant who sold it to him, and the witnesses before whom he bought it, and the owner shall bring witnesses who can identify his property. The judge shall examine their testimony—both of the witnesses before whom the price was paid, and of the witnesses who identify the lost article on oath. The merchant is then proved to be a thief and shall be put to death. The owner of the lost article receives his property, and he who bought it receives the money he paid from the estate of the merchant.

10. If the purchaser does not bring the merchant and the witnesses before whom he bought the article, but its owner bring witnesses who identify it, then the buyer is the thief and shall be put to death, and the owner receives the lost article.

11. If the owner do not bring witnesses to identify the lost article, he is an evil-doer, he has traduced, and shall be put to death. . . .

14. If any one steal the minor son of another, he shall be put to death.

15. If any one take a male or female slave of the court, or a male or female slave of a freed man, outside the city gates, he shall be put to death.

16. If any one receive into his house a runaway male or female slave of the court, or of a freedman, and does not bring it out at the public

proclamation of the major domus, the master of the house shall be put to death. . . .

19. If he hold the slaves in his house, and they are caught there, he shall be put to death. . . .

21. If any one break a hole into a house [with the intent to steal], he shall be put to death. . . .

22. If any one is committing a robbery and is caught, then he shall be put to death. . . .

25. If fire break out in a house, and some one who comes to put it out cast his eye upon the property of the owner of the house, and take the property of the master of the house, he shall be thrown into that self-same fire.

26. If a chieftain or a man [common soldier], who has been ordered to go upon the king's highway for war does not go, but hires a mercenary, if he withholds the compensation, then shall this officer or man be put to death, and he who represented him shall take possession of his house. . . .

109. If conspirators meet in the house of a tavern-keeper, and these conspirators are not captured and delivered to the court, the tavern-keeper shall be put to death.

110. If a "sister of a god" [a prostitute] open a tavern, or enter a tavern to drink, then shall this woman be burned to death. . . .

116. If the prisoner die in prison from blows or maltreatment, the master of the prisoner shall convict the merchant before the judge. If he was a free-born man, the son of the merchant shall be put to death; if it was a slave, he shall pay one-third of a mina of gold, and all that the master of the prisoner gave he shall forfeit. . . .

129. If a man's wife be surprised [having sex] with another man, both shall be tied and thrown into the water, but the husband may pardon his wife and the king his slaves.

130. If a man violate the wife [or fiancee] of another man, who has never known a man, and still lives in her father's house, and sleep with her and be surprised, this man shall be put to death, but the wife is blameless.

153. If the wife of one man on account of another man has their mates [her husband and the other man's wife] murdered, both of them shall be impaled.

154. If a man be guilty of incest with his daughter, he shall be driven from the place [exiled].

229. If a builder build a house for some one, and does not construct it properly, and the house which he built fall in and kill its owner, then that builder shall be put to death.

THE BIBLE, BOOK OF EXODUS, THE TEN COMMANDMENTS, C. 1300 B.C.

Moses received this list of laws, the Ten Commandments recorded in Exodus, chapter 20, around 1300 B.C.

1. I am the Lord thy God, which have brought thee out of the land of Egypt, out of the house of bondage. Thou shalt have no other gods before me.
2. Thou shalt not take the name of the Lord thy God in vain.
3. Thou shalt not make unto thee any graven image, or any likeness of anything that is in heaven above, or that is in the earth beneath, or that is in the water under the earth. Thou shalt not bow down thyself to them, nor serve them.
4. Remember the Sabbath day, to keep it holy.
5. Honor thy father and thy mother: that thy days may be long.
6. Thou shalt not kill.
7. Thou shalt not commit adultery.
8. Thou shalt not steal.
9. Thou shalt not bear false witness against thy neighbor.
10. Thou shalt not covet thy neighbor's house, thou shalt not covet thy neighbor's wife, nor his manservant, nor his maidservant, nor his ox, nor his ass, nor anything that is thy neighbor's.

The Book of Exodus follows the recitation of the Ten Commandments with a set of legal rules. Many resemble the "eye for an eye" legal philosophy of Hammurabi's Code.

Exodus 21. Anyone who strikes a man and kills him shall surely be put to death. However, if he does not do it intentionally, but God lets it happen, he is to flee to a place I will designate. But if a man schemes and kills another man deliberately, take him away from my altar and put him to death.

Anyone who kidnaps another and either sells him or still has him when he is caught must be put to death.

Anyone who curses his father or mother must be put to death.

If men quarrel and one hits the other with a stone or with his fist and he does not die but is confined to bed, the one who struck the blow will not be held responsible if the other gets up and walks around outside with his staff; however, he must pay the injured man for the loss of his time and see that he is completely healed.

If men who are fighting hit a pregnant woman and she gives birth prematurely but there is no serious injury, the offender must be fined whatever the woman's husband demands and the court allows. But if there is serious injury, you are to take life for life, eye for eye, tooth for tooth, hand for hand, foot for foot, burn for burn, wound for wound, bruise for bruise.

Exodus 22. If a thief is caught breaking in and is struck so that he dies, the defender is not guilty of bloodshed; but if it happens after sunrise, he is guilty of bloodshed.

A thief must certainly make restitution, but if he has nothing, he must be sold to pay for his theft. . . .

Code of Draco, c. 621 B.C.

Draco was an Athenian lawmaker who codified customary laws of his day. Only the section dealing with involuntary murder has been preserved. Writings of Aristotle, Plutarch, and others suggest that the death penalty was provided for even trivial offenses. For this reason, "draconian" has become synonymous with harsh legislation.

Even if a man unintentionally kills another, he is exiled. The kings are to adjudge responsible for the homicide either the killer or the planner; and the ephetai are to judge the case. If there is a father or brother or sons, pardon is to be agreed to by all, or the one who opposes is to prevail. But if none of these survives, by those up to the degree of first cousin once removed and first cousin, if all are willing to agree to a pardon; but the one who opposes is to prevail. But if not one of these survives, and if he killed unintentionally and the fifty-phratry members admit him to the country and let the fifty-one choose these by rank. And let also those who killed previously be bound by this law.

A proclamation is to be made against the killer in the market place by the victim's relatives as far as the degree of cousin's son and cousin. The prosecution is to be shared by the cousins and cousins' sons and by sons-in-law, fathers-in-law, and phratry members. . . . If anyone kills the killer or is responsible for his death, as long as he stays away from the frontier markets, games, and Amphictyonic sacrifices, he shall be liable to the same treatment as the one who kills an Athenian; and the ephetai are to judge the case. It is allowed to kill or arrest killers, if they are caught in the territory. . . . If a man defending himself straightway kills someone forcibly and unjustly plundering or seizing him, the killer shall pay no penalty."

THE MAGNA CARTA, JUNE 15, 1215

At Runneymede, England, on June 15, 1215, King John of England signed the Magna Carta.

. . . TO ALL FREE MEN OF OUR KINGDOM we have also granted, for us and our heirs for ever, all the liberties written out below, to have and to keep for them and their heirs, of us and our heirs:

Ordinary lawsuits shall not follow the royal court around, but shall be held in a fixed place.

. . .

For a trivial offence, a free man shall be fined only in proportion to the degree of his offence, and for a serious offence correspondingly, but not so heavily as to deprive him of his livelihood. In the same way, a merchant shall be spared his merchandise, and a husbandman the implements of his husbandry, if they fall upon the mercy of a royal court. None of these fines shall be imposed except by the assessment on oath of reputable men of the neighborhood.

Earls and barons shall be fined only by their equals, and in proportion to the gravity of their offence.

. . .

In future no official shall place a man on trial upon his own unsupported statement, without producing credible witnesses to the truth of it.

No free man shall be seized or imprisoned, or stripped of his rights or possessions, or outlawed or exiled, or deprived of his standing in any other way, nor will we proceed with force against him, or send others to do so, except by the lawful judgement of his equals or by the law of the land.

To no one will we sell, to no one deny or delay right or justice. . . .

All fines that have been given to us unjustly and against the law of the land, and all fines that we have exacted unjustly, shall be entirely remitted or the matter decided by a majority judgement of the twenty-five barons referred to below in the clause for securing the peace together with Stephen, archbishop of Canterbury, if he can be present, and such others as he wishes to bring with him.

Given by our hand in the meadow that is called Runnymede, between Windsor and Staines, on the fifteenth day of June in the seventeenth year of our reign [i.e., 1215].

The English Bill of Rights, 1689

This statute, a precursor to the American Bill of Rights, limited the Crown's power. Capping the "Glorious Revolution," it included protections against excessive bails and fines and cruel and unusual punishments.

An Act for declaring the rights and liberties of the subject and settling the succession of the crown.

. . .

Whereas the late King James the Second, . . . did endeavour to subvert and extirpate the protestant religion, and the laws and liberties of this kingdom . . . by assuming and exercising a power of dispensing with and suspending of laws, and the execution of laws, without consent of parliament . . . and excessive bail hath been required of persons committed in criminal cases, to elude the benefit of the laws made for the liberty of the subject.

And excessive fines have been imposed; and illegal and cruel punishments inflicted . . .

All of which are utterly and directly contrary to the known laws and statutes, and freedom of this realm:

. . . The lords spiritual and temporal, and commons . . . for the vindicating and asserting their ancient rights and liberties, declare:

That it is the right of the subjects to petition the King, and all commitments and prosecutions for such petitioning are illegal.

That the raising or keeping a standing army within the kingdom in time of peace, unless it be with consent of parliament, is against law.

That the subjects which are protestants, may have arms for their defence suitable to their conditions, and as allowed by law.

That the freedom of speech, and debates or proceedings in parliament, ought not to be impeached or questioned in any court or place out of parliament.

That excessive bail ought not to be required, nor excessive fines imposed; nor cruel and unusual punishments inflicted.

THE AMERICAN DECLARATION OF INDEPENDENCE, 1776

The Continental Congress approved a Resolution of Independence on July 2, 1776. Thomas Jefferson was charged with drafting a formal Declaration of Independence that would justify the American Revolution to the world. The final draft was approved on July 4, 1776.

The unanimous Declaration of the thirteen United States of America . . .

When in the course of human events, it becomes necessary for one people to dissolve the political bands which have connected them with another, and to assume among the powers of the earth, the separate and equal station to which the laws of nature and of nature's God entitle them, a decent respect to the opinions of mankind requires that they should declare the causes which impel them to the separation.

We hold these truths to be self-evident, that all men are created equal, that they are endowed by their Creator with certain unalienable rights, that among these are life, liberty, and the pursuit of happiness.

That to secure these rights, governments are instituted among men, deriving their just powers from the consent of the governed. That whenever any form of government becomes destructive of these ends, it is the right of the people to alter or to abolish it, and to institute new government, laying its foundation on such principles and organizing its powers in such form, as to them shall seem most likely to effect their safety and happiness.

Prudence, indeed, will dictate that governments long established should not be changed for light and transient causes; and accordingly all experience hath shewn, that mankind are more disposed to suffer, while evils are sufferable, than to right themselves by abolishing the forms to which they are accustomed.

But when a long train of abuses and usurpations, pursuing invariably the same object evinces a design to reduce them under absolute despotism, it is their right, it is their duty, to throw off such government, and to provide new guards for their future security.

Such has been the patient sufferance of these colonies; and such is now the necessity which constrains them to alter their former systems of government. The history of the present King of Great Britain [George III] is a history of repeated injuries and usurpations, all having in direct object the establishment of an absolute tyranny over these states. To prove this, let facts be submitted to a candid world.

He has refused his assent to laws, the most wholesome and necessary for the public good.

He has forbidden his governors to pass laws of immediate and pressing importance, unless suspended in their operation till his assent should be obtained, and when so suspended, he has utterly neglected to attend to them.

He has refused to pass other laws for the accommodation of large districts of people, unless those people would relinquish the right of representation in the legislature, a right inestimable to them and formidable to tyrants only.

He has called together legislative bodies at places unusual, uncomfortable, and distant from the depository of their public records, for the sole purpose of fatiguing them into compliance with his measures.

He has dissolved representative houses repeatedly, for opposing with manly firmness his invasions on the rights of the people.

He has refused for a long time, after such dissolutions, to cause others to be elected; whereby the legislative powers, incapable of annihilation, have returned to the people at large for their exercise; the State remaining in the meantime exposed to all the dangers of invasion from without, and convulsions within.

He has endeavoured to prevent the population of these States; for that purpose obstructing the laws for naturalization of foreigners; refusing to pass others to encourage their migrations hither, and raising the conditions of new appropriations of lands.

He has obstructed the administration of justice, by refusing his assent to laws for establishing judiciary powers.

He has made judges dependent on his will alone, for the tenure of their offices, and the amount and payment of their salaries.

He has erected a multitude of new offices, and sent hither swarms of officers to harass our people, and eat out their substance.

He has kept among us, in times of peace, standing armies, without the consent of our legislatures.

He has affected to render the military independent of and superior to the civil power.

He has combined with others to subject us to a jurisdiction foreign to our constitution and unacknowledged by our laws; giving his assent to their acts of pretended legislation:

For quartering large bodies of armed troops among us:

For protecting them, by a mock trial, from punishment for any murders which they should commit on the inhabitants of these States:

For cutting off our trade with all parts of the world:

For imposing taxes on us without our consent:

For depriving us in many cases of the benefits of trial by jury:

For transporting us beyond seas to be tried for pretended offences:

For abolishing the free system of English laws in a neighbouring province, establishing therein an arbitrary government, and enlarging its boundaries so as to render it at once an example and fit instrument for introducing the same absolute rule into these colonies:

For taking away our Charters, abolishing our most valuable laws and altering fundamentally the forms of our governments:

For suspending our own legislatures, and declaring themselves invested with power to legislate for us in all cases whatsoever.

He has abdicated government here by declaring us out of his protection and waging war against us.

He has plundered our seas, ravaged our coasts, burnt our towns, and destroyed the lives of our people.

He is at this time transporting large armies of foreign mercenaries to complete the works of death, desolation and tyranny, already begun with circumstances of cruelty and perfidy scarcely paralleled in the most barbarous ages, and totally unworthy the head of a civilized nation.

He has constrained our fellow citizens taken captive on the high seas to bear arms against their country, to become the executioners of their friends and brethren, or to fall themselves by their hands.

He has excited domestic insurrections amongst us, and has endeavoured to bring on the inhabitants of our frontiers, the merciless Indian savages, whose known rule of warfare is an undistinguished destruction of all ages, sexes and conditions.

In every stage of these oppressions, we have petitioned for redress in the most humble terms. Our repeated petitions have been answered only by repeated injury. A prince, whose character is thus marked by every act which may define a tyrant, is unfit to be the ruler of a free people. . . .

We, therefore, the Representatives of the United States of America, in General Congress, assembled, appealing to the Supreme Judge of the world for the rectitude of our intentions, do, in the name, and by the authority of the good people of these colonies, solemnly publish and declare,

That these United Colonies are, and of right ought to be free and independent States; that they are absolved from all allegiance to the British Crown, and that all political connection between them and the State of Great Britain is and ought to be totally dissolved; and that as free and independent States, they have full power to levy war, conclude peace, contract alliances, establish commerce, and to do all other acts and things which independent states may of right do.

And for the support of this Declaration, with a firm reliance on the protection of Divine Providence, we mutually pledge to each other our lives, our fortunes, and our sacred honor.

[Signed by representatives of New Hampshire, Massachusetts, Rhode Island, Connecticut, New York, New Jersey, Pennsylvania, Delaware, Maryland, Virginia, North Carolina, South Carolina, and Georgia.]

Ordinance of the Northwest Territory, 1787

The Articles of Confederation Congress passed this act to provide for the political organization of the Northwest territories. The act described the basic rights and liberties of settlers. Article II specified the rights of persons accused of crimes. The act also provided that states carved out of this region would be admitted to the Union on a equal footing with the original states.

An ordinance for the government of the Territory of the United States northwest of the river Ohio:

. . .

SECTION 8. For the prevention of crimes and injuries, the laws to be adopted or made shall have force in all parts of the district. . . .

SECTION 14. It is hereby ordained and declared, by the authority aforesaid, that the following articles shall be considered as articles of compact, between the original States and the people and States in the said territory, and forever remain unalterable, unless by common consent, to wit:

ARTICLE I

No person, demeaning himself in a peaceable and orderly manner, shall ever be molested on account of his mode of worship, or religious sentiments, in the said territory.

ARTICLE II

The inhabitants of the said territory shall always be entitled to the benefits of the writs of habeas corpus, and of the trial by jury; of a proportionate representation of the people in the legislature, and of judicial proceedings according to the course of the common law. All persons shall be bailable, unless for capital offences, where the proof shall be evident, or the presumption great. All fines shall be moderate; and no cruel or unusual punishments shall be inflicted. No man shall be deprived of his liberty or property, but by the judgment of his peers, or the law of the land, and should the public exigencies make it necessary, for the common preservation, to take any person's property, or to demand his particular services, full compensation shall be made for the same. And, in the just preservation of rights and property, it is understood and declared, that no law ought ever to be made or have force in the said territory, that shall, in any manner whatever, interfere with or affect private contracts, or engagements, bona fide, and without fraud previously formed.

ARTICLE III

Religion, morality, and knowledge being necessary to good government and happiness of mankind, schools and the means of education shall forever be encouraged. The utmost good faith shall always be observed towards the Indians; their lands and property shall never be taken from them without their consent; and in their property, rights, and liberty they never shall be invaded or disturbed, unless in just and lawful wars authorized by Congress; but laws founded in justice and humanity shall, from time to time, be made, for preventing wrongs being done to them, and for preserving peace and friendship with them.

. . .

AMENDMENTS TO THE U.S. CONSTITUTION

Amendment V (1791). No person shall be held to answer for a capital, or otherwise infamous crime, unless on a presentment or indictment of a grand jury, except in cases arising in the land or naval forces, or in the militia, when in actual service in time of war or public danger; nor shall any person be subject for the same offense to be twice put in jeopardy of life or limb; nor shall be compelled in any criminal case to be a witness against himself, nor be deprived of life, liberty, or property, without due process of law; nor shall private property be taken for public use, without just compensation.

Amendment VIII (1791). Excessive bail shall not be required, nor excessive fines imposed, nor cruel and unusual punishments inflicted.

Amendment XIV (1868). Section 1. All persons born or naturalized in the United States, and subject to the jurisdiction thereof, are citizens of the United States and of the state wherein they reside. No state shall make or enforce any law which shall abridge the privileges or immunities of citizens of the United States; nor shall any state deprive any person of life, liberty, or property, without due process of law; nor deny to any person within its jurisdiction the equal protection of the laws.

. . .

"Speech in Favor of Capital Punishment," John Stuart Mill, April 21, 1868

Mill delivered this speech before Parliament on April 21, 1868, in opposition to a bill banning capital punishment.

. . . It would be a great satisfaction to me if I were able to support this Motion. It is always a matter of regret to me to find myself . . . opposed to . . . the philanthropists. . . . On the very subject that is now occupying us we all know what signal service they have rendered. It is through their efforts that our criminal laws . . . have so greatly relaxed their most revolting and most impolitic ferocity, that aggravated murder is now practically the only crime which is punished with death by any of our lawful tribunals; and we are even now deliberating whether the extreme penalty should be retained in that solitary case. . . . When there has been brought home to any one, by conclusive evidence, the greatest crime known to the law; and when the attendant circumstances suggest no palliation of the guilt, no hope that the culprit may even yet not be unworthy to live among mankind, nothing to make it probable that the crime was an exception to his general character rather than a consequence of it, then I confess it appears to me that to deprive the criminal of the life of which he has proved himself to be unworthy—solemnly to blot him out from the fellowship of mankind and from the catalogue of the living—is the most appropriate . . . penal consequences. . . . I defend this penalty, when confined to atrocious cases, on the very ground on which it is commonly attacked—on that of humanity to the criminal; as beyond comparison the least cruel mode in which it is possible adequately to deter from the crime. If, in our horror of inflicting death, we endeavour to devise some punishment . . . which shall act on the human mind with a deterrent force at all comparable to that of death, we are driven to inflictions less severe indeed in appearance, and therefore less efficacious, but far more cruel in reality. Few, I think, would venture to propose, as a punishment for aggravated murder, less than imprisonment with hard labor for life; that is the fate to which a murderer would be consigned by the mercy which shrinks from putting him to death. But has it been sufficiently considered what sort of a mercy this is, and what kind of life it leaves to him? . . . What comparison can there really be, in point of severity, between consigning a man to the short pang of a rapid death, and immuring him in a living tomb, there to linger out what may be a long life in the hardest and most monotonous toil, without any of its alleviations or rewards—debarred from all pleasant sights and sounds, and cut off from all earthly hope, except a slight mitigation of bodily restraint, or a small improvement of diet? Yet even such a lot as this . . . is universally reputed a milder punishment than death . . . [I]t is characteristic of all punishments which depend on duration for their efficacy . . . that they are more rigorous than they seem; while it is, on the contrary, one of the strongest recommendations a punishment can have, that it should seem more rigorous than it is; for its practical power depends far less on what it is than on what it seems. There is not, I should think, any human infliction which makes an impression on the imagination so entirely out of proportion to its real severity as the punishment of death. . . . My Hon. Friend says that it does not inspire terror, and that experience proves it to be a failure. But the influence of a punishment is not to be estimated by its effect on hardened criminals. Those whose habitual way of life keeps them, so to speak, at all times within sight of the gallows, do grow to care less about it; as, to compare good things with bad, an old soldier is not much affected by the chance of dying in battle. I can afford to admit all that is often said about the indifference of professional criminals to the gallows. Though of that indifference one-third is probably bravado and another third confidence that they shall have the luck to escape, it is quite probable that the remaining third is real. But the efficacy of a punishment which acts principally through the imagination, is chiefly to be measured by the impression it makes on those who are still innocent; by the horror with which it surrounds the first promptings of guilt; the restraining influence it exercises over the beginning of the thought which, if indulged, would become a temptation. . . . As for what is called the failure of death punishment, who is able to judge of that? We partly know who those are whom it has not deterred; but who is there who knows whom it has deterred, or how many human beings it has saved who would have lived to be murderers if that awful association had not been thrown round the idea of murder from their earliest infancy? Let us not forget that the most imposing fact loses its power over the imagination if it is made too cheap. When a punishment fit only for the most atrocious crimes is lavished on small offences until human feeling recoils from it, then, indeed, it ceases to intimidate, because it ceases to be believed in. The failure of capital punishment in cases of theft is easily accounted for; the thief did not believe that it would be inflicted. He had learnt by experience that jurors would perjure themselves rather than find him guilty; that Judges would seize any excuse for not sentencing him to death, or for recommending him to mercy. . . . When it is impossible to inflict a punishment, or when its infliction becomes a public scandal, the idle threat cannot too soon disappear from the statute book. And in the case of the host of offences which were formerly capital, I heartily rejoice that it did become impracticable to execute the law. If the same state of public feeling comes to exist in the case of murder; if the time comes when jurors refuse to find a murderer guilty; when Judges will not sentence him to death, or will recommend him to mercy; or when, if juries and Judges do not flinch from their duty, Home Secretaries, under pressure of deputations and memorials, shrink from theirs, and the threat becomes, as it became in the other cases, a mere brutum fulmen; then, indeed, it may become necessary to do in this case what has been done in those—to abrogate the penalty. That time may come. . . .

Much has been said of the sanctity of human life, and the absurdity of supposing that we can teach respect for life by ourselves destroying it. But I am surprised at the employment of this argument, for it is one which might be brought against any punishment whatever. It is not human life only, not human life as such, that ought to be sacred to us, but human feelings. The human capacity of suffering is what we should cause to be respected, not the mere capacity of existing. And we may imagine somebody asking how we can teach people not to inflict suffering by ourselves inflicting it? But to this I should answer . . . that to deter by suffering from inflicting suffering is not only possible, but the very purpose of penal justice. Does fining a criminal show want of respect for property, or imprisoning him, for personal freedom? Just as unreasonable is it to think that to take the life of a man who has taken that of another is to show want of regard for human life. We show, on the contrary, most emphatically our regard for it, by the adoption of a rule that he who violates that right in another forfeits it for himself, and that while no other crime that he can commit deprives him of his right to live, this shall. There is one argument against capital punishment . . . which I cannot deny to have weight . . . and which never can be entirely got rid of. It is this—that if by an error of justice an innocent person is put to death, the mistake can never be corrected; all compensation, all reparation for the wrong is impossible. This would be indeed a serious objection if these miserable mistakes—among the most tragical occurrences in the whole round of human affairs—could not be made extremely rare. The argument is invincible where the mode of criminal procedure is dangerous to the innocent, or where the Courts of Justice are not trusted. . . . If our own procedure and Courts of Justice afforded ground for . . . apprehension, I should be the first to join in withdrawing the power of inflicting irreparable punishment from such tribunals. But we all know that the defects of our procedure are the very opposite. Our rules of evidence are even too favorable to the prisoner; and juries and Judges carry out the maxim, "It is better that ten guilty should escape than that one innocent person should suffer," not only to the letter, but beyond the letter. Judges are most anxious to point out, and juries to allow for, the barest possibility of the prisoner's innocence. No human judgment is infallible . . . but in so grave a case as that of murder, the accused, in our system, has always the benefit of the merest shadow of a doubt. . . .

I think, Sir, that in the case of most offences, except those against property, there is more need of strengthening our punishments than of weakening them. . . . I shall therefore vote against the Amendment.

Evangelium Vitae (The Gospel of Life), Encyclical of Pope John Paul II, March 25, 1995

These passages are from a papal encyclical on the death penalty.

9. And yet God, who is always merciful even when he punishes, "put a mark on Cain, lest any who came upon him should kill him" (Gen 4:15). He thus gave him a distinctive sign, not to condemn him to the hatred of others, but to protect and defend him from those wishing to kill him, even out of a desire to avenge Abel's death. Not even a murderer loses his personal dignity, and God himself pledges to guarantee this. And it is precisely here that the paradoxical mystery of the merciful justice of God is shown forth. As Saint Ambrose writes: " . . . God drove Cain out of his presence and sent him into exile far away from his native land, so that he passed from a life of human kindness to one which was more akin to the rude existence of a wild beast. God, who preferred the correction rather than the death of a sinner, did not desire that a homicide be punished by the exaction of another act of homicide."

27. Among the signs of hope we should also count the spread, at many levels of public opinion, of a new sensitivity ever more opposed to war as an instrument for the resolution of conflicts between peoples, and increasingly oriented to finding effective but "non-violent" means to counter the armed aggressor. In the same perspective there is evidence of a growing public opposition to the death penalty, even when such a penalty is seen as a kind of "legitimate defence" on the part of society. Modern society in fact has the means of effectively suppressing crime by rendering criminals harmless without definitively denying them the chance to reform.

40. The commandment regarding the inviolability of human life reverberates at the heart of the "ten words" in the covenant of Sinai (cf. Ex 34:28). In the first place that commandment prohibits murder: "You shall not kill" (Ex 20:13). . . . Of course we must recognize that in the Old Testament this sense of the value of life, though already quite marked, does not yet reach the refinement found in the Sermon on the Mount. This is apparent in some aspects of the current penal legislation,

which provided for severe forms of corporal punishment and even the death penalty. But the overall message, which the New Testament will bring to perfection, is a forceful appeal for respect for the inviolability of physical life and the integrity of the person. It culminates in the positive commandment which obliges us to be responsible for our neighbour as for ourselves: "You shall love your neighbour as yourself" (Lev 19:18).

55. Moreover, "legitimate defence can be not only a right but a grave duty for someone responsible for another's life, the common good of the family or of the State." Unfortunately it happens that the need to render the aggressor incapable of causing harm sometimes involves taking his life. In this case, the fatal outcome is attributable to the aggressor whose action brought it about, even though he may not be morally responsible because of a lack of the use of reason.

56. This is the context in which to place the problem of the death penalty. On this matter there is a growing tendency, both in the Church and in civil society, to demand that it be applied in a very limited way or even that it be abolished completely. The problem must be viewed in the context of a system of penal justice ever more in line with human dignity and thus, in the end, with God's plan for man and society. The primary purpose of the punishment which society inflicts is "to redress the disorder caused by the offence." Public authority must redress the violation of personal and social rights by imposing on the offender an adequate punishment for the crime, as a condition for the offender to regain the exercise of his or her freedom. In this way authority also fulfils the purpose of defending public order and ensuring people's safety, while at the same time offering the offender an incentive and help to . . . be rehabilitated.

It is clear that, for these purposes to be achieved, the nature and extent of the punishment . . . ought not go to the extreme of executing the offender except in cases of absolute necessity: in other words, when it would not be possible otherwise to defend society. Today, however, as a result of steady improvements in the organization of the penal system, such cases are very rare, if not practically non-existent.

AMERICAN BAR ASSOCIATION RESOLUTION ON THE DEATH PENALTY, FEBRUARY 3, 1997

This resolution was approved by the ABA House of Delegates on February 3, 1997.

RECOMMENDATION

RESOLVED, That the American Bar Association calls upon each jurisdiction that imposes capital punishment not to carry out the death penalty until the jurisdiction implements policies and procedures that are consistent with the following longstanding American Bar Association policies intended to (1) ensure that death penalty cases are administered fairly and impartially, in accordance with due process, and (2) minimize the risk that innocent persons may be executed:

(i) Implementing ABA "Guidelines for the Appointment and Performance of Counsel in Death Penalty Cases" (adopted Feb. 1989) and Association policies intended to encourage competency of counsel in capital cases (adopted Feb. 1979, Feb. 1988, Feb. 1990, Aug. 1996);

(ii) Preserving, enhancing, and streamlining state and federal courts' authority and responsibility to exercise independent judgment on the merits of constitutional claims in state post-conviction and federal habeas corpus proceedings (adopted Aug. 1982, Feb. 1990);

(iii) Striving to eliminate discrimination in capital sentencing on the basis of the race of either the victim or the defendant (adopted Aug. 1988, Aug. 1991); and

(iv) Preventing execution of mentally retarded persons (adopted Feb. 1989) and persons who were under the age of 18 at the time of their offenses (adopted Aug. 1983).

FURTHER RESOLVED, That in adopting this recommendation, apart from existing Association policies relating to offenders who are mentally retarded or under the age of 18 at the time of the commission of the offenses, the Association takes no position on the death penalty.

Message Supporting the Moratorium on the Death Penalty

His Holiness, Tenzin Gyatso, the Fourteenth Dalai Lama

In general, death is something none of us wants, in fact it is something we don't even like to think about. When death takes place naturally, it is a process beyond our control to stop, but where death is willfully and deliberately brought about, it is very unfortunate. Of course, within our legal systems there are said to be certain reasons and purposes for employing the death penalty. It is used to punish offenders, to prevent them ever repeating their misdeed and to deter others. However, if we examine the situation more carefully, we will find that these are not the real solutions.

Harmful actions and their tragic consequences all have their origin in disturbing emotions and negative thoughts, and these are a state of mind, whose potential we find within all human beings. From this point of view, every one of us has the potential to commit crimes, because we are all subject to negative disturbing emotions and negative mental qualities. And we will not overcome these by executing other people.

What is deemed criminal can vary greatly from country to country. In some countries, for example, speaking out for human rights is considered criminal, whereas in other countries preventing free speech is a crime. The punishments for crimes are also very different, but usually include various forms of imprisonment or hardship, financial penalties and, in a number of countries, physical pain. In some countries, crimes that the government considers very serious are punished by executing the person who committed the crime.

The death penalty fulfills a preventive function, but it is also very clearly a form of revenge. It is an especially severe form of punishment because it is so final. The human life is ended and the executed person is deprived of the opportunity to change, to restore the harm done or compensate for it. Before advocating execution we should consider whether criminals are intrinsically negative and harmful people or whether they will remain perpetually in the same state of mind in which they committed their crime or not. The answer, I believe, is definitely not. However horrible the act they have committed, I believe that everyone has the potential to improve and correct themselves. Therefore, I am optimistic that it remains possible to deter criminal activity, and prevent such harmful consequences of such acts in society, without having to resort to the death penalty.

My overriding belief is that it is always possible for criminals to improve and that by its very finality the death penalty contradicts this. Therefore, I support those organizations and individuals who are trying to bring an end to the use of the death penalty.

Today, in many societies very little importance is placed on education or the development of human values through social programs and entertainment. In fact, if we take television programming as an example, violence, including killing, is regarded as having a high entertainment value. This is indicative of how misguided we have become.

I believe human beings are not violent by nature. Unlike lions and tigers, we are not naturally equipped to kill with sharp teeth and claws. From a Buddhist viewpoint, I believe that the basic nature of every sentient being is pure, that the deeper nature of mind is something pure. Human beings become violent because of negative thoughts which arise as a result of their environment and circumstances.

I wholeheartedly support an appeal to those countries who at present employ the death penalty to observe an unconditional moratorium. At the same time we should give more support to education and encourage a greater sense of universal responsibility. We need to explain the importance of the practice of love and compassion for our own survival and to try to minimize those conditions which foster murderous tendencies, such as the proliferation of weapons in our societies. These are things even private individuals can work towards.

Gregg v. Georgia (1976)

In response to Furman v. Georgia *(1972), which held that, as applied, the death penalty violated the Eighth Amendment, thirty-five states passed revised death penalty statutes. Ten states attempted to eliminate jury discretion by making the death penalty mandatory for certain crimes; twenty-five states implemented two-stage procedures in capital cases: the first stage of the trial would determine guilt or innocence, and the second would determine punishment. In* Gregg, *the Supreme Court upheld the two-stage procedure.*

Judgment of the Court, and opinion of MR. JUSTICE STEWART, MR. JUSTICE POWELL, and MR. JUSTICE STEVENS, announced by MR. JUSTICE STEWART.

The issue in this case is whether the imposition of the sentence of death for the crime of murder under the law of Georgia violates the Eighth and Fourteenth Amendments.

I

The petitioner, Troy Gregg, was charged with committing armed robbery and murder. In accordance with Georgia procedure in capital cases, the trial was in two stages, a guilt stage and a sentencing stage. The evidence at the guilt trial established that on November 21, 1973, the petitioner and a traveling companion, Floyd Allen, while hitchhiking north in Florida were picked up by Fred Simmons and Bob Moore. . . . [T]he four men interrupted their journey for a rest stop along the highway. The next morning the bodies of Simmons and Moore were discovered in a ditch nearby.

. . . [T]he petitioner and Allen, while in Simmons' car, were arrested in Asheville, N.C. In the search incident to the arrest a .25-caliber pistol, later shown to be that used to kill Simmons and Moore, was found in the petitioner's pocket. After receiving the warnings required by *Miranda v. Arizona,* and signing a written waiver of his rights, the petitioner signed a statement in which he admitted shooting, then robbing Simmons and Moore. He justified the slayings on grounds of self-defense. . . .

The trial judge submitted the murder charges to the jury. . . . He also instructed on the issue of self-defense but declined to instruct on manslaughter. He submitted the robbery case to the jury. . . . The jury found the petitioner guilty of two counts of armed robbery and two counts of murder.

At the penalty stage, which took place before the same jury, neither the prosecutor nor the petitioner's lawyer offered any additional evidence. Both counsel, however, made lengthy arguments dealing generally with the propriety of capital punishment under the circumstances and with the weight of the evidence of guilt. The trial judge instructed the jury that it could recommend either a death sentence or a life prison sentence on each count. The judge further charged the jury that in determining what sentence was appropriate the jury was free to consider the facts and circumstances, if any, presented by the parties in mitigation or aggravation.

Finally, the judge instructed the jury that it "would not be authorized to consider [imposing] the penalty of death" unless it first found beyond a reasonable doubt one of these aggravating circumstances:

"One—That the offense of murder was committed while the offender was engaged in the commission of two other capital felonies, to wit the armed robbery of [Simmons and Moore].

"Two—That the offender committed the offense of murder for the purpose of receiving money and the automobile described in the indictment.

"Three—The offense of murder was outrageously and wantonly vile, horrible and inhuman, in that they [sic] involved the depravity of [the] mind of the defendant."

Finding the first and second of these circumstances, the jury returned verdicts of death on each count.

The Supreme Court of Georgia affirmed the convictions and the imposition of the death sentences for murder. . . . The death sentences imposed for armed robbery, however, were vacated on the grounds that the death penalty had rarely been imposed in Georgia for that offense and that the jury improperly considered the murders as aggravating circumstances for the robberies after having considered the armed robberies as aggravating circumstances for the murders. . . .

III. . . .

It is clear from [these] precedents that the Eighth Amendment has not been regarded as a static concept. As Mr. Chief Justice Warren said, in an oft-quoted phrase, "[t]he Amendment must draw its meaning from the evolving standards of decency that mark the progress of a maturing society." *Trop v. Dulles*. Thus, an assessment of contemporary values concerning the infliction of a challenged sanction is relevant to the application of the Eighth Amendment. . . . [T]his assessment does not call for a subjective judgment. It requires, rather, that we look to objective indicia that reflect the public attitude toward a given sanction.

But our cases also make clear that public perceptions of standards of decency with respect to criminal sanctions are not conclusive. A penalty also must accord with "the dignity of man," which is the "basic concept underlying the Eighth Amendment." This means, at least, that the punishment not be "excessive." When a form of punishment in the abstract (in this case, whether capital punishment may ever be imposed as a sanction for murder) rather than in the particular (the propriety of death as a penalty to be applied to a specific defendant for a specific crime) is under consideration, the inquiry into "excessiveness" has two aspects. First, the punishment must not involve the unnecessary and wanton infliction of pain. . . . Second, the punishment must not be grossly out of proportion to the severity of the crime. *Trop v. Dulles*. . . .

Of course, the requirements of the Eighth Amendment must be applied with an awareness of the limited role to be played by the courts. . . .

Therefore, in assessing a punishment selected by a democratically elected legislature against the constitutional measure, we presume its validity. We may not require the legislature to select the least severe penalty possible so long as the penalty selected is not cruelly inhumane or disproportionate to the crime involved. And a heavy burden rests on those who would attack the judgment of the representatives of the people. . . .

. . . We now consider specifically whether the sentence of death for the crime of murder is a per se violation of the Eighth and Fourteenth Amendments to the Constitution. We note first that history and precedent strongly support a negative answer to this question.

The imposition of the death penalty for the crime of murder has a long history of acceptance both in the United States and in England. . . .

It is apparent from the text of the Constitution itself that the existence of capital punishment was accepted by the Framers. At the time the Eighth Amendment was ratified, capital punishment was a common sanction in every State. Indeed, the First Congress of the United States enacted legislation providing death as the penalty for specified crimes. . . .

And the Fourteenth Amendment, adopted over three-quarters of a century later, similarly contemplates the existence of the capital sanction in providing that no State shall deprive any person of "life, liberty, or property" without due process of law. . . .

Four years ago, the petitioners in *Furman* and its companion cases predicated their argument primarily upon the asserted proposition that standards of decency had evolved to the point where capital punishment no longer could be tolerated. The petitioners in those cases said, in effect, that the evolutionary process had come to an end, and that standards of decency required that the Eighth Amendment be construed finally as prohibiting capital punishment for any crime regardless of its depravity and impact on society. This view was accepted by two Justices. Three other Justices were unwilling to go so far; focusing on the procedures by which convicted defendants were selected for the death penalty rather than on the actual punishment inflicted, they joined in the conclusion that the statutes before the Court were constitutionally invalid.

The petitioners in the capital cases before the Court today renew the "standards of decency" argument, but developments during the four years since *Furman* have undercut substantially the assumptions upon which their argument rested. . . .

The most marked indication of society's endorsement of the death penalty for murder is the legislative response to *Furman*. The legislatures of at least 35 States have enacted new statutes that provide for the death penalty for at least some crimes that result in the death of another person. And the Congress of the United States, in 1974, enacted a statute providing the death penalty for aircraft piracy that results in death. These recently adopted statutes have attempted to address the concerns expressed by the Court in *Furman* primarily (i) by specifying the factors to be weighed and the procedures to be followed in deciding when to impose a capital sentence, or (ii) by making the death penalty mandatory for specified crimes. But all of the post-*Furman* statutes make clear that capital punishment itself has not been rejected by the elected representatives of the people.

In the only statewide referendum occurring since *Furman* and brought to our attention, the people of California adopted a constitutional amendment that authorized capital punishment, in effect negating a prior ruling by the Supreme Court of California . . . that the death penalty violated the California Constitution. . . .

The jury also is a significant and reliable objective index of contemporary values because it is so directly involved. . . . It may be true that evolving standards have influenced juries in recent decades to be more discriminating in imposing the sentence of death. But the relative infrequency of jury verdicts imposing the death sentence does not indicate rejection of capital punishment per se. Rather, the reluctance of juries in many cases to impose the sentence may well reflect the humane feeling that this most irrevocable of sanctions should be reserved for a small number of extreme cases. . . .

As we have seen, however, the Eighth Amendment demands more than that a challenged punishment be acceptable to contemporary society. The Court also must ask whether it comports with the basic concept of human dignity at the core of the Amendment. . . .

The death penalty is said to serve two principal social purposes: retribution and deterrence of capital crimes by prospective offenders.

In part, capital punishment is an expression of society's moral outrage at particularly offensive conduct. This function may be unappealing to many, but it is essential in an ordered society that asks its citizens to rely on legal processes rather than self-help to vindicate their wrongs. . . .

Statistical attempts to evaluate the worth of the death penalty as a deterrent to crimes by potential offenders have occasioned a great deal of debate. The results simply have been inconclusive. . . .

In sum, we cannot say that the judgment of the Georgia Legislature that capital punishment may be necessary in some cases is clearly wrong. . . .

Finally, we must consider whether the punishment of death is disproportionate in relation to the crime for which it is imposed. There is no question that death as a punishment is unique in its severity and irrevocability. . . . But we are concerned here only with the imposition of capital punishment for the crime of murder, and when a life has been taken deliberately by the offender, we cannot say that the punishment is invariably disproportionate to the crime. It is an extreme sanction, suitable to the most extreme of crimes.

We hold that the death penalty is not a form of punishment that may never be imposed, regardless of the circumstances of the offense, regardless of the character of the offender, and regardless of the procedure followed in reaching the decision to impose it.

IV

We now consider whether Georgia may impose the death penalty on the petitioner in this case. . . .

Furman mandates that where discretion is afforded a sentencing body on a matter so grave as the determination of whether a human life should be taken or spared, that discretion must be suitably directed and limited so as to minimize the risk of wholly arbitrary and capricious action. . . .

Jury sentencing has been considered desirable in capital cases in order "to maintain a link between contemporary community values and the penal system—a link without which the determination of punishment could hardly reflect 'the evolving standards of decency that mark the progress of a maturing society.'" But it creates special problems. . . . Those who have studied the question suggest that a bifurcated procedure—one in which the question of sentence is not considered until the determination of guilt has been made—is the best answer. . . .

While some have suggested that standards to guide a capital jury's sentencing deliberation are impossible to formulate, the fact is that such standards have been developed. . . . While such standards are by necessity somewhat general, they do provide guidance to the sentencing authority and thereby reduce the likelihood that it will impose a sentence that fairly can be called capricious or arbitrary. Where the sentencing authority is required to specify the factors it relied upon in reaching its decision, the further safeguard of meaningful appellate review is available to ensure that death sentences are not imposed capriciously or in a freakish manner.

In summary, the concerns expressed in *Furman* that the penalty of death not be imposed in an arbitrary or capricious manner can be met by a carefully drafted statute that ensures that the sentencing authority is given adequate information and guidance. As a general proposition these concerns are best met by a system that provides for a bifurcated proceeding at which the sentencing authority is apprised of the information relevant to the imposition of sentence and provided with standards to guide its use of the information. . . .

We now turn to consideration of the constitutionality of Georgia's capital-sentencing procedures. In the wake of *Furman*, Georgia amended its capital punishment statute, but chose not to narrow the scope of its murder provisions. Thus, now as before *Furman*, in Georgia "[a] person commits murder when he unlawfully and with malice aforethought, either express or implied, causes the death of another human being." All persons convicted of murder "shall be punished by death or by imprisonment for life."

Georgia did act, however, to narrow the class of murderers subject to capital punishment by specifying statutory aggravating circumstances, one of which must be found by the jury to exist beyond a reasonable doubt before a death sentence can ever be imposed. In addition, the jury is authorized to consider any other appropriate aggravating or mitigating circumstances. The jury is not required to find any mitigating circumstance in order to make a recommendation of mercy that is binding on the trial court, but it must find a statutory aggravating circumstance before recommending a sentence of death.

These procedures require the jury to consider the circumstances of the crime and the criminal before it recommends sentence. No longer can a Georgia jury do as *Furman*'s jury did: reach a finding of the defendant's guilt and then, without guidance or direction, decide whether he should live or die. Instead, the jury's attention is directed to the specific circumstances of the crime: Was it committed in the course of another capital felony? Was it committed for money? Was it committed upon a peace officer or judicial officer? Was it committed in a particularly heinous way or in a manner that endangered the lives of many persons? In addition, the jury's attention is focused on the characteristics of the person who committed the crime: Does he have a record of prior convictions for capital offenses? Are there any special facts about this defendant that mitigate against imposing capital punishment (e.g., his youth, the extent of his cooperation with the police, his emotional state at the time of the crime). As a result, while some jury discretion still exists, "the discretion to be exercised is controlled by clear and objective standards so as to produce non-discriminatory application." . . .

Finally, the Georgia statute has an additional provision designed to assure that the death penalty will not be imposed on a capriciously selected group of convicted defendants. The new sentencing procedures require that the State Supreme Court review every death sentence. . . .

It is apparent that the Supreme Court of Georgia has taken its review responsibilities seriously. . . . [A]lthough armed robbery is a capital offense under Georgia law, the Georgia court concluded that the death sentences imposed in this case for that crime were "unusual in that they are rarely imposed for [armed robbery]. Thus, under the test provided by statute, . . . they must be considered to be excessive or disproportionate to the penalties imposed in similar cases." The court therefore vacated Gregg's death sentences for armed robbery and has followed a similar course in every other armed robbery death penalty case to come before it.

The provision for appellate review in the Georgia capital-sentencing system serves as a check against the random or arbitrary imposition of the death penalty. . . .

V. . . .

For the reasons expressed in this opinion, we hold that the statutory system under which Gregg was sentenced to death does not violate the Constitution. Accordingly, the judgment of the Georgia Supreme Court is affirmed. . . .

MR. JUSTICE BRENNAN, dissenting.

The Cruel and Unusual Punishments Clause "must draw its meaning from the evolving standards of decency that mark the progress of a maturing society." The [majority] opinions . . . hold that "evolving standards of decency" require focus not on the essence of the death penalty itself but primarily upon the procedures employed by the State to single out persons to suffer the penalty of death. Those opinions hold further that, so viewed, the Clause invalidates the mandatory infliction of the death penalty but not its infliction under sentencing procedures that . . . adequately safeguard against the risk that the death penalty was imposed in an arbitrary and capricious manner.

In *Furman v. Georgia*, I read "evolving standards of decency" as requiring focus upon the essence of the death penalty itself and not primarily or solely upon the procedures under which the determination to inflict the penalty upon a particular person was made....

This Court inescapably has the duty, as the ultimate arbiter of the meaning of our Constitution, to say whether, when individuals condemned to death stand before our Bar, "moral concepts" require us to hold that the law has progressed to the point where we should declare that the punishment of death, like punishments on the rack, the screw, and the wheel, is no longer morally tolerable in our civilized society. My opinion in *Furman v. Georgia* concluded that our civilization and the law had progressed to this point and that therefore the punishment of death, for whatever crime and under all circumstances, is "cruel and unusual" in violation of the Eighth and Fourteenth Amendments of the Constitution....

The fatal constitutional infirmity in the punishment of death is that it treats "members of the human race as nonhumans, as objects to be toyed with and discarded. [It is] thus inconsistent with the fundamental premise of the Clause that even the vilest criminal remains a human being possessed of common human dignity." As such it is a penalty that "subjects the individual to a fate forbidden by the principle of civilized treatment guaranteed by the [Clause]." I therefore would hold, on that ground alone, that death is today a cruel and unusual punishment prohibited by the Clause. "Justice of this kind is obviously no less shocking than the crime itself, and the new 'official' murder, far from offering redress for the offense committed against society, adds instead a second defilement to the first." ...

MR. JUSTICE MARSHALL, dissenting.

... In *Furman* I concluded that the death penalty is constitutionally invalid for two reasons. First, the death penalty is excessive. And second, the American people, fully informed as to the purposes of the death penalty and its liabilities, would in my view reject it as morally unacceptable.

Since the decision in *Furman*, the legislatures of 35 States have enacted new statutes authorizing the imposition of the death sentence for certain crimes, and Congress has enacted a law providing the death penalty for air piracy resulting in death. I would be less than candid if I did not acknowledge that these developments have a significant bearing on a realistic assessment of the moral acceptability of the death penalty to the American people. But if the constitutionality of the death penalty turns, as I have urged, on the opinion of an informed citizenry, then even the enactment of new death statutes cannot be viewed as conclusive. In *Furman*, I observed that the American people are largely unaware of the information critical to a judgment on the morality of the death penalty, and concluded that if they were better informed they would consider it shocking, unjust, and unacceptable. A recent study, conducted after the enactment of the post-*Furman* statutes, has confirmed that the American people know little about the death penalty, and that the opinions of an informed public would differ significantly from those of a public unaware of the consequences and effects of the death penalty. . . .

WOODSON V. NORTH CAROLINA (1976)

In Woodson v. North Carolina *and the companion case,* Roberts v. Louisiana, *the Court struck down state laws that made the death penalty mandatory for first-degree murder. The Court voted five to four, with Justices Brennan, Marshall, Stewart, Powell, and Stevens in the majority and Chief Justice Burger and Justices Blackmun, White, and Rehnquist in the minority.*

Judgment of the Court, and opinion of MR. JUSTICE STEWART, MR. JUSTICE POWELL, and MR. JUSTICE STEVENS, announced by MR. JUSTICE STEWART.

The question in this case is whether the imposition of a death sentence for the crime of first-degree murder under the law of North Carolina violates the Eighth and Fourteenth Amendments.

The petitioners were convicted of first-degree murder as the result of their participation in an armed robbery of a convenience food store, in the course of which the cashier was killed and a customer was seriously wounded. There were four participants in the robbery: the petitioners James Tyrone Woodson and Luby Waxton and two others, Leonard Tucker and Johnnie Lee Carroll. . . .

The evidence for the prosecution established that the four men had been discussing a possible robbery for some time. On the fatal day Woodson had been drinking heavily. About 9:30 P.M., Waxton and Tucker came to the trailer where Woodson was staying. When Woodson came out of the trailer, Waxton struck him in the face and threatened to kill him in an effort to make him sober up and come along on the robbery. . . . Upon arriving at their destination Tucker and Waxton went into the store while Carroll and Woodson remained in the car as lookouts. Once inside the store, Tucker purchased a package of cigarettes from the woman cashier. Waxton then also asked for a package of cigarettes, but as the cashier approached him he pulled the derringer out of his hip pocket and fatally shot her at point-blank range. Waxton then took the money tray from the cash register and gave it to Tucker, who carried it out of the store, pushing past an entering customer as he reached the door. After he was outside, Tucker heard a second shot from inside the store, and shortly thereafter Waxton emerged, carrying a handful of paper money. Tucker and Waxton got in the car and the four drove away.

The petitioners' testimony agreed in large part with this version of the circumstances of the robbery. It differed diametrically in one important respect: Waxton claimed that he never had a gun, and that Tucker had shot both the cashier and the customer.

During the trial Waxton asked to be allowed to plead guilty to the same lesser offenses to which Tucker had pleaded guilty, but the solicitor refused to accept the pleas. Woodson, by contrast, maintained throughout the trial that he had been coerced by Waxton, that he was therefore innocent, and that he would not consider pleading guilty to any offense.

The petitioners were found guilty on all charges, and, as was required by statute, sentenced to death. The Supreme Court of North Carolina affirmed. We granted certiorari to consider whether the imposition of the death penalties in this case comports with the Eighth and Fourteenth Amendments to the United States Constitution. . . .

The history of mandatory death penalty statutes in the United States thus reveals that the practice of sentencing to death all persons convicted of a particular offense has been rejected as unduly harsh and unworkably rigid. The two crucial indicators of evolving standards of decency respecting the imposition of punishment in our society—jury determinations and legislative enactments—both point conclusively to the repudiation of automatic death sentences. At least since the Revolution, American jurors have, with some regularity, disregarded their oaths and refused to convict defendants where a death sentence was the automatic consequence of a guilty verdict. . . . Thereafter, continuing evidence of jury reluctance to convict persons of capital offenses in mandatory death penalty jurisdictions resulted in legislative authorization of discretionary jury sentencing. . . .

It is now well established that the Eighth Amendment draws much of its meaning from "the evolving standards of decency that mark the progress of a maturing society." *Trop v. Dulles*. . . . [O]ne of the most significant developments in our society's treatment of capital punishment has been the rejection of the common-law practice of inexorably imposing a death sentence upon every person convicted of a specified offense. North Carolina's mandatory death penalty statute for first-degree murder departs markedly from contemporary standards respecting the imposition of the punishment of death and thus cannot be applied consistently with the Eighth and Fourteenth Amendments' requirement that the State's power to punish "be exercised within the limits of civilized standards." . . .

It is argued that North Carolina has remedied the inadequacies of the death penalty statutes held unconstitutional in *Furman* by withdrawing all sentencing discretion from juries in capital cases. But when one considers the long and consistent American experience with the death penalty in first-degree murder cases, it becomes evident that mandatory statutes enacted in response to *Furman* have simply papered over the problem of unguided and unchecked jury discretion. . . .

[Another] constitutional shortcoming of the North Carolina statute is its failure to allow the particularized consideration of relevant aspects of the character and record of each convicted defendant before the imposition upon him of a sentence of death. . . . A process that accords no significance to relevant facets of the character and record of the individual offender or the circumstances of the particular offense excludes from consideration in fixing the ultimate punishment of death the possibility of compassionate or mitigating factors stemming from the diverse frailties of humankind. It treats all persons convicted of a designated offense not as uniquely individual human beings, but as members of a faceless, undifferentiated mass to be subjected to the blind infliction of the penalty of death.

. . . While the prevailing practice of individualizing sentencing determinations generally reflects simply enlightened policy rather than a constitutional imperative, we believe that in capital cases the fundamental respect for humanity underlying the Eighth Amendment requires consideration of the character and record of the individual offender and the circumstances of the particular offense as a constitutionally indispensable part of the process of inflicting the penalty of death. . . .

For the reasons stated, we conclude that the death sentences imposed upon the petitioners under North Carolina's mandatory death sentence statute violated the Eighth and Fourteenth Amendments and therefore must be set aside. . . .

Coker v. Georgia (1977)

In Coker v Georgia, *the Court ruled that for rape of an adult, death is an excessive penalty.*

MR. JUSTICE WHITE announced the judgment of the Court and filed an opinion in which MR. JUSTICE STEWART, MR. JUSTICE BLACKMUN, and MR. JUSTICE STEVENS joined.

Georgia Code Ann. 26–2001 (1972) provides that "[a] person convicted of rape shall be punished by death or by imprisonment for life, or by imprisonment for not less than one nor more than 20 years." Punishment is determined by a jury in a separate sentencing proceeding in which at least one of the statutory aggravating circumstances must be found before the death penalty may be imposed. Petitioner Coker was convicted of rape and sentenced to death. Both the conviction and the sentence were affirmed by the Georgia Supreme Court. Coker was granted a writ of certiorari, limited to the single claim, rejected by the Georgia court, that the punishment of death for rape violates the Eighth Amendment, which proscribes "cruel and unusual punishments" and which must be observed by the States as well as the Federal Government.

I

While serving various sentences for murder, rape, kidnaping, and aggravated assault, petitioner escaped from the Ware Correctional Institution near Waycross, Ga., on September 2, 1974. At approximately 11 o'-clock that night, petitioner entered the house of Allen and Elnita Carver through an unlocked kitchen door. Threatening the couple with a "board," he tied up Mr. Carver in the bathroom, obtained a knife from the kitchen, and took Mr. Carver's money and the keys to the family car. Brandishing the knife and saying "you know what's going to happen to you if you try anything, don't you," Coker then raped Mrs. Carver.

Soon thereafter, petitioner drove away in the Carver car, taking Mrs. Carver with him. Mr. Carver, freeing himself, notified the police; and not long thereafter petitioner was apprehended. Mrs. Carver was unharmed.

Petitioner was charged with escape, armed robbery, motor vehicle theft, kidnaping, and rape. . . . The jury returned a verdict of guilty, rejecting his general plea of insanity. A sentencing hearing was then conducted in accordance with the procedures dealt with at length in *Gregg v. Georgia*. . . . The jury was instructed that it could consider as aggravating circumstances whether the rape had been committed by a person with a prior record of conviction for a capital felony and whether the rape had been committed in the course of committing another capital felony, namely, the armed robbery of Allen Carver. The court also instructed, pursuant to statute, that even if aggravating circumstances were present, the death penalty need not be imposed if the jury found they were outweighed by mitigating circumstances, that is, circumstances not constituting justification or excuse for the offense in question, "but which, in fairness and mercy, may be considered as extenuating or reducing the degree" of moral culpability or punishment. The jury's verdict on the rape count was death by electrocution. Both aggravating circumstances on which the court instructed were found to be present by the jury.

II

. . . It is now settled that the death penalty is not invariably cruel and unusual punishment within the meaning of the Eighth Amendment; it is not inherently barbaric or an unacceptable mode of punishment for crime; neither is it always disproportionate to the crime for which it is imposed. It is also established that imposing capital punishment, at least for murder, in accordance with the procedures provided under the Georgia statutes saves the sentence from the infirmities which led the Court to invalidate the prior Georgia capital punishment statute in *Furman v. Georgia*.

In sustaining the imposition of the death penalty in *Gregg*, however, the Court firmly embraced the holdings and dicta from prior cases . . . to the effect that the Eighth Amendment bars not only those punishments that are "barbaric" but also those that are "excessive" in relation to the crime committed. Under *Gregg*, a punishment is "excessive" and unconstitutional if it (1) makes no measurable contribution to acceptable goals of punishment and hence is nothing more than the purposeless and needless imposition of pain and suffering; or (2) is grossly out of proportion to the severity of the crime. A punishment might fail the test on either ground. Furthermore, these Eighth Amendment judgments should not be, or appear to be, merely the subjective views of individual Justices; judgment should be informed by objective factors to the maximum possible extent. To this end, attention must be given to the public attitudes concerning a particular sentence—history and precedent, legislative attitudes, and the response of juries reflected in their sentencing decisions are to be consulted. In *Gregg*, after giving due regard to such sources, the Court's judgment was that the death penalty for deliberate murder was neither the purposeless imposition of severe punishment nor a punishment grossly disproportionate to the crime. But the Court reserved the question of the constitutionality of the death penalty when imposed for other crimes.

III

That question, with respect to rape of an adult woman, is now before us. We have concluded that a sentence of death is grossly disproportionate and excessive punishment for the crime of rape and is therefore forbidden by the Eighth Amendment as cruel and unusual punishment.

As advised by recent cases, we seek guidance in history and from the objective evidence of the country's present judgment concerning the acceptability of death as a penalty for rape of an adult woman. At no time in the last 50 years have a majority of the States authorized death as a punishment for rape. . . . *Furman* then invalidated most of the capital punishment statutes in this country, including the rape statutes, because, among other reasons, of the manner in which the death penalty was imposed and utilized under those laws.

With their death penalty statutes for the most part invalidated, the States were faced with the choice of enacting modified capital punishment laws in an attempt to satisfy the requirements of *Furman* or of being satisfied with life imprisonment as the ultimate punishment for any offense. Thirty-five States immediately reinstituted the death penalty for at least limited kinds of crime. . . .

But if the "most marked indication of society's endorsement of the death penalty for murder is the legislative response to *Furman*," *Gregg v. Georgia,* it should also be a telling datum that the public judgment with respect to rape, as reflected in the statutes providing the punishment for that crime, has been dramatically different. In reviving death penalty laws to satisfy *Furman*'s mandate, none of the States that had not previously authorized death for rape chose to include rape among capital felonies. . . .

It should be noted that Florida, Mississippi, and Tennessee also authorized the death penalty in some rape cases, but only where the victim was a child and the rapist an adult. The Tennessee statute has since been invalidated because the death sentence was mandatory. The upshot is that Georgia is the sole jurisdiction in the United States at the present time that authorizes a sentence of death when the rape victim is an adult woman, and only two other jurisdictions provide capital punishment when the victim is a child.

The current judgment with respect to the death penalty for rape is not wholly unanimous among state legislatures, but it obviously weighs very heavily on the side of rejecting capital punishment as a suitable penalty for raping an adult woman.

It was also observed in *Gregg* that "[t]he jury . . . is a significant and reliable objective index of contemporary values. . . ."

According to the factual submissions in this Court, out of all rape convictions in Georgia since 1973 . . . in the vast majority of cases, at least 9 out of 10, juries have not imposed the death sentence.

IV

These recent events evidencing the attitude of state legislatures and sentencing juries do not wholly determine this controversy, for the Constitution contemplates that in the end our own judgment will be brought to bear on the question of the acceptability of the death penalty under the Eighth Amendment. Nevertheless, the legislative rejection of capital punishment for rape strongly confirms our own judgment, which is that death is indeed a disproportionate penalty for the crime of raping an adult woman.

We do not discount the seriousness of rape as a crime. It is highly reprehensible, both in a moral sense and in its almost total contempt for the personal integrity and autonomy of the female victim and for the latter's privilege of choosing those with whom intimate relationships are to be established. Short of homicide, it is the "ultimate violation of self." It is also a violent crime because it normally involves force, or the threat of force or intimidation, to overcome the will and the capacity of the victim to resist. Rape is very often accompanied by physical injury to the female and can also inflict mental and psychological damage. Because it undermines the community's sense of security, there is public injury as well.

Rape is without doubt deserving of serious punishment; but in terms of moral depravity and of the injury to the person and to the public, it does not compare with murder, which does involve the unjustified taking of human life. Although it may be accompanied by another crime, rape by definition does not include the death of or even the serious injury to another person. The murderer kills; the rapist, if no more than that, does not. Life is over for the victim of the murderer; for the rape victim, life may not be nearly so happy as it was, but it is not over and normally is not beyond repair. We have the abiding conviction that the death penalty, which "is unique in its severity and irrevocability," is an excessive penalty for the rapist who, as such, does not take human life....

MR. JUSTICE BRENNAN, concurring in the judgment.

Adhering to my view that the death penalty is in all circumstances cruel and unusual punishment prohibited by the Eighth and Fourteenth Amendments, *Gregg v. Georgia* (dissenting opinion), I concur in the judgment of the Court setting aside the death sentence imposed under the Georgia rape statute.

MR. JUSTICE MARSHALL, concurring in the judgment.

In *Gregg v. Georgia* (dissenting opinion), I stated: "In *Furman v. Georgia* (concurring opinion), I set forth at some length my views on the basic issue presented to the Court in these cases. The death penalty, I concluded, is a cruel and unusual punishment prohibited by the Eighth and Fourteenth Amendments. That continues to be my view." ...

MR. JUSTICE POWELL, concurring in the judgment in part and dissenting in part.

I concur in the judgment of the Court on the facts of this case, and also in the plurality's reasoning supporting the view that ordinarily death is disproportionate punishment for the crime of raping an adult woman. Although rape invariably is a reprehensible crime, there is no indication that petitioner's offense was committed with excessive brutality or that the victim sustained serious or lasting injury. The plurality, however, does not limit its holding to the case before us or to similar cases. Rather, in an opinion that ranges well beyond what is necessary, it holds that capital punishment always—regardless of the circumstances—is a disproportionate penalty for the crime of rape....

Today, in a case that does not require such an expansive pronouncement, the plurality draws a bright line between murder and all rapes—regardless of the degree of brutality of the rape or the effect upon the victim. I dissent because I am not persuaded that such a bright line is appropriate. As noted in *Snider v. Peyton*, "[t]here is extreme variation in the degree of culpability of rapists." The deliberate viciousness of the rapist may be greater than that of the murderer. Rape is never an act committed accidentally. Rarely can it be said to be unpremeditated. There also is wide variation in the effect on the victim. The plurality opinion says that "[l]ife is over for the victim of the murderer; for the rape victim, life may not be nearly so happy as it was, but it is not over and normally is not beyond repair." But there is indeed "extreme variation" in the crime of rape. Some victims are so grievously injured physically or psychologically that life is beyond repair.

Thus, it may be that the death penalty is not disproportionate punishment for the crime of aggravated rape. Final resolution of the question must await careful inquiry into objective indicators of society's "evolving standards of decency," particularly legislative enactments and the responses of juries in capital cases. . . . The plurality properly examines [precedents] which do support the conclusion that society finds the death penalty unacceptable for the crime of rape in the absence of excessive brutality or severe injury. But it has not been shown that society finds the penalty disproportionate for all rapes. In a proper case a more discriminating inquiry than the plurality undertakes well might discover that both juries and legislatures have reserved the ultimate penalty for the case of an outrageous rape resulting in serious, lasting harm to the victim. I would not prejudge the issue. To this extent, I respectfully dissent.

MR. CHIEF JUSTICE BURGER, with whom MR. JUSTICE REHNQUIST joins, dissenting.

In a case such as this, confusion often arises as to the Court's proper role in reaching a decision. Our task is not to give effect to our individual views on capital punishment; rather, we must determine what the Constitution permits a State to do under its reserved powers. In striking down the death penalty imposed upon the petitioner in this case, the Court has overstepped the bounds of proper constitutional adjudication by substituting its policy judgment for that of the state legislature. I accept that the Eighth Amendment's concept of disproportionality bars the death penalty for minor crimes. But rape is not a minor crime; hence the Cruel and Unusual Punishments Clause does not give the Members of this Court license to engraft their conceptions of proper public policy onto the considered legislative judgments of the States. Since I cannot agree that Georgia lacked the constitutional power to impose the penalty of death for rape, I dissent from the Court's judgment. . . .

Unlike the plurality, I would narrow the inquiry in this case to the question actually presented: Does the Eighth Amendment's ban against cruel and unusual punishment prohibit the State of Georgia from executing a person who has, within the space of three years, raped three separate women, killing one and attempting to kill another, who is serving prison terms exceeding his probable lifetime and who has not hesitated to escape confinement at the first available opportunity? Whatever one's view may be as to the State's constitutional power to impose the death penalty upon a rapist who stands before a court convicted for the first time, this case reveals a chronic rapist whose continuing danger to the community is abundantly clear. . . .

LOCKETT V. OHIO (1978)

An Ohio statute limited the range of mitigating factors that could be considered by a sentencing judge in capital cases. The United States Supreme Court ruled that the state death penalty law was unconstitutional because it did not permit consideration of a wide range of relevant mitigating factors. In Bell v. Ohio, *decided on the same day, the Court also held that a judge must be permitted to consider relevant mitigating factors. In Chief Justice Burger's words, a trial judge must not be precluded by a state law "from considering as a mitigating factor, any aspect of the defendant's character or record and any of the circumstances of the offense that the defendant proffers."*

CHIEF JUSTICE BURGER announced the Court's judgment and delivered an opinion of the Court with respect to Parts I and II, in which JUSTICES STEWART, WHITE, BLACKMUN, POWELL, REHNQUIST, and STEVENS joined, and an opinion with respect to Part III, in which JUSTICES STEWART, POWELL, and STEVENS joined.

We granted certiorari in this case to consider . . . whether Ohio violated the Eighth and Fourteenth Amendments by sentencing Sandra Lockett to death pursuant to a statute that narrowly limits the sentencer's discretion to consider the circumstances of the crime and the record and character of the offender as mitigating factors.

I

Lockett was charged with aggravated murder with the aggravating specifications (1) that the murder was "committed for the purpose of escaping detection, apprehension, trial, or punishment" for aggravated robbery, and (2) that the murder was "committed while . . . committing, attempting to commit, or fleeing immediately after committing or attempting to commit . . . aggravated robbery." That offense was punishable by death in Ohio. . . . She was also charged with aggravated robbery. The State's case against her depended largely upon the testimony of a coparticipant, one Al Parker, who gave the following account of her participation in the robbery and murder.

Lockett became acquainted with Parker and Nathan Earl Dew while she and a friend, Joanne Baxter, were in New Jersey. Parker and Dew then accompanied Lockett, Baxter, and Lockett's brother back to Akron, Ohio, Lockett's hometown. After they arrived in Akron, Parker and Dew needed money for the trip back to New Jersey. Dew suggested that he pawn his ring. Lockett . . . felt that the ring was too beautiful to pawn, and suggested instead that they could get some money by robbing a grocery store and a furniture store in the area. She warned that the grocery store's operator was a "big guy" who carried a "45" and that they would have "to get him real quick." She also volunteered to get a gun from her father's basement to aid in carrying out the robberies, but by that time, the two stores had closed and it was too late to proceed with the plan to rob them.

Someone, apparently Lockett's brother, suggested a plan for robbing a pawnshop. He and Dew would enter the shop and pretend to pawn a ring. Next Parker, who had some bullets, would enter the shop, ask to see a gun, load it, and use it to rob the shop. No one planned to kill the pawnshop operator in the course of the robbery. Because she knew the owner, Lockett was not to be among those entering the pawnshop, though she did guide the others to the shop that night.

The next day Parker, Dew, Lockett, and her brother gathered at Baxter's apartment. Lockett's brother asked if they were "still going to do it," and everyone, including Lockett, agreed to proceed. The four then drove by the pawnshop several times and parked the car. Lockett's brother and Dew entered the shop. Parker then left the car and told

Lockett to start it again in two minutes. The robbery proceeded according to plan until the pawnbroker grabbed the gun when Parker announced the "stickup." The gun went off with Parker's finger on the trigger, firing a fatal shot into the pawnbroker.

Parker went back to the car where Lockett waited with the engine running. While driving away from the pawnshop, Parker told Lockett what had happened. She took the gun from the pawnshop and put it into her purse. Lockett and Parker drove to Lockett's aunt's house and called a taxicab. Shortly thereafter, while riding away in a taxicab, they were stopped by the police. . . .

Parker was . . . charged with aggravated murder with specifications, an offense punishable by death, and aggravated robbery. Prior to trial, he pleaded guilty to the murder charge and agreed to testify against Lockett, her brother, and Dew. In return, the prosecutor dropped the aggravated robbery charge and the specifications to the murder charge, thereby eliminating the possibility that Parker could receive the death penalty.

Lockett's brother and Dew were later convicted of aggravated murder with specifications. Lockett's brother was sentenced to death, but Dew received a lesser penalty because it was determined that his offense was "primarily the product of mental deficiency," one of the three mitigating circumstances specified in the Ohio death penalty statute. . . .

At trial, the opening argument of Lockett's defense counsel summarized . . . Lockett's version of the events leading to the killing. He asserted . . . that, as far as Lockett knew, Dew and her brother had planned to pawn Dew's ring for $100 to obtain money for the trip back to New Jersey. Lockett had not waited in the car while the men went into the pawnshop but had gone to a restaurant for lunch and had joined Parker, thinking the ring had been pawned, after she saw him walking back to the car. . . .

[At trial], [t]he court instructed the jury that, before it could find Lockett guilty, it had to find that she purposely had killed the pawnbroker while committing or attempting to commit aggravated robbery. The jury was further charged that one who

"purposely aids, helps, associates himself or herself with another for the purpose of committing a crime is regarded as if he or she were the principal offender and is just as guilty as if the person performed every act constituting the offense. . . ."

Regarding the intent requirement, the court instructed:

"A person engaged in a common design with others to rob by force and violence an individual or individuals of their property is presumed to acquiesce in whatever may reasonably be necessary to accomplish the object of their enterprise. . . .

"If the conspired robbery and the manner of its accomplishment would be reasonably likely to produce death, each plotter is equally guilty with the principal offender as an aider and abettor in the homicide. . . . An intent to kill by an aider and abettor may be found to exist beyond a reasonable doubt under such circumstances."

The jury found Lockett guilty as charged.

Once a verdict of aggravated murder with specifications had been returned, the Ohio death penalty statute required the trial judge to impose a death sentence unless, after "considering the nature and circumstances of the offense" and Lockett's "history, character, and condition," he found by a preponderance of the evidence that (1) the victim had induced or facilitated the offense, (2) it was unlikely that Lockett would have committed the offense but for the fact that she "was under duress, coercion, or strong provocation," or (3) the offense was "primarily the product of [Lockett's] psychosis or mental deficiency."

In accord with the Ohio statute, the trial judge requested a presentence report as well as psychiatric and psychological reports. The reports contained detailed information about Lockett's intelligence, character, and background. The psychiatric and psychological reports described her as a 21-year-old with low-average or average intelligence, and not suffering from a mental deficiency. One of the psychologists reported that "her prognosis for rehabilitation" if returned to society was favorable. The presentence report showed that Lockett had committed no major offenses although she had a record of several minor ones as a juvenile and two minor offenses as an adult. It also showed that she had once used heroin but was receiving treatment at a drug abuse clinic and seemed to be "on the road to success" as far as her drug problem was concerned. It concluded that Lockett suffered no psychosis and was not mentally deficient.

After considering the reports and hearing argument on the penalty issue, the trial judge concluded that the offense had not been primarily the product of psychosis or mental deficiency. Without specifically addressing the other two statutory mitigating factors, the judge said that he had "no alternative, whether [he] like[d] the law or not" but to impose the death penalty. He then sentenced Lockett to death. . . .

III

. . . We find it necessary to consider only [Lockett's] contention that her death sentence is invalid because the statute under which it was imposed did not permit the sentencing judge to consider, as mitigating factors, her character, prior record, age, lack of specific intent to cause death, and her relatively minor part in the crime. . . .

. . . Essentially [Lockett] contends that the Eighth and Fourteenth Amendments require that the sentencer be given a full opportunity to consider mitigating circumstances in capital cases and that the Ohio statute does not comply with that requirement. . . .

We begin by recognizing that the concept of individualized sentencing in criminal cases generally, although not constitutionally required, has long been accepted in this country. . . .

The opinions of this Court going back many years in dealing with sentencing in capital cases have noted the strength of the basis for individualized sentencing. For example, Mr. Justice Black, writing for the Court in *Williams v. New York*—a capital case—observed that the

"whole country has traveled far from the period in which the death sentence was an automatic and commonplace result of convictions—even for offenses today deemed trivial."

Ten years later, in *Williams v. Oklahoma*, another capital case, the Court echoed Mr. Justice Black, stating that

"[i]n discharging his duty of imposing a proper sentence, the sentencing judge is authorized, if not required, to consider all of the mitigating and aggravating circumstances involved in the crime." . . .

Although legislatures remain free to decide how much discretion in sentencing should be reposed in the judge or jury in noncapital cases, the plurality opinion in *Woodson*, after reviewing the historical repudiation of mandatory sentencing in capital cases, concluded that

"in capital cases the fundamental respect for humanity underlying the Eighth Amendment . . . requires consideration of the character and record of the individual offender and the circumstances of the particular offense as a constitutionally indispensable part of the process of inflicting the penalty of death."

That declaration rested "on the predicate that the penalty of death is qualitatively different" from any other sentence. We are satisfied that this qualitative difference between death and other penalties calls for a greater degree of reliability when the death sentence is imposed. The mandatory death penalty statute in *Woodson* was held invalid because it permitted no consideration of "relevant facets of the character and record of the individual offender or the circumstances of the particular offense." The plurality did not attempt to indicate, however, which facets of an offender or his offense it deemed "relevant" in capital sentencing or what degree of consideration of "relevant facets" it would require.

We are now faced with those questions and we conclude that the Eighth and Fourteenth Amendments require that the sentencer, in all but the rarest kind of capital case, not be precluded from considering, as a mitigating factor, any aspect of a defendant's character or record and any of the circumstances of the offense that the defendant proffers as a basis for a sentence less than death. We recognize that, in noncapital cases, the established practice of individualized sentences rests not on constitutional commands, but on public policy enacted into statutes. The considerations that account for the wide acceptance of individualization of sentences in noncapital cases surely cannot be thought less important in capital cases. Given that the imposition of death by public authority is so profoundly different from all other penalties, we cannot avoid the conclusion that an individualized decision is essential in capital cases. The need for treating each defendant in a capital case with that degree of respect due the uniqueness of the individual is far more important than in noncapital cases. A variety of flexible techniques—probation, parole, work furloughs, to name a few—and various postconviction remedies may be available to modify an initial sentence of confinement in noncapital cases. The nonavailability of corrective or modifying mechanisms with respect to an executed capital sentence underscores the need for individualized consideration as a constitutional requirement in imposing the death sentence.

There is no perfect procedure for deciding in which cases governmental authority should be used to impose death. But a statute that prevents the sentencer in all capital cases from giving independent mitigating weight to aspects of the defendant's character and record and to circumstances of the offense proffered in mitigation creates the risk that the death penalty will be imposed in spite of factors which may call for a less severe penalty. When the choice is between life and death, that risk is unacceptable and incompatible with the commands of the Eighth and Fourteenth Amendments.

The Ohio death penalty statute does not permit the type of individualized consideration of mitigating factors we now hold to be required by the Eighth and Fourteenth Amendments in capital cases. . . .

The limited range of mitigating circumstances which may be considered by the sentencer under the Ohio statute is incompatible with the Eighth and Fourteenth Amendments. To meet constitutional requirements, a death penalty statute must not preclude consideration of relevant mitigating factors. Accordingly, the judgment under review is reversed to the extent that it sustains the imposition of the death penalty, and the case is remanded for further proceedings.

MR. JUSTICE MARSHALL, concurring in the judgment.

I continue to adhere to my view that the death penalty is, under all circumstances, a cruel and unusual punishment prohibited by the Eighth Amendment. . . . This case, as well, serves to reinforce my view.

When a death sentence is imposed under the circumstances presented here, I fail to understand how any of my Brethren—even those who believe that the death penalty is not wholly inconsistent with the Constitution—can disagree that it must be vacated. Under the Ohio death penalty statute, this 21-year-old Negro woman was sentenced to death for a killing that she did not actually commit or intend to commit. She was convicted under a theory of vicarious liability. The imposition of the death penalty for this crime totally violates the principle of proportionality embodied in the Eighth Amendment's prohibition; it makes no distinction between a willful and malicious murderer and an accomplice to an armed robbery in which a killing unintentionally occurs. . . .

MR. JUSTICE WHITE, concurring in part, dissenting in part, and concurring in the judgments of the Court. . . .

. . . It is clear from recent history that the infliction of death under circumstances where there is no purpose to take life has been widely rejected as grossly out of proportion to the seriousness of the crime.

The value of capital punishment as a deterrent to those lacking a purpose to kill is extremely attenuated. Whatever questions may be raised concerning the efficacy of the death penalty as a deterrent to intentional murder—and that debate rages on—its function in deterring individuals from becoming involved in ventures in which death may unintentionally result is even more doubtful. . . .

Under those circumstances the conclusion is unavoidable that the infliction of death upon those who had no intent to bring about the death of the victim is not only grossly out of proportion to the severity of the crime but also fails to contribute significantly to acceptable or, indeed, any perceptible goals of punishment. . . .

ENMUND V. FLORIDA (1982)

Earl Enmund aided and abetted felony murder by serving as the driver of a getaway car, but neither killed anyone nor intended the killings. The Court held that his death sentence was excessive.

JUSTICE WHITE delivered the opinion of the Court.

I

The facts of this case . . . are as follows. On April 1, 1975, at approximately 7:45 A.M., Thomas and Eunice Kersey, aged 86 and 74, were robbed and fatally shot at their farmhouse in central Florida. The evidence showed that Sampson and Jeanette Armstrong had gone to the back door of the Kersey house and asked for water for an overheated car. When Mr. Kersey came out of the house, Sampson Armstrong grabbed him, pointed a gun at him, and told Jeanette Armstrong to take his money. Mr. Kersey cried for help, and his wife came out of the house with a gun and shot Jeanette Armstrong, wounding her. Sampson Armstrong, and perhaps Jeanette Armstrong, then shot and killed both of the Kerseys, dragged them into the kitchen, and took their money and fled.

Two witnesses testified that they drove past the Kersey house between 7:30 and 7:40 A.M. and saw a large cream- or yellow-colored car parked beside the road about 200 yards from the house and that a man was sitting in the car. Another witness testified that at approximately 6:45 A.M. he saw Ida Jean Shaw, petitioner's common-law wife and Jeanette Armstrong's mother, driving a yellow Buick with a vinyl top which belonged to her and petitioner Earl Enmund. Enmund was a passenger in the car along with an unidentified woman. At about 8 A.M. the same witness saw the car return at a high rate of speed. Enmund was driving, Ida Jean Shaw was in the front seat, and one of the other two people in the car was lying down across the back seat.

Enmund, Sampson Armstrong, and Jeanette Armstrong were indicted for the first-degree murder and robbery of the Kerseys. Enmund and Sampson Armstrong were tried together. The prosecutor maintained in his closing argument that "Sampson Armstrong killed the old people." The judge instructed the jury that "[t]he killing of a human being while engaged in the perpetration of or in the attempt to perpetrate the offense of robbery is murder in the first degree even though there is no premeditated design or intent to kill." . . .

The jury found both Enmund and Sampson Armstrong guilty of two counts of first-degree murder and one count of robbery. A separate sentencing hearing was held and the jury recommended the death penalty for both defendants under the Florida procedure whereby the jury advises the trial judge whether to impose the death penalty. . . . The trial judge then sentenced Enmund to death on the two counts of first-degree murder. . . .

We granted Enmund's petition for certiorari, presenting the question whether death is a valid penalty under the Eighth and Fourteenth Amendments for one who neither took life, attempted to take life, nor intended to take life.

II

. . . [T]he Florida Supreme Court held that the record supported no more than the inference that Enmund was the person in the car by the side of the road at the time of the killings, waiting to help the robbers escape. This was enough under Florida law to make Enmund a constructive aider and abettor and hence a principal in first-degree murder upon whom the death penalty could be imposed. It was thus irrelevant to Enmund's challenge to the death sentence that he did not himself kill and was not present at the killings; also beside the point was whether he intended that the Kerseys be killed or anticipated that lethal force would or might be used if necessary to effectuate the robbery or a safe escape. We have concluded that imposition of the death penalty in these circumstances is inconsistent with the Eighth and Fourteenth Amendments.

The Cruel and Unusual Punishments Clause of the Eighth Amendment is directed, in part, "'against all punishments which by their excessive length or severity are greatly disproportioned to the offenses charged.'" . . . This Court most recently held a punishment excessive in relation to the crime charged in *Coker v. Georgia*. There the plurality opinion concluded that the imposition of the death penalty for the rape of an adult woman "is grossly disproportionate and excessive punishment for the crime of rape and is therefore forbidden by the Eighth Amendment as cruel and unusual punishment." In reaching this conclusion, it was stressed that our judgment "should be informed by objective factors to the maximum possible extent." Accordingly, the Court looked to the historical development of the punishment at issue, legislative judgments, international opinion, and the sentencing decisions juries have made before bringing its own judgment to bear on the matter. We proceed to analyze the punishment at issue in this case in a similar manner.

The Coker plurality observed that "[a]t no time in the last 50 years have a majority of the States authorized death as a punishment for rape." More importantly, in reenacting death penalty laws in order to satisfy the criteria established in *Furman v. Georgia*, only three States provided the death penalty for the rape of an adult woman in their revised statutes. The plurality therefore concluded that "[t]he current judgment with respect to the death penalty for rape . . . among state legislatures . . . weighs very heavily on the side of rejecting capital punishment as a suitable penalty for raping an adult woman."

Thirty-six state and federal jurisdictions presently authorize the death penalty. Of these, only eight jurisdictions authorize imposition of the death penalty solely for participation in a robbery in which another robber takes life. . . .

Thus only a small minority of jurisdictions—eight—allow the death penalty to be imposed solely because the defendant somehow participated in a robbery in the course of which a murder was committed. . . . Moreover, of the eight States which have enacted new death penalty statutes since 1978, none authorize capital punishment in such circumstances. . . . [T]he current legislative judgment . . . weighs on the side of rejecting capital punishment for the crime at issue.

Society's rejection of the death penalty for accomplice liability in felony murders is also indicated by the sentencing decisions that juries have made. As we have previously observed, "'[t]he jury . . . is a significant and reliable objective index of contemporary values because it is so directly involved.'" *Coker v. Georgia*. The evidence is overwhelming that American juries have repudiated imposition of the death penalty for crimes such as petitioner's. . . .

That juries have rejected the death penalty in cases such as this one where the defendant did not commit the homicide, was not present when the killing took place, and did not participate in a plot or scheme to murder is also shown by petitioner's survey of the Nation's death-row population. As of October 1, 1981, there were 796 inmates under sentences of death for homicide. Of the 739 for whom sufficient data are available, only 41 did not participate in the fatal assault on the victim. Of the 40 among the 41 for whom sufficient information was available, only 16 were not physically present when the fatal assault was committed. These 16 prisoners included only 3, including petitioner, who were sentenced to die absent a finding that they hired or solicited someone else to kill the victim or participated in a scheme designed to kill the victim. The figures for Florida are similar. . . . In only one case—Enmund's—there was no finding of an intent to kill and the defendant was not the triggerman. . . .

. . . The fact remains that we are not aware of a single person convicted of felony murder over the past quarter century who did not kill or attempt to kill, and did not intend the death of the victim, who has been executed, and that only three persons in that category are presently sentenced to die. . . . Petitioner's argument is that because he did not kill, attempt to kill, and he did not intend to kill, the death penalty is disproportionate as applied to him, and the statistics he cites are adequately tailored to demonstrate that juries—and perhaps prosecutors as well—consider death a disproportionate penalty for those who fall within his category.

III

Although the judgments of legislatures, juries, and prosecutors weigh heavily in the balance, it is for us ultimately to judge whether the Eighth Amendment permits imposition of the death penalty on one such as Enmund who aids and abets a felony in the course of which a murder is committed by others but who does not himself kill, attempt to kill, or intend that a killing take place or that lethal force will be employed. We have concluded, along with most legislatures and juries, that it does not.

We have no doubt that robbery is a serious crime deserving serious punishment. It is not, however, a crime "so grievous an affront to humanity that the only adequate response may be the penalty of death." *Gregg v. Georgia.* "[I]t does not compare with murder, which does involve the unjustified taking of human life. . . . As was said of the crime of rape in *Coker*, we have the abiding conviction that the death penalty, which is "unique in its severity and irrevocability," *Gregg v. Georgia*, is an excessive penalty for the robber who, as such, does not take human life.

Here the robbers did commit murder; but they were subjected to the death penalty only because they killed as well as robbed. The question before us is not the disproportionality of death as a penalty for murder, but rather the validity of capital punishment for Enmund's own conduct. The focus must be on his culpability, not on that of those who committed the robbery and shot the victims, for we insist on "individualized consideration as a constitutional requirement in imposing the death sentence," *Lockett v. Ohio*, which means that we must focus on "relevant facets of the character and record of the individual offender." *Woodson v. North Carolina*. Enmund himself did not kill or attempt to kill; and, as construed by the Florida Supreme Court, the record before us does not warrant a finding that Enmund had any intention of participating in or facilitating a murder. Yet under Florida law death was an authorized penalty because Enmund aided and abetted a robbery in the course of which murder was committed. It is fundamental that "causing harm intentionally must be punished more severely than causing the same harm unintentionally." Enmund did not kill or intend to kill and thus his culpability is plainly different from that of the robbers who killed; yet the State treated them alike and attributed to Enmund the culpability of those who killed the Kerseys. This was impermissible under the Eighth Amendment. . . .

In *Gregg v. Georgia* the opinion announcing the judgment observed that "[t]he death penalty is said to serve two principal social purposes: retribution and deterrence of capital crimes by prospective offenders." Unless the death penalty when applied to those in Enmund's position measurably contributes to one or both of these goals, it "is nothing more than the purposeless and needless imposition of pain and suffering," and hence an unconstitutional punishment. We are quite unconvinced, however, that the threat that the death penalty will be imposed for murder will measurably deter one who does not kill and has no intention or purpose that life will be taken. . . .

As for retribution as a justification for executing Enmund, we think this very much depends on the degree of Enmund's culpability—what Enmund's intentions, expectations, and actions were. . . . [T]he Court has found criminal penalties to be unconstitutionally excessive in the absence of intentional wrongdoing. . . .

For purposes of imposing the death penalty, Enmund's criminal culpability must be limited to his participation in the robbery, and his punishment must be tailored to his personal responsibility and moral guilt. Putting Enmund to death to avenge two killings that he did not commit and had no intention of committing or causing does not measurably contribute to the retributive end of ensuring that the criminal gets his just deserts. This is the judgment of most of the legislatures that have recently addressed the matter, and we have no reason to disagree with that judgment for purposes of construing and applying the Eighth Amendment.

IV

Because the Florida Supreme Court affirmed the death penalty in this case in the absence of proof that Enmund killed or attempted to kill, and regardless of whether Enmund intended or contemplated that life would be taken, we reverse the judgment upholding the death penalty and remand for further proceedings not inconsistent with this opinion. . . .

JUSTICE BRENNAN, concurring.

I join the Court's opinion. However, I adhere to my view that the death penalty is in all circumstances cruel and unusual punishment prohibited by the Eighth and Fourteenth Amendments. See *Gregg v. Georgia* (dissenting opinion).

JUSTICE O'CONNOR, with whom THE CHIEF JUSTICE, JUSTICE POWELL, and JUSTICE REHNQUIST join, dissenting.

Today the Court holds that the Eighth Amendment prohibits a State from executing a convicted felony murderer. I dissent from this holding. . . .

II

Earl Enmund's claim in this Court is that the death sentence imposed by the Florida trial court, and affirmed by the Florida Supreme Court, is unconstitutionally disproportionate to the role he played in the robbery and murders of the Kerseys. In particular, he contends that because he had no actual intent to kill the victims—in effect, because his behavior and intent were no more blameworthy than that of any robber—capital punishment is too extreme a penalty. . . .

Coker teaches . . . that proportionality—at least as regards capital punishment—not only requires an inquiry into contemporary standards as expressed by legislators and jurors, but also involves the notion that the magnitude of the punishment imposed must be related to the degree of the harm inflicted on the victim, as well as to the degree of the defendant's blameworthiness. . . .

In sum, in considering the petitioner's challenge, the Court should decide not only whether the petitioner's sentence of death offends contemporary standards as reflected in the responses of legislatures and juries, but also whether it is disproportionate to the harm that the petitioner caused and to the petitioner's involvement in the crime. . . .

I conclude that . . . the death penalty for felony murder does not fall short of our national "standards of decency."

Although the Court disingenuously seeks to characterize Enmund as only a "robber," it cannot be disputed that he is responsible, along with Sampson and Jeanette Armstrong, for the murders of the Kerseys. There is no dispute that their lives were unjustifiably taken, and that the petitioner, as one who aided and abetted the armed robbery, is legally liable for their deaths. Quite unlike the defendant in *Coker*, the petitioner cannot claim that the penalty imposed is "grossly out of proportion" to the harm for which he admittedly is at least partly responsible. . . .

The Court's holding today is especially disturbing because it makes intent a matter of federal constitutional law, requiring this Court both to review highly subjective definitional problems customarily left to state criminal law and to develop an Eighth Amendment meaning of intent. . . . Under the circumstances, the determination of the degree of blameworthiness is best left to the sentencer, who can sift through the facts unique to each case. . . .

In sum, the petitioner and the Court have failed to show that contemporary standards, as reflected in both jury determinations and legislative enactments, preclude imposition of the death penalty for accomplice felony murder. Moreover, examination of the qualitative factors underlying the concept of proportionality do not show that the death penalty is disproportionate as applied to Earl Enmund. In contrast to the crime in *Coker*, the petitioner's crime involves the very type of harm that this Court has held justifies the death penalty. Finally, because of the unique and complex mixture of facts involving a defendant's actions, knowledge, motives, and participation during the commission of a felony murder, I believe that the factfinder is best able to assess the defendant's blameworthiness. Accordingly, I conclude that the death penalty is not disproportionate to the crime of felony murder, even though the defendant did not actually kill or intend to kill his victims. . . .

Solem v. Helm (1983)

In Solem, *the Supreme Court invalidated a South Dakota recidivist statute that sentenced a repeat offender convicted of writing a bad check for $100 to life imprisonment without possibility of parole.*

JUSTICE POWELL delivered the opinion of the Court.

The issue presented is whether the Eighth Amendment proscribes a life sentence without possibility of parole for a seventh nonviolent felony.

I

By 1975 the State of South Dakota had convicted respondent Jerry Helm of six nonviolent felonies. In 1964, 1966, and 1969 Helm was convicted of third-degree burglary. In 1972 he was convicted of obtaining money under false pretenses. In 1973 he was convicted of grand larceny. And in 1975 he was convicted of third-offense driving while intoxicated. The record contains no details about the circumstances of any of these offenses, except that they were all nonviolent, none was a crime against a person, and alcohol was a contributing factor in each case.

In 1979 Helm was charged with uttering a "no account" check for $100. . . . Helm pleaded guilty.

Ordinarily the maximum punishment for uttering a "no account" check would have been five years' imprisonment in the state penitentiary and a $5,000 fine. . . . As a result of his criminal record, however, Helm was subject to South Dakota's recidivist statute:

"When a defendant has been convicted of at least three prior convictions [sic] in addition to the principal felony, the sentence for the principal felony shall be enhanced to the sentence for a Class 1 felony." S.D. Codified Laws 22–7–8 (1979) (amended 1981).

The maximum penalty for a "Class 1 felony" was life imprisonment in the state penitentiary and a $25,000 fine. Moreover, South Dakota law explicitly provides that parole is unavailable: "A person sentenced to life imprisonment is not eligible for parole by the board of pardons and paroles." The Governor is authorized to pardon prisoners, or to commute their sentences, but no other relief from sentence is available even to a rehabilitated prisoner.

Immediately after accepting Helm's guilty plea, the South Dakota Circuit Court sentenced Helm to life imprisonment. The court explained:

"'I think you certainly earned this sentence and certainly proven that you're an habitual criminal and the record would indicate that you're beyond rehabilitation and that the only prudent thing to do is to lock you up for the rest of your natural life, so you won't have further victims of your crimes, just be coming back before Courts. You'll have plenty of time to think this one over.'"

After Helm had served two years in the state penitentiary, he requested the Governor to commute his sentence to a fixed term of years. . . . of making Helm eligible to be considered for parole . . . The Governor denied Helm's request in May 1981.

In November 1981, Helm sought habeas relief in the United States District Court for the District of South Dakota. . . . [T]he District Court . . . denied the writ.

The United States Court of Appeals for the Eighth Circuit reversed . . . [and] concluded . . . that Helm's sentence was "grossly disproportionate to the nature of the offense." It therefore directed the District Court to issue the writ unless the State resentenced Helm.

We granted certiorari to consider the Eighth Amendment question presented by this case. We now affirm.

II

The Eighth Amendment declares: "Excessive bail shall not be required, nor excessive fines imposed, nor cruel and unusual punishments inflicted." The final clause prohibits not only barbaric punishments, but also sentences that are disproportionate to the crime committed.

The principle that a punishment should be proportionate to the crime is deeply rooted and frequently repeated in common-law jurisprudence. In 1215 three chapters of Magna Carta were devoted to the rule that "amercements" may not be excessive. And the principle was repeated and extended in the First Statute of Westminster (1275). These were not hollow guarantees, for the royal courts relied on them to invalidate disproportionate punishments. . . .

The English Bill of Rights repeated the principle of proportionality in language that was later adopted in the Eighth Amendment. . . .

When the Framers of the Eighth Amendment adopted the language of the English Bill of Rights, they also adopted the English principle of proportionality. Indeed, one of the consistent themes of the era was that Americans had all the rights of English subjects. . . . Thus our Bill of Rights was designed in part to ensure that these rights were preserved.

Although the Framers may have intended the Eighth Amendment to go beyond the scope of its English counterpart, their use of the language of the English Bill of Rights is convincing proof that they intended to provide at least the same protection—including the right to be free from excessive punishments.

The constitutional principle of proportionality has been recognized explicitly in this Court for almost a century. . . .

Most recently, the Court has applied the principle of proportionality to hold capital punishment excessive in certain circumstances. *Enmund v. Florida* (1982) (death penalty excessive for felony murder when defendant did not take life, attempt to take life, or intend that a life be taken or that lethal force be used); *Coker v. Georgia* (1977) ("sentence of death is grossly disproportionate and excessive punishment for the crime of rape"); . . . And the Court has continued to recognize that the Eighth Amendment proscribes grossly disproportionate punishments. . . .

There is no basis for the State's assertion that the general principle of proportionality does not apply to felony prison sentences. . . .

In sum, we hold as a matter of principle that a criminal sentence must be proportionate to the crime for which the defendant has been convicted. Reviewing courts, of course, should grant substantial deference to the broad authority that legislatures necessarily possess in determining the types and limits of punishments for crimes, as well as to the discretion that trial courts possess in sentencing convicted criminals. But no penalty is per se constitutional. . . .

III

When sentences are reviewed under the Eighth Amendment, courts should be guided by objective factors that our cases have recognized. First, we look to the gravity of the offense and the harshness of the penalty. . . .

Second, it may be helpful to compare the sentences imposed on other criminals in the same jurisdiction. If more serious crimes are subject to the same penalty, or to less serious penalties, that is some indication that the punishment at issue may be excessive. . . .

Third, courts may find it useful to compare the sentences imposed for commission of the same crime in other jurisdictions. . . .

In sum, a court's proportionality analysis under the Eighth Amendment should be guided by objective criteria. . . .

Application of these factors assumes that courts are competent to judge the gravity of an offense, at least on a relative scale. In a broad sense this assumption is justified, and courts traditionally have made these judgments—just as legislatures must make them in the first instance. Comparisons can be made in light of the harm caused or threatened to the victim or society, and the culpability of the offender. . . .

There are other accepted principles that courts may apply in measuring the harm caused or threatened to the victim or society. The absolute magnitude of the crime may be relevant. Stealing a million dollars is viewed as more serious than stealing a hundred dollars—a point recognized in statutes distinguishing petty theft from grand theft. . . . Few would dispute that a lesser included offense should not be punished more severely than the greater offense. Thus a court is justified in viewing assault with intent to murder as more serious than simple assault. . . . It also is generally recognized that attempts are less serious than completed crimes. . . . Similarly, an accessory after the fact should not be subject to a higher penalty than the principal. . . .

Turning to the culpability of the offender, there are again clear distinctions that courts may recognize and apply. In *Enmund* the Court looked at the petitioner's lack of intent to kill in determining that he was less culpable than his accomplices. Most would agree that negligent conduct is less serious than intentional conduct. South Dakota, for example, ranks criminal acts in ascending order of seriousness as follows: negligent acts, reckless acts, knowing acts, intentional acts, and malicious acts. A court, of course, is entitled to look at a defendant's motive in committing a crime. Thus a murder may be viewed as more serious when committed pursuant to a contract. . . .

This list is by no means exhaustive. It simply illustrates that there are generally accepted criteria for comparing the severity of different crimes on a broad scale, despite the difficulties courts face in attempting to draw distinctions between similar crimes.

Application of the factors that we identify also assumes that courts are able to compare different sentences. This assumption, too, is justified. The easiest comparison, of course, is between capital punishment and noncapital punishments, for the death penalty is different from other punishments in kind rather than degree. For sentences of imprisonment, the problem is not so much one of ordering, but one of line-drawing. It is clear that a 25-year sentence generally is more severe than a 15-year sentence, but in most cases it would be difficult to decide that the former violates the Eighth Amendment while the latter does not. Decisions of this kind, although troubling, are not unique to this area. The courts are constantly called upon to draw similar lines in a variety of contexts. . . .

IV

It remains to apply the analytical framework established by our prior decisions to the case before us. We first consider the relevant criteria, viewing Helm's sentence as life imprisonment without possibility of parole. We then consider the State's argument that the possibility of commutation is sufficient to save an otherwise unconstitutional sentence.

Helm's crime was "one of the most passive felonies a person could commit." It involved neither violence nor threat of violence to any person. The $100 face value of Helm's "no account" check was not trivial, but neither was it a large amount. One hundred dollars was less than half the amount South Dakota required for a felonious theft. It is easy to see why such a crime is viewed by society as among the less serious offenses. . . .

Helm, of course, was not charged simply with uttering a "no account" check, but also with being a habitual offender. And a State is justified in punishing a recidivist more severely than it punishes a first offender. Helm's status, however, cannot be considered in the abstract. His prior offenses, although classified as felonies, were all relatively minor. All were nonviolent and none was a crime against a person. . . .

Helm's present sentence is life imprisonment without possibility of parole. . . . Helm's sentence is the most severe punishment that the State could have imposed on any criminal for any crime. . . . Only capital punishment, a penalty not authorized in South Dakota when Helm was sentenced, exceeds it.

We next consider the sentences that could be imposed on other criminals in the same jurisdiction. . . .

[T]here were a handful of crimes that were necessarily punished by life imprisonment: murder, and, on a second or third offense, treason, first-degree manslaughter, first-degree arson, and kidnaping. There was a larger group for which life imprisonment was authorized in the discretion of the sentencing judge, including: treason, first-degree manslaughter, first-degree arson, and kidnaping; attempted murder, placing an explosive device on an aircraft, and first-degree rape on a second or third offense; and any felony after three prior offenses. Finally, there was a large group of very serious offenses for which life imprisonment was not authorized, including a third offense of heroin dealing or aggravated assault.

Criminals committing any of these offenses ordinarily would be thought more deserving of punishment than one uttering a "no account" check—even when the bad-check writer had already committed six minor felonies. Moreover, there is no indication in the record that any habitual offender other than Helm has ever been given the maximum sentence on the basis of comparable crimes. It is more likely that the possibility of life imprisonment under [the statute] generally is reserved for criminals such as fourth-time heroin dealers, while habitual bad-check writers receive more lenient treatment. In any event, Helm has been treated in the same manner as, or more severely than, criminals who have committed far more serious crimes.

Finally, we compare the sentences imposed for commission of the same crime in other jurisdictions. The Court of Appeals found that "Helm could have received a life sentence without parole for his offense in only one other state, Nevada," and we have no reason to doubt this finding. . . . At the very least, therefore, it is clear that Helm could not have received such a severe sentence in 48 of the 50 States. But even under Nevada law, a life sentence without possibility of parole is merely authorized in these circumstances. . . . We are not advised that any defendant such as Helm, whose prior offenses were so minor, actually has received the maximum penalty in Nevada. It appears that Helm was treated more severely than he would have been in any other State.

The State argues that the present case is essentially the same as *Rummel v. Estelle,* for the possibility of parole in that case is matched by the possibility of executive clemency here. The State reasons that the Governor could commute Helm's sentence to a term of years. We conclude, however, that the South Dakota commutation system is fundamentally different from the parole system that was before us in Rummel.

As a matter of law, parole and commutation are different concepts, despite some surface similarities. Parole is a regular part of the rehabilitative process. Assuming good behavior, it is the normal expectation in the vast majority of cases. . . . Thus it is possible to predict, at least to some extent, when parole might be granted. Commutation, on the other hand, is an ad hoc exercise of executive clemency. A Governor may commute a sentence at any time for any reason without reference to any standards. . . .

In South Dakota commutation is more difficult to obtain than parole. . . . In fact, no life sentence has been commuted in over eight years. . . . Furthermore, even if Helm's sentence were commuted, he merely would be eligible to be considered for parole. . . .

The possibility of commutation is nothing more than a hope for "an ad hoc exercise of clemency." . . .

V

The Constitution requires us to examine Helm's sentence to determine if it is proportionate to his crime. Applying objective criteria, we find that Helm has received the penultimate sentence for relatively minor criminal conduct. He has been treated more harshly than other criminals in the State who have committed more serious crimes. He has been treated more harshly than he would have been in any other jurisdiction, with the possible exception of a single State. We conclude that his sentence is significantly disproportionate to his crime, and is therefore prohibited by the Eighth Amendment. The judgment of the Court of Appeals is accordingly [a]ffirmed.

CHIEF JUSTICE BURGER, with whom JUSTICE WHITE, JUSTICE REHNQUIST, and JUSTICE O'CONNOR join, dissenting.

The controlling law governing this case is crystal clear, but today the Court blithely discards any concept of stare decisis, trespasses gravely on the authority of the states, and distorts the concept of proportionality of punishment by tearing it from its moorings in capital cases. Only three Terms ago, we held in *Rummel v. Estelle*, that a life sentence imposed after only a third nonviolent felony conviction did not constitute cruel and unusual punishment under the Eighth Amendment. Today, the Court ignores its recent precedent and holds that a life sentence imposed after a seventh felony conviction constitutes cruel and unusual punishment under the Eighth Amendment. Moreover, I reject the fiction that all Helm's crimes were innocuous or nonviolent. Among his felonies were three burglaries and a third conviction for drunken driving. By comparison Rummel was a relatively "model citizen." Although today's holding cannot rationally be reconciled with Rummel, the Court does not purport to overrule Rummel. I therefore dissent. . . .

FORD V. WAINWRIGHT (1986)

In this case, the Supreme Court held that the Constitution prohibits the execution of a prisoner who is insane.

JUSTICE MARSHALL announced the judgment of the Court and delivered the opinion of the Court with respect to Parts I and II and an opinion with respect to Parts III, IV, and V, in which JUSTICE BRENNAN, JUSTICE BLACKMUN, and JUSTICE STEVENS join.

For centuries no jurisdiction has countenanced the execution of the insane, yet this Court has never decided whether the Constitution forbids the practice. Today we keep faith with our common-law heritage in holding that it does.

I

Alvin Bernard Ford was convicted of murder in 1974 and sentenced to death. There is no suggestion that he was incompetent at the time of his offense, at trial, or at sentencing. In early 1982, however, Ford began to manifest gradual changes in behavior. They began as an occasional peculiar idea or confused perception, but became more serious over time. After reading in the newspaper that the Ku Klux Klan had held a rally in nearby Jacksonville, Florida, Ford developed an obsession focused upon the Klan. His letters to various people reveal endless brooding about his "Klan work," and an increasingly pervasive delusion that he had become the target of a complex conspiracy, involving the Klan and assorted others, designed to force him to commit suicide. He believed that the prison guards, part of the conspiracy, had been killing people and putting the bodies in the concrete enclosures used for beds. Later, he began to believe that his women relatives were being tortured and sexually abused somewhere in the prison. This notion developed into a delusion that the people who were tormenting him at the prison had taken members of Ford's family hostage. The hostage delusion took firm hold and expanded, until Ford was reporting that 135 of his friends and family were being held hostage in the prison, and that only he could help them. By "day 287" of the "hostage crisis," the list of hostages had expanded to include "senators, Senator Kennedy, and many other leaders." In a letter to the Attorney General of Florida, written in 1983, Ford appeared to assume authority for ending the "crisis," claiming to have fired a number of prison officials. He began to refer to himself as "Pope John Paul, III," and reported having appointed nine new justices to the Florida Supreme Court.

Counsel for Ford asked a psychiatrist who had examined Ford earlier, Dr. Jamal Amin, to continue seeing him and to recommend appropriate treatment. . . . Dr. Amin concluded in 1983 that Ford suffered from "a severe, uncontrollable, mental disease which closely resembles 'Paranoid Schizophrenia With Suicide Potential'"—a "major mental disorder . . . severe enough to substantially affect Mr. Ford's present ability to assist in the defense of his life."

Ford subsequently refused to see Dr. Amin again, believing him to have joined the conspiracy against him, and Ford's counsel sought assistance from Dr. Harold Kaufman, who interviewed Ford in November 1983. Ford told Dr. Kaufman that "I know there is some sort of death penalty, but I'm free to go whenever I want because it would be illegal and the executioner would be executed." When asked if he would be executed, Ford replied: "I can't be executed because of the landmark case. I won. *Ford v. State* will prevent executions all over." . . . Dr. Kaufman concluded that Ford had no understanding of why he was being executed, made no connection between the homicide of which he had been convicted and the death penalty, and indeed sincerely believed that he would not be executed because he owned the prisons and could control the Governor through mind waves. Dr. Kaufman found that there was "no reasonable possibility that Mr. Ford was dissembling, malingering or otherwise putting on a performance. . . . The following month, in an interview with his attorneys, Ford regressed further into nearly complete incomprehensibility. . . .

Counsel for Ford invoked the procedures of Florida law governing the determination of competency of a condemned inmate. Following the procedures set forth in the statute, the Governor of Florida appointed a panel of three psychiatrists to evaluate whether, under [State law], Ford had "the mental capacity to understand the nature of the death penalty and the reasons why it was imposed upon him." At a single meeting, the three psychiatrists together interviewed Ford for approximately 30 minutes. Each doctor then filed a separate two- or three-page report with the Governor, to whom the statute delegates the final decision. One doctor concluded that Ford suffered from "psychosis with paranoia" but had "enough cognitive functioning to understand the nature and the effects of the death penalty, and why it is to be imposed on him." Another found that, although Ford was "psychotic," he did "know fully what can happen to him." The third concluded that Ford had a "severe adaptational disorder," but did "comprehend his total situation including being sentenced to death, and all of the implications of that penalty." He believed that Ford's disorder, "although severe, seem[ed] contrived and recently learned." Thus, the interview produced three different diagnoses, but accord on the question of sanity as defined by state law.

The Governor . . . signed a death warrant for Ford's execution. Ford's attorneys unsuccessfully sought a hearing in state court to determine anew Ford's competency to suffer execution. Counsel then filed a petition for habeas corpus in the United States District Court for the Southern District of Florida, seeking an evidentiary hearing on the question of Ford's sanity, proffering the conflicting findings of the Governor-appointed commission and subsequent challenges to their methods by other psychiatrists. The District Court denied the petition without a hearing. The Court of Appeals granted a certificate of probable cause and stayed Ford's execution. . . . [It] addressed the merits of Ford's claim and a divided panel affirmed the District Court's denial of the writ. This Court granted Ford's petition for certiorari in order to resolve the important issue whether the Eighth Amendment prohibits the execution of the insane. . . .

II

Since this Court last had occasion to consider the infliction of the death penalty upon the insane, our interpretations of the Due Process Clause and the Eighth Amendment have evolved substantially. In *Solesbee v. Balkcom,* a condemned prisoner claimed a due process right to a judicial determination of his sanity, yet the Court did not consider the possible existence of a right under the Eighth Amendment, which had not yet been applied to the States. The sole question the Court addressed was whether Georgia's procedure for ascertaining sanity adequately effectuated that State's own policy of sparing the insane from execution. . . . Now that the Eighth Amendment has been recognized to affect significantly both the procedural and the substantive aspects of the death penalty, the question of executing the insane takes on a wholly different complexion. The adequacy of the procedures chosen by a State to determine sanity, therefore, will depend upon an issue that this Court has never addressed: whether the Constitution places a substantive restriction on the State's power to take the life of an insane prisoner.

There is now little room for doubt that the Eighth Amendment's ban on cruel and unusual punishment embraces, at a minimum, those modes or acts of punishment that had been considered cruel and unusual at the time that the Bill of Rights was adopted. . . .

Moreover, the Eighth Amendment's proscriptions are not limited to those practices condemned by the common law in 1789. . . . Not bound by the sparing humanitarian concessions of our forebears, the Amendment also recognizes the "evolving standards of decency that mark the progress of a maturing society." *Trop v. Dulles*. In addition to considering the barbarous methods generally outlawed in the 18th century, therefore, this Court takes into account objective evidence of contemporary values before determining whether a particular punishment comports with the fundamental human dignity that the Amendment protects. . . .

We begin, then, with the common law. The bar against executing a prisoner who has lost his sanity bears impressive historical credentials; the practice consistently has been branded "savage and inhuman." . . .

As is often true of common-law principles . . . the reasons for the rule are less sure and less uniform than the rule itself. One explanation is that the execution of an insane person simply offends humanity; another, that it provides no example to others and thus contributes nothing to whatever deterrence value is intended to be served by capital punishment. Other commentators postulate religious underpinnings. . . . It is also said that execution serves no purpose in these cases because madness is its own punishment. . . . More recent commentators opine that the community's quest for "retribution"—the need to offset a criminal act by a punishment of equivalent "moral quality"—is not served by execution of an insane person. . . . Unanimity of rationale, therefore, we do not find. "But whatever the reason of the law is, it is plain the law is so." We know of virtually no authority condoning the execution of the insane at English common law. . . .

This ancestral legacy has not outlived its time. Today, no State in the Union permits the execution of the insane. It is clear that the ancient and humane limitation upon the State's ability to execute its sentences has as firm a hold upon the jurisprudence of today as it had centuries ago in England. The various reasons put forth in support of the common-law restriction have no less logical, moral, and practical force than they did when first voiced. . . . Whether its aim be to protect the condemned from fear and pain without comfort of understanding, or to protect the dignity of society itself from the barbarity of exacting mindless vengeance, the restriction finds enforcement in the Eighth Amendment.

III

The Eighth Amendment prohibits the State from inflicting the penalty of death upon a prisoner who is insane. Petitioner's allegation of insanity in his habeas corpus petition, if proved, therefore, would bar his execution. The question before us is whether the District Court was under an obligation to hold an evidentiary hearing on the question of Ford's sanity. . . .

IV

The first deficiency in Florida's procedure lies in its failure to include the prisoner in the truth-seeking process. . . . [S]tate practice does not permit any material relevant to the ultimate decision to be submitted on behalf of the prisoner facing execution. . . .

A related flaw in the Florida procedure is the denial of any opportunity to challenge or impeach the state-appointed psychiatrists' opinions. " . . . Cross-examination of the psychiatrists, or perhaps a less formal equivalent, would contribute markedly to the process of seeking truth in sanity disputes by bringing to light the bases for each expert's beliefs, the precise factors underlying those beliefs, any history of error or caprice of the examiner, any personal bias with respect to the issue of capital punishment, the expert's degree of certainty about his or her own conclusions, and the precise meaning of ambiguous words used in the report. Without some questioning of the experts concerning their technical conclusions, a factfinder simply cannot be expected to evaluate the various opinions, particularly when they are themselves inconsistent. . . . The failure of the Florida procedure to afford the prisoner's representative any opportunity to clarify or challenge the state experts' opinions or methods creates a significant possibility that the ultimate decision made in reliance on those experts will be distorted.

Perhaps the most striking defect in the procedures of [the Florida statute] . . . is the State's placement of the decision wholly within the executive branch. Under this procedure, the person who appoints the experts and ultimately decides whether the State will be able to carry out the sentence that it has long sought is the Governor, whose subordinates have been responsible for initiating every stage of the prosecution of the condemned from arrest through sentencing. The commander of the State's corps of prosecutors cannot be said to have the neutrality that is necessary for reliability in the factfinding proceeding. . . .

V

Having identified various failings of the Florida scheme, we must conclude that the State's procedures for determining sanity are inadequate to preclude federal redetermination of the constitutional issue. We do not here suggest that only a full trial on the issue of sanity will suffice to protect the federal interests; we leave to the State the task of developing appropriate ways to enforce the constitutional restriction upon its execution of sentences. . . .

Yet the lodestar of any effort to devise a procedure must be the overriding dual imperative of providing redress for those with substantial claims and of encouraging accuracy in the factfinding determination. The stakes are high, and the "evidence" will always be imprecise. It is all the more important that the adversary presentation of relevant information be as unrestricted as possible. . . . Fidelity to these principles is the solemn obligation of a civilized society.

Today we have explicitly recognized in our law a principle that has long resided there. It is no less abhorrent today than it has been for centuries to exact in penance the life of one whose mental illness prevents him from comprehending the reasons for the penalty or its implications. In light of the clear need for trustworthiness in any factual finding that will prevent or permit the carrying out of an execution, we hold that [the Florida statute] provides inadequate assurances of accuracy. . . . Having been denied a factfinding procedure "adequate to afford a full and fair hearing" on the critical issue, petitioner is entitled to an evidentiary hearing in the District Court, de novo, on the question of his competence to be executed.

The judgment of the Court of Appeals is reversed, and the case is remanded for further proceedings consistent with this opinion. . . .

JUSTICE REHNQUIST, with whom THE CHIEF JUSTICE joins, dissenting.

The Court today holds that the Eighth Amendment prohibits a State from carrying out a lawfully imposed sentence of death upon a person who is currently insane. This holding is based almost entirely on two unremarkable observations. First, the Court states that it "know[s] of virtually no authority condoning the execution of the insane at English common law." Second, it notes that "[t]oday, no State in the Union permits the execution of the insane." Armed with these facts, and shielded by the claim that it is simply "keep[ing] faith with our common-law heritage," the Court proceeds to cast aside settled precedent and to significantly alter both the common-law and current practice of not executing the insane. It manages this feat by carefully ignoring the fact that the Florida scheme it finds unconstitutional, in which the Governor is assigned the ultimate responsibility of deciding whether a condemned prisoner is currently insane, is fully consistent with the "common-law heritage" and current practice on which the Court purports to rely.

The Court places great weight on the "impressive historical credentials" of the common-law bar against executing a prisoner who has lost his sanity. What it fails to mention, however, is the equally important and unchallenged fact that at common law it was the executive who passed upon the sanity of the condemned. . . . So when the Court today creates a constitutional right to a determination of sanity outside of the executive branch, it does so not in keeping with but at the expense of "our common-law heritage." . . .

Since no State sanctions execution of the insane, the real battle being fought in this case is over what procedures must accompany the inquiry into sanity. The Court reaches the result it does by examining the common law, creating a constitutional right that no State seeks to violate, and then concluding that the common-law procedures are inadequate to protect the newly created but common-law based right. I find it unnecessary to "constitutionalize" the already uniform view that the insane should not be executed, and inappropriate to "selectively incorporate" the common-law practice. I therefore dissent.

TISON V. ARIZONA (1987)

The Supreme Court narrowed Enmund v. Florida *in* Tison, *upholding the death penalty for accomplices if their participation in the crime was major and if they displayed reckless indifference to the value of human life.*

JUSTICE O'CONNOR delivered the opinion of the Court.

The question presented is whether the petitioners' participation in the events leading up to and following the murder of four members of a family makes the sentences of death imposed by the Arizona courts constitutionally permissible although neither petitioner specifically intended to kill the victims and neither inflicted the fatal gunshot wounds. We hold that the Arizona Supreme Court applied an erroneous standard . . . and, therefore, vacate the judgments below and remand the case for further proceedings not inconsistent with this opinion.

I

Gary Tison was sentenced to life imprisonment as the result of a prison escape during the course of which he had killed a guard. After he had been in prison a number of years, Gary Tison's wife, their three sons Donald, Ricky, and Raymond, Gary's brother Joseph, and other relatives made plans to help Gary Tison escape again. . . . The Tison family assembled a large arsenal of weapons for this purpose. Plans for escape were discussed with Gary Tison, who insisted that his cellmate, Randy Greenawalt, also a convicted murderer, be included in the prison break. The following facts are largely evidenced by petitioners' detailed confessions given as part of a plea bargain. . . . [T]he bargain was rescinded and [the defendants] were tried, convicted, and sentenced to death.

On July 30, 1978, the three Tison brothers entered the Arizona State Prison at Florence carrying a large ice chest filled with guns. The Tisons armed Greenawalt and their father, and the group, brandishing their weapons, locked the prison guards and visitors present in a storage closet. The five men fled the prison grounds in the Tisons' Ford Galaxy automobile. No shots were fired at the prison.

After leaving the prison, the men abandoned the Ford automobile and proceeded on to an isolated house in a white Lincoln automobile that the brothers had parked at a hospital near the prison. At the house, the Lincoln automobile had a flat tire; the only spare tire was pressed into service. After two nights at the house, the group drove toward Flagstaff. As the group traveled on back roads and secondary highways through the desert, another tire blew out. The group decided to flag down a passing motorist and steal a car. Raymond stood out in front of the Lincoln; the other four armed themselves and lay in wait by the side of the road . . . [A] Mazda occupied by John Lyons, his wife Donnelda, his 2-year-old son Christopher, and his 15-year-old niece, Theresa Tyson, pulled over to render aid.

As Raymond showed John Lyons the flat tire on the Lincoln, the other Tisons and Greenawalt emerged. The Lyons family was forced into the backseat of the Lincoln. Raymond and Donald drove the Lincoln down a dirt road off the highway and then down a gas line service road farther into the desert; Gary Tison, Ricky Tison, and Randy Greenawalt followed in the Lyons' Mazda. The two cars were parked trunk to trunk and the Lyons family was ordered to stand in front of the Lincoln's headlights. The Tisons transferred their belongings from the Lincoln into the Mazda. They discovered guns and money in the Mazda which they kept, and they put the rest of the Lyons' possessions in the Lincoln.

Gary Tison then told Raymond to drive the Lincoln still farther into the desert. Raymond did so, and, while the others guarded the Lyons and Theresa Tyson, Gary fired his shotgun into the radiator, presumably to completely disable the vehicle. The Lyons and Theresa Tyson were then escorted to the Lincoln and again ordered to stand in its headlights. Ricky Tison reported that John Lyons begged, in comments "more or less directed at everybody," "Jesus, don't kill me." Gary Tison said he was "thinking about it." John Lyons asked the Tisons and Greenawalt to "[g]ive us some water . . . just leave us out here, and you all go home." Gary Tison then told his sons to go back to the Mazda and get some water. Raymond later explained that his father "was like in conflict with himself. . . . What it was, I think it was the baby being there and all this, and he wasn't sure about what to do."

The petitioners' statements diverge to some extent, but it appears that both of them went back towards the Mazda, along with Donald, while Randy Greenawalt and Gary Tison stayed at the Lincoln guarding the victims. . . . [P]etitioners agree they saw Greenawalt and their father brutally murder their four captives with repeated blasts from their shotguns. Neither made an effort to help the victims, though both later stated they were surprised by the shooting. The Tisons got into the Mazda and drove away, continuing their flight. Physical evidence suggested that Theresa Tyson managed to crawl away from the bloodbath, severely injured. She died in the desert after the Tisons left.

Several days later the Tisons and Greenawalt were apprehended after a shootout at a police roadblock. Donald Tison was killed. Gary Tison escaped into the desert where he subsequently died of exposure. Raymond and Ricky Tison and Randy Greenawalt were captured and tried jointly for the crimes associated with the prison break itself and the shootout at the roadblock; each was convicted and sentenced.

The State then individually tried each of the petitioners for capital murder of the four victims as well as for the associated crimes of armed robbery, kidnaping, and car theft. The capital murder charges were based on Arizona felony-murder law providing that a killing occurring during the perpetration of robbery or kidnaping is capital murder and that each participant in the kidnaping or robbery is legally responsible for the acts of his accomplices. Each of the petitioners was convicted of the four murders under these accomplice liability and felony-murder statutes.

Arizona law also provided for a capital sentencing proceeding, to be conducted without a jury, to determine whether the crime was sufficiently aggravated to warrant the death sentence. The statute set out six aggravating and four mitigating factors. The judge found three statutory aggravating factors:

(1) the Tisons had created a grave risk of death to others (not the victims);

(2) the murders had been committed for pecuniary gain;

(3) the murders were especially heinous.

The judge found no statutory mitigating factor. Importantly, the judge specifically found that the crime was not mitigated by the fact that each of the petitioners' "participation was relatively minor." Rather, he found that the "participation of each [petitioner] in the crimes giving rise to the application of the felony murder rule in this case was very substantial." The trial judge also specifically found, that each "could reasonably have foreseen that his conduct . . . would cause or create a grave risk of . . . death." He did find, however, three nonstatutory mitigating factors:

(1) the petitioners' youth—Ricky was 20 and Raymond was 19;

(2) neither had prior felony records;

(3) each had been convicted of the murders under the felony-murder rule.

Nevertheless, the judge sentenced both petitioners to death.

On direct appeal, the Arizona Supreme Court affirmed. The Court found:

"The record establishes that both Ricky and Raymond Tison were present when the homicides took place and that they occurred as part of and in the course of the escape and continuous attempt to prevent recapture. The deaths would not have occurred but for their assistance. That they did not specifically intend that the Lyonses and Theresa Tyson die, that they did not plot in advance that these homicides would take place, or that they did not actually pull the triggers on the guns which inflicted the fatal wounds is of little significance."

In evaluating the trial court's findings of aggravating and mitigating factors, the Arizona Supreme Court found the first aggravating factor—

creation of grave risk to others—not supported by the evidence. All those killed were intended victims, and no one else was endangered. The Arizona Supreme Court, however, upheld the "pecuniary gain" and "heinousness" aggravating circumstances and the death sentences. This Court denied the Tisons' petition for certiorari.

Petitioners then collaterally attacked their death sentences in state postconviction proceedings alleging that *Enmund v. Florida*, which had been decided in the interim, required reversal. A divided Arizona Supreme Court, interpreting *Enmund* to require a finding of "intent to kill," declared in Raymond Tison's case "the dictate of *Enmund* is satisfied," writing:

"Intend [sic] to kill includes the situation in which the defendant intended, contemplated, or anticipated that lethal force would or might be used or that life would or might be taken in accomplishing the underlying felony.

"In the present case the evidence does not show that petitioner killed or attempted to kill. The evidence does demonstrate beyond a reasonable doubt, however, that petitioner intended to kill. Petitioner played an active part in preparing the breakout, including obtaining a getaway car and various weapons. At the breakout scene itself, petitioner played a crucial role by, among other things, holding a gun on prison guards. Petitioner knew that Gary Tison's murder conviction arose out of the killing of a guard during an earlier prison escape attempt. Thus petitioner could anticipate the use of lethal force during this attempt to flee confinement; in fact, he later said that during the escape he would have been willing personally to kill in a 'very close life or death situation,' and that he recognized that after the escape there was a possibility of killings.

"The use of lethal force that petitioner contemplated indeed occurred when the gang abducted the people who stopped on the highway to render aid. Petitioner played an active part in the events that led to the murders. He assisted in the abduction by flagging down the victims as they drove by, while the other members of the gang remained hidden and armed. He assisted in escorting the victims to the murder site. At the site, petitioner, Ricky Tison and Greenawalt placed the gang's possessions in the victims' Mazda and the victims' possessions in the gang's disabled Lincoln Continental. After Gary Tison rendered the Lincoln inoperable by firing into its engine compartment, petitioner assisted in escorting the victims to the Lincoln. Petitioner then watched Gary Tison and Greenawalt fire in the direction of the victims. Petitioner did nothing to interfere. After the killings, petitioner did nothing to disassociate himself from Gary Tison and Greenawalt, but instead used the victims' car to continue on the joint venture, a venture that lasted several more days.

"From these facts we conclude that petitioner intended to kill. Petitioner's participation up to the moment of the firing of the fatal shots was substantially the same as that of Gary Tison and Greenawalt. . . . Petitioner, actively participated in the events leading to death by . . . providing the murder weapons and helping abduct the victims. Also petitioner was present at the murder site, did nothing to interfere with the murders, and after the murders even continued on the joint venture.

" . . . In *Enmund*, unlike in the present case, the defendant did not actively participate in the events leading to death (by, for example, as in the present case, helping abduct the victims) and was not present at the murder site."

In Ricky Tison's case the Arizona Supreme Court relied on a similar recitation of facts to find intent. . . . We granted certiorari in order to consider the Arizona Supreme Court's application of *Enmund*.

II

In *Enmund v. Florida*, this Court reversed the death sentence of a defendant convicted under Florida's felony-murder rule. Enmund was the driver of the "getaway" car in an armed robbery of a dwelling. The occupants of the house, an elderly couple, resisted and Enmund's accomplices killed them. . . .

. . . [This] Court undertook its own proportionality analysis. Armed robbery is a serious offense, but one for which the penalty of death is plainly excessive; the imposition of the death penalty for robbery, therefore, violates the Eighth and Fourteenth Amendments' proscription "'against all punishments which by their excessive length or severity are greatly disproportioned to the offenses charged.'" Furthermore, the Court found that Enmund's degree of participation in the murders was so tangential that it could not be said to justify a sentence of death. It found that neither the deterrent nor the retributive purposes of the death penalty were advanced by imposing the death penalty upon Enmund. . . .

Enmund explicitly dealt with two distinct subsets of all felony murders in assessing whether Enmund's sentence was disproportional under the Eighth Amendment. At one pole was Enmund himself: the minor actor in an armed robbery, not on the scene, who neither intended to kill nor was found to have had any culpable mental state. . . . The Court held that capital punishment was disproportional in these cases. *Enmund* also clearly dealt with the other polar case: the felony murderer who actually killed, attempted to kill, or intended to kill. The Court clearly held that the . . . small minority of jurisdictions that limited the death penalty to these circumstances could continue to exact it in accordance with local law when the circumstances warranted. The Tison brothers' cases fall into neither of these neat categories.

Petitioners argue strenuously that they did not "intend to kill" as that concept has been generally understood in the common law. We accept this as true. . . . [T]here is no evidence that either Ricky or Raymond Tison took any act which he desired to, or was substantially certain would, cause death.

The Arizona Supreme Court did not attempt to argue that the facts of this case supported an inference of "intent" in the traditional sense. Instead, the Arizona Supreme Court attempted to reformulate "intent to kill" as a species of foreseeability. . . .

This definition of intent is broader than that described by the *Enmund* Court. Participants in violent felonies like armed robberies can frequently "anticipat[e] that lethal force . . . might be used . . . in accomplishing the underlying felony." Enmund himself may well have so anticipated. Indeed, the possibility of bloodshed is inherent in the commission of any violent felony and this possibility is generally foreseeable and foreseen; it is one principal reason that felons arm themselves. The Arizona Supreme Court's attempted reformulation of intent to kill amounts to little more than a restatement of the felony-murder rule itself. Petitioners do not fall within the "intent to kill" category of felony murderers for which *Enmund* explicitly finds the death penalty permissible under the Eighth Amendment.

On the other hand, it is equally clear that petitioners also fall outside the category of felony murderers for whom *Enmund* explicitly held the death penalty disproportional: their degree of participation in the crimes was major rather than minor, and the record would support a finding of the culpable mental state of reckless indifference to human life. . . .

. . . [T]he Tison brothers' participation in the crime was anything but minor. . . . [T]hey both subjectively appreciated that their acts were likely to result in the taking of innocent life. The issue raised by this case is whether the Eighth Amendment prohibits the death penalty in the intermediate case of the defendant whose participation is major and whose mental state is one of reckless indifference to the value of human life. Enmund does not specifically address this point. We now take up the task of determining whether the Eighth Amendment proportionality requirement bars the death penalty under these circumstances.

Like the *Enmund* Court, we find the state legislatures' judgment as to proportionality in these circumstances relevant to this constitutional inquiry. The largest number of States still fall into the two intermediate categories discussed in *Enmund*. Four States authorize the death penalty in felony-murder cases upon a showing of culpable mental state such as recklessness or extreme indifference to human life. Two jurisdictions require that the defendant's participation be substantial and the statutes of at least six more, including Arizona, take minor participation in the felony expressly into account in mitigation of the murder.... [T]he greater the defendant's participation in the felony murder, the more likely that he acted with reckless indifference to human life. At a minimum, however, it can be said that all these jurisdictions ... specifically authorize the death penalty in a felony-murder case where, though the defendant's mental state fell short of intent to kill, the defendant was a major actor in a felony in which he knew death was highly likely to occur.... [S]ubstantial and recent legislative authorization of the death penalty for the crime of felony murder regardless of the absence of a finding of an intent to kill powerfully suggests that our society does not reject the death penalty as grossly excessive under these circumstances....

A critical facet of the individualized determination of culpability required in capital cases is the mental state with which the defendant commits the crime. Deeply ingrained in our legal tradition is the idea that the more purposeful is the criminal conduct, the more serious is the offense, and, therefore, the more severely it ought to be punished....

A narrow focus on the question of whether or not a given defendant "intended to kill," however, is a highly unsatisfactory means of definitively distinguishing the most culpable and dangerous of murderers. Many who intend to, and do, kill are not criminally liable at all—those who act in self-defense or with other justification or excuse. Other intentional homicides, though criminal, are often felt undeserving of the death penalty—those that are the result of provocation. On the other hand, some nonintentional murderers may be among the most dangerous and inhumane of all—the person who tortures another not caring whether the victim lives or dies, or the robber who shoots someone in the course of the robbery, utterly indifferent to the fact that the desire to rob may have the unintended consequence of killing the victim as well as taking the victim's property. This reckless indifference to the value of human life may be every bit as shocking to the moral sense as an "intent to kill." Indeed it is for this very reason that the common law and modern criminal codes alike have classified behavior such as occurred in this case along with intentional murders. . . . *Enmund* held that when "intent to kill" results in its logical though not inevitable consequence—the taking of human life—the Eighth Amendment permits the State to exact the death penalty after a careful weighing of the aggravating and mitigating circumstances. Similarly, we hold that the reckless disregard for human life implicit in knowingly engaging in criminal activities known to carry a grave risk of death represents a highly culpable mental state, a mental state that may be taken into account in making a capital sentencing judgment when that conduct causes its natural, though also not inevitable, lethal result.

The petitioners' own personal involvement in the crimes was not minor, but rather, as specifically found by the trial court, "substantial." Far from merely sitting in a car away from the actual scene of the murders acting as the getaway driver to a robbery, each petitioner was actively involved in every element of the kidnaping-robbery and was physically present during the entire sequence of criminal activity culminating in the murder of the Lyons family and the subsequent flight. The Tisons' high level of participation in these crimes further implicates them in the resulting deaths. . . .

[W]e . . . hold that major participation in the felony committed, combined with reckless indifference to human life, is sufficient to satisfy the *Enmund* culpability requirement. The Arizona courts have clearly found that the former exists; we now vacate the judgments below and remand for determination of the latter in further proceedings not inconsistent with this opinion. . . .

McCleskey v. Kemp (1987)

The Supreme Court ruled that a study by Professor David Baldus showing that blacks who murdered white victims were the most likely defen-

dants to receive the death penalty did not invalidate McCleskey's death sentence. It was necessary for McCleskey to demonstrate that decision makers in this particular case acted with a racially discriminatory intent.

JUSTICE POWELL delivered the opinion of the Court.

This case presents the question whether a complex statistical study that indicates a risk that racial considerations enter into capital sentencing determinations proves that petitioner McCleskey's capital sentence is unconstitutional under the Eighth or Fourteenth Amendment.

I

McCleskey, a black man, was convicted of two counts of armed robbery and one count of murder in the Superior Court of Fulton County, Georgia. . . . McCleskey's convictions arose out of the robbery of a furniture store and the killing of a white police officer during the course of the robbery. The evidence at trial indicated that McCleskey and three accomplices planned and carried out the robbery. All four were armed. McCleskey entered the front of the store while the other three entered the rear. McCleskey secured the front of the store by rounding up the customers and forcing them to lie face down on the floor. The other three rounded up the employees in the rear and tied them up with tape. The manager was forced at gunpoint to turn over the store receipts, his watch, and $6. During the course of the robbery, a police officer, answering a silent alarm, entered the store through the front door. As he was walking down the center aisle of the store, two shots were fired. Both struck the officer. One hit him in the face and killed him.

Several weeks later, McCleskey was arrested in connection with an unrelated offense. He confessed that he had participated in the furniture store robbery, but denied that he had shot the police officer. At trial, the State introduced evidence that at least one of the bullets that struck the officer was fired from a .38 caliber Rossi revolver. This description matched the description of the gun that McCleskey had carried during the robbery. The State also introduced the testimony of two witnesses who had heard McCleskey admit to the shooting.

The jury convicted McCleskey of murder. At the penalty hearing, the jury heard arguments as to the appropriate sentence. Under Georgia law, the jury could not consider imposing the death penalty unless it found beyond a reasonable doubt that the murder was accompanied by one of the statutory aggravating circumstances. The jury in this case found two aggravating circumstances to exist beyond a reasonable doubt: the murder was committed during the course of an armed robbery; and the murder was committed upon a peace officer engaged in the performance of his duties.... McCleskey offered no mitigating evidence. The jury recommended that he be sentenced to death on the murder charge and to consecutive life sentences on the armed robbery charges. The court followed the jury's recommendation and sentenced McCleskey to death.

On appeal, the Supreme Court of Georgia affirmed the convictions and the sentences....

McCleskey ... filed a petition for a writ of habeas corpus in the Federal District Court for the Northern District of Georgia. His petition raised 18 claims, one of which was that the Georgia capital sentencing process is administered in a racially discriminatory manner in violation of the Eighth and Fourteenth Amendments to the United States Constitution. In support of his claim, McCleskey proffered a statistical study performed by Professors David C. Baldus, Charles Pulaski, and George Woodworth (the Baldus study) that purports to show a disparity in the imposition of the death sentence in Georgia based on the race of the murder victim and, to a lesser extent, the race of the defendant. The Baldus study is actually two sophisticated statistical studies that examine over 2,000 murder cases that occurred in Georgia during the 1970s. The raw numbers collected by Professor Baldus indicate that defendants charged with killing white persons received the death penalty in 11 percent of the cases, but defendants charged with killing blacks received the death penalty in only 1 percent of the cases....

Baldus also divided the cases according to the combination of the race of the defendant and the race of the victim. He found that the death penalty was assessed in 22 percent of the cases involving black defendants and white victims; 8 percent of the cases involving white defendants and white victims; 1 percent of the cases involving black defendants and black victims; and 3 percent of the cases involving white defendants and black victims....

Baldus subjected his data to an extensive analysis, taking account of 230 variables that could have explained the disparities on nonracial grounds. One of his models concludes that, even after taking account of 39 nonracial variables, defendants charged with killing white victims were 4.3 times as likely to receive a death sentence as defendants charged with killing blacks.... Thus, the Baldus study indicates that black defendants, such as McCleskey, who kill white victims have the greatest likelihood of receiving the death penalty.

The District Court . . . concluded that McCleskey's "statistics do not demonstrate a prima facie case in support of the contention that the death penalty was imposed upon him because of his race, because of the race of the victim, or because of any Eighth Amendment concern." . . .

The Court of Appeals for the Eleventh Circuit, sitting en banc, carefully reviewed the District Court's decision on McCleskey's claim. It assumed the validity of the study itself and addressed the merits of McCleskey's Eighth and Fourteenth Amendment claims. That is, the court assumed that the study "showed that systematic and substantial disparities existed in the penalties imposed upon homicide defendants in Georgia based on race of the homicide victim, that the disparities existed at a less substantial rate in death sentencing based on race of defendants, and that the factors of race of the victim and defendant were at work in Fulton County." Even assuming the study's validity, the Court of Appeals found the statistics "insufficient to demonstrate discriminatory intent or unconstitutional discrimination in the Fourteenth Amendment context, [and] insufficient to show irrationality, arbitrariness and capriciousness under any kind of Eighth Amendment analysis." . . .

The Court of Appeals affirmed the denial by the District Court of McCleskey's petition for a writ of habeas corpus. . . . We granted certiorari and now affirm.

II

McCleskey's first claim is that the Georgia capital punishment statute violates the Equal Protection Clause of the Fourteenth Amendment. He argues that race has infected the administration of Georgia's statute in two ways: persons who murder whites are more likely to be sentenced to death than persons who murder blacks, and black murderers are more likely to be sentenced to death than white murderers. As a black defendant who killed a white victim, McCleskey claims that the Baldus study demonstrates that he was discriminated against because of his race and because of the race of his victim. . . . We agree with the Court of Appeals, and every other court that has considered such a challenge, that this claim must fail.

Our analysis begins with the basic principle that a defendant who alleges an equal protection violation has the burden of proving "the existence of purposeful discrimination." A corollary to this principle is that a criminal defendant must prove that the purposeful discrimination "had a discriminatory effect" on him. Thus, to prevail under the Equal Protection Clause, McCleskey must prove that the decisionmakers in his case acted with discriminatory purpose. He offers no evidence specific to his own case that would support an inference that racial considerations played a part in his sentence. Instead, he relies solely on the Baldus study. McCleskey argues that the Baldus study compels an inference that his sentence rests on purposeful discrimination. McCleskey's claim that these statistics are sufficient proof of discrimination, without regard to the facts of a particular case, would extend to all capital cases in Georgia, at least where the victim was white and the defendant is black.

The Court has accepted statistics as proof of intent to discriminate in certain limited contexts. First, this Court has accepted statistical disparities as proof of an equal protection violation in the selection of the jury venire in a particular district. . . . Second, this Court has accepted statistics in the form of multiple-regression analysis to prove statutory violations under Title VII of the Civil Rights Act of 1964.

But the nature of the capital sentencing decision, and the relationship of the statistics to that decision, are fundamentally different from the corresponding elements in the venire-selection or Title VII cases. Most importantly, each particular decision to impose the death penalty is made by a petit jury selected from a properly constituted venire. Each jury is unique in its composition, and the Constitution requires that its decision rest on consideration of innumerable factors that vary according to the characteristics of the individual defendant and the facts of the particular capital offense. Thus, the application of an inference drawn from the general statistics to a specific decision in a trial and sentencing simply is not comparable to the application of an inference drawn from general statistics to a specific venire-selection or Title VII case. In those cases, the statistics relate to fewer entities, and fewer variables are relevant to the challenged decisions.

Another important difference between the cases in which we have accepted statistics as proof of discriminatory intent and this case is that, in the venire-selection and Title VII contexts, the decisionmaker has an opportunity to explain the statistical disparity. Here, the State has no practical opportunity to rebut the Baldus study. . . ."

Finally, McCleskey's statistical proffer must be viewed in the context of his challenge. McCleskey challenges decisions at the heart of the State's criminal justice system. "[O]ne of society's most basic tasks is that of protecting the lives of its citizens and one of the most basic ways in which it achieves the task is through criminal laws against murder." Implementation of these laws necessarily requires discretionary judgments. Because discretion is essential to the criminal justice process, we would demand exceptionally clear proof before we would infer that the discretion has been abused. The unique nature of the decisions at issue in this case also counsels against adopting such an inference from the disparities indicated by the Baldus study. Accordingly, we hold that the Baldus study is clearly insufficient to support an inference that any of the decisionmakers in McCleskey's case acted with discriminatory purpose. . . .

III

McCleskey also argues that the Baldus study demonstrates that the Georgia capital sentencing system violates the Eighth Amendment. . . .

Two principal decisions guide our resolution of McCleskey's Eighth Amendment claim. In *Furman v. Georgia,* the Court concluded that the death penalty was so irrationally imposed that any particular death sentence could be presumed excessive. . . .

In *Gregg*, the Court specifically addressed the question left open in *Furman*—whether the punishment of death for murder is "under all circumstances, 'cruel and unusual' in violation of the Eighth and Fourteenth Amendments of the Constitution." We noted that any punishment might be unconstitutionally severe if inflicted without penological justification, but concluded:

"Considerations of federalism, as well as respect for the ability of a legislature to evaluate, in terms of its particular State, the moral consensus concerning the death penalty and its social utility as a sanction, require us to conclude, in the absence of more convincing evidence, that the infliction of death as a punishment for murder is not without justification and thus is not unconstitutionally severe." . . .

In sum, our decisions since *Furman* have identified a constitutionally permissible range of discretion in imposing the death penalty. First, there is a required threshold below which the death penalty cannot be imposed. In this context, the State must establish rational criteria that narrow the decisionmaker's judgment as to whether the circumstances of a particular defendant's case meet the threshold. Moreover, a societal consensus that the death penalty is disproportionate to a particular offense prevents a State from imposing the death penalty for that offense. Second, States cannot limit the sentencer's consideration of any relevant circumstance that could cause it to decline to impose the penalty. In this respect, the State cannot channel the sentencer's discretion, but must allow it to consider any relevant information offered by the defendant.

IV

In light of our precedents under the Eighth Amendment, McCleskey cannot argue successfully that his sentence is "disproportionate to the crime in the traditional sense." He does not deny that he committed a murder in the course of a planned robbery, a crime for which this Court has determined that the death penalty constitutionally may be imposed. His disproportionality claim "is of a different sort." McCleskey argues that the sentences in his case is disproportionate to the sentences in other murder cases.

On the one hand, he cannot base a constitutional claim on an argument that his case differs from other cases in which defendants did receive the death penalty. On automatic appeal, the Georgia Supreme Court found that McCleskey's death sentence was not disproportionate to other death sentences imposed in the State. . . .

On the other hand, absent a showing that the Georgia capital punishment system operates in an arbitrary and capricious manner, McCleskey cannot prove a constitutional violation by demonstrating that other defendants who may be similarly situated did not receive the death penalty. In *Gregg*, the Court confronted the argument that "the opportunities for discretionary action that are inherent in the processing of any murder case under Georgia law," specifically the opportunities for discretionary leniency, rendered the capital sentences imposed arbitrary and capricious. We rejected this contention. . . .

Because McCleskey's sentence was imposed under Georgia sentencing procedures that focus discretion "on the particularized nature of the crime and the particularized characteristics of the individual defendant," we lawfully may presume that McCleskey's death sentence was not "wantonly and freakishly" imposed, and thus that the sentence is not disproportionate within any recognized meaning under the Eighth Amendment.

Although our decision in *Gregg* as to the facial validity of the Georgia capital punishment statute appears to foreclose McCleskey's disproportionality argument, he further contends that the Georgia capital punishment system is arbitrary and capricious in application, and therefore his sentence is excessive, because racial considerations may influence capital sentencing decisions in Georgia. We now address this claim.

To evaluate McCleskey's challenge, we must examine exactly what the Baldus study may show. Even Professor Baldus does not contend that his statistics prove that race enters into any capital sentencing decisions or that race was a factor in McCleskey's particular case. Statistics at most may show only a likelihood that a particular factor entered into some decisions. There is, of course, some risk of racial prejudice influencing a jury's decision in a criminal case. There are similar risks that other kinds of prejudice will influence other criminal trials. . . . McCleskey asks us to accept the likelihood allegedly shown by the Baldus study as the constitutional measure of an unacceptable risk of racial prejudice influencing capital sentencing decisions. This we decline to do. . . .

McCleskey's argument that the Constitution condemns the discretion allowed decisionmakers in the Georgia capital sentencing system is antithetical to the fundamental role of discretion in our criminal justice system. Discretion in the criminal justice system offers substantial benefits to the criminal defendant. Not only can a jury decline to impose the death sentence, it can decline to convict or choose to convict of a lesser offense. Whereas decisions against a defendant's interest may be reversed by the trial judge or on appeal, these discretionary exercises of leniency are final and unreviewable. Similarly, the capacity of prosecutorial discretion to provide individualized justice is "firmly entrenched in American law." As we have noted, a prosecutor can decline to charge, offer a plea bargain, or decline to seek a death sentence in any particular case. Of course, "the power to be lenient [also] is the power to discriminate," but a capital punishment system that did not allow for discretionary acts of leniency "would be totally alien to our notions of criminal justice."

At most, the Baldus study indicates a discrepancy that appears to correlate with race. Apparent disparities in sentencing are an inevitable part of our criminal justice system. The discrepancy indicated by the Baldus study is "a far cry from the major systemic defects identified in *Furman*." As this Court has recognized, any mode for determining guilt or punishment "has its weaknesses and the potential for misuse." . . .

Specifically, "there can be 'no perfect procedure for deciding in which cases governmental authority should be used to impose death.'" Despite these imperfections, our consistent rule has been that constitutional guarantees are met when "the mode [for determining guilt or punishment] itself has been surrounded with safeguards to make it as fair as possible." Where the discretion that is fundamental to our criminal process is involved, we decline to assume that what is unexplained is invidious. In light of the safeguards designed to minimize racial bias in the process, the fundamental value of jury trial in our criminal justice system, and the benefits that discretion provides to criminal defendants, we hold that the Baldus study does not demonstrate a constitutionally significant risk of racial bias affecting the Georgia capital sentencing process.

V

Two additional concerns inform our decision in this case. First, McCleskey's claim, taken to its logical conclusion, throws into serious question the principles that underlie our entire criminal justice system. The Eighth Amendment is not limited in application to capital punishment, but applies to all penalties. Thus, if we accepted McCleskey's claim that racial bias has impermissibly tainted the capital sentencing decision, we could soon be faced with similar claims as to other types of penalty. Moreover, the claim that his sentence rests on the irrelevant factor of race easily could be extended to apply to claims based on unexplained discrepancies that correlate to membership in other minority groups, and even to gender. Similarly, since McCleskey's claim relates to the race of his victim, other claims could apply with equally logical force to statistical disparities that correlate with the race or sex of other actors in the criminal justice system, such as defense attorneys or judges. Also, there is no logical reason that such a claim need be limited to racial or sexual bias. If arbitrary and capricious punishment is the touchstone under the Eighth Amendment, such a claim could—at least in theory—be based upon any arbitrary variable, such as the defendant's facial characteristics, or the physical attractiveness of the defendant or the victim, that some statistical study indicates may be influential in jury decisionmaking. As these examples illustrate, there is no limiting principle to the type of challenge brought by McCleskey. The Constitution does not require that a State eliminate any demonstrable disparity that correlates with a potentially irrelevant factor in order to operate a criminal justice system that includes capital punishment. As we have stated specifically in the context of capital punishment, the Constitution does not "plac[e] totally unrealistic conditions on its use."

Second, McCleskey's arguments are best presented to the legislative bodies. It is not the responsibility—or indeed even the right—of this Court to determine the appropriate punishment for particular crimes. . . . Legislatures also are better qualified to weigh and "evaluate the results of statistical studies in terms of their own local conditions and with a flexibility of approach that is not available to the courts." Capital punishment is now the law in more than two-thirds of our States. It is the ultimate duty of courts to determine on a case-by-case basis whether these laws are applied consistently with the Constitution. Despite McCleskey's wide-ranging arguments that basically challenge the validity of capital punishment in our multiracial society, the only question before us is whether in his case, the law of Georgia was properly applied. We agree with the District Court and the Court of Appeals for the Eleventh Circuit that this was carefully and correctly done in this case.

VI

Accordingly, we affirm the judgment of the Court of Appeals for the Eleventh Circuit. . . .

JUSTICE BRENNAN, with whom JUSTICE MARSHALL joins, and with whom JUSTICE BLACKMUN and JUSTICE STEVENS join in all but Part I, dissenting.

I

Adhering to my view that the death penalty is in all circumstances cruel and unusual punishment forbidden by the Eighth and Fourteenth Amendments, I would vacate the decision below insofar as it left undisturbed the death sentence imposed in this case. . . . [M]urder defendants in Georgia with white victims are more than four times as likely to receive the death sentence as are defendants with black victims. Nothing could convey more powerfully the intractable reality of the death penalty: "that the effort to eliminate arbitrariness in the infliction of that ultimate sanction is so plainly doomed to failure that it—and the death penalty—must be abandoned altogether." . . .

Even if I did not hold this position, however, I would reverse the Court of Appeals, for petitioner McCleskey has clearly demonstrated that his death sentence was imposed in violation of the Eighth and Fourteenth Amendments. . . .

II

At some point in this case, Warren McCleskey doubtless asked his lawyer whether a jury was likely to sentence him to die. A candid reply to this question would have been disturbing. First, counsel would have to tell McCleskey that few of the details of the crime or of McCleskey's past criminal conduct were more important than the fact that his victim was white. Furthermore, counsel would feel bound to tell McCleskey that defendants charged with killing white victims in Georgia are 4.3 times as likely to be sentenced to death as defendants charged with killing blacks. In addition, frankness would compel the disclosure that it was more likely than not that the race of McCleskey's victim would determine whether he received a death sentence: 6 of every 11 defendants convicted of killing a white person would not have received the death penalty if their victims had been black, while, among defendants with aggravating and mitigating factors comparable to McCleskey's, 20 of every 34 would not have been sentenced to die if their victims had been black. Finally, the assessment would not be complete without the information that cases involving black defendants and white victims are more likely to result in a death sentence than cases featuring any other racial combination of defendant and victim. The story could be told in a variety of ways, but McCleskey could not fail to grasp its essential narrative line: there was a significant chance that race would play a prominent role in determining if he lived or died.

The Court today holds that Warren McCleskey's sentence was constitutionally imposed. It finds no fault in a system in which lawyers must tell their clients that race casts a large shadow on the capital sentencing process. . . .

The statistical evidence in this case . . . relentlessly documents the risk that McCleskey's sentence was influenced by racial considerations. This evidence shows that there is a better than even chance in Georgia that race will influence the decision to impose the death penalty: a majority of defendants in white-victim crimes would not have been sentenced to die if their victims had been black. . . . [P]etitioner's statistics on their face are a powerful demonstration of the type of risk that our Eighth Amendment jurisprudence has consistently condemned. . . .

IV

The Court . . . maintains that accepting McCleskey's claim would pose a threat to all sentencing because of the prospect that a correlation might be demonstrated between sentencing outcomes and other personal characteristics. . . . Race is a consideration whose influence is expressly constitutionally proscribed. . . . That a decision to impose the death penalty could be influenced by race is . . . a particularly repugnant prospect, and evidence that race may play even a modest role in levying a death sentence should be enough to characterize that sentence as "cruel and unusual."

Certainly, a factor that we would regard as morally irrelevant, such as hair color, at least theoretically could be associated with sentencing results to such an extent that we would regard as arbitrary a system in which that factor played a significant role. . . . [H]owever, the evaluation of evidence suggesting such a correlation must be informed not merely by statistics, but by history and experience. One could hardly contend that this Nation has on the basis of hair color inflicted upon persons deprivation comparable to that imposed on the basis of race. Recognition of this fact would necessarily influence the evaluation of data suggesting the influence of hair color on sentencing, and would require evidence of statistical correlation even more powerful than that presented by the Baldus study.

Furthermore, the Court's fear of the expansive ramifications of a holding for McCleskey in this case is unfounded because it fails to recognize the uniquely sophisticated nature of the Baldus study. . . .

The Court's projection of apocalyptic consequences for criminal sentencing is thus greatly exaggerated. . . .

Finally, the Court justifies its rejection of McCleskey's claim by cautioning against usurpation of the legislatures' role in devising and monitoring criminal punishment. . . . The judiciary's role in this society counts for little if the use of governmental power to extinguish life does not elicit close scrutiny. . . . Those whom we would banish from society or from the human community itself often speak in too faint a voice to be heard above society's demand for punishment. It is the particular role of courts to hear these voices, for the Constitution declares that the majoritarian chorus may not alone dictate the conditions of social life. The Court thus fulfills, rather than disrupts, the scheme of separation of powers by closely scrutinizing the imposition of the death penalty, for no decision of a society is more deserving of "sober second thought."

V

. . . The Court's decision today will not change what attorneys in Georgia tell other Warren McCleskeys about their chances of execution. Nothing will soften the harsh message they must convey, nor alter the prospect that race undoubtedly will continue to be a topic of discussion. McCleskey's evidence will not have obtained judicial acceptance, but that will not affect what is said on death row. However many criticisms of today's decision may be rendered, these painful conversations will serve as the most eloquent dissents of all.

JUSTICE BLACKMUN, with whom JUSTICE MARSHALL and JUSTICE STEVENS join, and with whom JUSTICE BRENNAN joins in all but Part IV-B, dissenting.

The Court today sanctions the execution of a man despite his presentation of evidence that establishes a constitutionally intolerable level of racially based discrimination leading to the imposition of his death sentence. I am disappointed with the Court's action not only because of its denial of constitutional guarantees to petitioner McCleskey individually, but also because of its departure from what seems to me to be well-developed constitutional jurisprudence.

JUSTICE BRENNAN has thoroughly demonstrated that, if one assumes that the statistical evidence presented by petitioner McCleskey is valid, as we must in light of the Court of Appeals' assumption, there exists in the Georgia capital sentencing scheme a risk of racially based discrimination that is so acute that it violates the Eighth Amendment. His analysis of McCleskey's case in terms of the Eighth Amendment is consistent with this Court's recognition that because capital cases involve the State's imposition of a punishment that is unique both in kind and degree, the decision in such cases must reflect a heightened degree of reliability under the Amendment's prohibition of the infliction of cruel and unusual punishments. . . .

Yet McCleskey's case raises concerns that are central not only to the principles underlying the Eighth Amendment, but also to the principles underlying the Fourteenth Amendment. Analysis of his case in terms of the Fourteenth Amendment is consistent with this Court's recognition that racial discrimination is fundamentally at odds with our constitutional guarantee of equal protection. The protections afforded by the Fourteenth Amendment are not left at the courtroom door. Nor is equal protection denied to persons convicted of crimes. The Court in the past has found that racial discrimination within the criminal justice system is particularly abhorrent. . . .

JUSTICE STEVENS, with whom JUSTICE BLACKMUN joins, dissenting.

. . . The Court's decision appears to be based on a fear that the acceptance of McCleskey's claim would sound the death knell for capital punishment in Georgia. If society were indeed forced to choose between a racially discriminatory death penalty (one that provides heightened protection against murder "for whites only") and no death penalty at all, the choice mandated by the Constitution would be plain. But the Court's fear is unfounded. One of the lessons of the Baldus study is that there exist certain categories of extremely serious crimes for which prosecutors consistently seek, and juries consistently impose, the death penalty without regard to the race of the victim or the race of the offender. If Georgia were to narrow the class of death-eligible defendants to those categories, the danger of arbitrary and discriminatory imposition of the death penalty would be significantly decreased, if not eradicated. . . . [S]uch a restructuring of the sentencing scheme is surely not too high a price to pay. . . .

PENRY V. LYNAUGH (1989)

The Supreme Court held that executing mentally retarded individuals who are convicted of capital crimes does not necessarily violate the Eighth Amendment. In this case, however, the Court struck down Johnny Paul Penry's death sentence because the jury had not been properly instructed about how to take into account his mental retardation and other mitigating factors.

JUSTICE O'CONNOR delivered the opinion of the Court, except as to Part IV-C.

In this case, we must decide whether petitioner, Johnny Paul Penry, was sentenced to death in violation of the Eighth Amendment because the jury was not instructed that it could consider and give effect to his mitigating evidence in imposing its sentence. We must also decide whether the Eighth Amendment categorically prohibits Penry's execution because he is mentally retarded.

I

On the morning of October 25, 1979, Pamela Carpenter was brutally raped, beaten, and stabbed with a pair of scissors in her home in Livingston, Texas. She died a few hours later in the course of emergency treatment. Before she died, she described her assailant. Her description led two local sheriff's deputies to suspect Penry, who had recently been released on parole after conviction on another rape charge. Penry subsequently gave two statements confessing to the crime and was charged with capital murder.

At a competency hearing held before trial, a clinical psychologist, Dr. Jerome Brown, testified that Penry was mentally retarded. As a child, Penry was diagnosed as having organic brain damage, which was probably caused by trauma to the brain at birth. Penry was tested over the years as having an IQ between 50 and 63, which indicates mild to moderate retardation. Dr. Brown's own testing before the trial indicated that Penry had an IQ of 54. Dr. Brown's evaluation also revealed that Penry, who was 22 years old at the time of the crime, had the mental age of a 6 1/2-year-old . . . Penry's social maturity, or ability to function in the world, was that of a 9- or 10-year-old. Dr. Brown testified that "there's a point at which anyone with [Penry's] IQ is always incompetent, but, you know, this man is more in the borderline range."

The jury found Penry competent to stand trial. . . . The trial court determined that Penry's confessions were voluntary, and they were introduced into evidence. At trial, Penry raised an insanity defense and presented the testimony of a psychiatrist, Dr. Jose Garcia. Dr. Garcia testified that Penry suffered from organic brain damage and moderate retardation, which resulted in poor impulse control and an inability to learn from experience. . . . In Dr. Garcia's judgment, Penry was suffering from an organic brain disorder at the time of the offense which made it impossible for him to appreciate the wrongfulness of his conduct or to conform his conduct to the law.

Penry's mother testified at trial that Penry was unable to learn in school and never finished the first grade. Penry's sister testified that their mother had frequently beaten him over the head with a belt when he was a child. Penry was also routinely locked in his room without access to a toilet for long periods of time. As a youngster, Penry was in and out of a number of state schools and hospitals, until his father removed him from state schools altogether when he was 12. Penry's aunt subsequently struggled for over a year to teach Penry how to print his name.

The State introduced the testimony of two psychiatrists to rebut the testimony of Dr. Garcia. Dr. Kenneth Vogtsberger testified that although Penry was a person of limited mental ability, he was not suffering from any mental illness or defect at the time of the crime, and that he knew the difference between right and wrong and had the potential to honor the law. . . .

Dr. Felix Peebles also testified for the State that Penry was legally sane at the time of the offense and had a "full-blown anti-social personality." . . . Although they disagreed with the defense psychiatrist over the extent and cause of Penry's mental limitations, both psychiatrists for the State acknowledged that Penry was a person of extremely limited mental ability, and that he seemed unable to learn from his mistakes.

The jury rejected Penry's insanity defense and found him guilty of capital murder. The following day, at the close of the penalty hearing, the jury decided the sentence to be imposed on Penry by answering three "special issues":

"(1) whether the conduct of the defendant that caused the death of the deceased was committed deliberately and with the reasonable expectation that the death of the deceased or another would result;

"(2) whether there is a probability that the defendant would commit criminal acts of violence that would constitute a continuing threat to society; and

"(3) if raised by the evidence, whether the conduct of the defendant in killing the deceased was unreasonable in response to the provocation, if any, by the deceased."

If the jury unanimously answers "yes" to each issue submitted, the trial court must sentence the defendant to death. Otherwise, the defendant is sentenced to life imprisonment. . . .

The jury answered "yes" to all three special issues, and Penry was sentenced to death. The Texas Court of Criminal Appeals affirmed his conviction and sentence on direct appeal. . . . This Court denied certiorari on direct review.

Penry then filed this federal habeas corpus petition challenging his death sentence. . . . The District Court denied relief, and Penry appealed to the Court of Appeals for the Fifth Circuit.

The Court of Appeals affirmed the District Court's judgment. . . .

We granted certiorari to resolve two questions. First, was Penry sentenced to death in violation of the Eighth Amendment because the jury was not adequately instructed to take into consideration all of his mitigating evidence and because the terms in the Texas special issues were not defined in such a way that the jury could consider and give effect to his mitigating evidence in answering them? Second, is it cruel and unusual punishment under the Eighth Amendment to execute a mentally retarded person with Penry's reasoning ability? . . .

II

B

. . . . Citing *Lockett* [v. Ohio] and *Eddings* [v. Oklahoma], Penry argues that he was sentenced to death in violation of the Eighth Amendment because, in light of the jury instructions given, the jury was unable to fully consider and give effect to the mitigating evidence of his mental retardation and abused background, which he offered as the basis for a sentence less than death. . . .

[A]t the time Penry's conviction became final, it was clear from *Lockett* and *Eddings* that a State could not, consistent with the Eighth and Fourteenth Amendments, prevent the sentencer from considering and giving effect to evidence relevant to the defendant's background or character or to the circumstances of the offense that mitigate against imposing the death penalty. . . . Penry argues that those assurances were not fulfilled in his particular case because, without appropriate instructions, the jury could not fully consider and give effect to the mitigating evidence of his mental retardation and abused childhood in rendering its sentencing decision. . . .

III

Underlying *Lockett* and *Eddings* is the principle that punishment should be directly related to the personal culpability of the criminal defendant. If the sentencer is to make an individualized assessment of the appropriateness of the death penalty, "evidence about the defendant's background and character is relevant because of the belief, long held by this society, that defendants who commit criminal acts that are attributable to a disadvantaged background, or to emotional and mental problems, may be less culpable than defendants who have no such excuse." Moreover, *Eddings* makes clear that it is not enough simply to allow the defendant to present mitigating evidence to the sentencer. The sentencer must also be able to consider and give effect to that evidence in imposing sentence. . . .

Although Penry offered mitigating evidence of his mental retardation and abused childhood as the basis for a sentence of life imprisonment rather than death, the jury that sentenced him was only able to express its views on the appropriate sentence by answering three questions: Did Penry act deliberately when he murdered Pamela Carpenter? Is there a probability that he will be dangerous in the future? Did he act unreasonably in response to provocation? The jury was never instructed that it could consider the evidence offered by Penry as mitigating evidence and that it could give mitigating effect to that evidence in imposing sentence. . . .

Penry argues that his mitigating evidence of mental retardation and childhood abuse has relevance to his moral culpability beyond the scope of the special issues, and that the jury was unable to express its "reasoned moral response" to that evidence in determining whether death was the appropriate punishment. We agree. Thus, we reject the State's contrary argument that the jury was able to consider and give effect to all of Penry's mitigating evidence in answering the special issues without any jury instructions on mitigating evidence.

The first special issue asks whether the defendant acted "deliberately and with the reasonable expectation that the death of the deceased . . . would result." Neither the Texas Legislature nor the Texas Court of Criminal Appeals have defined the term "deliberately," and the jury was not instructed on the term, so we do not know precisely what meaning the jury gave to it. . . .

In the absence of jury instructions defining "deliberately" . . . a juror who believed that Penry's retardation and background diminished his moral culpability and made imposition of the death penalty unwarranted would be unable to give effect to that conclusion if the juror also believed that Penry committed the crime "deliberately." Thus, we cannot be sure that the jury's answer to the first special issue reflected a "reasoned moral response" to Penry's mitigating evidence.

The second special issue asks "whether there is a probability that the defendant would commit criminal acts of violence that would constitute a continuing threat to society." The mitigating evidence concerning Penry's mental retardation indicated that one effect of his retardation is his inability to learn from his mistakes. Although this evidence is relevant to the second issue, it is relevant only as an aggravating factor because it suggests a "yes" answer to the question of future dangerousness. . . .

Penry's mental retardation and history of abuse is thus a two-edged sword: it may diminish his blameworthiness for his crime even as it indicates that there is a probability that he will be dangerous in the future. . . .

The second special issue, therefore, did not provide a vehicle for the jury to give mitigating effect to Penry's evidence of mental retardation and childhood abuse.

The third special issue asks "whether the conduct of the defendant in killing the deceased was unreasonable in response to the provocation, if any, by the deceased." On this issue, the State argued that Penry stabbed Pamela Carpenter with a pair of scissors not in response to provocation, but "for the purpose of avoiding detection." Penry's own confession indicated that he did not stab the victim after she wounded him superficially with a scissors during a struggle. . . . Thus, a juror who believed Penry lacked the moral culpability to be sentenced to death could not express that view in answering the third special issue if she also concluded that Penry's action was not a reasonable response to provocation. . . .

. . . [A] reasonable juror could well have believed that there was no vehicle for expressing the view that Penry did not deserve to be sentenced to death based upon his mitigating evidence. . . .

In this case, in the absence of instructions informing the jury that it could consider and give effect to the mitigating evidence of Penry's mental retardation and abused background by declining to impose the death penalty, we conclude that the jury was not provided with a vehicle for expressing its "reasoned moral response" to that evidence in rendering its sentencing decision. Our reasoning in *Lockett* and *Eddings* thus compels a remand for resentencing so that we do not "risk that the death penalty will be imposed in spite of factors which may call for a less severe penalty." . . .

IV

Penry's second claim is that it would be cruel and unusual punishment, prohibited by the Eighth Amendment, to execute a mentally retarded person like himself with the reasoning capacity of a 7-year-old. He argues that because of their mental disabilities, mentally retarded people do not possess the level of moral culpability to justify imposing the death sentence. He also argues that there is an emerging national consensus against executing the mentally retarded. The State responds that there is insufficient evidence of a national consensus against executing the retarded, and that existing procedural safeguards adequately protect the interests of mentally retarded persons such as Penry. . . .

B

The Eighth Amendment categorically prohibits the infliction of cruel and unusual punishments. At a minimum, the Eighth Amendment prohibits punishment considered cruel and unusual at the time the Bill of Rights was adopted. The prohibitions of the Eighth Amendment are not limited, however, to those practices condemned by the common law in 1789. The prohibition against cruel and unusual punishments also recognizes the "evolving standards of decency that mark the progress of a maturing society." In discerning those "evolving standards," we have looked to objective evidence of how our society views a particular punishment today. The clearest and most reliable objective evidence of contemporary values is the legislation enacted by the country's legislatures. We have also looked to data concerning the actions of sentencing juries. . . .

The common law prohibition against punishing "idiots" for their crimes suggests that it may indeed be "cruel and unusual" punishment to execute persons who are profoundly or severely retarded and wholly lacking the capacity to appreciate the wrongfulness of their actions. Because of the protections afforded by the insanity defense today, such a person is not likely to be convicted or face the prospect of punishment. Moreover, under *Ford v. Wainwright*, someone who is "unaware of the punishment they are about to suffer and why they are to suffer it" cannot be executed.

Such a case is not before us today. Penry was found competent to stand trial. In other words, he was found to have the ability to consult with his lawyer with a reasonable degree of rational understanding, and was found to have a rational as well as factual understanding of the proceedings against him. In addition, the jury rejected his insanity defense, which reflected their conclusion that Penry knew that his conduct was wrong and was capable of conforming his conduct to the requirements of the law.

Penry argues, however, that there is objective evidence today of an emerging national consensus against execution of the mentally retarded, reflecting the "evolving standards of decency that mark the progress of a maturing society." Only one State [Georgia], however, currently bans execution of retarded persons who have been found guilty of a capital offense. Maryland has enacted a similar statute which will take effect on July 1, 1989.

In contrast, in *Ford v. Wainwright*, which held that the Eighth Amendment prohibits execution of the insane, considerably more evidence of a national consensus was available. No State permitted the execution of the insane, and 26 States had statutes explicitly requiring suspension of the execution of a capital defendant who became insane. . . . In our view, the two state statutes prohibiting execution of the mentally retarded, even when added to the 14 States that have rejected capital punishment completely, do not provide sufficient evidence at present of a national consensus. . . .

. . . [A]t present, there is insufficient evidence of a national consensus against executing mentally retarded people convicted of capital offenses for us to conclude that it is categorically prohibited by the Eighth Amendment.

C

On the record before the Court today . . . I cannot conclude that all mentally retarded people of Penry's ability—by virtue of their mental retardation alone, and apart from any individualized consideration of their personal responsibility—inevitably lack the cognitive, volitional, and moral capacity to act with the degree of culpability associated with the death penalty. Mentally retarded persons are individuals whose abilities and experiences can vary greatly. . . .

Not surprisingly, courts have long been reluctant to rely on the concept of mental age as a basis for exculpating a defendant from criminal responsibility. Moreover, reliance on mental age to measure the capabilities of a retarded person for purposes of the Eighth Amendment could have a disempowering effect if applied in other areas of the law. Thus, on that premise, a mildly mentally retarded person could be denied the opportunity to enter into contracts or to marry by virtue of the fact that he had a "mental age" of a young child. In light of the inherent problems with the mental age concept, and in the absence of better evidence of a national consensus against execution of the retarded, mental age should not be adopted as a line-drawing principle in our Eighth Amendment jurisprudence.

In sum, mental retardation is a factor that may well lessen a defendant's culpability for a capital offense. But we cannot conclude today that the Eighth Amendment precludes the execution of any mentally retarded person of Penry's ability convicted of a capital offense simply by virtue of his or her mental retardation alone. So long as sentencers can consider and give effect to mitigating evidence of mental retardation in imposing sentence, an individualized determination whether "death is the appropriate punishment" can be made in each particular case. While a national consensus against execution of the mentally retarded may someday emerge reflecting the "evolving standards of decency that mark the progress of a maturing society," there is insufficient evidence of such a consensus today.

Accordingly, the judgment below is affirmed in part and reversed in part, and the case is remanded for further proceedings consistent with this opinion. . . .

JUSTICE BRENNAN, with whom JUSTICE MARSHALL joins, concurring in part and dissenting in part.

I agree that the jury instructions given at sentencing in this case deprived petitioner of his constitutional right to have a jury consider all mitigating evidence that he presented before sentencing him to die. I would also hold, however, that the Eighth Amendment prohibits the execution of offenders who are mentally retarded and who thus lack the full degree of responsibility for their crimes that is a predicate for the constitutional imposition of the death penalty. . . .

Stanford v. Kentucky (1989)

The Supreme Court held in Thompson v. Oklahoma *(1988) that William Wayne Thompson, who had participated in a murder when he was 15 years old, could not be executed. In* Stanford v. Kentucky, *the Supreme Court upheld death sentences for Kevin Stanford, who was 17 years old when he committed a murder in Kentucky, and Heath Wilkins, who was 16 years old when he committed a murder in Missouri.*

JUSTICE SCALIA announced the judgment of the Court and delivered the opinion of the Court with respect to Parts I, II, III, and IV-A, and an opinion with respect to Parts IV-B and V, in which THE CHIEF JUSTICE, JUSTICE WHITE, and JUSTICE KENNEDY join.

These two consolidated cases require us to decide whether the imposition of capital punishment on an individual for a crime committed at 16 or 17 years of age constitutes cruel and unusual punishment under the Eighth Amendment.

I

The first case involves the shooting death of 20-year-old Barbel Poore in Jefferson County, Kentucky. Petitioner Kevin Stanford committed the murder on January 7, 1981, when he was approximately 17 years and 4 months of age. Stanford and his accomplice repeatedly raped and sodomized Poore during and after their commission of a robbery at a gas station where she worked as an attendant. They then drove her to a secluded area near the station, where Stanford shot her point-blank in the face and then in the back of her head. The proceeds from the robbery were roughly 300 cartons of cigarettes, two gallons of fuel, and a small amount of cash. A corrections officer testified that petitioner explained the murder as follows: "'[H]e said, I had to shoot her, [she] lived next door to me and she would recognize me. . . . I guess we could have tied her up or something or beat [her up] . . . and tell her if she tells, we would kill her. . . . Then after he said that he started laughing.'"

After Stanford's arrest, a Kentucky juvenile court conducted hearings to determine whether he should be transferred for trial as an adult under [Kentucky law]. . . . Stressing the seriousness of petitioner's offenses and the unsuccessful attempts of the juvenile system to treat him for numerous instances of past delinquency, the juvenile court found certification for trial as an adult to be in the best interest of petitioner and the community.

Stanford was convicted of murder, first-degree sodomy, first-degree robbery, and receiving stolen property, and was sentenced to death and 45 years in prison. The Kentucky Supreme Court affirmed the death sentence. . . .

The second case before us today involves the stabbing death of Nancy Allen, a 26-year-old mother of two who was working behind the sales counter of the convenience store she and David Allen owned and operated in Avondale, Missouri. Petitioner Heath Wilkins committed the murder on July 27, 1985, when he was approximately 16 years and 6 months of age. The record reflects that Wilkins' plan was to rob the store and murder "whoever was behind the counter" because "a dead person can't talk." While Wilkins' accomplice, Patrick Stevens, held Allen, Wilkins stabbed her, causing her to fall to the floor. When Stevens had trouble operating the cash register, Allen spoke up to assist him, leading Wilkins to stab her three more times in her chest. Two of these wounds penetrated the victim's heart. When Allen began to beg for her life, Wilkins stabbed her four more times in the neck, opening her carotid artery. After helping themselves to liquor, cigarettes, rolling papers, and approximately $450 in cash and checks, Wilkins and Stevens left Allen to die on the floor.

Because he was roughly six months short of the age of majority for purposes of criminal prosecution [under Missouri law], Wilkins could not automatically be tried as an adult under Missouri law. Before that could happen, the juvenile court was required to terminate juvenile court jurisdiction and certify Wilkins for trial as an adult. . . . Relying on the "viciousness, force and violence" of the alleged crime, petitioner's maturity, and the failure of the juvenile justice system to rehabilitate him after previous delinquent acts, the juvenile court made the necessary certification.

Wilkins was charged with first-degree murder, armed criminal action, and carrying a concealed weapon. After the court found him competent, petitioner entered guilty pleas to all charges. A punishment hearing was held, at which both the State and petitioner himself urged imposition of the death sentence. Evidence at the hearing revealed that petitioner had been in and out of juvenile facilities since the age of eight for various acts of burglary, theft, and arson, had attempted to kill his mother by putting insecticide into Tylenol capsules, and had killed several animals in his neighborhood. Although psychiatric testimony indicated that Wilkins had "personality disorders," the witnesses agreed that Wilkins was aware of his actions and could distinguish right from wrong.

Determining that the death penalty was appropriate, the trial court entered the following order:

"[T]he court finds beyond reasonable doubt that the following aggravating circumstances exist:

"1. The murder in the first degree was committed while the defendant was engaged in the perpetration of the felony of robbery, and

"2. The murder in the first degree involved depravity of mind and that as a result thereof, it was outrageously or wantonly vile, horrible or inhuman."

. . . [T]he Supreme Court of Missouri affirmed. . . .

We granted certiorari in these cases to decide whether the Eighth Amendment precludes the death penalty for individuals who commit crimes at 16 or 17 years of age.

II

The thrust of both Wilkins' and Stanford's arguments is that imposition of the death penalty on those who were juveniles when they committed their crimes falls within the Eighth Amendment's prohibition against "cruel and unusual punishments." Wilkins would have us define juveniles as individuals 16 years of age and under; Stanford would draw the line at 17. . . .

[P]etitioners . . . argue that their punishment is contrary to the "evolving standards of decency that mark the progress of a maturing society." . . . In determining what standards have "evolved," . . . we have looked not to our own conceptions of decency, but to those of modern American society as a whole. As we have said, "Eighth Amendment judgments should not be, or appear to be, merely the subjective views of individual Justices; judgment should be informed by objective factors to the maximum possible extent." . . .

III

"[F]irst" among the "'objective indicia that reflect the public attitude toward a given sanction'" are statutes passed by society's elected representatives. Of the 37 States whose laws permit capital punishment, 15 decline to impose it upon 16-year-old offenders and 12 decline to impose it on 17-year-old offenders. This does not establish the degree of national consensus this Court has previously thought sufficient to label a particular punishment cruel and unusual. In invalidating the death penalty for rape of an adult woman, we stressed that Georgia was the sole jurisdiction that authorized such a punishment. In striking down capital punishment for participation in a robbery in which an accomplice takes a life, we emphasized that only eight jurisdictions authorized similar punishment. In finding that the Eighth Amendment precludes execution of the insane and thus requires an adequate hearing on the issue of sanity, we relied upon (in addition to the common-law rule) the fact that "no State in the Union" permitted such punishment. And in striking down a life sentence without parole under a recidivist statute, we stressed that "[i]t appears that [petitioner] was treated more severely than he would have been in any other State."

Since a majority of the States that permit capital punishment authorize it for crimes committed at age 16 or above, petitioners' cases are more analogous to *Tison v. Arizona* than *Coker, Enmund, Ford,* and *Solem*. In *Tison*, which upheld Arizona's imposition of the death penalty for major participation in a felony with reckless indifference to human life, we noted that only 11 of those jurisdictions imposing capital punishment rejected its use in such circumstances. . . . We think the same conclusion as in *Tison* is required in these cases. . . .

IV

Wilkins and Stanford argue, however, that even if the laws themselves do not establish a settled consensus, the application of the laws does. That contemporary society views capital punishment of 16- and 17-year-old offenders as inappropriate is demonstrated, they say, by the reluctance of juries to impose, and prosecutors to seek, such sentences. Petitioners are quite correct that a far smaller number of offenders under 18 than over 18 have been sentenced to death in this country. . . . And it appears that actual executions for crimes committed under age 18 accounted for only about two percent of the total number of executions that occurred between 1642 and 1986. . . . These statistics, however, carry little significance. Given the undisputed fact that a far smaller percentage of capital crimes are committed by persons under 18 than over 18, the discrepancy in treatment is much less than might seem. Granted, however, that a substantial discrepancy exists, that does not establish the requisite proposition that the death sentence for offenders under 18 is categorically unacceptable to prosecutors and juries. To the contrary, it is not only possible, but overwhelmingly probable, that the very considerations which induce petitioners and their supporters to believe that death should never be imposed on offenders under 18 cause prosecutors and juries to believe that it should rarely be imposed.

This last point suggests why there is also no relevance to the laws cited by petitioners and their amici which set 18 or more as the legal age for engaging in various activities, ranging from driving to drinking alcoholic beverages to voting. It is, to begin with, absurd to think that one must be mature enough to drive carefully, to drink responsibly, or to vote intelligently, in order to be mature enough to understand that murdering another human being is profoundly wrong, and to conform one's conduct to that most minimal of all civilized standards. But even if the requisite degrees of maturity were comparable, the age statutes in question would still not be relevant. They do not represent a social judgment that all persons under the designated ages are not responsible enough to drive, to drink, or to vote, but at most a judgment that the vast majority are not. These laws set the appropriate ages for the operation of a system that makes its determinations in gross, and that does not conduct individualized maturity tests for each driver, drinker, or voter. The criminal justice system, however, does provide individualized testing. In the realm of capital punishment in particular, "individualized consideration [is] a constitutional requirement" and one of the individualized mitigating factors that sentencers must be permitted to consider is the defendant's age.... The application of this particularized system to the petitioners can be declared constitutionally inadequate only if there is a consensus, not that 17 or 18 is the age at which most persons, or even almost all persons, achieve sufficient maturity to be held fully responsible for murder; but that 17 or 18 is the age before which no one can reasonably be held fully responsible....

V

Having failed to establish a consensus against capital punishment for 16- and 17-year-old offenders through state and federal statutes and the behavior of prosecutors and juries, petitioners seek to demonstrate it through other indicia, including public opinion polls, the views of interest groups, and the positions adopted by various professional associations. We decline the invitation to rest constitutional law upon such uncertain foundations....

We also reject petitioners' argument that we should invalidate capital punishment of 16- and 17-year-old offenders on the ground that it fails to serve the legitimate goals of penology. According to petitioners, it fails to deter because juveniles, possessing less developed cognitive skills than adults, are less likely to fear death; and it fails to exact just retribution because juveniles, being less mature and responsible, are also less morally blameworthy....

But ... it is not demonstrable that no 16-year-old is "adequately responsible" or significantly deterred. It is rational, even if mistaken, to think the contrary....

We reject the dissent's contention that our approach, by "largely return[ing] the task of defining the contours of Eighth Amendment protection to political majorities," leaves "'[c]onstitutional doctrine [to] be formulated by the acts of those institutions which the Constitution is supposed to limit.'" When this Court cast loose from the historical moorings consisting of the original application of the Eighth Amendment, it did not embark rudderless upon a wide-open sea. Rather, it limited the Amendment's extension to those practices contrary to the "evolving standards of decency that mark the progress of a maturing society." It has never been thought that this was a shorthand reference to the preferences of a majority of this Court. By reaching a decision supported neither by constitutional text nor by the demonstrable current standards of our citizens, the dissent displays a failure to appreciate that "those institutions which the Constitution is supposed to limit" include the Court itself. To say, as the dissent says, that "'it is for us ultimately to judge whether the Eighth Amendment permits imposition of the death penalty'"—and to mean that as the dissent means it, i.e., that it is for us to judge, not on the basis of what we perceive the Eighth Amendment originally prohibited, or on the basis of what we perceive the society through its democratic processes now overwhelmingly disapproves, but on the basis of what we think "proportionate" and "measurably contributory to acceptable goals of punishment"—to say and mean that, is to replace judges of the law with a committee of philosopher-kings. . . .

We discern neither a historical nor a modern societal consensus forbidding the imposition of capital punishment on any person who murders at 16 or 17 years of age. Accordingly, we conclude that such punishment does not offend the Eighth Amendment's prohibition against cruel and unusual punishment.

The judgments of the Supreme Court of Kentucky and the Supreme Court of Missouri are therefore Affirmed.

JUSTICE O'CONNOR, concurring in part and concurring in the judgment.

Last Term, in *Thompson v. Oklahoma*, . . . I concluded that Oklahoma's imposition of a death sentence on an individual who was 15 years old at the time he committed a capital offense should be set aside. Applying the same standard today, I conclude that the death sentences for capital murder imposed by Missouri and Kentucky on petitioners Wilkins and Stanford respectively should not be set aside because it is sufficiently clear that no national consensus forbids the imposition of capital punishment on 16- or 17-year-old capital murderers.

In *Thompson* I noted that " . . . every single American legislature that has expressly set a minimum age for capital punishment has set that age at 16 or above." It is this difference between *Thompson* and these cases, more than any other, that convinces me there is no national consensus forbidding the imposition of capital punishment for crimes committed at the age of 16 and older. As the Court indicates, "a majority of the States that permit capital punishment authorize it for crimes committed at age 16 or above. . . .

JUSTICE BRENNAN, with whom JUSTICE MARSHALL, JUSTICE BLACKMUN, and JUSTICE STEVENS join, dissenting.

I believe that to take the life of a person as punishment for a crime committed when below the age of 18 is cruel and unusual and hence is prohibited by the Eighth Amendment.

. . . [W]e begin the task of deciding whether a punishment is unconstitutional by reviewing legislative enactments and the work of sentencing juries relating to the punishment in question to determine whether our Nation has set its face against a punishment to an extent that it can be concluded that the punishment offends our "evolving standards of decency." The Court undertakes such an analysis in this case. But JUSTICE SCALIA, in his plurality opinion on this point, would treat the Eighth Amendment inquiry as complete with this investigation. . . . [A] more searching inquiry is mandated by our precedents interpreting the Cruel and Unusual Punishments Clause. . . . Only then can we be in a position to judge, as our cases require, whether a punishment is unconstitutionally excessive, either because it is disproportionate given the culpability of the offender, or because it serves no legitimate penal goal.

I

Our judgment about the constitutionality of a punishment under the Eighth Amendment is informed, though not determined by an examination of contemporary attitudes toward the punishment, as evidenced in the actions of legislatures and of juries. The views of organizations with expertise in relevant fields and the choices of governments elsewhere in the world also merit our attention as indicators whether a punishment is acceptable in a civilized society.

The Court's discussion of state laws concerning capital sentencing gives a distorted view of the evidence of contemporary standards that these legislative determinations provide. Currently, 12 of the States whose statutes permit capital punishment specifically mandate that offenders under age 18 not be sentenced to death. When one adds to these 12 States the 15 (including the District of Columbia) in which capital punishment is not authorized at all, it appears that the governments in fully 27 of the States have concluded that no one under 18 should face the death penalty. A further three States explicitly refuse to authorize sentences of death for those who committed their offense when under 17, making a total of 30 States that would not tolerate the execution of petitioner Wilkins. . . .

The fact that juries have on occasion sentenced a minor to death shows, the Court says, that the death penalty for adolescents is not categorically unacceptable to juries. This, of course, is true; but it is not a conclusion that takes Eighth Amendment analysis very far. . . . [W]e have never adopted the extraordinary view that a punishment is beyond Eighth Amendment challenge if it is sometimes handed down by a jury. . . .

Both in absolute and in relative terms, imposition of the death penalty on adolescents is distinctly unusual. . . .

The Court speculates that this very small number of capital sentences imposed on adolescents indicates that juries have considered the youth of the offender when determining sentence, and have reserved the punishment for rare cases in which it is nevertheless appropriate. . . . It is certainly true that in the vast majority of cases, juries have not sentenced juveniles to death, and it seems to me perfectly proper to conclude that a sentence so rarely imposed is "unusual."

Further indicators of contemporary standards of decency that should inform our consideration of the Eighth Amendment question are the opinions of respected organizations. . . . There is no dearth of opinion from such groups that the state-sanctioned killing of minors is unjustified. A number, indeed, have filed briefs amicus curiae in these cases, in support of petitioners. The American Bar Association has adopted a resolution opposing the imposition of capital punishment upon any person for an offense committed while under age 18, as has the National Council of Juvenile and Family Court Judges. The American Law Institute's Model Penal Code similarly includes a lower age limit of 18 for the death sentence. And the National Commission on Reform of the Federal Criminal Laws also recommended that 18 be the minimum age.

Our cases recognize that objective indicators of contemporary standards of decency in the form of legislation in other countries is also of relevance to Eighth Amendment analysis. Many countries, of course—over 50, including nearly all in Western Europe—have formally abolished the death penalty, or have limited its use to exceptional crimes such as treason. Twenty-seven others do not in practice impose the penalty. Of the nations that retain capital punishment, a majority—65—prohibit the execution of juveniles. Sixty-one countries retain capital punishment and have no statutory provision exempting juveniles, though some of these nations are ratifiers of international treaties that do prohibit the execution of juveniles. . . . In addition to national laws, three leading human rights treaties ratified or signed by the United States explicitly prohibit juvenile death penalties. Within the world community, the imposition of the death penalty for juvenile crimes appears to be overwhelmingly disapproved.

Together, the rejection of the death penalty for juveniles by a majority of the States, the rarity of the sentence for juveniles . . ., the decisions of respected organizations in relevant fields that this punishment is unacceptable, and its rejection generally throughout the world, provide to my mind a strong grounding for the view that it is not constitutionally tolerable that certain States persist in authorizing the execution of adolescent offenders. . . . [Furthermore,] the execution of juveniles fails to satisfy two well-established and independent Eighth Amendment requirements—that a punishment not be disproportionate, and that it make a contribution to acceptable goals of punishment.

II

JUSTICE SCALIA forthrightly states in his plurality opinion that Eighth Amendment analysis is at an end once legislation and jury verdicts relating to the punishment in question are analyzed as indicators of contemporary values. A majority of the Court rejected this revisionist view as recently as last Term, see *Thompson*, and does so again in this case and in *Penry v. Lynaugh*. . . .

The Court has explicitly stated that "the attitude of state legislatures and sentencing juries do not wholly determine" a controversy arising under the Eighth Amendment because "the Constitution contemplates that in the end our own judgment will be brought to bear on the question of the [constitutional] acceptability of" a punishment. . . .

JUSTICE SCALIA's approach would largely return the task of defining the contours of Eighth Amendment protection to political majorities. But

"[t]he very purpose of a Bill of Rights was to withdraw certain subjects from the vicissitudes of political controversy, to place them beyond the reach of majorities and officials and to establish them as legal principles to be applied by the courts. One's right to life, liberty, and property, to free speech, a free press, freedom of worship and assembly, and other fundamental rights may not be submitted to vote; they depend on the outcome of no elections."

. . . The promise of the Bill of Rights goes unfulfilled when we leave "[c]onstitutional doctrine [to] be formulated by the acts of those institutions which the Constitution is supposed to limit," as is the case under JUSTICE SCALIA'S positivist approach to the definition of citizens' rights. This Court abandons its proven and proper role in our constitutional system when it hands back to the very majorities the Framers distrusted the power to define the precise scope of protection afforded by the Bill of Rights, rather than bringing its own judgment to bear on that question. . . .

III

. . . Proportionality analysis requires that we compare "the gravity of the offense," understood to include not only the injury caused, but also the defendant's culpability, with "the harshness of the penalty." In my view, juveniles so generally lack the degree of responsibility for their crimes that is a predicate for the constitutional imposition of the death penalty that the Eighth Amendment forbids that they receive that punishment. . . .

. . . [Age] 18 is the dividing line that society has generally drawn, the point at which it is thought reasonable to assume that persons have an ability to make, and a duty to bear responsibility for their, judgments. . . .

There may be exceptional individuals who mature more quickly than their peers, and who might be considered fully responsible for their actions prior to the age of 18, despite their lack of the experience upon which judgment depends. In my view, however, . . . it is constitutionally inadequate that a juvenile offender's level of responsibility be taken into account only along with a host of other factors that the court or jury may decide outweigh that want of responsibility. . . .

Juveniles very generally lack that degree of blameworthiness that is, in my view, a constitutional prerequisite for the imposition of capital punishment under our precedents concerning the Eighth Amendment proportionality principle. . . . I would hold that the Eighth Amendment prohibits the execution of any person for a crime committed below the age of 18. . . .

HARMELIN V. MICHIGAN (1991)

Five members of the Court voted to uphold a sentence of life imprisonment without possibility of parole for possession of more than 650 grams of cocaine. Justice Scalia, joined by Chief Justice Rehnquist, wanted to overturn Solem's *proportionality rule in noncapital cases. Justice Kennedy, joined by Justices O'Connor and Souter, distinguished* Harmelin *from* Solem *and found that the Michigan law satisfied the proportionality requirement.*

JUSTICE SCALIA announced the judgment of the Court and delivered the opinion of the Court with respect to Part IV, and an opinion with respect to Parts I, II, and III, in which THE CHIEF JUSTICE joins.

Petitioner was convicted of possessing 672 grams of cocaine and sentenced to a mandatory term of life in prison without possibility of parole. . . . [W]e granted certiorari.

Petitioner claims that his sentence is unconstitutionally "cruel and unusual" for two reasons: first, because it is "significantly disproportionate" to the crime he committed; second, because the sentencing judge was statutorily required to impose it, without taking into account the particularized circumstances of the crime and of the criminal.

I

The Eighth Amendment, which applies against the States by virtue of the Fourteenth Amendment, provides: "Excessive bail shall not be required, nor excessive fines imposed, nor cruel and unusual punishments inflicted." In *Rummel v. Estelle*, we held that it did not constitute "cruel and unusual punishment" to impose a life sentence, under a recidivist statute, upon a defendant who had been convicted, successively, of fraudulent use of a credit card to obtain $80 worth of goods or services, passing a forged check in the amount of $28.36, and obtaining $120.75 by false pretenses. . . . We specifically rejected the proposition asserted by the dissent, that unconstitutional disproportionality could be established by weighing three factors: (1) gravity of the offense compared to severity of the penalty, (2) penalties imposed within the same jurisdiction for similar crimes, and (3) penalties imposed in other jurisdictions for the same offense. A footnote in the opinion, however, said: "This is not to say that a proportionality principle would not come into play in the extreme example mentioned by the dissent, . . . if a legislature made overtime parking a felony punishable by life imprisonment."

Two years later, in *Hutto v. Davis*, we similarly rejected an Eighth Amendment challenge to a prison term of 40 years and fine of $20,000 for possession and distribution of approximately nine ounces of marijuana. . . .

A year and a half after *Davis* we uttered what has been our last word on this subject to date. *Solem v. Helm* set aside under the Eighth Amendment, because it was disproportionate, a sentence of life imprisonment without possibility of parole, imposed under a South Dakota recidivist statute for successive offenses that included three convictions of third-degree burglary, one of obtaining money by false pretenses, one of grand larceny, one of third-offense driving while intoxicated, and one of writing a "no account" check with intent to defraud. . . . Having decreed that a general principle of disproportionality exists, the Court used as the criterion for its application the three-factor test that had been explicitly rejected in both *Rummel* and *Davis*. . . .

. . . [O]ur 5-to-4 decision . . . in *Solem* was scarcely the expression of clear and well accepted constitutional law. We have long recognized, of course, that the doctrine of stare decisis is less rigid in its application to constitutional precedents, and we think that to be especially true of a constitutional precedent that is both recent and in apparent tension with other decisions. Accordingly, we have addressed anew, and in greater detail, the question whether the Eighth Amendment contains a proportionality guarantee—with particular attention to the background of the Eighth Amendment . . . and to the understanding of the Eighth Amendment before the end of the 19th century. . . . We conclude from this examination that Solem was simply wrong; the Eighth Amendment contains no proportionality guarantee.

Solem based its conclusion principally upon the proposition that a right to be free from disproportionate punishments was embodied within the "cruell and unusuall Punishments" provision of the English Declaration of Rights of 1689, and was incorporated, with that language, in the Eighth Amendment. . . .

As *Solem* observed, the principle of proportionality was familiar to English law at the time the Declaration of Rights was drafted. . . . Despite this familiarity, the drafters of the Declaration of Rights did not explicitly prohibit "disproportionate" or "excessive" punishments. Instead, they prohibited punishments that were "cruell and unusuall." The *Solem* Court simply assumed, with no analysis, that the one included the other. As a textual matter, of course, it does not: a disproportionate punishment can perhaps always be considered "cruel," but it will not always be (as the text also requires) "unusual." . . .

Most historians agree that the "cruell and unusuall Punishments" provision of the English Declaration of Rights was prompted by the abuses attributed to the infamous Lord Chief Justice Jeffreys of the King's Bench during the Stuart reign of James II. . . .

But the vicious punishments for treason decreed in the Bloody Assizes (drawing and quartering, burning of women felons, beheading, disemboweling, etc.) were common in that period—indeed, they were specifically authorized by law and remained so for many years afterwards. . . .

In sum, we think it most unlikely that the English Cruell and Unusuall Punishments Clause was meant to forbid "disproportionate" punishments. There is even less likelihood that proportionality of punishment was one of the traditional "rights and privileges of Englishmen" apart from the Declaration of Rights, which happened to be included in the Eighth Amendment. . . .

Unless one accepts the notion of a blind incorporation, however, the ultimate question is not what "cruell and unusuall punishments" meant in the Declaration of Rights, but what its meaning was to the Americans who adopted the Eighth Amendment. . . .

Wrenched out of its common-law context, and applied to the actions of a legislature, the word "unusual" could hardly mean "contrary to law." But it continued to mean (as it continues to mean today) "such as [does not] occu[r] in ordinary practice," Webster's American Dictionary (1828), "[s]uch as is [not] in common use." According to its terms, then, by forbidding "cruel and unusual punishments," the Clause disables the Legislature from authorizing particular forms or "modes" of punishment—specifically, cruel methods of punishment that are not regularly or customarily employed. . . .

The early commentary on the Clause contains no reference to disproportionate or excessive sentences, and again indicates that it was designed to outlaw particular modes of punishment. . . .

Perhaps the most persuasive evidence of what "cruel and unusual" meant, however, is found in early judicial constructions of the Eighth Amendment and its state counterparts. . . .

Throughout the 19th century, state courts interpreting state constitutional provisions with identical or more expansive wording (i.e., "cruel or unusual") concluded that these provisions did not proscribe disproportionality but only certain modes of punishment. . . .

II

We think it enough that those who framed and approved the Federal Constitution chose, for whatever reason, not to include within it the guarantee against disproportionate sentences that some State Constitutions contained. It is worth noting, however, that there was good reason for that choice—a reason that reinforces the necessity of overruling *Solem.* While there are relatively clear historical guidelines and accepted practices that enable judges to determine which modes of punishment are "cruel and unusual," proportionality does not lend itself to such analysis. . . . The real function of a constitutional proportionality principle, if it exists, is to enable judges to evaluate a penalty that some assemblage of men and women has considered proportionate—and to say that it is not. For that real-world enterprise, the standards seem so inadequate that the proportionality principle becomes an invitation to imposition of subjective values.

This becomes clear, we think, from a consideration of the three factors that Solem found relevant to the proportionality determination: (1) the inherent gravity of the offense, (2) the sentences imposed for similarly grave offenses in the same jurisdiction, and (3) sentences imposed for the same crime in other jurisdictions. As to the first factor: of course some offenses, involving violent harm to human beings, will always and everywhere be regarded as serious, but that is only half the equation. The issue is what else should be regarded to be as serious as these offenses, or even to be more serious than some of them. On that point, judging by the statutes that Americans have enacted, there is enormous variation—even within a given age, not to mention across the many generations ruled by the Bill of Rights. . . .

The second factor suggested in *Solem* fails for the same reason. One cannot compare the sentences imposed by the jurisdiction for "similarly grave" offenses if there is no objective standard of gravity. . . .

As for the third factor mentioned by *Solem*—the character of the sentences imposed by other States for the same crime—it must be acknowledged that that can be applied with clarity and ease. The only difficulty is that it has no conceivable relevance to the Eighth Amendment. That a State is entitled to treat with stern disapproval an act that other States punish with the mildest of sanctions follows a fortiori from the undoubted fact that a State may criminalize an act that other States do not criminalize at all. . . . Diversity not only in policy, but in the means of implementing policy, is the very raison d'etre of our federal system. . . .

IV

Petitioner claims that his sentence violates the Eighth Amendment for a reason in addition to its alleged disproportionality. He argues that it is "cruel and unusual" to impose a mandatory sentence of such severity, without any consideration of so-called mitigating factors such as, in his case, the fact that he had no prior felony convictions. . . .

. . . [T]his claim has no support in the text and history of the Eighth Amendment. Severe, mandatory penalties may be cruel, but they are not unusual in the constitutional sense, having been employed in various forms throughout our Nation's history. . . . [M]andatory death sentences abounded in our first Penal Code. They were also common in the several States—both at the time of the founding and throughout the 19th century. There can be no serious contention, then, that a sentence which is not otherwise cruel and unusual becomes so simply because it is "mandatory." . . .

It is true that petitioner's sentence is unique in that it is the second most severe known to the law; but life imprisonment with possibility of parole is also unique in that it is the third most severe. And if petitioner's sentence forecloses some "flexible techniques" for later reducing his sentence, it does not foreclose all of them, since there remain the possibilities of retroactive legislative reduction and executive clemency. In some cases, moreover, there will be negligible difference between life without parole and other sentences of imprisonment—for example, a life sentence with eligibility for parole after 20 years, or even a lengthy term sentence without eligibility for parole, given to a 65-year-old man. But even where the difference is the greatest, it cannot be compared with death. We have drawn the line of required individualized sentencing at capital cases, and see no basis for extending it further.

The judgment of the Michigan Court of Appeals is Affirmed.

JUSTICE KENNEDY, with whom JUSTICE O'CONNOR and JUSTICE SOUTER join, concurring in part and concurring in the judgment.

I concur in Part IV of the Court's opinion and in the judgment. I write this separate opinion because my approach to the Eighth Amendment proportionality analysis differs from JUSTICE SCALIA'S.... Stare decisis counsels our adherence to the narrow proportionality principle that has existed in our Eighth Amendment jurisprudence for 80 years. Although our proportionality decisions have not been clear or consistent in all respects, they can be reconciled, and they require us to uphold petitioner's sentence.

I

Our decisions recognize that the Cruel and Unusual Punishments Clause encompasses a narrow proportionality principle....

Though our decisions recognize a proportionality principle, its precise contours are unclear. This is so in part because we have applied the rule in few cases and even then to sentences of different types. Our most recent pronouncement on the subject in *Solem*, furthermore, appeared to apply a different analysis than in *Rummel* and *Davis. Solem* twice stated, however, that its decision was consistent with *Rummel* and thus did not overrule it. Despite these tensions, close analysis of our decisions yields some common principles that give content to the uses and limits of proportionality review.

The first of these principles is that the fixing of prison terms for specific crimes involves a substantive penological judgment that, as a general matter, is "properly within the province of legislatures, not courts." ...

The second principle is that the Eighth Amendment does not mandate adoption of any one penological theory. "The principles which have guided criminal sentencing ... have varied with the times." The federal and state criminal systems have accorded different weights at different times to the penological goals of retribution, deterrence, incapacitation, and rehabilitation....

Third, marked divergences both in underlying theories of sentencing and in the length of prescribed prison terms are the inevitable, often beneficial, result of the federal structure.... State sentencing schemes may embody different penological assumptions, making interstate comparison of sentences a difficult and imperfect enterprise.... Thus, the circumstance that a State has the most severe punishment for a particular crime does not by itself render the punishment grossly disproportionate....

The fourth principle at work in our cases is that proportionality review by federal courts should be informed by "'objective factors to the maximum possible extent.'" The most prominent objective factor is the type of punishment imposed. . . . [O]ur decisions recognize that we lack clear objective standards to distinguish between sentences for different terms of years. Although "no penalty is per se constitutional," the relative lack of objective standards concerning terms of imprisonment has meant that" '[o]utside the context of capital punishment, successful challenges to the proportionality of particular sentences [are] exceedingly rare.'"

All of these principles—the primacy of the legislature, the variety of legitimate penological schemes, the nature of our federal system, and the requirement that proportionality review be guided by objective factors—inform the final one: The Eighth Amendment does not require strict proportionality between crime and sentence. Rather, it forbids only extreme sentences that are "grossly disproportionate" to the crime.

II

With these considerations stated, it is necessary to examine the challenged aspects of petitioner's sentence: its severe length and its mandatory operation.

Petitioner's life sentence without parole is the second most severe penalty permitted by law. It is the same sentence received by the petitioner in *Solem*. Petitioner's crime, however, was far more grave than the crime at issue in Solem.

The crime of uttering a no account check at issue in *Solem* was "'one of the most passive felonies a person could commit.'" It 'involved neither violence nor threat of violence to any person," and was "viewed by society as among the less serious offenses." . . .

Petitioner was convicted of possession of more than 650 grams (over 1.5 pounds) of cocaine. This amount of pure cocaine has a potential yield of between 32,500 and 65,000 doses. From any standpoint, this crime falls in a different category from the relatively minor, nonviolent crime at issue in *Solem*. Possession, use, and distribution of illegal drugs represent "one of the greatest problems affecting the health and welfare of our population." Petitioner's suggestion that his crime was nonviolent and victimless, echoed by the dissent, is false to the point of absurdity. To the contrary, petitioner's crime threatened to cause grave harm to society. . . .

. . . [R]eports detailing the pernicious effects of the drug epidemic in this country do not establish that Michigan's penalty scheme is correct or the most just in any abstract sense. But they do demonstrate that the Michigan Legislature could with reason conclude that the threat posed to the individual and society by possession of this large an amount of cocaine—in terms of violence, crime, and social displacement—is momentous enough to warrant the deterrence and retribution of a life sentence without parole. . . .

. . . *Solem* is best understood as holding that comparative analysis within and between jurisdictions is not always relevant to proportionality review. The Court stated that "it may be helpful to compare sentences imposed on other criminals in the same jurisdiction," and that "courts may find it useful to compare the sentences imposed for commission of the same crime in other jurisdictions." It did not mandate such inquiries.

A better reading of our cases leads to the conclusion that intrajurisdictional and interjurisdictional analyses are appropriate only in the rare case in which a threshold comparison of the crime committed and the sentence imposed leads to an inference of gross disproportionality. In *Solem* and *Weems*, decisions in which the Court invalidated sentences as disproportionate, we performed a comparative analysis of sentences after determining that the sentence imposed was grossly excessive punishment for the crime committed. By contrast, *Rummel* and *Davis*, decisions in which the Court upheld sentences against proportionality attacks, did not credit such comparative analyses. In rejecting this form of argument, *Rummel* noted that "[e]ven were we to assume that the statute employed against Rummel was the most stringent found in the 50 States, that severity hardly would render Rummel's punishment 'grossly disproportionate' to his offenses."

The proper role for comparative analysis of sentences, then, is to validate an initial judgment that a sentence is grossly disproportionate to a crime. This conclusion neither "eviscerate[s]" *Solem*, nor "abandon[s]" its second and third factors, as the dissent charges, and it takes full account of *Rummel* and *Davis*, cases ignored by the dissent. In light of the gravity of petitioner's offense, a comparison of his crime with his sentence does not give rise to an inference of gross disproportionality, and comparative analysis of his sentence with others in Michigan and across the Nation need not be performed.

Petitioner also attacks his sentence because of its mandatory nature. Petitioner would have us hold that any severe penalty scheme requires individualized sentencing so that a judicial official may consider mitigating circumstances. Our precedents do not support this proposition, and petitioner presents no convincing reason to fashion an exception or adopt a new rule in the case before us. The Court demonstrates that our Eighth Amendment capital decisions reject any requirement of individualized sentencing in noncapital cases. . . .

In asserting the constitutionality of this mandatory sentence, I offer no judgment on its wisdom. Mandatory sentencing schemes can be criticized for depriving judges of the power to exercise individual discretion when remorse and acknowledgment of guilt, or other extenuating facts, present what might seem a compelling case for departure from the maximum. On the other hand, broad and unreviewed discretion exercised by sentencing judges leads to the perception that no clear standards are being applied, and that the rule of law is imperiled by sentences imposed for no discernible reason other than the subjective reactions of the sentencing judge. The debate illustrates that, as noted at the outset, arguments for and against particular sentencing schemes are for legislatures to resolve. . . .

III

. . . Reasonable minds may differ about the efficacy of Michigan's sentencing scheme, and it is far from certain that Michigan's bold experiment will succeed. The accounts of pickpockets at Tyburn hangings are a reminder of the limits of the law's deterrent force, but we cannot say the law before us has no chance of success and is on that account so disproportionate as to be cruel and unusual punishment. The dangers flowing from drug offenses and the circumstances of the crime committed here demonstrate that the Michigan penalty scheme does not surpass constitutional bounds. Michigan may use its criminal law to address the issue of drug possession in wholesale amounts in the manner that it has in this sentencing scheme. For the foregoing reasons, I conclude that petitioner's sentence of life imprisonment without parole for his crime of possession of more than 650 grams of cocaine does not violate the Eighth Amendment.

JUSTICE WHITE, with whom JUSTICE BLACKMUN and JUSTICE STEVENS join, dissenting.

The Eighth Amendment provides that "[e]xcessive bail shall not be required, nor excessive fines imposed, nor cruel and unusual punishments inflicted." JUSTICE SCALIA concludes that "the Eighth

Amendment contains no proportionality guarantee." Accordingly, he says *Solem v. Helm* "was simply wrong" in holding otherwise, as would be the Court's other cases interpreting the Amendment to contain a proportionality principle. JUSTICE KENNEDY, on the other hand, asserts that the Eighth Amendment's proportionality principle is so "narrow" that *Solem*'s analysis should be reduced from three factors to one. With all due respect, I dissent.

The language of the Amendment does not refer to proportionality in so many words, but it does forbid "excessive" fines, a restraint that suggests that a determination of excessiveness should be based at least in part on whether the fine imposed is disproportionate to the crime committed. Nor would it be unreasonable to conclude that it would be both cruel and unusual to punish overtime parking by life imprisonment, or, more generally, to impose any punishment that is grossly disproportionate to the offense for which the defendant has been convicted. . . .

. . . [T]he [Eighth] Amendment as ratified contained the words "cruel and unusual," and there can be no doubt that prior decisions of this Court have construed these words to include a proportionality principle. . . .

. . . Indeed, *Rummel v. Estelle*, the holding of which JUSTICE SCALIA does not question, itself recognized that the Eighth Amendment contains a proportionality requirement, for it did not question *Coker* and indicated that the proportionality principle would come into play in some extreme, nonfelony cases.

. . . JUSTICE SCALIA . . . appears to accept that the Amendment does indeed insist on proportional punishments in . . . cases . . . that involve sentences of death. His fallback position is that outside the capital cases, proportionality review is not required by the Amendment. With the exception of capital cases, the severity of the sentence for any crime is a matter that the Amendment leaves to the discretion of legislators. Any prison sentence, however severe, for any crime, however petty, will be beyond review under the Eighth Amendment. This position . . . ignores the generality of the Court's several pronouncements about the Eighth Amendment's proportionality component. And it fails to explain why the words "cruel and unusual" include a proportionality requirement in some cases but not in others. . . . The Court's capital punishment cases requiring proportionality reject JUSTICE SCALIA'S notion that the Amendment bars only cruel and unusual modes or methods of punishment. Under that view, capital punishment—a mode of punishment—would either be completely barred or left to the discretion of the legislature. Yet neither is true. The death penalty is appropriate in some cases and not in others. The same should be true of punishment by imprisonment. . . .

The Court . . . has recognized that a punishment may violate the Eighth Amendment if it is contrary to the "evolving standards of decency that mark the progress of a maturing society." In evaluating a punishment under this test, "we have looked not to our own conceptions of decency, but to those of modern American society as a whole" in determining what standards have "evolved," and thus have focused not on "the subjective views of individual Justices," but on "objective factors to the maximum possible extent." It is this type of objective factor which forms the basis for the tripartite proportionality analysis set forth in *Solem*.

Contrary to JUSTICE SCALIA'S suggestion, the *Solem* analysis has worked well in practice. Courts appear to have had little difficulty applying the analysis to a given sentence, and application of the test by numerous state and federal appellate courts has resulted in a mere handful of sentences being declared unconstitutional. Thus, it is clear that reviewing courts have not baldly substituted their own subjective moral values for those of the legislature. . . . *Solem* is wholly consistent with this approach, and when properly applied, its analysis affords "substantial deference to the broad authority that legislatures necessarily possess in determining the types and limits of punishments for crimes, as well as to the discretion that trial courts possess in sentencing convicted criminals" and will only rarely result in a sentence failing constitutional muster. The fact that this is one of those rare instances is no reason to abandon the analysis. . . .

Two dangers lurk in JUSTICE SCALIA'S analysis. First, he provides no mechanism for addressing a situation such as that proposed in *Rummel*, in which a legislature makes overtime parking a felony punishable by life imprisonment. He concedes that "one can imagine extreme examples"—perhaps such as the one described in *Rummel*—"that no rational person, in no time or place, could accept," but attempts to offer reassurance by claiming that "for the same reason these examples are easy to decide, they are certain never to occur." This is cold comfort indeed, for absent a proportionality guarantee, there would be no basis for deciding such cases should they arise.

Second, . . . JUSTICE SCALIA'S position that the Eighth Amendment addresses only modes or methods of punishment is quite inconsistent with our capital punishment cases, which do not outlaw death as a mode or method of punishment, but instead put limits on its application. If the concept of proportionality is downgraded in the Eighth Amendment calculus, much of this Court's capital penalty jurisprudence will rest on quicksand.

While JUSTICE SCALIA seeks to deliver a swift death sentence to Solem, JUSTICE KENNEDY prefers to eviscerate it, leaving only an empty shell. The analysis JUSTICE KENNEDY proffers is contradicted by the language of *Solem* itself and by our other cases interpreting the Eighth Amendment. . . .

Because there is no justification for overruling or limiting *Solem*, it remains to apply that case's proportionality analysis to the sentence imposed on petitioner. Application of the *Solem* factors to the statutorily mandated punishment at issue here reveals that the punishment fails muster under *Solem* and, consequently, under the Eighth Amendment to the Constitution. . . .

Application of *Solem*'s proportionality analysis leaves no doubt that the Michigan statute at issue fails constitutional muster. The statutorily mandated penalty of life without possibility of parole for possession of narcotics is unconstitutionally disproportionate in that it violates the Eighth Amendment's prohibition against cruel and unusual punishment. Consequently, I would reverse the decision of the Michigan Court of Appeals.

JUSTICE STEVENS, with whom JUSTICE BLACKMUN joins, dissenting.

While I agree wholeheartedly with JUSTICE WHITE'S dissenting opinion, I believe an additional comment is appropriate.

The severity of the sentence that Michigan has mandated for the crime of possession of more than 650 grams of cocaine, whether diluted or undiluted, does not place the sentence in the same category as capital punishment. I remain convinced that Justice Stewart correctly characterized the penalty of death as "unique" because of "its absolute renunciation of all that is embodied in our concept of humanity." Nevertheless, a mandatory sentence of life imprisonment without the possibility of parole does share one important characteristic of a death sentence: The offender will never regain his freedom. Because such a sentence does not even purport to serve a rehabilitative function, the sentence must rest on a rational determination that the punished "criminal conduct is so atrocious that society's interest in deterrence and retribution wholly outweighs any considerations of reform or rehabilitation of the perpetrator." Serious as this defendant's crime was, I believe it is irrational to conclude that every similar offender is wholly incorrigible. . . .

ATKINS V. VIRGINIA (2002)

In a six-to-three decision, the Supreme Court reversed its stance in Penry v. Lynaugh *(1989), and ruled that it is cruel and unusual to execute mentally retarded individuals.*

JUSTICE STEVENS delivered the opinion of the Court.

Those mentally retarded persons who meet the law's requirements for criminal responsibility should be tried and punished when they commit crimes. Because of their disabilities in areas of reasoning, judgment, and control of their impulses, however, they do not act with the level of moral culpability that characterizes the most serious adult criminal conduct. Moreover, their impairments can jeopardize the reliability and fairness of capital proceedings against mentally retarded defendants. Presumably for these reasons, in the 13 years since we decided *Penry v. Lynaugh*, the American public, legislators, scholars, and judges have deliberated over the question whether the death penalty should ever be imposed on a mentally retarded criminal. The consensus reflected in those deliberations informs our answer to the question presented by this case: whether such executions are cruel and unusual punishments prohibited by the Eighth Amendment to the Federal Constitution.

Petitioner, Daryl Renard Atkins, was convicted of abduction, armed robbery, and capital murder, and sentenced to death. At approximately midnight on August 16, 1996, Atkins and William Jones, armed with a semiautomatic handgun, abducted Eric Nesbitt, robbed him of the money on his person, drove him to an automated teller machine in his pickup truck where cameras recorded their withdrawal of additional cash, then took him to an isolated location where he was shot eight times and killed.

Jones and Atkins both testified in the guilt phase of Atkins' trial. Each confirmed most of the details in the other's account of the incident, with the important exception that each stated that the other had actually shot and killed Nesbitt. Jones' testimony, which was both more coherent and credible than Atkins', was obviously credited by the jury and was sufficient to establish Atkins' guilt. At the penalty phase of the trial, the State introduced victim impact evidence and proved two aggravating circumstances: future dangerousness and vileness of the offense. . . .

In the penalty phase, the defense relied on one witness, Dr. Evan Nelson, a forensic psychologist who had evaluated Atkins before trial and concluded that he was mildly mentally retarded. His conclusion was based on interviews with people who knew Atkins, a review of school and court records, and the administration of a standard intelligence test which indicated that Atkins had a full scale IQ of 59.5

The jury sentenced Atkins to death. . . .

The Supreme Court of Virginia affirmed the imposition of the death penalty. Atkins . . . contend[ed] that he is mentally retarded and thus cannot be sentenced to death. The majority of the state court rejected this contention, relying on our holding in *Penry*. The Court was not willing to commute Atkins' sentence of death to life imprisonment merely because of his IQ score.

Justice Hassell and Justice Koontz dissented. They . . . concluded that the imposition of the sentence of death upon a criminal defendant who has the mental age of a child between the ages of 9 and 12 is excessive. In their opinion, it is indefensible to conclude that individuals who are mentally retarded are not to some degree less culpable for their criminal acts. By definition, such individuals have substantial limitations not shared by the general population. A moral and civilized society diminishes itself if its system of justice does not afford recognition and consideration of those limitations in a meaningful way.

Because of the gravity of the concerns expressed by the dissenters, and in light of the dramatic shift in the state legislative landscape that has occurred in the past 13 years, we granted certiorari to revisit the issue that we first addressed in the *Penry* case.

The Eighth Amendment succinctly prohibits excessive sanctions. . . . In *Weems v. United States*, we held that a punishment of 12 years jailed in irons at hard and painful labor for the crime of falsifying records was excessive. We explained that it is a precept of justice that punishment for crime should be graduated and proportioned to the offense. We have repeatedly applied this proportionality precept in later cases interpreting the Eighth Amendment. . . . Thus, even though imprisonment for ninety days is not, in the abstract, a punishment which is either cruel or unusual, it may not be imposed as a penalty for the status of narcotic addiction because such a sanction would be excessive. . . .

A claim that punishment is excessive is judged not by the standards that prevailed in 1685 when Lord Jeffreys presided over the Bloody Assizes or when the Bill of Rights was adopted, but rather by those that currently prevail. As Chief Justice Warren explained in his opinion in *Trop v. Dulles*: The basic concept underlying the Eighth Amendment is nothing less than the dignity of man. The Amendment must draw its meaning from the evolving standards of decency that mark the progress of a maturing society.

Proportionality review under those evolving standards should be informed by objective factors to the maximum possible extent. . . . [T]he clearest and most reliable objective evidence of contemporary values is the legislation enacted by the country's legislatures. Relying in part on such legislative evidence, we have held that death is an impermissibly excessive punishment for the rape of an adult woman, *Coker v. Georgia*, or for a defendant who neither took life, attempted to take life, nor intended to take life, *Enmund v. Florida*. . . .

We also acknowledged in *Coker* that the objective evidence, though of great importance, did not wholly determine the controversy, for the Constitution contemplates that in the end our own judgment will be brought to bear on the question of the acceptability of the death penalty under the Eighth Amendment. . . .

Thus, in cases involving a consensus, our own judgment is brought to bear by asking whether there is reason to disagree with the judgment reached by the citizenry and its legislators.

Guided by our approach in these cases, we shall first review the judgment of legislatures that have addressed the suitability of imposing the death penalty on the mentally retarded and then consider reasons for agreeing or disagreeing with their judgment.

. . . In [1986], the public reaction to the execution of a mentally retarded murderer in Georgia apparently led to the enactment of the first state statute prohibiting such executions. In 1988, when Congress enacted legislation reinstating the federal death penalty, it expressly provided that a sentence of death shall not be carried out upon a person who is mentally retarded. In 1989, Maryland enacted a similar prohibition. It was in that year that we decided *Penry*, and concluded that those two state enactments, even when added to the 14 States that have rejected capital punishment completely, do not provide sufficient evidence at present of a national consensus.

Much has changed since then. Responding to the national attention received by the *Bowden* execution and our decision in *Penry*, state legislatures across the country began to address the issue. In 1990 Kentucky and Tennessee enacted statutes similar to those in Georgia and Maryland, as did New Mexico in 1991, and Arkansas, Colorado, Washington, Indiana, and Kansas in 1993 and 1994. In 1995, when New York reinstated its death penalty, it emulated the Federal Government by expressly exempting the mentally retarded. Nebraska followed suit in 1998. There appear to have been no similar enactments during the next two years, but in 2000 and 2001 six more States, South Dakota, Arizona, Connecticut, Florida, Missouri, and North Carolina joined the procession. The Texas Legislature unanimously adopted a similar bill, and bills have passed at least one house in other States, including Virginia and Nevada.

It is not so much the number of these States that is significant, but the consistency of the direction of change. Given the well-known fact that anti-crime legislation is far more popular than legislation providing protections for persons guilty of violent crime, the large number of States prohibiting the execution of mentally retarded persons (and the complete absence of States passing legislation reinstating the power to conduct such executions) provides powerful evidence that today our society views mentally retarded offenders as categorically less culpable than the average criminal. . . . Moreover, even in those States that allow the execution of mentally retarded offenders, the practice is uncommon. . . . The practice, therefore, has become truly unusual, and it is fair to say that a national consensus has developed against it.

To the extent there is serious disagreement about the execution of mentally retarded offenders, it is in determining which offenders are in fact retarded. In this case, for instance, the Commonwealth of Virginia disputes that Atkins suffers from mental retardation. Not all people who claim to be mentally retarded will be so impaired as to fall within the range of mentally retarded offenders about whom there is a national consensus. As was our approach in *Ford v. Wainwright*, with regard to insanity, we leave to the State[s] the task of developing appropriate ways to enforce the constitutional restriction upon its execution of sentences.

This consensus unquestionably reflects widespread judgment about the relative culpability of mentally retarded offenders, and the relationship between mental retardation and the penological purposes served by the death penalty. Additionally, it suggests that some characteristics of mental retardation undermine the strength of the procedural protections that our capital jurisprudence steadfastly guards.

As discussed above, clinical definitions of mental retardation require not only subaverage intellectual functioning, but also significant limitations in adaptive skills such as communication, self-care, and self-direction that became manifest before age 18. Mentally retarded persons frequently know the difference between right and wrong and are competent to stand trial. Because of their impairments, however, by definition they have diminished capacities to understand and process information, to communicate, to abstract from mistakes and learn from experience, to engage in logical reasoning, to control impulses, and to understand the reactions of others. There is no evidence that they are more likely to engage in criminal conduct than others, but there is abundant evidence that they often act on impulse rather than pursuant to a premeditated plan, and that in group settings they are followers rather than leaders. Their deficiencies do not warrant an exemption from criminal sanctions, but they do diminish their personal culpability.

In light of these deficiencies, our death penalty jurisprudence provides two reasons consistent with the legislative consensus that the mentally retarded should be categorically excluded from execution. First, there is a serious question as to whether either justification that we have recognized as a basis for the death penalty applies to mentally retarded offenders. *Gregg v. Georgia* identified retribution and deterrence of capital crimes by prospective offenders as the social purposes served by the death penalty. Unless the imposition of the death penalty on a mentally retarded person measurably contributes to one or both of these goals, it is nothing more than the purposeless and needless imposition of pain and suffering, and hence an unconstitutional punishment.

With respect to retribution . . . the severity of the appropriate punishment necessarily depends on the culpability of the offender. . . . Thus, pursuant to our narrowing jurisprudence, which seeks to ensure that only the most deserving of execution are put to death, an exclusion for the mentally retarded is appropriate.

With respect to deterrence . . . it seems likely that capital punishment can serve as a deterrent only when murder is the result of premeditation and deliberation. Exempting the mentally retarded from that punishment will not affect the cold calculus that precedes the decision of other potential murderers. Indeed, that sort of calculus is at the opposite end of the spectrum from behavior of mentally retarded offenders. The theory of deterrence in capital sentencing is predicated upon the notion that the increased severity of the punishment will inhibit criminal actors from carrying out murderous conduct. Yet it is the same cognitive and behavioral impairments that make these defendants less morally culpable for example, the diminished ability to understand and process information, to learn from experience, to engage in logical reasoning, or to control impulses that also make it less likely that they can process the information of the possibility of execution as a penalty and, as a result, control their conduct based upon that information. Nor will exempting the mentally retarded from execution lessen the deterrent effect of the death penalty with respect to offenders who are not mentally retarded. Such individuals are unprotected by the exemption and will continue to face the threat of execution. Thus, executing the mentally retarded will not measurably further the goal of deterrence.

The reduced capacity of mentally retarded offenders provides a second justification for a categorical rule making such offenders ineligible for the death penalty. The risk that the death penalty will be imposed in spite of factors which may call for a less severe penalty is enhanced, not only by the possibility of false confessions, but also by the lesser ability of mentally retarded defendants to make a persuasive showing of mitigation in the face of prosecutorial evidence of one or more aggravating factors. Mentally retarded defendants may be less able to give meaningful assistance to their counsel and are typically poor witnesses, and their demeanor may create an unwarranted impression of lack of remorse for their crimes. . . . Mentally retarded defendants in the aggregate face a special risk of wrongful execution.

Our independent evaluation of the issue reveals no reason to disagree with the judgment of the legislatures that have recently addressed the matter and concluded that death is not a suitable punishment for a mentally retarded criminal. We are not persuaded that the execution of mentally retarded criminals will measurably advance the deterrent or the retributive purpose of the death penalty. Construing and applying the

Eighth Amendment in the light of our evolving standards of decency, we therefore conclude that such punishment is excessive and that the Constitution places a substantive restriction on the States' power to take the life of a mentally retarded offender.

CHIEF JUSTICE REHNQUIST, with whom JUSTICE SCALIA and JUSTICE THOMAS join, dissenting.

The question presented by this case is whether a national consensus deprives Virginia of the constitutional power to impose the death penalty on capital murder defendants like petitioner, i.e., those defendants who indisputably are competent to stand trial, aware of the punishment they are about to suffer and why, and whose mental retardation has been found an insufficiently compelling reason to lessen their individual responsibility for the crime. The Court pronounces the punishment cruel and unusual primarily because 18 States recently have passed laws limiting the death eligibility of certain defendants based on mental retardation alone, despite the fact that the laws of 19 other States besides Virginia continue to leave the question of proper punishment to the individuated consideration of sentencing judges or juries familiar with the particular offender and his or her crime.

. . . I write separately . . . to call attention to the defects in the Court's decision to place weight on foreign laws, the views of professional and religious organizations, and opinion polls in reaching its conclusion. The Court's suggestion that these sources are relevant to the constitutional question finds little support in our precedents and, in my view, is antithetical to considerations of federalism, which instruct that any permanent prohibition upon all units of democratic government must [be apparent] in the operative acts (laws and the application of laws) that the people have approved. *Stanford v. Kentucky*. The Court's uncritical acceptance of the opinion poll data brought to our attention, moreover, warrants additional comment, because we lack sufficient information to conclude that the surveys were conducted in accordance with generally accepted scientific principles or are capable of supporting valid empirical inferences about the issue before us. . . .

There are strong reasons for limiting our inquiry into what constitutes an evolving standard of decency under the Eighth Amendment to the laws passed by legislatures and the practices of sentencing juries in America. Here, the Court goes beyond these well-established objective indicators of contemporary values. It finds further support to [its] conclusion that a national consensus has developed against imposing the death penalty on all mentally retarded defendants in international opinion, the views of professional and religious organizations, and opinion polls not demonstrated to be reliable. Believing this view to be seriously mistaken, I dissent.

JUSTICE SCALIA, with whom the CHIEF JUSTICE and JUSTICE THOMAS join, dissenting.

Today's decision is the pinnacle of our Eighth Amendment death-is-different jurisprudence. Not only does it, like all of that jurisprudence, find no support in the text or history of the Eighth Amendment; it does not even have support in current social attitudes regarding the conditions that render an otherwise just death penalty inappropriate. Seldom has an opinion of this Court rested so obviously upon nothing but the personal views of its members. . . .

. . . [P]etitioner's mental retardation was a central issue at sentencing. The jury concluded, however, that his alleged retardation was not a compelling reason to exempt him from the death penalty in light of the brutality of his crime and his long demonstrated propensity for violence. In upsetting this particularized judgment on the basis of a constitutional absolute, the Court concludes that no one who is even slightly mentally retarded can have sufficient moral responsibility to be subjected to capital punishment for any crime. As a sociological and moral conclusion that is implausible; and it is doubly implausible as an interpretation of the United States Constitution. . . .

The Court . . . argue[s] . . . that execution of the mildly retarded is inconsistent with the evolving standards of decency that mark the progress of a maturing society. Before today, our opinions consistently emphasized that Eighth Amendment judgments regarding the existence of social standards should be informed by objective factors to the maximum possible extent and should not be, or appear to be, merely the subjective views of individual Justices. First among these objective factors are the statutes passed by society's elected representatives. . . .

The Court pays lip service to these precedents as it miraculously extracts a national consensus forbidding execution of the mentally retarded, from the fact that 18 . . . have very recently enacted legislation barring execution of the mentally retarded. . . . If one is to say, as the Court does today, that all executions of the mentally retarded are so morally repugnant as to violate our national standards of decency, surely the consensus it points to must be one that has set its righteous face against all such executions. . . .

The Court attempts to bolster its embarrassingly feeble evidence of consensus with the following: It is not so much the number of these States that is significant, but the consistency of the direction of change. But in what other direction could we possibly see change? Given that 14 years ago all the death penalty statutes included the mentally retarded, any change (except precipitate undoing of what had just been done) was bound to be in the one direction the Court finds significant enough to overcome the lack of real consensus. . . .

Even less compelling (if possible) is the Court's argument that evidence of national consensus is to be found in the infrequency with which retarded persons are executed in States that do not bar their execution. To begin with, what the Court takes as true is in fact quite doubtful. It is not at all clear that execution of the mentally retarded is uncommon. . . . If, however, execution of the mentally retarded is uncommon; and if it is not a sufficient explanation of this that the retarded comprise a tiny fraction of society (1 percent to 3 percent), then surely the explanation is that mental retardation is a constitutionally mandated mitigating factor at sentencing. For that reason, even if there were uniform national sentiment in favor of executing the retarded in appropriate cases, one would still expect execution of the mentally retarded to be uncommon. . . .

But the Prize for the Court's Most Feeble Effort to fabricate national consensus must go to its appeal . . . to the views of assorted professional and religious organizations, members of the so-called world community, and respondents to opinion polls. I agree with the Chief Justice (dissenting opinion) that the views of professional and religious organizations and the results of opinion polls are irrelevant. Equally irrelevant are the practices of the world community, whose notions of justice are (thankfully) not always those of our people. We must never forget that it is a Constitution for the United States of America that we are expounding. [W]here there is not first a settled consensus among our own people, the views of other nations, however enlightened the Justices of this Court may think them to be, cannot be imposed upon Americans through the Constitution. . . .

Beyond the empty talk of a national consensus, the Court gives us a brief glimpse of what really underlies today's decision: pretension to a power confined neither by the moral sentiments originally enshrined in the Eighth Amendment (its original meaning) nor even by the current moral sentiments of the American people. [T]he Constitution, the Court says, contemplates that in the end our own judgment will be brought to bear on the question of the acceptability of the death penalty under the Eighth Amendment. . . . The arrogance of this assumption of power takes one's breath away. And it explains, of course, why the Court can be so cavalier about the evidence of consensus. It is just a game, after all. [I]n the end, it is the feelings and intuition of a majority of the Justices that count the perceptions of decency, or of penology, or of mercy, entertained by a majority of the small and unrepresentative segment of our society that sits on this Court. . . .

The Court throws one last factor into its grab bag of reasons why execution of the retarded is excessive in all cases: Mentally retarded offenders face a special risk of wrongful execution because they are less able to make a persuasive showing of mitigation, to give meaningful assistance to their counsel, and to be effective witnesses. Special risk is pretty flabby language (even flabbier than less likely) and I suppose a similar special risk could be said to exist for just plain stupid people, inarticulate people, even ugly people. If this unsupported claim has any substance to it (which I doubt) it might support a due process claim in all criminal prosecutions of the mentally retarded; but it is hard to see how it has anything to do with an Eighth Amendment claim that execution of the mentally retarded is cruel and unusual. We have never before held it to be cruel and unusual punishment to impose a sentence in violation of some other constitutional imperative. . . .

I respectfully dissent.

Ring v. Arizona (2002)

In a seven-to-two decision, the Supreme Court ruled that under the Sixth Amendment's right to a jury trial, juries and not judges must find the facts that determine whether capital punishment can be imposed. The Court held that Arizona's "judge only" sentencing procedure was unconstitutional.

JUSTICE GINSBURG delivered the opinion of the Court.

This case concerns the Sixth Amendment right to a jury trial in capital prosecutions. In Arizona, following a jury adjudication of a defendant's guilt of first-degree murder, the trial judge, sitting alone, determines the presence or absence of the aggravating factors required by Arizona law for imposition of the death penalty.

In *Walton v. Arizona* (1990), this Court held that Arizona's sentencing scheme was compatible with the Sixth Amendment because the additional facts found by the judge qualified as sentencing considerations, not as element[s] of the offense of capital murder. Ten years later, however, we decided *Apprendi v. New Jersey* (2000), which held that the Sixth Amendment does not permit a defendant to be expose[d] to a penalty exceeding the maximum he would receive if punished according to the facts reflected in the jury verdict alone. This prescription governs, *Apprendi* determined, even if the State characterizes the additional findings made by the judge as sentencing factor[s].

Apprendi's reasoning is irreconcilable with *Walton*'s holding in this regard, and today we overrule *Walton* in relevant part. Capital defendants, no less than non-capital defendants, we conclude, are entitled to a jury determination of any fact on which the legislature conditions an increase in their maximum punishment.

At the trial of petitioner Timothy Ring for murder, armed robbery, and related charges, . . . the jury [found] the facts here recounted. On November 28, 1994, a Wells Fargo armored van pulled up to the Dillards department store at Arrowhead Mall in Glendale, Arizona. Courier Dave Moss left the van to pick up money inside the store. When he returned, the van, and its driver, John Magoch, were gone.

Later that day, Maricopa County Sheriffs Deputies found the van its doors locked and its engine running in the parking lot of a church in Sun City, Arizona. Inside the vehicle they found Magoch, dead from a single gunshot to the head. According to Wells Fargo records, more than $562,000 in cash and $271,000 in checks were missing from the van.

Prompted by an informant's tip, Glendale police sought to determine whether Ring and his friend James Greenham were involved in the robbery. The police investigation [resulted in criminal charges]. . . .

The trial judge instructed the jury on alternative charges of premeditated murder and felony murder. The jury deadlocked on premeditated murder, with 6 of 12 jurors voting to acquit, but convicted Ring of felony murder occurring in the course of armed robbery. . . .

As later summed up by the Arizona Supreme Court, the evidence admitted at trial failed to prove, beyond a reasonable doubt, that [Ring] was a major participant in the armed robbery or that he actually murdered Magoch. Although clear evidence connected Ring to the robbery's proceeds, nothing submitted at trial put him at the scene of the robbery. Furthermore, [f]or all we know from the trial evidence, the Arizona court stated, [Ring] did not participate in, plan, or even expect the killing. This lack of evidence no doubt explains why the jury found [Ring] guilty of felony, but not premeditated, murder.

Under Arizona law, Ring could not be sentenced to death, the statutory maximum penalty for first-degree murder, unless further findings were made. The State's first-degree murder statute . . . directs the judge who presided at trial to conduct a separate sentencing hearing to determine the existence or nonexistence of [certain enumerated] circumstances for the purpose of determining the sentence to be imposed. The statute further instructs: The hearing shall be conducted before the court alone. The court alone shall make all factual determinations required by this section or the constitution of the United States or this state.

At the conclusion of the sentencing hearing, the judge is to determine the presence or absence of the enumerated aggravating circumstances and any mitigating circumstances. The State's law authorizes the judge to sentence the defendant to death only if there is at least one aggravating circumstance and there are no mitigating circumstances sufficiently substantial to call for leniency. . . .

On October 29, 1997, the trial judge entered his Special Verdict sentencing Ring to death. Because Ring was convicted of felony murder, not premeditated murder, the judge recognized that Ring was eligible for the death penalty only if he was Magoch's actual killer or if he was a major participant in the armed robbery that led to the killing and exhibited a reckless disregard or indifference for human life. . . .

Citing Greenham's testimony at the sentencing hearing, the judge concluded that Ring is the one who shot and killed Mr. Magoch. The judge also found that Ring was a major participant in the robbery and that armed robbery is unquestionably a crime which carries with it a grave risk of death.

The judge then turned to the determination of aggravating and mitigating circumstances. He found two aggravating factors. First, the judge determined that Ring committed the offense in expectation of receiving something of pecuniary value . . . [t]aking the cash from the armored car was the motive and reason for Mr. Magoch's murder and not just the result. Second, the judge found that the offense was committed in an especially heinous, cruel or depraved manner. In support of this finding, he cited Ring's comment, as reported by Greenham at the sentencing hearing, expressing pride in his marksmanship. The judge found one non-statutory mitigating factor: Ring's minimal criminal record. In his judgment, that mitigating circumstance did not call for leniency; he therefore sentenced Ring to death.

On appeal, Ring argued that Arizona's capital sentencing scheme violates the Sixth and Fourteenth Amendments to the U.S. Constitution because it entrusts to a judge the finding of a fact raising the defendant's maximum penalty. The State, in response, noted that this Court had upheld Arizona's system in *Walton v. Arizona* and had stated in Apprendi that *Walton* remained good law.

... [T]he Arizona Supreme Court ... rejected Ring's constitutional attack on the State's capital murder judicial sentencing system ... and affirmed the death sentence.

We granted Ring's petition for a writ of certiorari. ... We now reverse the judgment of the Arizona Supreme Court.

Based solely on the jury's verdict finding Ring guilty of first-degree felony murder, the maximum punishment he could have received was life imprisonment. This was so because, in Arizona, a death sentence may not legally be imposed unless at least one aggravating factor is found to exist beyond a reasonable doubt. The question presented is whether that aggravating factor may be found by the judge, as Arizona law specifies, or whether the Sixth Amendment's jury trial guarantee, made applicable to the States by the Fourteenth Amendment, requires that the aggravating factor determination be entrusted to the jury. ...

... [In] *Apprendi v. New Jersey*, [t]he defendant-petitioner ... was convicted of second-degree possession of a firearm, an offense carrying a maximum penalty of ten years under New Jersey law. On the prosecutor's motion, the sentencing judge found by a preponderance of the evidence that Apprendi's crime had been motivated by racial animus. That finding triggered application of New Jersey's hate crime enhancement, which doubled Apprendi's maximum authorized sentence. The judge sentenced Apprendi to 12 years in prison, 2 years over the maximum that would have applied but for the enhancement.

We held that Apprendi's sentence violated his right to a jury determination that [he] is guilty of every element of the crime with which he is charged, beyond a reasonable doubt. That right attached not only to Apprendi's weapons offense but also to the hate crime aggravating circumstance. New Jersey, the Court observed, threatened Apprendi with certain pains if he unlawfully possessed a weapon and with additional pains if he selected his victims with a purpose to intimidate them because of their race. Merely using the label sentence enhancement to describe the [second act] surely does not provide a principled basis for treating [the two acts] differently.

The dispositive question, we said, is one not of form, but of effect. If a State makes an increase in a defendant's authorized punishment contingent on the finding of a fact, that fact, no matter how the State labels it, must be found by a jury beyond a reasonable doubt. A defendant may not be expose[d] to a penalty exceeding the maximum he would receive if punished according to the facts reflected in the jury verdict alone. . . .

Arizona suggests that judicial authority over the finding of aggravating factors may be a better way to guarantee against the arbitrary imposition of the death penalty. The Sixth Amendment jury trial right, however, does not turn on the relative rationality, fairness, or efficiency of potential fact finders. Entrusting to a judge the finding of facts necessary to support a death sentence might be an admirably fair and efficient scheme of criminal justice designed for a society that is prepared to leave criminal justice to the State. The founders of the American Republic were not prepared to leave it to the State, which is why the jury-trial guarantee was one of the least controversial provisions of the Bill of Rights. It has never been efficient; but it has always been free.

In any event, the superiority of judicial fact finding in capital cases is far from evident. Unlike Arizona, the great majority of States responded to this Court's Eighth Amendment decisions requiring the presence of aggravating circumstances in capital cases by entrusting those determinations to the jury. . . .

Because Arizona's enumerated aggravating factors operate as the functional equivalent of an element of a greater offense, the Sixth Amendment requires that they be found by a jury.

The guarantees of jury trial in the Federal and State Constitutions reflect a profound judgment about the way in which law should be enforced and justice administered. If the defendant preferred the commonsense judgment of a jury to the more tutored but perhaps less sympathetic reaction of the single judge, he was to have it.

. . . The judgment of the Arizona Supreme Court is therefore reversed, and the case is remanded for further proceedings not inconsistent with this opinion.

Chronology of Capital Punishment

The following information is reprinted with permission from the *Congressional Quarterly Researcher,* March 10, 1995, vol. 5, no. 9 (May 2, 2002), as cited in "Frontline: Angel on Death Row," at http://www.pbs.org/wgbh/pages/frontline/angel/.

17th Century	England prescribes death for fourteen offenses, but the American colonies impose the death sentence for fewer crimes.
1636	The Massachusetts Bay Colony lists thirteen crimes punishable by death, including idolatry and witchcraft.
1682	Under William Penn's Great Act, the death penalty is prescribed only for murder and treason in Pennsylvania.
19th Century	Politics and advances in technology influence use of the death penalty.
Dec. 2, 1859	Abolitionist John Brown is hanged for treason, conspiracy, and murder at Charles Town, Virginia.
August 6, 1890	Murderer William Kemmler is the first person executed in the electric chair, at New

	York state's Auburn Prison. The "chair" is later installed at Sing Sing Prison.
1900s	A short-lived abolition movement leads to the repeal of numerous state death penalty statutes.
1907	Kansas abolishes capital punishment. Eight more states follow suit over the next ten years.
1920s	Two sensational murder cases spark renewed debate over the death penalty.
September 10, 1924	Defense attorney Clarence Darrow wins life sentences for Chicago "thrill killers" Richard Loeb and Nathan Leopold, Jr.
August 22, 1927	Nicola Sacco and Bartolomeo Vanzetti, Italian immigrants with anarchist sympathies, are electrocuted in Massachusetts for two murders.
1930s	U.S. executions reach an all-time peak, averaging 167 a year.
1960s	Growing doubts about the death penalty and legal challenges lead to a decline in executions.
June 2, 1967	After Luis Jose Monge dies in the gas chamber at Colorado State Penitentiary, an unofficial moratorium on executions begins.
1970s	An eventful decade for capital punishment sees the death penalty invalidated by the U.S. Supreme Court and then reinstated.
June 29, 1972	Supreme Court rules in *Furman v. Georgia* that the death penalty amounts to cruel and unusual punishment because juries impose sentences arbitrarily. The decision overturns all existing death penalty laws and death sentences.

July 2, 1976	The Supreme Court holds in *Gregg v. Georgia* that under the state's new two-stage trial system, the death penalty no longer violates the Eighth Amendment.
January 17, 1977	A Utah firing squad makes Gary Gilmore the first person executed in the United States in almost ten years.
1977	Oklahoma becomes the first state to adopt lethal injection.
1980s	The Supreme Court further clarifies its views on the death penalty.
1986	Supreme Court bars executing insane persons in *Ford v. Wainwright.*
1989	In *Perry v. Lynaugh,* the Supreme Court holds that executing mentally retarded persons does not violate the Eighth Amendment. However, the Court reverses this in 2002.
1990s	Death penalty provisions in anticrime bills stir sharp debate in Congress.
September 13, 1994	President Clinton signs crime bill making dozens of federal crimes subject to death penalty.
February 8, 1995	The House votes 297–132 to limit inmate appeals of death sentences to one year in state cases.
March 7, 1995	New York Governor George E. Pataki signs new death penalty law.
February 1997	American Bar Association calls for moratorium on executions until death penalty fairness is assured.
2000	Illinois Governor George Ryan imposes moratorium on executions in that state, citing high number of invalid death penalty sentences.

2001 On his last day in office, President Clinton commutes the federal death sentence of drug kingpin Ronnie Chandler to life imprisonment. On June 11, Timothy McVeigh becomes the first person executed under federal death penalty since 1963.

2002 Ray Krone leaves prison, the 100th person given the death penalty to be freed as innocent, after DNA testing establishes probable guilt of another person.

In *Atkins v. Virginia*, the Court reverses its 1989 *Perry* decision that mentally retarded persons can be executed.

January 2003 Three days before his term expires, Governor George Ryan, quoting President Abraham Lincoln's second inaugural address and Justice Harry Blackmun's "machinery of death" dissent in *Callins v. Collins*, commutes all 167 death sentences to life imprisonment.

Table of Cases

Ake v. Oklahoma, 470 U.S. 68 (1985)
Arave v. Creech, 507 U.S. 463 (1993)
Arizona v. Rumsey, 467 U.S. 203 (1984)
Atkins v. Virginia, 122 S.Ct. 2242 (2002)
Bearden v. Georgia, 461 U.S. 660 (1983)
Beck v. Alabama, 447 U.S. 625 (1980)
Blystone v. Pennsylvania, 494 U.S. 299 (1990)
Booth v. Maryland, 482 U.S. 496 (1987)
Boykin v. Alabama, 395 U.S. 238 (1969)
Brown v. Board of Education, 347 U.S. 483 (1954)
Brown v. Mississippi, 297 U.S. 278 (1936)
Buchanan v. Angelone, 522 U.S. 269 (1998)
Buchanan v. Kentucky, 483 U.S. 402 (1987)
Bullington v. Missouri, 451 U.S. 430 (1981)
Caldwell v. Mississippi, 472 U.S. 320 (1985)
California v. Brown, 479 U.S. 538 (1987)
Callins v. Collins, 510 U.S. 1141 (1994)
Campbell v. Wood, 18 F.3d 662 (9th Cir.), *cert. denied,* 511 U.S. 1119 (1994)
Chicago, Burlington & Quincy Railroad Co. v. Chicago, 166 U.S. 226 (1897)
Coker v. Georgia, 433 U.S. 584 (1977)
Coleman v. Thompson, 501 U.S. 722 (1991)
Collins v. Johnston, 237 U.S. 502 (1915)

Cooper v. Oklahoma, 517 U.S. 348 (1996)
Corbitt v. New Jersey, 439 U.S. 212 (1978)
Dawson v. Delaware, 503 U.S. 159 (1992)
Enmund v. Florida, 458 U.S. 782 (1982)
Estelle v. Gamble, 429 U.S. 97 (1976)
Fay v. Noia, 372 U.S. 391 (1963)
Felker v. Turpin, 518 U.S. 651 (1996)
Fierro v. Gomez, 77 F.3d 301 (9th Cir.1996)
Fong Yue Ting v. United States, 149 U.S. 698 (1893)
Ford v. Wainwright, 477 U.S. 399 (1986)
Furman v. Georgia, 408 U.S. 238 (1972)
Gilmore v. Utah, 429 U.S. 1012 (1976)
Godfrey v. Georgia, 446 U.S. 420 (1980)
Gomez v. United States District Court, 503 U.S. 653 (1992)
Gregg v. Georgia, 428 U.S. 153 (1976)
Hale v. Kentucky, 303 U.S. 613 (1938)
Harmelin v. Michigan, 501 U.S. 957 (1991)
Herrera v. Collins, 506 U.S. 390 (1993)
Hitchcock v. Dugger, 481 U.S. 393 (1987)
Holden v. Minnesota, 137 U.S. 483 (1890)
Hope v. Pelzer, U.S. (June 27, 2002)
Hopt v. Utah, 110 U.S. 584 (1884)
Hudson v. McMillian, 503 U.S. 1 (1992)
Hurtado v. California, 110 U.S. 516 (1884)
Hutto v. Davis, 454 U.S. 370 (1982)
Hutto v. Finney, 437 U.S. 678 (1978)
Ingraham v. Wright, 430 U.S. 651 (1977)
In re Kemmler, 136 U.S. 436 (1890)
In re Medley, 134 U.S. 160 (1890)
Johnson v. Dye, 175 F.2d 250 (3d Cir.), *rev'd,* 338 U.S. 864 (1949)
Johnson v. Mississippi, 486 U.S. 356 (1988)
Johnson v. Texas, 509 U.S. 350 (1993)
Jones v. United States, 527 U.S. 373 (1999)
Jurek v. Texas, 428 U.S. 262 (1976)

Kansas v. Hendricks, 521 U.S. 346 (1997)
Knight v. Florida, 528 U.S. 990 (1999)
Lambert v. Barrett, 159 U.S. 660 (1895)
Lockett v. Ohio, 438 U.S. 586 (1978)
Lockhart v. McCree, 476 U.S. 162 (1986)
Louisiana ex. rel. Francis v. Resweber, 329 U.S. 459 (1947)
Lowenfield v. Phelps, 484 U.S. 231 (1988)
Maxwell v. Bishop, 398 U.S. 262 (1970)
Maynard v. Cartwright, 486 U.S. 356 (1988)
McCleskey v. Kemp, 481 U.S. 279 (1987)
McGautha v. California, 402 U.S. 183 (1971)
McKoy v. North Carolina, 494 U.S. 433 (1990)
Medina v. California, 505 U.S. 437 (1992)
Mills v. Maryland, 486 U.S. 367 (1988)
Miranda v. Arizona, 384 U.S. 436 (1966)
Missouri Pacific Railway v. Nebraska, 164 U.S. 403 (1896)
Moore v. Dempsey, 261 U.S. 86 (1923)
Morgan v. Illinois, 504 U.S. 719 (1992)
Murray v. Giarratano, 492 U.S. 1 (1989)
Norris v. Alabama, 294 U.S. 587 (1935)
O'Neil v. Vermont, 144 U.S. 323 (1892)
Palko v. Connecticut, 302 U.S. 319 (1937)
Payne v. Tennessee, 501 U.S. 808 (1991)
Penry v. Lynaugh, 492 U.S. 302 (1989)
People v. Anderson, 6 Cal.3d 628, *cert. denied,* 406 U.S. 958 (1972)
Perry v. Louisiana, 498 U.S. 38 (1990)
Poland v. Arizona, 476 U.S. 147 (1986)
Powell v. Alabama, 287 U.S. 45 (1932)
Powell v. Texas, 392 U.S. 514 (1968)
Plessy v. Ferguson, 163 U.S. 537 (1896)
Profitt v. Florida, 428 U.S. 242 (1976)
Pulley v. Harris, 465 U.S. 37 (1984)
Rhodes v. Chapman, 452 U.S. 337 (1981)
Riggins v. Nevada, 504 U.S. 127 (1992)

Ring v. Arizona, U.S. (June 24, 2002)
Roberts v. Louisiana 428 U.S. 325 (1976)
Robinson v. California, 370 U.S. 660 (1962)
Romano v. Oklahoma, 512 U.S. 1 (1994)
Rudolph v. Alabama, 375 U.S. 889 (1963)
Ruffin v. Commonwealth, 62 Va. 790 (1871)
Rummel v. Estelle, 445 U.S. 263 (1980)
Sandin v. Conner, 515 U.S. 472 (1995)
Shafer v. South Carolina, 532 U.S. 36 (2001)
Simmons v. South Carolina, 512 U.S. 154 (1994)
Skinner v. Oklahoma, 316 U.S. 535 (1942)
Skipper v. South Carolina, 476 U.S. 1 (1986)
Solem v. Helm, 463 U.S. 277 (1983)
South Carolina v. Gathers, 490 U.S. 805 (1989)
Spaziano v. Florida, 468 U.S. 447 (1984)
Stanford v. Kentucky, 492 U.S. 361 (1989)
State v. Driver, 78 N.C. 423 (1878)
Strickland v. Washington, 466 U.S. 668 (1984)
Stroud v. Swope, 187 F.2d 850 (9th Cir.), *cert. denied,* 342 U.S. 829 (1951)
Sumner v. Shuman, 483 U.S. 66 (1987)
Territory v. Ketchum, 10 N.M. 718 (1901)
Thompson v. Oklahoma, 487 U.S. 815 (1988)
Tison v. Arizona, 481 U.S. 137 (1987)
Trop v. Dulles, 356 U.S. 86 (1958)
Turner v. Murray, 476 U.S. 28 (1986)
United States v. Bailey, 444 U.S. 394 (1980)
United States v. Bajakajian, 524 U.S. 321 (1998)
United States v. Hudson and Goodwin, 11 U.S. 32 (1812)
United States v. Jackson, 390 U.S. 570 (1968)
United States v. Reynolds, 235 U.S. 133 (1914)
United States v. Salerno, 481 U.S. 739 (1987)
Uphaus v. Wyman, 360 U.S. 72 (1959)
Wainwright v. Witt, 469 U.S. 412 (1985)

Walton v. Arizona, 497 U.S. 639 (1990)
Weems v. United States, 217 U.S. 349 (1910)
Whitley v. Albers, 475 U.S. 312 (1986)
Whitmore v. Arkansas, 495 U.S. 149 (1990)
Wilkerson v. Utah, 99 U.S. 130 (1878)
Williams v. New York, 337 U.S. 241 (1949)
Winston v. United States, 172 U.S. 303 (1899)
Witherspoon v. Illinois, 391 U.S. 510 (1968)
Wolff v. McDonnell, 418 U.S. 539 (1974)
Woodson v. North Carolina, 428 U.S. 280 (1976)

Appendix: Data

Bureau of Justice Summary Findings on Executions and Death Row, 2001

In 2001, sixty-six inmates were executed, nineteen fewer than in 2000. In 2000, eighty-five persons in fourteen states were executed—forty in Texas, eleven in Oklahoma, eight in Virginia, six in Florida, five in Missouri, four in Alabama, three in Arizona, two in Arkansas, and one each in Delaware, Louisiana, North Carolina, South Carolina, Tennessee, and California.

Of persons executed in 2000:

- Forty-nine were white
- Thirty-five were black
- One was American Indian

Of those executed in 2000:

- Eighty-three were men
- Two were women

Eighty of the executions in 2000 were carried out by lethal injection and five by electrocution. Thirty-eight states and the federal government in 2000 had capital statutes.

TABLE A.1 Number of People Executed in the United States, 1930–2001

Year	*Executions*	*Year*	*Executions*
1930	155	1966	1
1931	153	1967	2
1932	140	1968	0
1933	160	1969	0
1934	168	1970	0
1935	199	1971	0
1936	195	1972	0
1937	147	1973	0
1938	190	1974	0
1939	160	1975	0
1940	124	1976	0
1941	123	1977	1
1942	147	1978	0
1943	131	1979	2
1944	120	1980	0
1945	117	1981	1
1946	131	1982	2
1947	153	1983	5
1948	119	1984	21
1949	119	1985	18
1950	82	1986	18
1951	105	1987	25
1952	83	1988	11
1953	62	1989	16
1954	81	1990	23
1955	76	1991	14
1956	65	1992	31
1957	65	1993	38
1958	49	1994	31
1959	49	1995	56
1960	56	1996	45
1961	42	1997	74
1962	47	1998	68
1963	21	1999	98
1964	15	2000	85
1965	7	2001	66

SOURCE: "Capital Punishment 2000" (November 13, 2002), U.S. Department of Justice, Bureau of Justice Statistics, at http://www.ojp.usdoj.gov.

TABLE A.2 Number of Executions by State, 1976–2002

	Total	*2002*	*2001*
Texas	285	29	17
Virginia	86	3	2
Missouri	58	5	7
Florida	52	1	1
Oklahoma	52	4	18
Georgia	30	3	4
S. Carolina	28	3	0
Louisiana	27	1	0
Arkansas	24	0	1
Alabama	24	1	0
Arizona	22	0	0
N. Carolina	21	0	5
Delaware	13	0	1
Illinois	12	0	0
California	10	1	1
Nevada	9	0	1
Indiana	9	0	2
Utah	6	0	0
Mississippi	5	1	0
Ohio	5	3	1
Washington	4	0	1
Maryland	3	0	0
Nebraska	3	0	0
Pennsylvania	3	0	0
Kentucky	2	0	0
Montana	2	0	0
Oregon	2	0	0
Colorado	1	0	0
Idaho	1	0	0
New Mexico	1	0	1
Tennessee	1	0	0
Wyoming	1	0	0
Federal	2	0	2

SOURCE: Death Penalty Information Center (November 13, 2002), at http://www.deathpenaltyinfo.org

The number of prisoners on death row has been increasing. At year's end in 2000, thirty-seven states and the federal prison system held 3,593 prisoners under sentence of death, 1.5 percent more than at year's end in 1999. All had committed murder. Since the death penalty was reinstated by the U.S. Supreme Court in 1976, white inmates have made up the majority of those under sentence of death.

Of persons under sentence of death in 2000:

- 1,990 were white
- 1,535 were black
- 339 were Hispanic (accounting for 11 percent of inmates with a known ethnicity)
- 29 were American Indian
- 27 were of Asian descent
- 12 were of unknown race

Fifty-four women were under a sentence of death.

Among inmates under sentence of death and with available criminal histories:

- nearly two in three had a prior felony conviction
- about one in twelve had a prior homicide conviction

Among persons for whom arrest information was available, the average age at time of arrest was twenty-eight; 2 percent of inmates were age seventeen or younger. At year's end, the youngest inmate under sentence of death was eighteen; the oldest was eighty-five.

Source: U.S. Department of Justice, Bureau of Justice Statistics (November 13, 2002) at http://www.ojp.usdoj.gov/BJS/.

State Executions by Region, 1976–2002

- South: 656
- West: 59

TABLE A.3 Prisoners under Sentence of Death, 1953–2000

Year	*Number of prisoners*	*Year*	*Number of prisoners*
1953	131	1977	423
1954	147	1978	482
1955	125	1979	593
1956	146	1980	692
1957	151	1981	860
1958	147	1982	1,066
1959	164	1983	1,209
1960	212	1984	1,420
1961	257	1985	1,575
1962	267	1986	1,800
1963	297	1987	1,967
1964	315	1988	2,117
1965	331	1989	2,243
1966	406	1990	2,346
1967	435	1991	2,465
1968	517	1992	2,580
1969	575	1993	2,727
1970	631	1994	2,905
1971	642	1995	3,064
1972	334	1996	3,242
1973	134	1997	3,328
1974	244	1998	3,465
1975	488	1999	3,540
1976	420	2000	3,593

SOURCE: "Capital Punishment 2000" (November 13, 2002), U.S. Department of Justice, Bureau of Justice Statistics, at http://www.ojp.usdoj.gov.

- Midwest: 87
- Northeast: 3
- Texas and Virginia alone: 371

Federal executions are listed in the state in which the crime was committed.

Source: Death Penalty Information Center (November 13, 2002), at http://www.deathpenaltyinfo.org/.

TABLE A.4 Prisoners on Death Row by Race, 1968–2000

Year	*White*	*Black*	*Other*
1968	243	271	3
1969	263	310	2
1970	293	335	3
1971	306	332	4
1972	167	166	1
1973	64	68	2
1974	110	128	6
1975	218	262	8
1976	225	195	0
1977	229	192	2
1978	281	197	4
1979	354	236	3
1980	424	264	4
1981	499	353	8
1982	613	441	12
1983	692	505	12
1984	806	598	16
1985	896	664	15
1986	1,013	762	25
1987	1,128	813	26
1988	1,235	848	34
1989	1,308	898	37
1990	1,368	940	38
1991	1,449	979	37
1992	1,511	1,031	38
1993	1,575	1,111	41
1994	1,653	1,203	49
1995	1,732	1,284	48
1996	1,833	1,358	51
1997	1,864	1,408	56
1998	1,917	1,489	59
1999	1,960	1,515	65
2000	1,990	1,535	68

SOURCE: "Capital Punishment 2000" (November 13, 2002), U.S. Department of Justice, Bureau of Justice Statistics, at http://www.ojp.usdoj.gov.

States with the Death Penalty

Jurisdictions marked with an asterisk have had no executions since 1976. There are currently thirty-eight states with the death penalty (along with the U.S. government and the U.S. military*): Alabama, Arizona, Arkansas, California, Colorado, Connecticut*, Delaware, Florida, Georgia, Idaho, Illinois, Indiana, Kansas*, Kentucky, Louisiana, Maryland, Mississippi, Missouri, Montana, Nebraska, Nevada, New Hampshire*, New Jersey*, New Mexico, New York*, North Carolina, Ohio, Oklahoma, Oregon, Pennsylvania, South Carolina, South Dakota*, Tennessee, Texas, Utah, Virginia, Washington, and Wyoming.

The death row data are valid as of April 1, 2002, and are taken from the NAACP Legal Defense Fund's "Death Row USA" unless otherwise noted.

Source: Death Penalty Information Center (November 13, 2002), at http://www.deathpenaltyinfo.org/.

Bureau of Justice: Key Crime and Justice Facts at a Glance

Serious violent crime levels continued to decline in 2000. Property crime rates continue to decline. Violent crime levels declined between 1999 and 2000. Rates for men and women are more similar in recent years.

The number of arrests for drug abuse violations increased from 1999 to 2000 for both juveniles and adults. The proportion of those convicted in federal court who are sentenced to prison has been increasing. Of cases concluded in federal district court in every year since 1989, there have been more drug cases than other types of cases.

Almost 928,000 adults were convicted of a felony in state courts in 1998. Of the felons convicted in state court, more than two-thirds were sentenced to prison or jail in 1998. The number of

TABLE A.5 Public Opinion and the Death Penalty, 1936–1998 (percent)

Date	*Favor*	*Oppose*	*Don't Know*
Apr. 1936	62	33	5
Dec. 1936	59	38	3
Nov. 1937	61	33	7
Oct. 1953	68	26	6
Apr. 1956	53	34	13
Sep. 1957	47	34	18
Mar. 1960	53	36	11
Feb. 1965	45	43	12
Jul. 1966	42	47	11
Jun. 1967	54	38	8
Jan. 1969	51	40	9
Oct. 1971	48	41	11
Feb. 1972	51	41	8
Mar. 1972	53	39	8
Nov. 1972	60	30	10
Mar. 1973	60	35	5
Mar. 1974	63	32	5
Mar. 1975	60	33	7
Mar. 1976	66	30	5
Apr. 1976	67	27	7
Mar. 1977	67	26	6
Mar. 1978	66	28	6
Jul. 1979	65	27	8
Mar. 1980	67	27	6
Mar. 1981	66	25	9
Mar. 1982	74	21	6
Jun. 1982	71	20	9
Mar. 1983	73	22	5
Mar. 1984	70	24	6
Jan. 1985	72	20	8
Mar. 1985	76	19	5
Nov. 1985	75	17	8
Jan. 1986	70	22	8
Mar. 1986	71	23	5
Mar. 1987	70	24	6
Mar. 1988	71	22	7
Sep. 1988	79	16	5

(continued)

Date	*Favor*	*Oppose*	*Don't Know*
Mar. 1989	74	20	6
Mar. 1990	75	19	6
Mar. 1991	72	22	6
Mar. 1993	72	21	7
Mar. 1994	74	19	6
Sep. 1994	80	16	4
Mar. 1996	71	22	7
Mar. 1998	68	25	8

NOTE: Question wording: 1936–1937—"Are you in favor of the death penalty for murder?"; 1953–February 1972, November 1972, April 1976, January 1981, January 1985, November 1985, September 1994—"Are you in favor of the death penalty for persons [or "a person"] convicted of murder?"; All others—"Do you favor or oppose the death penalty for persons [or "people"] convicted of murder?"

SOURCES: 1936 through February 1972, November 1972, April 1976, January 1981, January 1985, November 1985, September 1988, and September 1994: Gallup surveys; others: General Social Survey, pp. 152–153 in Harold W. Stanley and Richard G. Niemi, *Vital Statistics on American Politics 1999–2000*, Washington, DC: Congressional Quarterly Inc (2000).

adults in the correctional population has been increasing. Over half of the increase in the prison population since 1990 is due to an increase in the prisoners convicted of violent offenses. The incarceration rate has more than tripled since 1980. The number of prisoners on death row has been increasing.

Direct expenditure for each of the major criminal justice functions (police, corrections, judicial) has been increasing. States spend more on criminal justice than municipalities, counties, or the federal government.

Source: "Capital Punishment 2000" (November 13, 2002), U.S. Department of Justice, Bureau of Justice Statistics at http://www/ojp.usdoj.gov/bjs.

Annotated Bibliography

Books, Documents, and Articles

"ABA Calls for Moratorium on Executions Until Death Penalty Fairness Assured." http://www.pbs.org/wgbh/pages/frontline/angel/procon/aba.html (June 15, 2002). At its February 1997 meeting, the American Bar Association House of Delegates passed, 280 to 119, a resolution calling for a halt to executions until courts can ensure that such cases are administered "fairly and impartially" and with minimal risk of executing innocent people. The resolution specified that the ABA takes no position on the death penalty itself.

Adler, Mortimer, ed. 1976. ***The Annals of America, 1493–1754***, vol. 1. Chicago: Encyclopaedia Brittanica. First of a multivolume collection of documents from American history.

Allen, Francis A. 1981. ***The Decline of the Rehabilitative Ideal.*** New Haven: Yale University Press. Asserts that rehabilitative punishment is failing as a result of loss of social cohesion in the United States.

American Law Institute. 1980. ***Model Penal Code and Commentaries, Part II.*** 3 vols. Philadelphia: American Law Institute. As the title suggests, this is a proposed model penal code. The commentary on the death penalty in vol. 1 (pp. 110–171) is valuable.

Bailyn, Bernard. 1992 (enlarged edition). ***The Ideological Origins of the American Revolution.*** Cambridge, MA: Belknap Press of the Harvard University Press. First published in 1967, this is the Pulitzer Prize–winning explanation of how the framers thought, and why.

Banner, Stuart. 2002. ***The Death Penalty: An American History.*** Cambridge, MA: Harvard University Press. Good new treatment of how the present death penalty stalemate evolved in American history.

Bedau, Hugo Adam. **"The Case Against the Death Penalty."** American Civil Liberties Union Freedom Network, at http://www.aclu.org/liberty/case_against_death.html (February 12, 2002). A pamphlet prepared for the American Civil Liberties Union's Capital Punishment Project presenting major arguments against the death penalty.

———, ed. 1964. ***The Death Penalty in America.*** Chicago: Aldine Publishing. The influential collection of essays by the prolific death penalty scholar and opponent.

———. 1982. ***The Death Penalty in America.*** New York: Oxford University Press. Updated third edition of the original.

Bennett, James V. 1970. ***I Choose Prison.*** New York: Alfred Knopf. Personal account of life as director of the federal prison system by one of the twentieth century's most influential prison administrators.

Berger, Raoul. 1977. ***Government By Judiciary: The Transformation of the Fourteenth Amendment.*** Cambridge, MA: Harvard University Press. The history of the incorporation doctrine from its most eminent historical critic.

Bessler, John. 1996. **"The Midnight Assassination Law and Minnesota's Anti–Death Penalty Movement, 1849–1911."** *William Mitchell Law Review* 22: 577. Good survey of the history of the death penalty in a single state.

Best, Harry. 1930. ***Crime and the Criminal Law in the United States.*** New York: Macmillan Company. Standard textbook from the era of rehabilitative punishment.

Bleich, Jeff, Kelly Klaus, and Deborah Pearlstine. 2001. **"The Clinton Court."** *Oregon State Bar Bulletin* 61(July): 9. Former Supreme Court clerks discuss President Clinton's influence on federal law.

Bradford, M. E. 1993. ***Original Intentions: On the Making and Ratification of the United States Constitution.*** Athens: University of Georgia Press. Essays on the conservative history of the Constitution, including a good one on the Fourteenth Amendment.

Branham, Lynn S. 2001. **"The Prison Litigation Reform Act's Enigmatic Exhaustion Requirement."** *Cornell Law Review* 86(March): 483. History and interpretation of attempt to control prison inmate lawsuits.

Brant, Irving. 1965. ***The Bill of Rights: Its Origin and Meaning.*** Indianapolis: Bobbs-Merrill Company. Concentrates on the First Amendment, but excellent general guide to English antecedents of Bill of Rights.

Bright, Stephen B. 1996. **"The Electric Chair and the Chain Gang: Choices and Challenges for America's Future."** *Notre Dame Law Re-*

view 71(July): 845. Scathing critique of American death penalty and incarceration practices, by the director of the Southern Center for Human Rights.

———. 1999. **"Death in Texas."** *The Champion* 23(July): 16. Discusses inadequacies in judicial oversight of death penalty cases in Texas.

Broom, Jack. 1994. **"Judge Says Rupe Is Too Heavy to Hang."** *Seattle Times,* September 20.

Burton-Rose, Daniel, Dan Pens, and Paul Wright, eds. 1998. ***The Celling of America.*** Monroe, ME: Common Courage Press. Essays about the modern American prison system, many from prisoners.

Cardozo, Benjamin N. 1921. ***The Nature of the Judicial Process.*** New Haven: Yale University Press. Lectures on judging by one of the twentieth century's most influential judges, later appointed to the Supreme Court.

Carrington, Frank. 1978. ***Neither Cruel Nor Unusual.*** New Rochelle, NY: Arlington House. Appeals for death penalty by emphasizing the fates of the victims of crimes.

Christian, Karen. 2001. **"Note: And the DNA Shall Set You Free."** *Ohio State Law Journal* 62: 1195. Case histories of DNA testing with proposal that access to testing be created by statute.

Clark, Phyllis E., and Robert Lehrman. 1980. ***Doing Time: A Look at Crime and Prisons.*** New York: Hastings House. Readable exposition of the rehabilitative theory of punishment from the end of the era.

Closen, Michael L., and Robert J. Dzielak. 1996. **"The History and Influence of the Law Review Institution."** *Akron Law Review* 30(Fall): 15. Good introduction to the evolution of legal scholarship presented in law reviews.

Cogan, Neil H., ed. 1997. ***The Complete Bill of Rights.*** New York: Oxford University Press. One-volume source for the congressional debates, revisions, and ratification debates of the Bill of Rights.

Cohen, Bernard L. 1970. ***Law Without Order: Capital Punishment and the Liberals.*** New Rochelle, NY: Arlington House. A popular and somewhat heated defense of the retributive theory of punishment.

Corwin, Edward S. 1928. **"The 'Higher Law' Background of American Constitutional Law,"** in *The Rights Retained By the People,* ed. Randy E. Barnett, 1989. Fairfax, VA: George Mason University Press. Reprint of seminal essay on American constitutional theory.

———. 1958. ***The Constitution and What it Means Today.*** Princeton, NJ: Princeton University Press. The mid–twentieth century successor to

Cooley and Story's commentaries on the Constitution, first published in 1920.

Cover, Robert M., and T. Alexander Aleinikoff. 1977. **"Dialectical Federalism: Habeas Corpus and the Court."** *Yale Law Journal* 86: 1035. Intensely technical account of the transformation of criminal law by the habeas corpus ruling in *Fay v. Noia.*

Cristman, Bill. 2001. **"*Chandler v. United States:* Does the Defense Attorney Have an Obligation to Present Mitigation Evidence in Eleventh Circuit Death Penalty Cases?"** *Georgia State University Law Review* 18(Winter): 563. Discusses effective assistance of counsel cases in federal court.

Crosskey, William W. 1954. **"Charles Fairman, Legislative History, and the Constitutional Limits on State Authority."** *University of Chicago Law Review* 22(Autumn): 1. Response to Fairman's article (q.v.) arguing that the Fourteenth Amendment does incorporate the Bill of Rights.

Curran, Nadine. 2000. **"Note: Blue Hairs in the Big House."** *New England Journal on Criminal and Civil Confinement* 26(Summer): 225. Exposition of the rapid growth in geriatric issues confronting prison administration.

DeMaio, Jerry R. 2001. **"If You Build It They Will Come: The Threat of Overclassification in Wisconsin's Supermax Prison."** *Wisconsin Law Review* 2001: 207. Introduction to the concept of the supermaximum prison.

Dow, David R. 1996. **"The State, The Death Penalty, and Carl Johnson."** *Boston College Law Review* 37(July): 691. Problems of representing a capital defendant after the trial are presented by lawyer who represented an executed murderer.

Dubber, Markus D. 1998. **"The Right to Be Punished: Autonomy and Its Demise in Modern Penal Thought."** *Law and History Review* 16(Spring): 113. Interesting analysis of the conflict between rehabilitative and punitive theories of criminal sentencing.

Dulles, Avery. 2001. **"Catholicism and Capital Punishment."** *First Things* 112(April): 30. Informative summary of the orthodox Roman Catholic position on the death penalty by an American cardinal and theologian.

Elliot, Jonathan, ed. 1937. ***Debates in the Several State Conventions on the Adoption of the Federal Constitution.*** 5 vols. Philadelphia: J. B. Lippincott Company. Reprint of the 1836 compilation of the constitutional ratification debates.

Fabian, John. 2001. **"The Paradox of Elected Judges: Tension in the American Judicial System."** *Georgetown Journal of Legal Ethics* 15(Fall): 155.

The recent history of elections decided on the basis of the death penalty issue.

Fairman, Charles. 1949. **"Does the Fourteenth Amendment Incorporate the Bill of Rights?"** *Stanford Law Review* 2(December): 5. The classic article denying that the Fourteenth Amendment was intended to apply the Bill of Rights to the states.

Fish, Peter G. 2002. ***Federal Justice in the Mid-Atlantic South: United States Courts from Maryland to the Carolinas, 1789–1835.*** Washington, DC: Administrative Office of the United States Courts. Massively researched and fascinating account of federal court implementation of the new United States' criminal and civil laws in the first generations after ratification of the constitution.

Foley, Daniel J. 2001. **"Death by Election?"** *Tennessee Bar Journal* 37 (December): 12. How the political vulnerability of judges perceived as soft on the death penalty has altered rulings by Tennessee's Supreme Court.

Frank, Jerome. 1947. **"Words and Music."** *Columbia Law Review* 47: 1259. Reflections on methodologies of judging by a member of Court of Appeals for the Second Circuit and influential scholar.

Friedman, Lawrence M. 1973. ***A History of American Law.*** New York: Touchstone Books, Simon & Schuster. The best single survey of American law in the eighteenth and nineteenth centuries.

Garofalo, Andrew F. 2000. **"*Brennan v. State:* The Constitutionality of Executing Sixteen-Year-Old Offenders in Florida."** *Nova Law Review* 24: 855. Good illustration of the application of Supreme Court precedent in a state court system.

Glaser, Daniel. 1969. ***The Effectiveness of a Prison and Parole System.*** Indianapolis: Bobbs-Merrill Company. Abridged edition of the 1964 study of rehabilitative effect of prison and parole on criminals.

Golberg, Arthur J. 1986. **"Memorandum to the Conference Re: Capital Punishment."** *South Texas Law Review* 27: 493. Reprint of Justice Goldberg's 1963 memorandum calling for the Supreme Court to hold that the death penalty is cruel and unusual punishment.

Greenberg, Jack. 1986. **"Against the American System of Capital Punishment."** *Harvard Law Review* 99(May): 1670. An article by anti–death penalty advocate criticizing the American system of capital punishment as it actually operates.

Grossman, Mark. 1998. ***Encyclopedia of Capital Punishment.*** Santa Barbara, CA: ABC-CLIO. Reference book providing an overview of capital punishment from the seventeenth century B.C. through the present.

Hall, Daniel E. 1995. **"When Caning Meets the Eighth Amendment: Whipping Offenders in the United States."** *Widener Journal of Public Law* 4: 403. Concludes, in wake of Michael Fay incident, that public whipping may still be constitutional in United States.

Hamilton, Alexander, James Madison, and John Jay. 1966. ***The Federalist Papers,*** ed. Roy P. Fairfield. Garden City, NY: Anchor Books, Doubleday & Co. Judicial papers on the judiciary branch in the proposed constitution provide a readable exposition of the rehabilitative theory of punishment from the end of the era.

Herman, Peter G., ed. 2001. ***The American Prison System.*** New York: H. W. Wilson. Well-chosen collection of essays and news articles covering the spectrum of modern prison issues.

Hirsch, Alan, and Diane Sheehey. 1993. ***The Bail Reform Act of 1984.*** Washington, DC: Federal Judicial Center. Analysis of the federal law of pretrial detention, for use by the federal judiciary.

Holmes, Oliver Wendell, Jr. 1881. ***The Common Law.*** Boston: Little, Brown and Company. Lectures explaining Holmes's philosophy of law before his appointment to the Supreme Court.

Horwitz, Robert. 1987. **"John Dewey,"** in *History of Political Philosophy,* ed. Leo Strauss and Joseph Cropsey. Chicago: University of Chicago Press. An introduction to the thought of the foremost American philosopher of the twentieth century.

Howard, Roscoe C. 1996. **"The Defunding of the Post-Conviction Defense Organizations as a Denial of the Right to Counsel."** *West Virginia Law Review* 98(Spring): 863. An argument that Congress's 1996 elimination of funding for death penalty attorneys is unwise and ultimately more costly.

Hudson, Daniel. 2000. ***Managing Death-sentenced Inmates: A Survey of Practices.*** Lanham, MD: American Correctional Association. Useful basic survey of issues for death row corrections officials by corrections professional.

Ignatieff, Michael. 1978. ***A Just Measure of Pain: The Penitentiary in the Industrial Revolution, 1750–1850.*** New York: Pantheon Books. First-rate history of the prison system and theories of punishment.

Jackson, Jesse. 1996. ***Legal Lynching: Racism, Injustice, and the Death Penalty.*** New York: Marlowe & Company. Popular treatment of argument that the death penalty is unjust and unevenly applied.

Joyce, James A. 1961. ***Capital Punishment: A World View.*** New York: Thomas Nelson & Sons. A call for a worldwide end to capital punishment by a committed rehabilitationist.

Kenyon, J. P. 1966. ***The Stuart Constitution, 1603–1688: Documents and Commentary.*** Cambridge: Cambridge University Press. Presents relevant materials from English law before the Bill of Rights.

Kirchmeier, Jeffrey L. 2000. **"Let's Make a Deal: Waiving the Eighth Amendment by Selecting a Cruel and Unusual Punishment."** *Connecticut Law Review* 32(Winter): 615. Questions whether waiver of prohibition against cruel and unusual punishment should be waivable.

———. 2002. **"Another Place Beyond Here: The Death Penalty Moratorium Movement in the United States."** *University of Colorado Law Review* 73(Winter): 1. History and current support for moratorium on executions.

Klarman, Michael J. 1998. **"Race and the Court in the Progressive Era."** *Vanderbilt Law Review* 51: 881. Enlightening article about a neglected period of Supreme Court history.

Koosed, Margery M. 2001. **"Averting Mistaken Executions by Adopting the Model Penal Code's Exclusion of Death in the Presence of Lingering Doubt."** *Northern Illinois University Law Review* 21(Spring): 41. Article pointing up the role of uncertainty in verdicts recommending the death penalty.

Kronenwetter, Michael. 1993. ***Capital Punishment.*** Santa Barbara: ABC-CLIO. Comprehensive treatment of the death penalty: its history, court rulings, and arguments from supporters and opponents.

Laurence, John. 1960. ***A History of Capital Punishment.*** New York: Citadel Press. An informative book on famous executions and executioners throughout history.

Lawes, Lewis E. 1969. ***Man's Judgment of Death.*** Montclair, NJ: Patterson Smith. Reprint of anti–capital punishment tract by the warden of Sing Sing Prison.

Ledewitz, Bruce, and Scott Staples. 1993. **"No Punishment without Cruelty."** *George Mason University Civil Rights Law Journal* 4 (Winter): 41. Good distinction between revenge and retribution by two opponents of the death penalty and life without parole.

Lee, Robert W. **"Deserving to Die."** *New American,* August 13, 1990. An article contending that capital punishment is the only appropriate way for society to respond to heinous crimes.

Liebman, James S., Jeffrey Fagan, Valerie West, and Jonathan Lloyd. 2000. **"Capital Attrition: Error Rates in Capital Cases, 1973–1995."** *Texas Law Review* 78(June): 1839. Brief, statistics-packed article concluding that the high error rate in capital cases requires overhaul of the system.

Lifton, Robert J., and Greg Mitchell. 2000. ***Who Owns Death?*** New York: HarperCollins Publishers. Social and psychological treatment of the death penalty from abolitionist perspective.

Little, Rory K. 1999. **"The Federal Death Penalty: History and Some Thoughts about the Department of Justice's Role."** *Fordham Urban Law Journal* 26(March): 347. Excellent history and insider's appraisal of the administration of the Federal Death Penalty Act of 1994.

Locke, John. 1924. ***Two Treatises of Civil Government.*** London: J. M. Dent & Sons Ltd. Everyman's Library edition of Locke's classic essays of 1690.

Logan, Wayne A. 2000. **"Opining on Death: Witness Sentence Recommendations in Capital Trials"** *Boston College Law Review* 41(May): 517. Discusses cases from *Booth v. Maryland* to *Payne v. Tennessee.*

Maitland, F. W. 1908 (H. A. L. Fisher, editor). ***The Constitutional History of England.*** Cambridge: Cambridge University Press. The development of English constitutional law by its foremost nineteenth-century expositor.

Margulies, Joseph. 2002. **"Memories of an Execution."** *Law and Inequality: A Journal of Theory and Practice* 20(Winter): 125. Perspective by counsel on Texas's execution of his client, "The Black Widow," in 2000.

McCafferty, James A. 1972. ***Capital Punishment.*** Chicago: Aldine-Atherton. A superior collection of essays for and against the death penalty, including valuable contributions by Jacques Barzun and Jack Greenberg.

McClellan, Grant S., ed. 1961. ***Capital Punishment.*** New York: H. W. Wilson. Collection of essays, worthwhile for statements by Ohio governor Michael DiSalle and California governor Edmund G. (Pat) Brown.

McCormick, John. **"The Wrongly Condemned: How Many Capital Cases End in False Convictions?"** *Newsweek,* November 9, 1998. An article chronicling false convictions in capital cases.

McDonald, Forrest. 1985. ***Novus Ordo Seclorum: The Intellectual Origins of the Constitution.*** Lawrence: University of Kansas Press. Intelligent treatise on the sources of principles believed by the framers.

McKelvey, Blake. 1977. ***American Prisons: A History of Good Intentions.*** Montclair, NJ: Patterson Smith. Excellent narrative history of America's experiences with prisons.

Melusky, Joseph. 2000. ***The American Political System: An Owner's Manual.*** New York: McGraw-Hill. A political science textbook providing background discussion on the framing, ratification, and interpretation of the U.S. Constitution.

Mencken, H. L. 1926. **"The Penalty of Death,"** in *Elements of Argument,* ed. Annette T. Rottenberg. New York: St. Martin's Press, 1985. pp.

394–396. The master of American satire derides the retributive theory of capital punishment.

Mill, John Stuart. **"Speech In Favor of Capital Punishment,"** *Ethics Updates,* at http://ethics.acusd.edu/Mill.html (19 February 2002). A speech delivered before Parliament on April 21, 1868 in opposition to a bill banning capital punishment.

Nygaard, Richard L. 1988. **"Crime, Pain, and Punishment: A Skeptic's View."** *Dickinson Law Review* 102(Winter): 355. Judge of Court of Appeals for the Third Circuit explains why he rejects punishment for crime.

Owens, John B. 2000. **"Book Review"** *California Law Review* 88(January): 233. Humorous review of suspense fiction about the Court by a former law clerk sheds light on Court's decision-making process.

Paduano, Anthony, and Clive A. S. Smith. 1991. **"The Unconscionability of Sub-minimum Wages Paid Appointed Counsel in Capital Cases."** *Rutgers Law Review* 43(Winter): 281. Argues that indigent capital defendants too often get the defense they pay for.

Parker, Frank J. 1975. ***Caryl Chessman: The Red Light Bandit.*** Chicago: Nelson-Hall, Inc. Summing up of one of twentieth century's most controversial death penalty cases.

Pope John Paul II. 1995. ***Evangelium Vitae (The Gospel of Life).*** Papal encyclical stating that the death penalty is morally acceptable when it is necessary to defend society, but that in view of improvements to penal systems, such cases are extremely rare if not nonexistent.

Post, Albert. 1944. **"Early Efforts to Abolish Capital Punishment in Pennsylvania."** *The Pennsylvania Magazine of History and Biography* 68(January): 38. Early survey of abolitionism in a single state.

Pound, Roscoe. 1957. ***The Development of Constitutional Guarantees of Liberty.*** New Haven: Yale University Press. Sources of American freedoms presented by influential legal scholar and educator.

———. 1999. ***The Spirit of the Common Law.*** New Brunswick, NJ: Transaction Publishers. Reissue of Pound's 1921 lectures on legal philosophy.

Prejean, Sister Helen. 1993. ***Dead Man Walking: An Eyewitness Account of the Death Penalty in the United States.*** New York: Vintage Books/Random House. Sister Helen Prejean's experiences as a spiritual adviser to death row prisoners in Louisiana'a Angola State Prison, source of the hit 1995 film.

Prettyman, Barrett, Jr. 1961. ***Death and the Supreme Court.*** New York: Harcourt, Brace & World. Prizewinning examination of the stories behind six capital punishment cases at the Supreme Court by a former law clerk.

Robbins, Ira P. 1993. **"The Prisoners' Mail Box and the Evolution of Federal Inmate Rights."** *Federal Rules Decisions* 144: 127. History of federal prisons in twentieth century presented through the development of a grievance system.

Roleff, Tamara, ed. 1999. ***Crime and Criminals: Opposing Viewpoints.*** San Diego: Greenhaven Press. Collection of essays on the death penalty and other sentencing issues.

Romano, Sally Ann. 1996. **"If the SHU Fits: Cruel and Unusual Punishment at California's Pelican Bay State Prison."** *Emory Law Journal* 45(Summer): 1089. History of prison systems, concluding that supermax facilities violate the Eighth Amendment.

Sarat, Austin. 1998. **"Recapturing the Spirit of *Furman*: The American Bar Association and the New Abolitionist Politics."** *Law and Contemporary Problems* 61(Autumn): 5. Presents the view that the abolitionist movement is gaining political strength.

Schwartz, Bernard, ed. 1980. ***The Roots of the Bill of Rights.*** 5 vols. New York: Chelsea House. Source documents for the Bill of Rights, from Magna Carta to notes of state ratifying conventions, edited and introduced by noted New York University law professor.

Semeraro, Steven. 2002. **"Responsibility in Capital Sentencing."** *San Diego Law Review* 39(Winter): 79. Charges that appellate review of death sentences is inadequate.

Skelton, Meghan S. 1997. **"Lethal Injection in the Wake of *Fierro v. Gomez*."** *Thomas Jefferson Law Review* 19(Spring): 1. A history of methods of execution with a call for lethal injection to go the way of the electric chair and gas chamber.

Stephens, Matthew L. 1990. **"Instrument of Justice or Tool of Vengeance?"** *Christian Social Action* 3(November): no. 10. An article written by a prison chaplain criticizing capital punishment on grounds that it is motivated by revenge and it is applied in an arbitrary and racist fashion.

Stephenson, D. Grier. 1994. **"Justice Blackmun's Eighth Amendment Pilgrimage."** *BYU Journal of Public Law* 8: 271. A comprehensive account of the evolution of the jurisprudence of the most famous convert to the position that the Eighth Amendment bars capital punishment.

Story, Joseph. 1987. ***Commentaries on the Constitution of the United States.*** Durham, NC: Carolina Academic Press. Reprint of Story's treatise with valuable introduction by Ronald D. Rotunda and John E. Nowak.

Stuntz, William J. 1998. **"Race, Class, and Drugs."** *Columbia Law Review* 98: 1795. Explains how even racially neutral law enforcement can be rationally perceived as discriminatory and why perception of fairness is important to successful drug laws.

Surrency, Erwin C. 1987. ***History of the Federal Courts.*** New York: Oceana Publications. Presents the evolution of the jurisdiction and procedures of federal courts.

Thompson, E. P. 1975. ***Whigs and Hunters: The Origin of the Black Act.*** New York: Pantheon Books/Random House. In-depth look at one capital punishment statute and how it was applied in Georgian England.

"U.S. Catholic Bishops' Statement on Capital Punishment." 1980. Available at http://www.pbs.org/wgbh/pages/frontline/angel/procon/bishopstate.html (13 February 2002). A 1980 statement issued by U.S. Roman Catholic bishops explaining their opposition to capital punishment.

U.S. Department of Justice. 2000. ***Survey of the Federal Death Penalty System, 1988–2000.*** Washington, DC: U.S. Department of Justice. Internal document reviewing performance of the Department of Justice's Review Committee on Capital Cases.

Van den Haag, Ernest. 1986. **"The Ultimate Punishment: A Defense."** *Harvard Law Review* 99(May): 1662. Defends capital punishment against various criticisms.

Veall, Donald. 1970. ***The Popular Movement for Law Reform, 1640–1660.*** Oxford: Clarendon Press. Changes in English criminal law and procedure are set in the history of the English Civil War.

Weinstein, Henry. 2002. **"Death Penalty Foes Mark A Milestone."** *Los Angeles Times,* April 10.

Wekesser, Carol, ed. 1991. ***The Death Penalty: Opposing Viewpoints.*** San Diego: Greenhaven Press. Collection of essays, including classics by Beccaria, Mill, and Horace Greeley.

White, Ahmed A. 2001. **"Rule of Law and the Limits of Sovereignty: The Private Prison in Jurisprudential Perspective."** *American Criminal Law Review* 38(May): 111. The modern phenomenon of private prisons is traced to its roots and found wanting.

Wiener, Scott. 1996. **"Popular Justice: State Judicial Elections and Procedural Due Process."** *Harvard Civil Rights–Civil Liberties Law Review* 31(Winter): 187. Can elected judges decide death penalty cases impartially? The author argues that the answer is no.

Williams, Kenneth. 2000. **"The Deregulation of the Death Penalty."** *Santa Clara Law Review* 40: 677. Post-1976 limitations on appellate and habeas corpus relief from the death penalty are criticized.

Internet Resources

Given the speed with which online resources evolve, it is not possible to produce an exhaustive list of relevant Web sites. Nevertheless, in addition to the sites listed in Chapter 5, the following are representative Web sites with a range of information.

Professor Lawrence Hinman of the University of San Diego's Values Institute maintains the **Ethics Updates** Web site at http://ethics.acusd.edu/Applied/deathpenalty (June 15, 2002). Statistical information, references to and texts of new and old speeches, essays, books, and law review and journal articles on the death penalty.

The **Justice Center** Web site is maintained by the University of Alaska, Anchorage, at http://www.uaa.alaska.edu/just/death (June 15, 2002). In addition to information about Alaska law, the site provides links to other sites and general resources on the death penalty.

Index

Abolitionists
versus deferentialists, 113–114, 139–140
ACA. *See* American Correctional Association
ACLU. *See* American Civil Liberties Union
Adams, John Quincy, 51
AEDPA. *See* Antiterrorism and Effective Death Penalty Act
AFL-CIO. *See* American Federation of Labor and Congress of Industrial Organizations
Age minimum, and death penalty, 123–125
Ake v. Oklahoma, 117
Alabama, 115, 129, 158, 172
Alcatraz, 94
ALI. *See* American Law Institute
Alien Act, 57
Aliens, deportation of, 156
Amadeo, Tony, 6
Amendments to the U.S. Constitution, 9, 208–209 (document). *See also individual amendments*
American Bar Association, 146, 177
American Bar Association House of Delegates, 17
American Bar Association Resolution on the Death Penalty, 214–215 (document)
American Civil Liberties Union (ACLU), 14, 177
American colonies
and transportation, sentence of, 33, 34, 35
American Correctional Association (ACA), 95, 178
American Federation of Labor and Congress of Industrial Organizations (AFL-CIO), 98
American law
versus English law, 36–38
American Law Institute (ALI), 22, 93, 195
American Prison Association, 95, 186
American Revolution, 39
American Society for the Abolition of Capital Punishment, 51
Ames, Aldrich, 123
Amherst College, 141
Amnesty International, 178
Amsterdam, Anthony, 103, 178, 185–186
Andrade, Leandro, 161
Angola State Prison, 191
Antihijacking law, 107

Antiterrorism and Effective Death Penalty Act (AEDPA), 145–146, 178, 184
Appeals, 114–115, 141–142, 179
 cost of, 16, 22
Arave v. Creech, 119–120
Aristotle, 32, 74, 82
Arizona, 129–130, 149
Arizona v. Rumsey, 116
Arkansas, 161, 173
 prison system, 166–167
Articles of Confederation, 40–41
"Aryan Brotherhood," 116
Assault and battery, 58–59
Assistance of counsel, 91. *See also* Sixth Amendment
Athelstan, King, 35
Atkins, Daryl, 128
Atkins v. Virginia, 128, 179, 314–323 (document)
Atlanta, Georgia, 48
Attica, New York, 164
Attorney general, 179
Auburn State Prison, 61

Bail, 40, 62
Bail Reform Act of 1984, 86, 156–157, 179
Bajakajian, Hosep, 161–162
Baldus, David, 152–154, 270–283
Banishment, 31–32, 33, 34, 35, 97
Barron v. Biltmore, 48
Barrow, Samuel J., 48
Bates, Sanford, 94, 180
Beard, Charles A., 77
Bearden v. Georgia, 102
Beccaria, Cesare, 39, 179
Beck v. Alabama, 115
Bedau, Hugo Adam, 14, 16–17, 180
Beheading, 59
Bell v. Cone, 148
Bellamy, Edward, 81
Benefit of clergy, 34
Bennett, James, 94, 180
Bentham, Jeremy, 81
Bethea, Rainey, 41, 180
Bible, 29–30, 35
Bill of Rights, 9, 48, 91, 92, 95, 155, 180, 186
 framers of, 10
Bird, Rose, 180
Black, Hugo, 82–83, 92, 95, 104
Black Act of 1723, 34
Blackmun, Harry, 23–26, 99, 103, 105, 109, 110, 112, 122, 139, 156, 168, 181
Blackstone, William, 33–35, 49, 52, 94, 125
Bloody Assizes, 44–45, 47, 186
Blystone v. Pennsylvania, 118
Bonaparte, Napoleon, 56
Book of Exodus, 32, 200–201 (document)
Booth v. Maryland, 115, 132, 133–134
Bork, Robert, 22, 181
Boykin v. Alabama, 103
Branch, Elmer, 105
Brandeis, Louis, 90–91
Breaking on the wheel, 10, 62
Brennan, William, 7, 95, 96, 100, 104–105, 106, 109, 111, 113, 122, 124, 133, 139, 168, 181
Breyer, Stephen, 80, 134, 135, 140
Bright, Stephen, 193
Brooks, Charles, Jr., 181
Brown, Debra, 2, 3
Brown v. Board of Education, 73, 95, 96, 194
Brown v. Mississippi, 73–74, 186
Buchanan, Douglas, 125
Buchanan v. Angelone, 125
Buchanan v. Kentucky, 130, 152
Bullington v. Missouri, 115–116
Bureau of Prisons, 84, 163

Burger, Warren, 7, 105, 107, 108, 110, 111, 113, 122
Burgess, Anthony, 86
Burglary tools, possession of, 101
Burke, Edmund, 33
Burning, of heretics, 149
Burning at the stake, 10, 60, 62
Burr, Aaron, 30
Bush, George H. W., 86–87, 140
Bush, Jeb, 155
Bush v. Gore, 69
Butch Cassidy and the Sundance Kid, 85

Calderon v. Thompson, 146
Caldwell v. Mississippi, 131
California, 89, 104, 106, 144, 157, 160
California prison system, 94
California v. Brown, 131
Callins, Bruce Edwin, 23–24
Callins v. Collins, 23–26
Campaign platform
  pro-death penalty, 112–113
Campbell v. Wood, 150
Canada, 15
Cannon, Joe Frank, 181–182
Capital cases
  cost of, 16
  and lawyers, 141
Capital punishment
  arguments against, 12–17, 143–144
  arguments for, 17–23, 143–144
  cost of, 15, 22
  See also Death penalty; Executions
Cardozo, Benjamin, 75, 77, 78, 79, 91
"The Case Against the Death Penalty" (ACLU), 14
Case method, 78
Cell 2455, Death Row, 182
Centralization of power, 70
Chain gangs, 163
The Champion, 189
Charles I, 56
Charles II, 44–45, 46, 186, 190
Chessman, Caryl, 97–98, 182
Chicago, Burlington, and Quincy Railroad Co. v. Chicago, 90
Cicero, 76
Circuit Courts of Appeal, 183
Citizenship, loss of
  and court martial, 156
Civil contempt, 156
Civil rights, 92
Civil Rights Act of 1964
  Title VII, 153
Civil Rights of Institutionalized Persons Act, 168
Civil War, 48, 50, 96
Civilized society, 14
Clark, Ramsey, 102
Clark, Tom, 102
Clifford, Nathan, 59–60
Clinton, Bill, 68, 112–113, 140
A Clockwork Orange (Burgess), 86
Code of Draco, 32, 201–202 (document)
Code of Hammurabi, 32, 197–200 (document)
Coker, Ehrlich, 122
Coker v. Georgia, 122, 123, 127, 152, 182, 229–235 (document)
Coleman, Alton, 2–3
Coleman v. Thompson, 147
Collateral attack, 182
Collateral review process, 142
Collazo, Oscar, 85
Collins v. Johnston, 91
Colorado, 50–51, 129–130
Columbia University, 185–186, 187, 195
Columbia University Law School, 79, 93, 95, 143

Commentaries on the Constitution (Story), 52–53
Commentaries on the Laws of England (Blackstone), 33, 52, 125
Common law, 182
Community treatment program, 84
Commutation, 189
Concurrence, 182
Cone, Gary, 148
Congress, 41, 153–154
versus Parliament, 54–57
Connecticut, 41
Connecticut Currant, 56
Constitution, 8–12, 23–26, 41, 42, 43, 54, 155
framers of, 9–10, 39, 77
Constitutional Limitations. *See* A Treatise on the Constitutional Limitations Which Rest upon the Legislative Power of the States of the American Union
Continental Congress, 40
Cooley, Thomas, 53, 88
Cooper v. Oklahoma, 126–127
Corbitt v. New Jersey, 115
Corporal punishment, 11
in schools, 156
Corrections officers
and prisoners, abuse of, 171–173
Counsel
ineffective assistance of, 186
See also Lawyers
County jail, 59
Court martial
and citizenship, loss of, 156
Court of Star Chamber, 38
Courts, 54–55
abolitionists versus deferentialists in, 113–114, 139–140
Courts of Appeals, 113–114
Creech, Thomas, 119–120
Criminal code, 55–58
The Criminal Man (Lombroso), 82, 187
Criminals, hardened, 20
Crucifixion, 62
Cruel and unusual punishments, 4, 9–12
Cruel and Unusual Punishments Clause, 4
Cummins Farm, 166–167
Curtis, Newton M., 52

Dalai Lama. *See* Qyatso, Tenin
Dallas, George M., 41
Darwin, Charles, 81
Darwinism, 82
Dawson v. Delaware, 116
Dead Man Walking: An Eyewitness Account of the Death Penalty in the United States (Prejean), 191
Deadlock, jury, 132
Death and the Supreme Court (Prettyman), 191
Death penalty
and abolitionists versus deferentialists, and Supreme Court, 113–114, 139–140
and age minimum, 123–125
alternatives to, lack of, 32–33
history of, 7–8
overturn of, 106–108
and public opinion, 346–347 (table)
states with, 345
See also Capital punishment; Executions
The Death Penalty in America (Bedau), 180
Death Penalty Information Center, 183
Death Penalty Review Unit, 183

Death qualification
  and jury service, 103–104, 130
Death row, 8, 13–14, 19, 103, 106, 114, 143
  excessive delay on, 134–135
  prisoners on, number of, by race (1968–2000), 344 (table)
  prisoners on, number of (2000), 342
  and volunteering for death, 13–14, 114–115, 143, 194
  Web site, 13
"Death Row U.S.A.," 188
Declaration of Independence, 49, 77, 192, 204–207 (document)
  signers of, 39–41
Declaration of Rights, 42
Defendants
  and incompetence, 125–127
  insanity of, 125–127
  sanity of, 117
Deferentialists
  versus abolitionists, 113–114, 139–140
Delaware, 42, 129–130
Delaying tactics
  cost of, 22
Denning, Lord, 23
Deportation, of aliens, 156
Deterrence, 5–6, 13–14, 15, 18–19, 20–21, 22, 39, 76, 102
  and increase in violent crimes, 16
Dewey, John, 75
Direct appeal process, 142
Disrespect
  for human dignity, 19–20, 39
  for human life, 14, 20–21
District courts, 183
District of Columbia, 52, 168
Double Jeopardy Clause, 91, 115–116. *See also* Fifth Amendment
Douglas, William, 7, 79, 95, 97, 100, 102, 106–108, 183
Draco. *See* Code of Draco
Drawing and quartering, 10, 60, 149
Dred Scott decision, 68
Driver, Giles, 58
Drug addiction, 101, 102, 157
Drug crimes
  number of arrests for, 345
  and revenue, raising of, 38
Due process, 11, 14, 89–91, 186
Due Process Clause, 90–91, 95, 106, 155, 158, 164
  and incorporation of rights, 91
  See also Fifth Amendment
Duffy, Clinton, 94
Dukakis, Michael, 86–87
Dunne, Finley Peter, 69

An Economic Interpretation of the Constitution of the United States (Beard), 77
Edison, Thomas, 61
Education, 14
Edwards, Jonathan, 30–31
Ehrlich, Isaac, 22
Eighth Amendment, 9–12
Eisenhower, Dwight D., 95
Electric chair, 10, 149, 150
Electrocution, 61–62, 92–93
Elmira Chamber of Commerce, 78
England, 46–47
Engler, John, 160
English Bill of Rights, 43, 180, 203–204 (document)
English Civil War, 44
English Declaration of Rights, 42
English law, 31–32, 33–38, 39, 42, 44–45, 50, 149
  versus American law, 36–38
English Revolution, 39
Enmund, Earl, 121

Enmund v. Florida, 121, 187, 242–248 (document)
Equal distribution, 14, 17–18
Equal Employment Opportunity Commission, 153
Equal protection, 14
Equal Protection Clause, 96, 158
Escape
  and prisons, conditions of, 168
Essay on Crimes and Punishments (Beccaria), 39
Estelle v. Gamble, 165–166
Eugenics movement, 158
European Union, 15
Evangelium Vitae (The Gospel of Life) (John Paul II), 213–214 (document)
Evarts, William, 70, 183
Evarts Act, 70
Evidence, forensic, 154–155
Excessive Fines Clause, 161
Execution, stay of, 101, 144–146, 194
Executions
  cost of, 16
  and methods, 149–151
  number of, by region (1976–2002), 342 (table)
  number of, by state (1976–2001), 341 (table)
  number of (1927–1963), 94
  number of (1930–2001), 340 (table)
  number of (1960s), 101
  number of (2000), 339
  See also Capital punishment; Death penalty
Executions, military, 7
Executions, public, 41
Executive branch, 151
Exodus. *See* Book of Exodus
Fay, Michael, 11, 183
Fay v. Noia, 98–99, 101, 144
Federal Bureau of Prisons, 94
Federal court system, three-tier, 70, 183
Federal crime bill, 50
Federal crimes, 48–50, 51–52
Federal Death Penalty Act of 1994, 132, 184
Federal government, 70
Federal habeas corpus statutes, 49, 142–144, 144–146, 184
Federal legislator, 151
Federal prisons, 48, 70, 94, 163. *See also* Prisons
Federalist Paper No. 51, 75
Federalist Paper No. 78, 56
Federalist Paper No. 84, 43
Feguer, Victor, 94, 99, 187
Felker v. Turpin, 145, 178
Felony convictions, 345
Field, Stephen, 62–64
Fierro v. Gomez, 150
Fifth Amendment, 11, 25, 89–90, 91, 115–116, 155. *See also* Due Process Clause
Filing fee
  and litigation, inmate, 174
Fines, 32, 161–162
  excessive, 40, 62
Firing squad, 59–60, 149, 150
First Amendment, 116
Florida, 109, 114, 122, 128–129, 129–130, 150, 155
Fong Yue Ting v. United States, 156
Ford, Gerald, 108
Ford v. Wainwright, 126, 256–262 (document)
Fordham University, 194
Forensic evidence, 154–155
Forfeiture laws, 161–162

Forgery, 50
Fort Leavenworth, Kansas, 48
Fourteenth Amendment, 48, 61–62, 88–89, 90, 92, 104, 106, 155, 158, 164, 186
Fourth Amendment, 10
Frame of Government (Penn), 36, 190
Francis, Willie, 92
Frank, Daniel, 7, 184
Frank, Jerome, 78–79
Frankfurter, Felix, 79, 92–93, 96, 184, 191
Freedom of speech, 91
Freedom of the press, 91
French Revolution, 39
Fuller, Melville, 61–62, 64
Furman, William, 105
Furman v. Georgia, 7–8, 71, 105–109, 111, 112, 121, 130, 132–133, 148, 155, 162, 178, 185, 195

Garza, Juan, 184
Gas chamber, 149, 150
"Gee Officer Krupke" (song), 84
George I, 34
George III, 39, 44
Georgia, 105, 108–109, 122, 127, 150, 152
Gilmore, Bessie, 114
Gilmore, Gary, 8, 13, 114, 185
Gilmore v. Utah, 114–115
Ginsburg, Ruth, 140, 148
Glaser, Daniel, 84
Glendening, Parris, 154–155
Glorious Revolution, 35, 44–45
The Godfather, 85
Godfrey v. Georgia, 119
Goldberg, Arthur, 80, 81, 98, 99–101, 102, 106, 185
Gomez v. United States District Court, 144
Gore, Al, Jr., 86
Government
  and law, 76–77
Governmental power
  versus individual rights, 155–156
Graham, Barbara, 98
Grand juries, 89
Grand larceny, 35
Great Britain, 20, 93
Great Society, 75
Greenberg, Jack, 12, 103, 185
Gregg, Troy, 108
Gregg v. Georgia, 8, 22, 108, 112, 114, 130, 135, 148, 181, 185, 193, 217–226 (document)
"Greyhound therapy," 97
Grotius, Hugo, 32
Guards, and prisons, conditions of, 166–167
Guided discretion, 8
Guillotine, 10
Gyatso, Tenzin
  Message Supporting the Moratorium on the Death Penalty, 215–217 (document)

Habeas corpus statutes. *See* Federal habeas corpus statutes
Hale v. Kentucky, 72
Hamilton, Alexander, 43, 56
Hammer, David Paul, 13
Hammurabi. *See* Code of Hammurabi
Hanging, 41, 59, 61, 149, 150
Hangman, 41
Hanssen, Robert, 123
Hard labor, 20, 62
Harding, Warren, 194
Harlan, John Marshall, 89–90, 95, 104, 191
Harmelin v. Michigan, 160–161, 302–314 (document)
Harris, Robert Alton, 113, 144

Harvard Law School, 52, 78, 79
Hawaii, 70
Hawkins, Steven, 189
Hayes, Rutherford, 183
Hayward, Susan, 98
Helsinki Accords, 186
Henry, Patrick, 42
Heresy, 34
Heretics, burning of, 149
Herrera v. Collins, 144–145
High treason, 34
Hitchcock v. Dugger, 119
Hobbes, Thomas, 35
Hofstadter, Richard, 77
Holden v. Minnesota, 51
Holmes, Abraham, 42–43
Holmes, Oliver Wendell, 75, 77
Homicide, 13. *See also* Murder
Hoover, Herbert, 94
Hope v. Pelzer, 172–173
Hopt v. Utah, 49
House of Burgesses, 42
Houston, Texas, 114
Hudson v. McMillian, 172
Hughes, Charles Evans, 78, 185–186
Human dignity, disrespect for, 19–20, 39
Human life, disrespect for, 14, 20–21
Human Rights Watch, 186
Hurtado v. California, 89–90, 91
Hutto v. Davis, 159
Hutto v. Finney, 166–168, 173

I Want to Live, 98
Idaho, 129, 150
Idaho State Penitentiary, 120
Ignatieff, Michael, 33
Illinois, 154
Imprisonment, 32–33, 33, 39, 62
  life, 52
In re Kemmler, 61, 88, 112, 150
In re Medley, 169
Incompetence, of defendants, 125–127
Incorporation, 91, 186
Indentured servant, 31–32
Indeterminate sentences, 83–84
Indiana, 129
Indifference, deliberate, 172
  and medical needs, in prison, 165–167
Individual rights
  versus governmental power, 155–156
Ingraham v. Wright, 156
Inmates
  and litigation, 173–174
  murder by, 174
  See also Prisoners
Innocence Protection Act, 3
Insanity, of defendants, 125–127
Interdiction, 5
Intoxicating liquors, selling of, illegal, 62–63
Iowa, 50–51
IQ, 15–16
Isolation
  and prisons, conditions of, 168–171

Jackson, Andrew, 49
Jackson, Lucious, 105
Jackson, Robert, 80, 191
Jail
  cost of, 16
  idleness in, 59
James II (Duke of York), 44–45, 46, 186
Jay, John, 43, 49
Jefferson, Thomas, 49, 56
Jeffreys, George, 45–47, 186
Jesuits, 46
John, King, 36

John Paul II
and *Evangelium Vitae (The Gospel of Life)*, 213–214 (document)
Johnson, Andrew, 183
Johnson, Lyndon B., 101, 104
Johnson, Samuel, 75–76
Johnson administration, 102
Johnson v. Dye, 163–164
Johnson v. Mississippi, 131
Johnson v. Texas, 125
Johnston, James, 94
Jones, Edith, 141
Jones v. United States, 132
Jones'El v. Berge, 170–171
"The Judge as Legislator" (Cardozo), 78
Judges, 54–55, 77–80
Judges Bill. *See* Judiciary Act
Judicial branch
versus legislative branch, 54–59
Judiciary Act of 1925, 70, 194
Jurek, Jerry, 110
Jurek v. Texas, 108, 110, 127
Juries, 35, 52
Jury deadlock, 132
Jury of peers, 40
Jury selection, 116–117
Jury service
and death qualification, 103–104, 130
Jury trial. *See* Trial by jury
Just war model, 87
Justice, 19, 77
miscarriage of, 18, 21–22, 71–72
Justice Department, 168, 179, 183, 188
Justices, of Supreme Court, 56. *See also individual justices*

Kansas, 157
Kansas v. Hendricks, 157
Kemmler, William, 61, 62
"Kemmler Process," 61
Kennedy, Anthony, 133, 140, 160, 162
Kennedy, John F., 85, 98
Kennedy, Robert F., 84, 85
King, Coretta Scott, 14
King, Martin Luther, Jr., 14, 85
Knight v. Florida, 134–135
Krone, Ray, 1–2, 3
Krull, George, 94
Krull, Michael, 94
Kubrick, Stanley, 86

Lambert v. Barrett, 64
Langdell, Charles, 78
Law, and government, 76–77
Law clerks, 79–80
Law of evidence, 131
Law schools, 78
Lawes, Lewis E., 94–95, 186
Lawyers
and capital cases, 141
competence of, 140–141, 146–149, 186
court-appointed, 16
Leahy, Patrick, 3
Leavenworth, 94
Lee, Robert, 22–23
Legal codes, 32
Legal philosophy, 74
Legal realism, 78
Legislative branch
vs. judicial branch, 54–59
Lethal injection, 10, 149, 151
Leviathan (Hobbes), 35
Libel, 56–57
Lie detector, 187
Liebman, James, 143, 187
Life imprisonment, 52
Life without parole, 15, 132
Lincoln, Abraham, 49, 68
Lindbergh, Charles, 99

"Lindbergh law," 99
Lindh, "Taliban John" Walker, 123
Litigation, inmate, 173–174
Livermore, Samuel, 44, 47
Locke, John, 35, 76–77
Lockett v. Ohio, 118, 235–242 (document)
Lockhart v. McCree, 130, 152
Loitering, 101
Lombroso, Cesare, 82, 187
Looking Backward (Bellamy), 81
Los Angeles, 114
Louisiana, 111, 115, 122, 126, 157
Louisiana ex. rel. Francis v. Resweber, 92–93, 112
"Lousy-lawyering," 16
Lowenfield, Leslie, 120
Lowenfield v. Phelps, 120

Madison, James, 41, 43, 75, 187
Magna Carta, 34, 36, 37, 40, 89, 202–203 (document)
Maine, 50–51
Mandatory sentences, 8, 11, 159–160. *See also* Sentencing
Mandatory sterilization laws, 158–159
Mandatory treatment, 11–12
Man's Judgment of Death (Lawes), 186
Manslaughter, 50
Manson, Charles, 85
Marshall, John, 49, 77–78, 88
Marshall, Thurgood, 7, 104–105, 106–107, 109, 111, 122, 139, 165, 187, 188
Mary II, 46, 56
Maryland, 42, 127, 169
Mason, George, 42–43
Massachusetts, 41, 42–43, 169
  and Salem witch trials, 37–38
Massachusetts Body of Liberties, 38
Massachusetts state prison system, 94
Matthews, Stanley, 89–90
Maxwell v. Bishop, 103–104, 105, 150
Maynard v. Cartwright, 119
McCarver, Ernest, 128
McCleskey, Warren, 152
McCleskey v. Kemp, 152–153, 270–283 (document)
McGautha v. California, 104, 106, 108
McGee, Richard A., 94
McKenna, Joseph, 87–89
McKoy v. North Carolina, 119
McNeil Island, Washington, 48
McNulty, Paul, 125
McVeigh, Timothy, 13, 99, 184, 187
Medical needs, deliberate indifference to
  in prison, 165–167
Medicinal rehabilitative model, 81–85
Medina v. California, 126
Mencken, H. L., 75
Mental illness, 102
  and prisoners, 170
Mental retardation, 15–16, 127–128
Mercer University, 6
Mercy, 22
Message Supporting the Moratorium on the Death Penalty (Gyatso), 215–217 (document)
Michigan, 50
Milan, Michigan, 94
Military executions, 7, 150
Mill, John Stuart, 20–22, 188
  "Speech in Favor of Capital Punishment," 209–213 (document)
Mills v. Maryland, 118–119
Miranda v. Arizona, 73, 114

Miscarriage of justice, 18, 21–22, 71–72
Mississippi, 122, 173
Missouri Pacific Railway v. Nebraska, 90
Model Penal Code, 93, 104, 108, 184, 195
Moderate middle, 188
Monetary penalty, 32
Money laundering, 38
Montana, 129
Moore v. Dempsey, 71
Moral degradation, 39
More, Thomas, 32, 82
Morgan v. Illinois, 130
Murder, 50, 52
  accomplices to, 121–122
  by inmates, 174
  premeditated, 50
Murderers, 117–121, 149
Murray v. Giarratano, 147

NAACP. *See* National Association for the Advancement of Colored People
National Association for the Advancement of Colored People (NAACP), 149, 188
  Legal Defense and Educational Fund, 101, 104, 178, 185, 187
National Association of Attorneys General, 173, 188
National Association of Criminal Defense Attorneys, 189
National Coalition to Abolish the Death Penalty, 14, 189
National Prison Association, 178
National standard, 70
Natural selection, 81
Nebraska, 129
Neck verse, 34
New Deal, 75, 92
New Hampshire, 42, 44
New Jersey, 169
New York, 42, 43, 48
New York University, 178
1984 (Orwell), 86
Nixon, Richard, 85, 104–105, 190
Norris v. Alabama, 72, 186
North Carolina, 42, 43, 59, 110–111, 118–119, 128, 148
Northwest Ordinance. *See* Ordinance of the Northwest Territory

Oates, Titus, 46–47
O'Connor, Sandra Day, 121, 124, 129, 140, 148, 160, 188, 189
Ohio, 104, 108
Oklahoma, 124, 127, 158
Old Bailey, 33
On Crimes and Punishments (Beccaria), 179
On the Origin of Species (Darwin), 81
O'Neil, John, 62
O'Neil v. Vermont, 62–64, 88
Ordinance for the Governance of the Northwest Territories. *See* Ordinance of the Northwest Territory
Ordinance of the Northwest Territory, 40–41, 47, 207–208 (document)
"Orgy of confiscations," 38
Orwell, George, 86
Oswald, Lee Harvey, 85
Overcrowding
  and prisons, conditions of, 167–168

Palko, Frank, 91
Palko v. Connecticut, 91
Panama, 70
Pardon, 189

Parliament, 34
  versus Congress, 54–57
Parole boards, 83–84
Parole, life without, 15, 132
Payne v. Tennessee, 133
PCDOs. *See* Post-Conviction Defender Organizations
Peers, jury of. *See* Jury of peers
Penalty phase
  and trial by jury, 131–132
Penitentiaries, 59. *See also* Prisons
Penn, William, 36, 190
Pennsylvania, 42, 43, 48, 50, 131
  Constitution of 1776, 36
Pennsylvania colony, 190
Penry, Johnny Paul, 127
Penry v. Lynaugh, 127–128, 283–291 (document)
People v. Anderson, 106, 108
Per Curiam, 72, 190
Perjury, 46
Perry, Rick, 127
Perry v. Louisiana, 126
Philadelphia, 41, 114
Philadelphia Society for Ameliorating the Miseries of Public Prisons, 169
Philippine criminal law, 87
Philippines, 70
Philosophers, 32
Pillory, 46, 47
Pious perjury, 35
Piracy, 50
Plessy v. Ferguson, 73
PLRA. *See* Prison Litigation Reform Act
Plurality, 190
Poland v. Arizona, 116
Politics (Aristotle), 32
Polk, James K., 41
Posner, Richard, 80
Post-Conviction Defender Organizations (PCDOs), 190
Pound, Roscoe, 75
Poverty, 14, 15–16, 102
Powell, Lewis, 104–105, 107, 108, 110, 111, 122, 132, 133, 159–160, 188, 190–191
Powell Commission, 144, 145–146
Powell v. Alabama, 72, 73, 91
Powell v. Texas, 102
Prejean, Sister Helen, 68, 191
Pressing, 37–38
Prettyman, Barrett, 141, 191
Princeton University, 30
Prison construction, 173
Prison grievance system, 174
Prison labor, 163
Prison Litigation Reform Act (PLRA), 174, 191
Prison population
  increase in, 347
Prison riots, 164
Prison trade programs, 163
Prisoners
  abuse of, and corrections officers, 171–173
  death row, number on (1968–2000), 344 (table)
  death row, number on (2000), 342. *See also* Death row
  medical needs of, and deliberate indifference to, 165–167
  and mental illness, 170
  See also Inmates
Prisons, 33
  federal, 48, 70, 94, 163
  state, 41, 48, 163
  See also individual prisons; Prisons, conditions of
Prisons, conditions of, 11, 162–175
  and corrections officers, 171–173
  and escape, 168
  and guards, 166–167
  and isolation, 168–171

and overcrowding, 167–168
See also Prisons
Probation, 83
Probation officer, 84
Pro-death penalty, as campaign platform, 112–113
Profitt v. Florida, 108, 109, 128–129
Property crime, 36, 345
Property, forfeiture of, 37
Proportionality, 134, 152, 158–161
Public defender, 141, 191–192
Public dissection, 60
Public executions, 41
Public intoxication, 102
Public opinion
and death penalty, 346–347 (table)
and Supreme Court, 80–81
Public order, 36
Puerto Rico, 70
Pulley v. Harris, 134
Punishment, 155–157
justifications of, 6–7

Quakers, 36, 190

Racial discrimination, 7, 8, 12, 14, 15–16, 18, 71–72, 82, 102–104, 116–117, 152–154
Radelet, Michael, 16–17
Rape, 50, 52
Rapists, 122
Reade, Justice, 58–59
Reagan, Ronald, 68, 140
Reconstruction, 48, 50, 71
"Red Light Bandit," 97
Reform, theories of, 48
Rehabilitation, 6, 12, 75–76, 85–86, 102
Rehnquist, William, 22, 80, 104, 108, 110, 111, 113, 122, 128, 129, 140, 143–144, 192
Reinhardt, Stephen, 192
Religious beliefs, 102
Reno, Janet, 183
Resolution on the Death Penalty (American Bar Association), 214–215 (document)
Retribution, 5, 14, 23, 75–76, 81, 83, 109
Revenue, raising of, 36–38
and drug crimes, 38
Review process, 141–146
cost of, 143
Revolutionary War, 31
Rhode Island, 50
Rhodes v. Chapman, 168
Ridge, Tom, 112–113
Riggins v. Nevada, 126
Ring v. Arizona, 129–130, 193, 323–328 (document)
Roberts, Stanislaus, 111
Roberts v. Louisiana, 108, 111, 115, 178
Robinson v. California, 101–102, 157–158
Roe v. Wade, 69
Roman Catholic Church, 37
Romano v. Oklahoma, 131
Roosevelt, Franklin D., 48, 79, 92, 95
Rosenberg, Ethel, 97, 123
Rosenberg, Julius, 97, 123
Royal Commission, 93
Royal trial, 37
Ruby, Jack, 85
Rudolph v. Alabama, 100–101
Ruffin v. Commonwealth, 162
Rummel, William, 159
Rummel v. Estelle, 159
Rupe, Mitchell, 149
Rush, Benjamin, 39, 67, 192
Russia, 15
Russian Revolution, 39
Rutledge, John, 49
Rutledge, Wiley, 80

Ryan, George, 3, 154–155
Ryan, John, 94

Salem witch trials, 37–38
San Quentin, 94, 97
Sandin v. Conner, 164–165
Sanity, of defendants, 117
Sarandon, Susan, 191
Sarat, Austin, 141
Scalia, Antonin, 24–26, 80–81, 124, 128, 140, 160, 192–193
Schools
  corporal punishment in, 156
Scott, James (Duke of Monmouth), 45
Scottsboro Boys case, 72
Second Treatise on Government (Locke), 35
Securities and Exchange Commission, 95
Sedition Act, 57
Sellin, Thorsten, 93
Senate Judiciary Committee, 102
Sentencing, 8, 83–84
  cost of, 16
  See also Mandatory sentences
Sentencing Reform Act of 1984, 86, 193
Sex offenders, 11–12, 157
Sexually Violent Predator Act, 157
Shafer v. South Carolina, 131–132
Shays's Rebellion, 41
Sidney, Algernon, 45–47
Simmons, Ronald, 114–115
Simmons v. South Carolina, 131–132
Sing Sing Prison, 62, 94, 186
Singapore, 183
"Sinners in the Hands of an Angry God" (Edwards), 30
Sixth Amendment, 91, 129, 147, 186
Skinner v. Oklahoma, 158–159
Skipper v. South Carolina, 116
Slavery, 32, 50
Sociological jurisprudence, 78
Socrates, 149
Soledad, California, 164
Solem v. Helm, 159–160, 249–255 (document)
Solicitor general, 193
Solitary confinement, 11
Souter, David, 133, 140, 160
South Africa, 15
South Carolina, 42, 131, 133
South Carolina v. Gathers, 133
South Dakota, 159
Southern Center for Human Rights, 193
"Southern strategy," 190
Spanish law, 88
Spaziano v. Florida, 129, 193
"Speech in Favor of Capital Punishment" (Mill), 209–213 (document)
Spenkelink, John, 193
Stanford, Kevin, 124
Stanford v. Kentucky, 124, 125, 130, 291–301 (document)
Starvation, 37
State constitutions, 57–58
State legislature, 151
State prisons, 41, 48, 163. *See also* Prisons
State review, mandatory, 16. *See also* Review process
State v. Driver, 58–59
Status crimes, 102
Stay of execution, 101, 144–146, 194
Stephens, Matthew, 15–16
Sterilization, mandatory, 158–159
Stevens, John Paul, 80, 108, 110–111, 122–124, 127–128, 140, 148, 188
Stewart, Potter, 7, 95, 104–108, 110–111, 121–122, 188
The Sting, 85

Story, Joseph, 52–53, 88
Strickland v. Washington, 147, 195
Stroud v. Swope, 163
Sumner v. Shuman, 117–118
Supermax Correctional Institution, 170–171
Supremacy Clause, 48
Supreme Court, 56–57, 68–70, 70–74, 183
  abolitionists versus deferentialists in, 113–114, 139–140
  and nineteenth century, lack of importance in, 49
  and public opinion, 80–81
  See also individual cases; individual justices
Suspended sentences, 83

Taft, Robert, Jr., 3
Taft, William Howard, 70, 194
Taney, Roger, 49
Tarver, Robert Lee, 150
Television age, 85
Ten Commandments, 200 (document)
Tennessee, 127, 148
Territory v. Ketchum, 58–59
Texas, 105, 110, 114, 125, 127, 159
Theft, 35
Third Amendment, 52
Thirteenth Amendment, 158
Thomas, Clarence, 116, 134–135, 140, 162, 165
Thompson, Thomas, 113
Thompson, William, 123
Thompson v. Oklahoma, 123–125
Thoughts on Government (Sidney), 46
Three strikes laws, 11, 160, 194
Three-tier federal court system, 70, 183
Thumbscrews, 37
Tison v. Arizona, 121–122, 262–270 (document)
Torture, 37–38, 60
Traitors, 122–123, 149
Transportation, sentence of, 31–35
Treason, 50, 52
A Treatise on the Constitutional Limitations Which Rest upon the Legislative Power of the States of the American Union (Cooley), 53
Trial
  by battle, 37
  cost of, 16
  by judge, 128–130
  by jury, 37, 128–130
  by ordeal, 37
  and penalty phase, 131–132
  two-stage, 8
Trop, Albert, 95–97, 106
Trop v. Dulles, 80, 95–97, 100, 106, 111, 122–123, 127–128, 152, 156, 194–195
Truman, Harry, 85, 95
Tufts University, 180
Turner v. Murray, 116–117
Twelve Tables of the Roman Republic, 32
Twenty Thousand Years in Sing Sing (Lawes), 186

Union Army, 96
United Nations General Assembly, 15
United States Sentencing Commission, 193
United States v. Bailey, 168
United States v. Bajakajian, 161–162
United States v. Hudson and Goodwin, 57
United States v. Jackson, 103, 115

United States v. Reynolds, 158
United States v. Salerno, 157
University of Pennsylvania, 79, 93
Unreasonable searches and seizures, 10
Uphaus v. Wyman, 156
U.S. Army
  and executions, 7
U.S. Navy
  and executions, 7
Utah, 150
Utopia (More), 32

Van den Haag, Ernest, 17–20, 194
Vermont, 62–63
Victim impact statement, 132–134
Victimless crimes, 36
Violent crimes, 345
  increase in, and deterrence, 16
Virgin Islands, 70
Virginia, 43, 131, 147, 162
Virginia Colonial Convention, 42
Virginia Declaration of Rights, 43
Volunteering for death, 13–14, 114–115, 143, 194
Voters, 151

Wainwright v. Witt, 130
Walnut Street Penitentiary, 169
Walters, Marlene, 2
Walton v. Arizona, 129
Wardens, 48, 94–94
Warren, Earl, 95–97, 105, 194–195
Washington, David, 195
Waxton, Luby, 110–111
Weaver, Richard, 69
Wechsler, Herbert, 93, 195
Weems, Paul, 87
Weems v. United States, 80, 87–89, 91, 99–100, 112, 122, 152, 158
West Side Story, 84
Western Europe, 15
"Westinghousing," 61
Westinghouse, George, 61
White, Byron, 7, 98, 104–105, 106–108, 110–111, 117, 121–122, 132–133, 188, 195
Whitley v. Albers, 171–172
Whitmore v. Arkansas, 114–115
Wilkerson v. Utah, 59–60, 88, 112, 150
Wilkins, Heath, 124
William III, 46, 56
William of Orange, 45
Williams v. New York, 82–83, 100
"Willie Horton" ads, 86–87
Wilson, Woodrow, 90
Winston v. United States, 52
Winthrop, John, 31
Wisconsin, 50, 170
Witherspoon v. Illinois, 103, 130
Wolff v. McDonnell, 164
Woodson, James, 110
Woodson v. North Carolina, 108, 110–111, 115, 178, 226–229 (document)
World War I, 48
Writ of certiorari, 71, 195

Yale Law School, 78, 79

Zero tolerance laws, 62